POLANSKI

CHRISTOPHER SANDFORD

POLANSKI

palgrave
macmillan

POLANSKI

First published in Great Britain in 2007 by Century.

First published in the U.S.A. in 2008 by PALGRAVE MACMILLAN® — a division of St. Martin's Press LLC, 175 Fifth Avenue, New York, NY 10010.

Where this book is distributed in the UK, Europe and the rest of the world, this is by Palgrave Macmillan, a division of Macmillan Publishers Limited, registered in England, company number 785998, of Houndmills, Basingstoke, Hampshire RG21 6XS.

Palgrave Macmillan is the global academic imprint of the above companies and has companies and representatives throughout the world.

Palgrave® and Macmillan® are registered trademarks in the United States, the United Kingdom, Europe and other countries.

ISBN: 978–0–230–61176–4

Library of Congress Cataloging-in-Publication Data.

Sandford, Christopher, 1956–
    Polanski / Christopher Sandford.
        p. cm.
    ISBN-13: 978–0–230–60778–1 (hardcover)
    ISBN-10: 0–230–60778–0 (hardcover)
        1. Polanski, Roman. 2. Motion picture producers and directors—France—Biography. I. Title.

PN1998.3.P65S26 2008   [B]
791.4302'33092—dc22   2008024578

A catalogue record of the book is available from the British Library.

Design by Newgen Imaging Systems.

First PALGRAVE MACMILLAN paperback edition: December 2009

10 9 8 7 6 5 4 3 2 1

Printed in the United States of America.

To Dad
and Sue

To KDS
and NSS

CONTENTS

LIST OF ILLUSTRATIONS

ACKNOWLEDGEMENTS

FIRST, A CONFESSION. WHEN I STARTED THIS BOOK, I rather fondly thought that it might go some small way to helping rescue Roman Polanski from his detractors – particularly those, still quite vociferous thirty years on, for whom he'll always be tainted by the events of 1977–8. While in no way excusing his crime, it seemed that the time might have come for all parties to move on, a view shared by Polanski's now middle-aged victim in the case, Samantha Geimer. It soon became clear that this alleged rehabilitation would have to proceed without the director's help. Polanski himself declined to meet, and several of his friends I approached for interviews told me that, 'after checking', they'd prefer not to talk. At one point I was told that Polanski (I stress this is hearsay) apparently considered me a 'nosy fellow', enough to give pause to anyone who happens to recall him using that same phrase to Jack Nicholson immediately prior to slicing open the actor's nose, although not, I hope, ultimately prejudicial to the research. This, then, is an 'unauthorised' biography, so I'm particularly grateful to the 270 people who did speak either by phone or email, or in various restaurants where Polanski was discussed, usually fondly, over a meal – which is how these things should be.

For recollections, input or advice I should thank, institutionally: Abacus, ABC News, Academy of Motion Picture Arts and Sciences, Amazon.com, *Atlantic Monthly*, Bookcase, Bookends, Borders, the British Library, British Newspaper Library, California Vital Records, *Chronicles*, the Cinema Store, Columbia Pictures, Companies House, Creative Artists, the *Daily Mail*, the David Lawrence Show, Directors Guild, Family Records Centre, FBI, Focus Fine Arts, General Register Office, Golem, Hollywood Roosevelt Hotel, IMDbPro.com, Inca, *Kamera*, Krakow@wp.pl, LipService, Los Angeles District Attorney's Office, the

Margaret Herrick Library, the *New York Times*, Orbis, Pages of Fun, Playboy Enterprises International, Producers Guild, Public Record Office, Renton Library, Roman Polanski Productions, Readings, the *Seattle Post-Intelligencer*, Seattle Public Library, Second Hand Books, *Slate*, the Smoking Gun, *Spotlight*, *The Times*, United Talent Agency, *Vanity Fair*, Variety.com.

Professionally: Isabelle Adjani, Polly Andrews, Tim Andrews, Terence Bayler, Tony Bill, Jacqueline Bisset, Mark Booth, Paul Bradley, Paul Brooke, Curtis Brown, Joan Brown, Vincent Bugliosi, Timothy Burrill Productions, the late William Burroughs, Jean Cazes, Charles Champlin, Michael Cimino, Gemma Cox, Bud Crowe, Valerie Cutko, Paul Darlow, Christian Darvin, Ariel Dorfman, Richard Dysart, Jozef Ebert, Roger Ebert, Hilly Elkins, the late Michael Elphick, 'Doc' Erickson, Jo Evans, Juliet Ewers, Peter Falk, Mike Fargo, Irene Fawkes, Mike Fenton, Judy Flanders, Adam Fleming, Kathryn Fleming, Tom Fleming, Jamie Foreman, Emilia Fox, John Fraser, Hugh Futcher, Toni Gahl, Corinne Garcia, John Gavin, Jim Geller, Sandi Gibbons, William Goldman, Don Gordon, Pytor Gorsky, Herman Graf, James Graham, Chris Green, Jeff Gross, Stefan Hansen, Alain Haultcoeur, Alan Hazen, Michael Heath, William Hobbs, Jim Hoven, Emily Hunt, Ernst Jaenecke, Roy Jenson, Norman Jewison, Iain Johnstone, Dean Jones, David Kelly, John M. Kelso, Frank Knox, the late Ronald Lacey, Leigh Lawson, Christopher Lee, Barbara Leigh, Barbara Levy, Daniel Metcalfe, Don Murray, Barry Norman, Sven Nykvist, Carole O'Shea, Josef Oziecka, Max Paley, Lucia Pallaris, James Robert Parish, John Pavlik, Michele Pay, Richard Pearson, Bruce Perret, Valli Pfohl, the late Donald Pleasence, Jennifer Prather, the late Anthony Quayle, Katharina Rae, Neil Rand, Marian Reid, Robert Relyea, Sol Rizzo, Jenny Romero, Suzanna Ruiz, James Russo, Mariella Ryecart, Andrei Sbytov, Denny Sevier, Paul Shelley, Tad Slowacki, Ed Strauss, Marshall Terrill, Damien Thomas, Sharon Thomas, John Thurley, Victor Tomei, the late Delli Colli Tonino, Louisa Towne, Robert Towne, the late Kenneth Tynan, Julia Tyrell, Eli Wallach, Ken Wilson, the late Shelley Winters, the late Robert Wise, Józef Wolski, Dora Yanni, Tony Yeo, Burt Young.

Personally: Adis, Air Canada, Amanuel, the Attic, Pete Barnes, Ray Bates, Benaroya Hall, Lucinda Bredin, Hilary and Robert Bruce, Changelink, Noel Chelberg, Cocina, the late Ernst Cohn, the late Steve Cox (senselessly murdered on 2 December 2006), Ken Crabtrey, the late *Cricket Lore*, the Cricketers Club of London, Celia Culpan, Deb K. Das, the Davenport, Monty Dennison, the Dowdall family, Milan Drdos, John and Barbara Dungee, Fairmont Waterfront Hotel, Malcolm Galfe, the Gay

Hussar, the Gees, Jim Gillespie, Audrey Godwin, Tom and Jackie Graveney, Peter Griffin, Grumbles, Patrice Haultcoeur, Charles Hillman, Alison Hooker, the late Amy Hostetter, Hotel Vancouver, Ivar's, JCC, Jo Jacobius, Lincoln Kamell, Tom Keylock, Terry Lambert, Jenny Lao, Belinda Lawson, Cindy Link, Todd Linse, Vince Lorimer, Ruth and Angie McCartney, the Macris, Lee Mattson, Jim Meyersahm, Sheila Mohn, the Morgans, John and Colleen Murray, Jonathan Naumann, Chuck Ogmund, the Revd Larry Olsen, Valya Page, Robin Parish, Peter Perchard, Chris Pickrell, George Plumptre, Prins family, Queen Anne Office Supply, Tim Rice, Keith Richards, Malcolm Robinson, the late Comte Flemming de Rosenborg, Ailsa Rushbrooke, Debbie Saks, Delia Sandford, Karen Sandford, my father Sefton Sandford, Sue Sandford, Peter Scaramanga, Seattle CC, the Revd Kempton Segerhammar, Jan Shawe, Fred and Cindy Smith, the *Spectator*, the Stanleys, Thaddeus Stuart, Subway 3674, Swedish Medical Center, the Travel Team, William Underhill, Roger and Di Villar, Lisbeth Vogl, West London Chemists, Jim Wheal, Katharina Whone, Richard Wigmore, the late Tom Willis Fleming, the Willis Flemings, Tad Wolanski; and a special doffed hat to my son Nicholas.

Thanks, McKelvey law firm.

C. S.
2007

'We should like to have some towering geniuses, to reveal us to ourselves in colour and fire, but of course they'd have to fit into the pattern of our society and be able to take direction from sound administrative types.'

J. B. Priestley

'I am the man of the spectacle. I'm playing.'

Roman Polanski

CHAPTER 1
DIRECTOR'S CUT

As THE CUSTOMS OFFICIALS AT THE SMALL SUDETEN town of Zittau stamped his coveted Polish 'consular' passport – allowing the holder, described as an 'Independent Film-maker', to live and work abroad – the 28-year-old man in the battered Mercedes convertible might have been struck by the cinematic potential of the scene. He was a trim, youthful figure whose upturned nose and pinched, quizzical expression gave him a vaguely feral air – in one ex-lover's uncharitable view, like that of an 'evil mole'. Inside the car, along with the director's pet black poodle, were virtually his entire worldly possessions: several boxes of German and French books, a Chubby Checker album, two velvet suits, some skis and a print of his first full-length feature, called *Knife in the Water*. Released on 9 March 1962, it enjoyed a mixed domestic reception, the state party secretary, Wladyslaw Gomulka, expressing his own reservations on the subject by hurling an ashtray at the screen. To compound his problems, the emigrant currently had no cash (his fee having been paid him in unconvertible Polish zloty), few if any prospects and only the vaguest of plans to make a life for himself in the West, more specifically Paris. His wife had recently left him and he was suffering from the after-effects of a fractured skull sustained in a late-night car crash. None of these blows had, however, impaired his legendary self-confidence. According to a retired East German 'Vopo' named Josip Sats, who made a note of the incident, he 'very categorically assured us "I'll be back,"' nodding his head towards Poland with a show of distaste, before adding, '"Someday, they'll remember me."' Years later, the director would recall how he had actually felt he was 'leaving one limbo for another'.

Roman Polanski was right. They did remember him, and, after a brief private visit, he returned in triumph nineteen years later to direct and star in a Polish stage version of *Amadeus*. Some of the same critics who had ignored or panned *Knife in the Water* now hailed him as 'a genius', 'our prodigal son' and 'on a par with Mozart'. 'Imagine,' added the party newspaper, in a wrenching editorial, the 'solitude of such [a] soul exiled in places like Los Angeles.'

There appear to be various mysteries about Polanski, polymath, felon, and reluctant subject of countless PhD theses: the chief one being that he seems to be several different people. The notorious swinger who defied social conventions, slept around, and liked his partners young if not legally underage, or the distinguished *artiste engagé*, fluent in five languages? ('He's extremely intelligent' and 'He's a freak' are the two phrases that crop up time and again in research.) Because people hold such distinct views of him, the first question a Polanski biographer tends to hear is, 'Is it a hatchet job?' It's a fair point, but not one, perhaps, that would be asked of a similar book on Steven Spielberg or Martin Scorsese, or even Oliver Stone. Thanks to the events of August 1969 and of March 1977–February 1978, millions of people who never go to a film would come to know of Polanski. To many of his friends and admirers he remains a rare example of someone who can entertain as well as challenge his audiences, with a life story even stranger than his fiction. Sharing the mystical aura of the Polish underground, he'd survived the Second World War but lost his mother to the horrors of Auschwitz. In the mid-Sixties his exhilaratingly odd films were part of the general revolution underway against the Hollywood establishment, with its grinding conformity and studio systems largely untouched since the days of Louis B. Mayer. No one seemed to bear more of the hope of young, irreverent talent.

His second wife's murder was, as Polanski stresses, both his worst and his most prolonged blow. 'It changed everything,' he's said. Even before Sharon Tate and her fellow victims of the Manson cult were buried, and for years afterwards, reporters openly speculated about the Polanskis' home life, where a wide knowledge of drugs, black magic and unorthodox sexual practices was thought to have somehow contributed to the tragedy. As the press competed to play up some of the couple's more exotic hobbies, a combination of Hollywood gossip and Roman's own provocations brought a rash of unflattering articles about what *Life* dubbed his 'Olympic ego'. (When you talk to people who knew him at the time, the word 'humility' comes up a lot. They say he was extremely sparing with it.)

Events nine years later, when Polanski fled the US immediately before sentencing on a child-sex charge, were to prove a gift to the same reporters, one of whom wrote that the award-winning director was 'someone you'd want to touch only with a pair of tongs'.

At about this same time, a court-ordered probation report noted of Polanski, 'Jail is not being recommended . . . It is believed that incalculable emotional damage could result from incarcerating the defendant, whose very existence has been a seemingly unending series of punishments.' Asked subsequently by a French reporter how it felt to be a fugitive, Polanski shrugged and said, 'I'm used to it. I've been a fugitive all my life.'

Tempting as it is for a Polanski biographer to 'explain' his career in terms of his being a perpetual outsider, I think the precise opposite is the case. A close London friend at the time of his wedding to Sharon Tate, reflecting on the 'somewhat ad hoc' planning of the event, recalls 'Roman remark[ing] that, [despite] familiarity with both Jewish and Catholic ritual, he was personally an agnostic. What he shared with truly religious people was a sense of exile, and this sprang not from his foreign ancestry, but from being a human being. The essential strangeness of life on this planet, particularly in places like Hollywood in the Sixties, would create this sense in anyone but a complete idiot.'

For the past thirty years, the name Polanski has become attached to two kinds of headline: first, a series of shrill variants of the word 'Monster!' with which both the *Globe* and *Star* greeted his arrest for statutory rape, and subsequent flight; and secondly, some equally rich stuff claiming him to be a victim of the various unsavoury and narrow-minded thugs pulling the levers of the American justice system, quite possibly in cahoots with the CIA, a view that, particularly in recent years, endears itself to many in his adopted home of France. (To get some of the gist of the debate, the reader has only to compare Mia Farrow's statement describing Polanski as 'a brave and brilliant man important to all humanity', and the Los Angeles *Facts* editorial calling for him to be castrated.) Between the paroxysms of these two groups, the man himself seems to have slipped away. One possible reason fans and critics alike mine his films for the slightest scraps of biographical detritus is that Polanski himself is so private. He rarely gives interviews, has never opened his beautiful home to *Hello!*, and even when successfully pursuing a libel action in the High Court appeared only via videolink, the first time in British legal history that a claimant has participated solely by TV monitor.

When Polanski sat down to write his life story in 1983, he began with this reflection: 'For as far back as I can remember, the line between fantasy and reality has been hopelessly blurred.' Some of the more enduring myths may have been, like rogue biographies, beyond his control, but others appear to be fully authorised. It would be fair to assume that Polanski's extraordinary success over the years as both a writer and director has at least something to do with his fertile imagination. The role playing, and attendant mimicry, an eminently practical way to cope with the uniquely appalling facts of his early life, seem to have begun with the war. Polanski speaks of an occasion shortly after the imposition of the Krakow ghetto when he and a friend were able to visit a cinema reserved for members of the *Wehrmacht* and their families by 'pretending we were German children' – only the first of many such ruses, some of them exercises in survival, one or two of which perhaps improved with telling down the years. Subsequent fame and power, coming on top of professional acting experience, enormously magnified and dramatised the way in which he seemed to adapt to the needs of every situation. Shortly before his fiftieth birthday, a colleague of Polanski's in Paris decided to make a surprise video tribute with which to amuse their mutual friends at a lavish party. The man spent 'several agonising days' planning how to go about it, before finally abandoning the idea. 'The only thing that would have worked would have been to get a chameleon, and then let it walk across the screen,' he says.

In 1970, at the height of his fame for *Rosemary's Baby* and, by association, the slaughter of his wife and friends, Polanski filmed a peculiarly haunting version of *Macbeth*. As part of the casting process he approached a 41-year-old New Zealand-born actor named Terence Bayler, who had acquitted himself with distinction in *Doctor Who* and other TV series, but was, as he concedes, 'no movie star'. Bayler provides an odd and touching example of Polanski's little-known talent for personal modesty, provided it simultaneously served the interests of the film, when the two of them found themselves sitting on the floor of an office sharing some fruit. 'I told him I was already under contract to do another job at the same time,' says Bayler. 'Roman said, "Well, we can buy you out." I told him no, that wouldn't be possible. Roman thought about this and then told me he would reschedule a chunk of *Macbeth* to accommodate me. I thought that was an extraordinary thing for him to do, whether because he really wanted me or because I'd initially resisted him. In either case, he certainly didn't need to do it, particularly given his fame.' Indeed, Bayler seems to have had a clearer notion of Polanski's status than Polanski himself, who frequently insisted he would be simply 'one of the gang' on *Macbeth*. (He was as good as his word.) In one of the sudden reversals that constitute the basic pattern of his life, the director then went directly from there to a Roman palazzo where he would shoot the woefully self-indulgent *What?*, an S&M romp that floored the filmgoing public even in the sexually libertine days of the mid-Seventies.

'Someday they'll remember me.' Such was Polanski's ability to 'seethe with chutzpah' as Ken Tynan observed, that one almost forgets how much of his life has been a sort of identity crisis. In 1978, some of the Los Angeles district attorneys' best minds were forced to work long hours to determine his exact nationality, while other personal details, such as his name, proved equally elusive over the years, even in an industry where skinny 'Stechetto' Scicolone could become Sophia Loren and Marion Morrison saddled up as John Wayne. According to the passport he presented that spring morning in 1962, he was born Rajmund Roman Thierry Polañski, his father, apparently as an artistic nom de plume, having changed the original family name from Liebling. As a boy he answered to Romek or Remo Polanski, until the Nazi occupation of Poland converted him into Roman Wilk, a practising Catholic. With the onset of adolescence, he then gloried in the striking alias 'Puker' for several months, before a later girlfriend dubbed him 'The Brat'. California state records list him variously as 'Rajmund R.', 'Raymund R.' or 'R. Thierry' Polanski in 1969 and 1970, while in 1977 he was formally charged as Roman Raymond Polanski, the name which remains on his file today.

There has always been an element of fantasy attached to Polanski. Among the rumours swirling around the Manson carnage and its aftermath were two to which he took particular exception. In August 1970, the *Daily Telegraph* alleged that Polanski had declined to appear as a witness in the killers' trial because the prosecution wouldn't pay his airfare from London to Los Angeles. Thirty-two years later, *Vanity Fair* was to rashly claim that the director had stopped in New York while on his way to California, where his wife's funeral was to be held, and propositioned a 'Swedish beauty' with the words, 'I can put you in movies. I can make you the next Sharon Tate.' Polanski sued, disproved the stories, and won damages from both publications. By scouring the internet, meanwhile, it's possible to read such 'indisputable' facts as that Polanski once sold his soul to the devil, that he has a hang-up for group sex, among other combinations, and – most startling of all – that he enjoyed his secondary education at Charterhouse School in Surrey.

A faint sense of schizophrenia seems to similarly pervade Polanski's career, which has rarely been burdened by consistency, let alone sequels, or by a need to pander to what the risk management consultants running most film studios call the 'great average'. As well as two satanic-cult pictures, his canon includes psychological thrillers, faithful adaptations of Shakespeare and Dickens, a costume melodrama, matinee swashbuckling, Hitchcockian suspense, Thirties noir, excursions in absurdism and soft porn, sometimes concurrently, and a deranged Dracula spoof in which a Jewish vampire hunter, played by Polanski himself, repeatedly peers through a keyhole at a naked woman who happens to be Sharon Tate. It's hard to even imagine the director of *Chinatown* and *The Tenant* as the same man. In 1974, Polanski shot his hard-boiled saga of big-city corruption, whose backdrop, ironically, is a vast, often sunny countryside, peopled by Raymond Chandler wiseguys; he followed it by his dark examination of one man (Polanski again) going mad in his Parisian apartment while clad in a wig, suspenders and high-heeled shoes, a film he finished just before it finished him, in 1976.

At the risk of hyperbole, or of sounding like an apologist, it could be said that there's no such thing as a truly bad Roman Polanski movie: weaker ones, certainly, pictures that, despite some brilliant sequences, are inanely plotted, comedies that aren't quite funny enough, meandering dramas in need of an editor – but never a really epic flop, one that's begging to be walked out on. Even the relative duds like *What?* are redeemed by Polanski's great artistic virtue: ruthlessness. With the possible exception of 2005's *Oliver Twist*, his films are never mawkish, maudlin or 'escapist'. Anyone looking to them for an emotional pick-me-up is in for a sorry disappointment. (That's emphatically not to say that they lack humour: even *The Pianist* has moments of black comedy.) With their flawed heroes, hallucinatory set pieces and unflinching treatment of paranoia, hysteria and violence, Polanski's movies would seem to offer no easy answers to the human condition; instead, they invite us to take a closer look. Few filmmakers have cherished the phrase 'this may hurt a little' quite like he does.

LEAVING ASIDE POLANSKI'S PRIVATE LIFE, the secret of his enduring fame is relatively simple: he deals exclusively in real people; he makes films about men and women who seem to be, at heart, 'just like us', even if their home lives are unusually rich, even by contemporary standards, in murders, frauds and sexual perversions; and he's done this while carrying his art into a high complexity, across a range of genres. As the critic Barry Norman says, 'In an industry that worships the routine, he never brings the rabbit out of the same hat twice.'

As well as imagination and technique, Polanski, as noted, also had his fair share of ambition. Keenly aware of his status as a foreigner (or, as one French critic put it, a 'jug-eared runt with a lisp') he sought 'power in craft . . . He drove both himself and his casts to the brink,' said his friend and colleague Carlo Ponti, even if this brought occasional grief along the way. A member of the *Chinatown* crew still recalls 'Roman suddenly starting to argue with Faye Dunaway about a bedroom scene', although the word 'argue' is somehow entirely inadequate to describe the peak-decibel abuse that then rocked the set for the next several minutes. After peace had been temporarily restored, Polanski went on to another sequence altogether in which he was to shoot his leading lady meeting Jack Nicholson in a restaurant. After the first take, it was noticed that a small strand of Dunaway's otherwise perfectly lacquered hair was catching the light. Stylists were summoned, but to no avail. Various personal assistants similarly failed to correct the problem, until Polanski himself, noting dryly that this was costing '$200 a minute', walked over, took hold of the offending hair and extracted it. Dunaway went nuts. 'I don't believe it!' she shrieked. 'I just don't believe it! That motherfucker pulled my hair out!' This was the cue for a lively exchange about the terms under which Dunaway would continue to work on *Chinatown*, if at all, until Polanski ended the debate by calmly announcing, 'You can fight with me, Faye, but I can never be wrong. I'm the director.'

Several of Polanski's films have, unlike *Chinatown*, enjoyed instant cult status without much commercial success. A classic example is 1965's *Repulsion*, another claustrophobic horror tale, in which a young Belgian woman living in London loses it and bludgeons to death her boyfriend, played by John Fraser. Fraser has fond memories of 'Roman prepar[ing] me for a particular close-up by saying, "John, I want you to do nothing." So I did nothing. I literally stood there. After the take, Roman shook his head and walked over. I could see that he wasn't happy. "John, I want you to do absolutely *nothing*," he said. I told him I'd done that. Without missing a beat, Roman responded, "But I can see you *thinking*. You must be blank. Blank, blank, blank." I tried the shot again, and back came Roman: "*Blank*, I said."' After several more takes, Polanski solved the problem by filming the back of Fraser's head.

'That's the great thing about Roman,' says a long-time colleague. 'It's all a challenge. That's what makes it fun. If he thinks there's no chance that you'll hate him, he's not interested in doing it.'

POLANSKI LEFT POLAND IN VIRTUAL ANONYMITY, stinging from reviews like the one calling *Knife in the Water* 'irrelevant' and berating the director for having an 'international driving licence but no film-school diploma.' Although his arrival in Paris similarly failed to rouse much excitement, he did meet a frustrated 34-year-old writer with cropped hair and a freshly gashed forehead, named Gérard Brach. Brach himself was so broke that he'd been reduced to sleeping on the floor of a friend's office and existing on a diet of bread and vinegar. Small and sickly-looking, a TB sufferer, like Polanski he was in the throes of a divorce; the gashed forehead was the result of a blow from a shoe, delivered by his wife. When the two men then sat down to collaborate on a screenplay, the leading female character was, Polanski notes, 'born out of a slight sense of revenge'.

Their property, which they called *If Katelbach Comes*, was given to the producer Pierre Roustang, who passed on it. Two other producers and an agent in turn read the script. They also passed. Someone then mentioned that there was a West German film distributor on the top floor of Roustang's office building. The manager in residence there read *If Katelbach Comes* and offered Polanski a $2,000 screenwriter's fee and a director's fee of $8,000 against a two per cent cut of the notional profits, but the whole deal fell through once budgets came to be discussed. After that, there were no serious takers.

For Polanski, Paris was an education in culture. 'It didn't so much define him as refine his eye,' a local friend recalls. Although destitute, he was able to enjoy long walks up the Champs-Élysées with his poodle Jules, dallying by the shop windows and haunting the galleries and museums where he was to exploit his youthful appearance by requesting a student's discount. In a strikingly generous arrangement, he was also to enjoy the run of Roustang's Left Bank home on the weekends when the producer was out of town. Polanski told the girls he invited up to the luxurious apartment that he owned the place. Paris, old and new, the city of his birth, assumed an 'air of magnificence', a 'grand tone' it was apparently always to have for him in spite of its slums and squalor, and of his own chronic poverty. According to Roustang, Polanski imagined it as a beautiful woman, which suggests that he might have thought of himself as her suitor. What he liked best about Western life, he once remarked, was the challenge. Kenneth Tynan said that his friend the 'magnetic Pole' conceived of cities, and Paris in particular, as places to be 'seduced, conquered [and] possessed'.

Later in the spring, Polanski learnt that another French producer, named Pierre Braunberger, had secured the domestic rights in perpetuity to *Knife in the Water*, for which he paid $9,700. Like most of the cinema-going public, the 57-year-old Braunberger had never seen the film. His young wife, however, had attended a late-night screening of *Knife* as part of a Polish arts fair and subsequently raved about its treatment of 'unbridled sexuality' – the future, as she insisted – with the result that Braunberger both bought the movie and invited Polanski and Brach to write him another one. A month later they sent him a script loosely based on *Snow White*, featuring a sexually ambiguous heroine, a gay yodelling choir and a troupe of midget wrestlers to depict the seven dwarfs. Braunberger declined to commission the project. *Knife*, too, did only modest business in Paris cinemas, selling a mere 12,400 seats in its six-week run there. Polanski endured one 'gala performance' where he sat in mounting despair amongst a small but vocally derisive crowd of drunks, the source of a subsequently heated debate with Braunberger over the latter's promotional efforts.

Across the Atlantic, meanwhile, *Knife* would eventually come to enjoy a midnight-cult status in arts clubs and on university campuses. It owed its American presence to a small import company called Kanawha, who bought the distribution rights and entered the picture in the first New York Film Festival. Polanski was flown in for the event, lodged at the Hilton on Sixth Avenue, and spoke, through a translator, to a number of reporters, most of whom took the now 30-year-old director for someone a decade younger. To the *New York Post*, which described him as 'cherubic', Polanski confided, 'I feel old . . . I'm a combination of an old man and a baby.' The paper concluded that 'it [was] entirely possible that Polanski will be an unnaturally brilliant boy for the next thirty years until suddenly he will be decrepit. Meanwhile, what a life!'

Polanski had mixed first impressions of New York. Even though he was reasonably fluent in English, or perhaps because of that, he was acutely conscious of his erratic grammar and thick accent. So he said little, instead walking around among 'seedy little bars, novelty shops and discount stores [on] streets that were potholed, filthy and narrower than I'd imagined.' In a town in which several public facilities were still marked 'White' and 'Colored', there were also to be various cultural shocks. When Kanawha threw a small party in his honour, Polanski asked if he could bring his new girlfriend, a dark-skinned usherette in the cinema where *Knife* was being shown. His hosts objected, so Polanski sent his own regrets.

Manning the front desk at the Lincoln Center, a festival organiser named Judy Flanders remembers Polanski appearing one morning 'down in the dumps about it all . . . As far as I could gather, he had no money and he was relying on the press receptions to get a free meal.' To compound his misery, a bottle of shampoo had leaked in his suitcase on the flight over and ruined his one good suit. The whole visit seemed to have raised the 'brilliant boy's' hopes only to dash them again. Then, a night or two later, as the festival was coming to a close, Flanders got an urgent phone call to meet up with some friends from Kanawha in Polanski's hotel room over a bottle of champagne. *Knife in the Water* was on the cover of *Time* magazine, and everyone wanted to celebrate.

CHAPTER 2
HITLER

THERE WERE SEVERAL MORE OCCASIONS OVER THE NEXT forty years when Roman Polanski was to imagine himself as an old man, something like his hero Bertrand Russell, 'rocking back and forth in [his] chair and musing on the state of the world.'

It's a curious image for Hollywood's *enfant terrible*, but Polanski has always had his reflective side, especially when holding forth with his version of art history – quoting everyone from Democritus to the Rolling Stones – while running off at tangents about politics and terrorism and firing his one-liners at the mainstream film industry, which he calls the 'kingdom of mediocrity'. Growing up smart yet horribly persecuted seems to have nurtured his sense of ego, as well as his lifelong fatalism. 'My characters' destinies [are] the result of apparently meaningless coincidence,' he once said, which would appear to apply to much of his own career. A still more sombre theme, one rarely far from the surface in Polanski's scripts, is the subject of betrayal, and, by extension, death – of compelling significance for the man whose mother, wife and unborn son were all murdered – and the inevitable survivor's guilt. When asked about the violence in his films, muted as it is by today's standards, Polanski invariably notes that he does no more than show the world around him, and certainly he's one of the few directors to have experienced quite as many of the twentieth century's homicidal monsters at first hand. 'People talk about the autobiographical aspect of Roman's work,' said Ken Tynan. 'But his life's much more interesting than that. The cliffhangers end with real falls.'

★

Rajmund Roman Thierry Polański was born in Paris on Friday night, 18 August 1933. His father, Ryszard, was a Jewish émigré from Krakow who had moved to the West in an ultimately failed bid to become a painter. According to a friend and fellow expatriate named Jan Solski, Ryszard was 'modestly gifted' but 'thoroughly dedicated' to his art, eventually leaving behind some sixty or seventy 'huge' portraits, most charitably described as abstract – red-brown acrylic splotches and semi-figurative works with titles such as *Weeping Woman*. In this commercially frustrating but personally eventful French exile, Ryszard would shed both his first wife and his family name, Liebling (an ornamental German version of the word 'darling'), adopting Polański, or its Westernised form, from early 1932. Six months later, he married a beautiful, divorced Russian half-Jewess named Bula Katz. When their only child was born in the summer of the following year, the family took rooms up three flights of stairs in a draughty apartment house at 5 rue Saint-Hubert, a then cobbled street lit by two sodium lamps, one either end, just west of Père Lachaise cemetery.

Roman Polanski was later impatient with the idea that he was 'particularly unlucky' or put-upon as a boy. One can only admire his resilience. As subsequent events were to prove, he was born not only into a world of violent change, but at the worst possible time to be Jewish, or even partly Jewish, in much of Europe. Hitler had become German chancellor on 30 January 1933, and within a month had contrived to suspend the articles of the Weimar constitution guaranteeing personal liberty, freedom of expression, freedom of the press, and the rights to hold meetings and form associations, while 'actively review[ing]' the whole question of disarmament. Rule by bayonet had arrived.

In defiance of an international convention forbidding troop movements in the area, the Polish government would in turn dispatch units to its Westerplatte munitions depot and other strategic points, in recognition of the 'state of disquiet existing [to] the west'. Soon after these events, Hitler was to adopt a noticeably more conciliatory policy towards Warsaw, apparently realising the advantages to be gained from the worsening of Franco-Polish relations and the disintegration of the French system of alliances. The result was the Declaration of Non-aggression and Understanding, signed on 26 January 1934, whose preamble referred to 'a hundred years of future co-operation' between Germany and Poland, but which broke down immediately following Hitler's dismemberment of Czechoslovakia in March 1939.

The national census of 1933 indicated that there were 3,114,000 Jews or 'Semitic sub-types' in Poland. They made up ten per cent of the entire Polish population, by far the largest such percentage of any nation in the world. The 355,000 Jews who lived in Warsaw equalled the number of Jews in all of France. These were not statistics likely to be ignored by the newly elected *Reichschancellor*, who, as early as September 1919, had written that anti-Semitism should be based not on emotion but on 'facts', and would, by the same logic, lead to the 'systematic removal' of Jewish rights. 'Its final aim,' he concluded, 'must inevitably be the removal of the Jews altogether.'

A SMALL, TACITURN, CYNICALLY HUMOROUS MAN, Ryszard – augmenting his few art commissions by taking poorly paid work in a record-pressing factory – came to regret his departure from Poland. In 1933 he wrote to his youngest brother Stefan that, after several years of living in the French capital, he still felt like a 'complete stranger'. We know that Ryszard was well dressed, irrepressibly proud of his looks, responsible and honest, but also gruff, bad-tempered and stingy – a 'clenched fist' in one account; not a natural parent. Fifty years later, shortly before his father was stricken with cancer, Roman Polanski was to write in his memoirs that 'he often hurt my feelings in little ways'. He went on to paint a picture of an emotionally vacant man whose one real attachment was to his ancient Underwood typewriter. Ryszard had, it's agreed, a way with women, a talent Roman would inherit from him. Mostly, though, the son consciously tried to be as unlike his father as possible. Where Ryszard was frugal, Roman prided himself on spending money the second he earned it, and often even earlier. The older man lived long enough to be flown to California as his rich and famous son's house guest, but would spend much of his time there complaining, not without cause, that Roman's friends were 'parasites'.

Polanski's mother was a more formidable proposition, a tall, elegant brunette who wore the most fashionable pillbox hats and sported a fox fur on all but the warmest days. Forty years later, Bula Polanski would be the physical model for Dunaway's character in *Chinatown*, with her exquisitely plucked eyebrows and vivid red lipstick shaped into a cupid's bow. Bula also took great pride in her housework, employed a maid whenever circumstances allowed, enjoyed a night out and charmed her many friends by 'turn[ing] a conversation around so that you would talk about yourself'. It was a curious pairing: Ryszard was the pragmatic and proverbially dour working-class Pole who made his wife accountable for every penny and was cool towards children; Bula the stylish and energetic

Russian with faint aristocratic connections and a 10-year-old daughter, Annette, from her first marriage.

The father's disposition and the heavy atmosphere he created in the house cast a deep shadow over Roman's early childhood. He was acutely aware of Ryszard's financial struggles, which seem to have had a singular motivational effect: the sense that the world of *praca zwyczajowy*, or conventional graft, wasn't for him. Meanwhile, Romek (the diminutive he answered to through adolescence) grew up under the handicap of being small, with extravagant ears, and features that were variously described as 'gnarled' or 'ferrety'. At least one friend suggests that Polanski's family life, to the extent that he had one, 'produced the basic anxiety, [the] sense of being adrift in a hostile world.' Kenneth Tynan would note that 'things were apparently pretty dark for Roman for seven or eight years, at which stage they turned black.'

At some point in June or early July 1936, in a fatefully ill-timed move, Ryszard would leave Paris and take his family back to Krakow. As he later conceded, with characteristic black humour, it was a 'truly exquisite' blunder on his part. That same summer, the gauleiter of Danzig, one Albert Förster, launched an aggressive campaign to expel the League of Nations high commissioner for the so-called 'free city', Sean Lester. Receiving no support from the League powers, Lester duly resigned. Förster then made a speech in which he announced that Germany was preparing for war, that Hitler would be entering Danzig within a few months, and that the Poles as well as the League would be 'eliminated'. Back in Berlin, the propaganda ministry, in a sorry departure from the Declaration of Non-aggression, confirmed that should the German minorities living there suffer the 'slightest abuse', the Führer would ensure that not a trace of Poland remained.

THE POLANSKIS SETTLED AT 9 KOMOROWSKI STREET, a three-roomed flat with low ceilings and a malodorous tiled stove, located between a Catholic church and one of Krakow's numerous open-air markets. There were few pretensions to elegance. The facade of the building was undistinguished, except for an heraldic beast of satanic demeanour, still intact today, carved over the doorway. Ryszard found temporary work as a freelance builder and carpenter before opening his own plastics business, manufacturing and selling ashtrays, dolls and inexpensive religious figurines.

In September 1938, Romek was enrolled at the local kindergarten, but lasted only one day. He was expelled for saying *'Pocatuj mnie w dupa'* – roughly translated as 'Kiss my ass' – to the 5-year-old girl seated next to him. Years later, his head teacher would remark that, even on that brief evidence, Polanski, who looked 'barely older than a baby', had been a curious mixture of the precocious and the backward. 'I couldn't make him out,' she admitted. 'I thought he would either be a cretin or a man of genius.' Much of Romek's subsequent education was at the hands of his teenage half-sister, who both encouraged him to draw and took him to the numerous cinemas around Rynek Główny, the town's central plaza, whose incredible visual patisserie of medieval towers and squat, redbrick apartment blocks was symbolic of the two Krakows: the ancient city with its baroque castle and churches, the so-called 'Pearl of Europe', and its gaudily modern Thirties facelift. The word between the wars was 'renewal', the result acres of dead tramway lines and rubble dumped into the green, still hair-oil of the Vistula river. In later years, the Krakow city planners would finish the job by erecting the country's largest steel mill in the town's eastern suburbs, bringing with it entire, prefabricated neighbourhoods whose chief physical characteristics were endless one-way systems and mortuaries.

One morning early in 1939, a middle-aged lady knocked on the door of the Polanskis' apartment. She was a giant of a woman; her bulging figure was swathed in a black crêpe dress and her feet overflowed in red shoes. She had applied a perhaps overgenerous blue rinse, topped off by a floral hat. She carried with her a thick loose-leaf notebook, which she consulted while enquiring about the family's religious habits. More specifically, was the small 5-year-old boy who gazed up at her with his 'extremely crafty' and 'wizened' grin a good, baptised Catholic?

Both Ryszard and Bula Polanski were lapsed Jews. Apart from on feast days, they rarely ventured the two miles south into Krakow's Kazimierz district, where the synagogues were packed together, in one contemporary account, as 'closely as dominoes ready to fall'. The surviving city records list neither parent among the register of 'Known Temple-goers'. As a boy, Romek had little or no concept of what it was to be Jewish. He was later able to be 'farmed out', for long periods, with a succession of Gentile families. This lack of orthodoxy perhaps put him in good stead when, even after the war, he was to convincingly pass himself off as a Catholic, if only to evade the Soviet census-takers. As a teenager he was gradually to adopt at least some of the trappings of Jewish ritual, wary as he was that 'a great deal of anti-Semitism still existed in Poland. Pogroms took place at this period, at least one of them in Krakow.' Several film critics have overextended themselves in seeking to explain Polanski's work in terms of a vast spiritual crisis – his 'question[ing] the whole connection between God's will and the course of history', one wrote. That would probably be going too far, if not, perhaps, going entirely in the wrong direction. It seems fair to say that Polanski was understandably curious about religion, violence and the interaction between the two as experienced in Poland, and that he alluded to this in some of his films. 'What did we do wrong?' Romek asked Ryszard one day shortly after the war.

That summer of 1939 Polanski spent slipping in and out of the cinema with Annette, eventually teaching himself to read, after a fashion, by deciphering the films' Polish subtitles. He was largely free to wander around Krakow, enjoying other organised entertainments such as fist-fighting competitions. In August the family were able to take a small holiday chalet in the mountain resort of Szczyrk, where Romek amused himself by collecting and sketching butterflies.

All the survivors agree that it was a golden summer, and figures prove that this wasn't mere nostalgia for an old-fashioned, deferential, secure, comparatively simple and happy world. Not only was it unusually hot; the diplomatic situation seemed to improve, at least while talks continued between Britain, France and the Soviet Union. To the semi-official Warsaw *Gazetta*, it appeared that these nations would 'never permit Germany to make direct contact with Polish troops . . . Our sovereignty is assured.'

The next day – Tuesday 22 August – it was announced in Moscow that the German foreign minister, Ribbentrop, was flying to the Soviet capital the following morning. It would be almost impossible to exaggerate the widespread astonishment at what followed. Late on the night of the 23rd Ribbentrop and his Soviet counterpart Molotov signed their non-aggression pact, ostensibly to 'desist from any act of violence, any threatening action, and any attack on each other', and, more pertinently, to partition Eastern Europe into spheres of influence for each to do with what it wished. It was agreed that whether or not Poland was to continue to exist as a state would be 'determined in the course of further political developments'.

The world was unaware, at this stage, that precise battle plans had already been drawn up in Berlin and Moscow that called for their two armies to meet on the banks of the Vistula, the river that flowed through Krakow.

A DAY OR TWO LATER, walking down Komorowski Street towards the park, Romek came across a crowd queuing up in front of a kiosk to buy a cartoon showing Hitler and the Nazi top brass which ingeniously folded out into the shape of a pig. It was the first time that he realised that there was a tangible threat to his country's well-being. With the outbreak of war now believed imminent, Ryszard sent his family into hiding in

Warsaw, some 150 miles further from the Reich border and thus, he thought, safe from immediate danger. It was another grave miscalculation. At 4.30 a.m. on 1 September 1939, the German battleship *Schleswig-Holstein* turned its heavy guns on Danzig, while ground troops poured across the frontier. Exactly a week later, panzer elements of Army Group South arrived at the outskirts of Warsaw.

The massacre that ensued was swift, efficient and of unparalleled ferocity. Polish defences were rapidly overrun, their army making a hasty strategic withdrawal south-east towards Rumania, where, abandoned by their commander and headquarters staff, the troops either surrendered or fled. With air defences similarly in disarray, the Germans were able to carry out round-the-clock bombing raids at little or no risk to themselves. Like tens of thousands of others, the Polanskis spent their nights huddled together in the nearest basement, where 6-year-old Romek dozed, fully clothed, in his mother's arms, a gauze pad strapped to his face as a makeshift gas mask. The small room would typically hold some forty or fifty fellow evac-uees. Those who shared the experience later chiefly remembered the noise, reminiscent of a lunatic asylum, with 'shouted warnings, screams [and] whimperings' in between the actual explosions. The Luftwaffe having efficiently destroyed the city's water supply system and road networks, the family took to scavenging for supplies, surviving for several days on a jar of pickles, whose salty-tasting juice they drank to the last drop, an event that Polanski would recall sixty-three years later in *The Pianist*.

The Polish agony lasted until 27 September, when the military commander of Warsaw surrendered the city and the civilian government fled. Some 22,000 non-combatants, among them an estimated 7,500 children, had died in the bombardment. The few remaining pockets of resistance in the south of the country crumbled within hours. Poland (the Soviets having invaded, largely unopposed, on 17 September) effectively no longer existed. In less than a month of fighting, the Germans had destroyed a major European army, killing some 70,000 troops and making prisoners of 700,000 more, at negligible cost to themselves. The humili-ated population of Warsaw stood watching the enemy forces enter their city on the morning of 28 September, some greeting their occupiers with a pathetically weary Nazi salute, many more breaking down in tears.

Clutching his father's hand, Romek now struggled out through streets – or what had once been streets – heaped with blackened bodies, broken glass, crockery, furniture and other debris. In a cobbled square in Old Town, he watched one group of elderly women hacking away the decaying flesh of a dead carthorse. There were numerous unclaimed human corpses of all ages, some of them apparently suicides. Rounding the corner by the royal castle, Ryszard Polanski pointed to the columns of German infantry approaching from the distance, their boots kicking up a thick cloud of dust ahead of them. As the troops streamed past, Ryszard squeezed his son's hand hard, turned his head and screwed up his nose like a pig's, muttering, 'Swine, swine!'

SHORTLY AFTER THAT, the Polanskis returned to Krakow. At least initially, they were able to live something approaching a normal life in a designated 'Jew sector'. Romek attended primary school for several weeks, until all Jewish children were abruptly expelled. This initiative was followed by the compulsory adoption of a white armband with the Star of David stencilled in blue, by all those, aged 12 and over, deemed 'impure' by the military government. In short order, signs went up in the windows of all public buildings declaring 'No Jews or Dogs Allowed'. 'The Hebrews', it was officially minuted in December 1939, 'spoil[ed] not just the appearance but the mood' of the city. They were to be treated 'without any sentimentality'. After that, Romek would not see the inside of another classroom for six years.

He used his spare time in reading, drawing and tinkering with a small epidiascope, a crude but surprisingly durable device for projecting pictures on to a wall. Early that winter, Romek, his parents and half-sister were moved again, to a large ground-floor flat, ample for the four of them but which they shared with three other families, across the Vistula on Podgorze Square. This was explained as being part of a citywide 'rationalisation' of resources, a notable euphemism for what followed.

The operation that would incarcerate Krakow's remaining Jewish population in a ghetto came as a shock even to those, like Ryszard, who had feared the worst from the German occupation. There had been, it's true, certain indications of official Nazi distaste and disapproval of their victims along the way. In April 1940, the Reich's so-called 'legal expert' Hans Frank announced that Krakow was to become the 'cleanest' city in Europe – that is, one without Jews. Following that, regulations went into effect prohibiting the ownership of 'luxury items' (including Ryszard's prized typewriter) among the 'minority classes'. In some cases, entire businesses were seized. The clothing and petrol rations were both subsequently cut. In two brutally efficient round-ups carried out in May and September 1940, the authorities expelled as many as two-thirds of the town's 68,000

Jews, resettling most of them in and around the Lublin district to the north-east. It was then decided that the Star of David armband, which the wearer himself bought, would be issued to young children. On a Friday night that December, fourteen synagogues were vandalised or looted, and a rabbi was accosted by a mob who removed his hair and beard while German soldiers watched impassively. But, even after these indignities, most of Krakow's surviving Jews greeted the events of 3 March 1941 with a kind of numb disbelief. Early that morning, hundreds of troops, armoured personnel carriers, equipment and workers simply appeared from their staging area on the far side of the Vistula. As *Wehrmacht* officers read out Edict 44/91 from the district governor, Dr Otto Wächter, denouncing the 'contamination' of the Aryan races, workmen began to rip up asphalt and cobblestones, unloading piles of bricks and bales of barbed wire, which were quickly made into a barrier running immediately in front of the Polanskis' flat on Podgorze Square. Some inhabitants were imprisoned immediately, and others given a two-week 'grace period' in which to relocate behind a rough-hewn wall mockingly built in the shape of Jewish gravestones. Either way, the entire district of some 18,000 people was effectively encircled and sealed off.

From then on the ghetto became a self-contained town with its own civil administration, or *Judenrat*, and a local police force that relied on a network of paid informers. Throughout 1941–2, 'stooges' were officially encouraged to report anyone suspected of 'deviation', which in most cases meant hoarding food. At this stage of the war, the official allocation, which would drop, was 100 grams of bread per day per person, and 200 grams of sugar monthly; the staple diet was potatoes. Acting on one such tip-off, a German officer in full leather regalia searched the Polanskis' flat, where, after seizing the 7-year-old's teddy bear, which he swung menacingly by the neck, he quickly discovered a box of bread rolls, freshly baked by Bula. With the tip of his swagger stick, the visitor scattered the rolls on to the floor, laughed and strode out. Polanski would remember this incident when he came to film the scene in *Macbeth* where two of the king's murderous henchmen surprise Lady Macduff and her young son. A day later, the family received a notice warning them that any future such breach of the regulations would be dealt with 'in the severest terms' – deportation or imprisonment – allowed for under *Judenrat* law.

While such threats remained a way of life, Romek, a highly imaginative youth, was able to take childlike pleasure in at least some of the ordeal. He enjoyed watching and sketching the local tram, the seats segregated between Jews and non-Jews, and playing in the rubble with other ghetto boys. On summer weekends there were open-air films in Podgorze Square, which he could illicitly watch by peering between strands of barbed wire, a seminal association he never forgot; during intermissions, the projectionist entertained his audiences by flashing up messages such as JEWS=LICE=TYPHUS! on the screen. Both the Jewish and non-Jewish populations were becoming increasingly dehumanised. Scenes that would have been greeted with utter disbelief in 1939 were met with a weary indifference two years later. At the slightest provocation, entire families were 'resettled' or 'evacuated', to use the Nazi terms, if not otherwise disposed of; a ghetto survivor named Pytor Gorsky recalls walking home one evening through an area 'where dogs prowled around with body parts in their jaws'. Perhaps the cruellest part of the whole experience, though, was the tantalising proximity of everyday life. Residents of the ghetto could look out of their windows at the traffic on the far side of the wall, and even walk up to one of the relatively open stretches constructed only of wood and barbed wire. Friends stood facing one another, trying to make themselves heard across the few yards separating them without attracting attention to themselves. Some were able to furtively pass notes and small packages to and fro. In time, without his parents' knowledge, Romek even managed to slip out of the ghetto, squeezing around the fence to enjoy a 'glorious adventure' exploring the 'other side'. His principal reaction to the bombings, the isolation and the worsening hunger was that it was all a huge misunderstanding; surely, he felt, 'something would be done'.

To most adults, the ghetto was a very different proposition. Survivors would later recall conditions as 'godforsaken', 'pitiless', and above all cramped – the official census of 320 dwellings with 3,167 rooms, compressed into sixteen city blocks, making for an average of six residents per room. In one of many such daily humiliations, a German officer once slapped Ryszard, out strolling with his family, either because the Polanskis had been walking on the pavement (as opposed to in the gutter, the prescribed path for Jews), or for the sheer fun of it. By mid-1941, Romek's father was earning a slave wage as a metalworker in a factory turning out munitions largely destined for the Eastern Front. Bula, for her part, having had her money, jewellery and most of her clothes legally confiscated, was forced to take work as a cleaning woman at Wawel Castle, the headquarters of the German staff. Like her husband, she was to enjoy the limited privileges of a *Kennkarte*, allowing her to pass in and out of the ghetto 'for professional purposes'. Although stoic about the ordeal, it must have been exquisitely galling to her to spend her days performing the most menial duties for the senior Nazis.

No one incident, however, quite brought home the horror of the situation like the warm summer day in 1941 when Romek watched a squad of German soldiers frogmarching some Jewish families near Podgorze Square. One elderly woman, unable to keep up, fell to her knees and began pleading with the officer in charge. In response, he calmly drew his pistol and shot her in the back. As the woman collapsed, Romek ran to the nearest building, squeezed himself under the staircase, and wept.

He didn't, as yet, seem particularly bothered by the periodic raids and deportations, since, as he later said, 'Children don't have any point of reference – they're optimistic. After each German round-up I told myself that things would improve.' In the most recent case, an SS captain named Krüger had personally shot twenty-five of the senior professors at Jagiellonian University and then driven off while still screaming anti-Polish insults. The ghetto itself, under Nazi control, was kept desperately short of food, but remained to some extent at work. For long periods it seemed to slide into a sort of apathy, until the next disaster. Pending that, the Polanskis made plans for Romek to be taken in by a suburban Catholic couple named Wilk, who in turn found a peasant family living outside Krakow willing to board him for a deposit of 2,000 zloty. But this arrangement lasted only a few days, the third party complaining bitterly that they hadn't intended to give refuge to a 'little Jew'. They did, however, retain both the Polanskis' down payment and the two battered suitcases containing Romek's wordly belongings.

The Germans' steady constriction of the ghetto tightened in the winter of 1941–2. Under the governorship of Otto Wächter, a man whose reputation for Teutonic efficiency was more than matched by his fanaticism and ruthlessness, the wholesale liquidation continued of 'intellectuals, academics, artists, poets [and] social deviants', while the remaining population was reduced to starvation level. Many of the relatively able-bodied were assigned to slave for the local Nazi overseer Amon Goeth (later hanged for war crimes) at his Plaszów 'enterprise camp' on the outskirts of Krakow. After the German invasion of Russia in June 1941, which stretched manpower resources so catastrophically, thousands more predominantly Jewish men and women were to vanish overnight, deported to the Reich for compulsory labour or to extermination camps like those located thirty miles west of Krakow in the sprawling suburbs of Oswiecim and Brzezinka, now known collectively as Auschwitz.

As the ghetto shrank, the Polanskis were moved again, sharing two cramped rooms with an elderly man, a couple with a small son named Stefan, and an incontinent dog. This latest accommodation to Wächter's master plan came into effect in January 1943, by which time the ghetto had been repeatedly decimated, with only 2,000–2,500 surviving inhabitants. Six months earlier, acting in his capacity as *Reichskommissar für die Festigung der deutschen Volkstums* (Reich Commissar for the Strengthening of Germanism), Heinrich Himmler had set out his plans for 'the resettlement of the entire Jewish population of the General Government [i.e. Poland]', 'resettlement' being a euphemism for genocide. The orders were executed, with brutal thoroughness, to a fixed schedule. On 13 February 1943, Pytor Gorsky and other ghetto dwellers were warned by an apparently sympathetic German guard that another raid was imminent. Early the next morning, Valentine's Day, Bula Polanski used her *Kennkarte* to take Romek out with her through the least heavily patrolled of the ghetto's four gates. An hour later she deposited him and a small heart-shaped box of dried fruits with the Wilk family, passing them another envelope of money and promising to collect him when circumstances allowed. Bula then travelled on to Wawel Castle. Several days later, it was Ryszard, instead, who appeared at the door and silently took his son home on the tram. The boy apparently thought his father's face looked 'roughed up', as if he had just been in one of the ghetto's frequent brawls, though in fact it reflected only sleeplessness. As they were walking the final few yards across Podgorze Bridge into the ghetto, Ryszard suddenly began sobbing uncontrollably. Turning to Romek, he said, 'They took your mother.'

Years later, it was learnt that Bula Polanski had been transported directly to Auschwitz, where, within days, she would be one of an estimated 980,000 Jews murdered in the gas chamber. She had been four months pregnant at the time. Her condition, it is thought, would have been immediately noted at the initial 'selection' process, in which SS doctors separated those who were useful for work from those who were 'unfit' and would be executed as soon as practical.

In the two weeks ahead, the storm troopers came for Romek's grandmother and his half-sister Annette, while his eldest and favourite uncle, Bernard, was interned at Buchenwald, where he was eventually beaten to death. Young Stefan's parents were also deported, so Ryszard undertook to feed both the boys as best he could. As an example of what that meant in practice, one warmed-up potato served as dinner for three, while the occasional crust of bread and rancid butter struck them as a Babylonian luxury.

At each fresh round-up, Romek was either walked through the gate or slipped alone through the fence and made his way by tram and foot to the Wilk family. Returning home one sunny March day, he ran up one empty street after another to find the entire ghetto ominously deserted until, panic-ridden, he turned the corner to the cobbled central square, the Plac Zgody. A wretched sight greeted him. A large crowd of men, women and children were lined up, some already silently shuffling forward to the wagons of a waiting train some 200 yards in the distance. The 500–600 members of this sombre parade were thin, pale and unkempt, of apparently all races and professions, and surrounded by German and Polish guards, with a plump SS officer barking orders from off a clipboard in his hand. In one account, 'names, articles and accusations rang over the square'; over and over again, with monotonous rhythm, came the carefully bureaucratic phrases: 'Repatriation of persons of German race ... Elimination of the injurious influences of those constituting a danger to the Reich and German community ... Continuing transfer of populations and immediate transport to that effect.' In plain language, this meant the accelerated expulsion of the native Polish or Slav populations, and the wholesale extermination of the Jews.*

After a futile search for his father, Romek eventually found his young friend Stefan wandering around the square by himself, crying for his own parents. The two boys were able to talk their way out of the area by promising a teenaged Pole on sentry duty that they were going home for some food and would be 'right back'. As the guard stood aside, he muttered imperceptibly, 'Don't run.' The boys spent the next week at the Wilks' before a homesick Romek got up the nerve to return to the ghetto. It was now all but vacant, the streets rubble-strewn, with only a few broken sticks of furniture and an overturned pram as evidence of the latest raid. In the midst of this wasteland, several doors bore an official-looking notice, printed

---

* A local kitchenware magnate and black-marketeer, Oskar Schindler, had intervened over the preceding year to save some 1,200 deportees from the death camps by employing them at his factory, the Deutsche Emailwaren Fabrik, which was soon converted to making field equipment (and ultimately munitions) for the German war effort. In September 1944, Schindler persuaded the authorities to let him take these 'specialist guest workers' with him from Krakow to a new plant in Czechoslovakia; this was his famous list. Despite some imaginative press coverage on the subject, there's no evidence that either Schindler or his managers ever encountered the Polanskis.

in Polish and German, with the most recent directives from Berlin: 'Having read the report submitted to him, on Jews, bandits and subhumans, the *Reichsführer-SS* decrees ... deprivation of all civic rights ... deportation to penal servitude ... indefinitely ... in the penalty companies of the *Reichsarbeitsdienst* ...', and so on. Almost incredibly, Ryszard himself had survived the mass round-up, and was reunited with Romek and young Stefan for several more days: the boys were put to work in a local factory manufacturing paper bags.

Early on the morning of 14 March 1943, the Krakow ghetto was finally liquidated. It was exactly a month since Bula Polanski had disappeared; the destruction of families 'one Jew at a time' was specifically encouraged in the German plan. Ryszard was able to smuggle Romek out of the immediate area, Stefan being left to his fate, before the SS came for him. From there the 9-year-old took to his heels, crossing Podgorze Bridge and riding the tram out of town to the Wilks, who happened to have been away. Unsure of what to do next, Romek doubled back to the bridge, where he found a column of men being marched off to the waiting trains. Among them was Ryszard.

Romek came as close as he dared and gestured to his father. As the long line of prisoners went by, Ryszard was able to slip back through the ranks to a position furthest from the guards. Like all the detainees, he had had his tie, belt and shoelaces removed. It was standard procedure.

For several seconds, the irregular-looking squad shuffled on in silence towards the wagons. Then Ryszard's lips moved, though just barely, and he spoke in a voice so low that Romek had to strain to hear it from six feet away.

'Zjeźdźaj,' he said. 'Get lost.'

NINE DAYS LATER, Ryszard was transferred to Mauthausen, a group of forty-nine German concentration camps located near Hitler's childhood home of Linz in Upper Austria. It was among the harshest outposts of a penal system known for its barbarism. On his official admission card, Ryszard denied having a wife or children and gave his age as six years younger than he actually was, presumably to present himself as being fit for work. At Mauthausen this chiefly entailed the notorious 'stairs of death', a vertiginous rock quarry up whose 186 steps prisoners struggled carrying concrete slabs weighing as much as 50 kg each. When an exhausted prisoner collapsed he fell backwards into the man immediately behind him, creating an horrific domino effect. Of the 335,000 inmates who passed through the Mauthausen sub-camps, an estimated 122,000 died while in captivity.

On the very day Ryszard was interned, the Germans announced that their occupying forces in Russia had come across huge mass graves in the Katyn Forest near Smolensk. There they found more than 4,000 bodies, which were identified as those of the Polish army officers listed as 'missing' since the outbreak of war. The subsequent discovery of two further sites brought the number of dead to 27,500. All had been shot through the back of the head. The officers had been swiftly arrested or captured in September 1939, tried *in absentia*, and shortly thereafter found guilty of being 'counter-Revolutionary landowners . . . spies and saboteurs . . . hardened . . . enemies of Soviet power.' The men had been individually murdered in a hut with padded, soundproofed walls, at a quota of 275 'erasures' a night, by Stalin's favourite executioner V. M. Blokhin. The Germans blamed the Russians. The Russians blamed the Germans, and, on a note of near farcical indignation, announced that they were severing diplomatic relations with the rump Polish government in London, who had had the temerity to protest. At that same time, the Nazis were efficiently quelling the Warsaw ghetto uprising, in which 7,000 Jewish residents were shot and a further 6,000 burnt alive or gassed in bunkers.

This was the backdrop at the time Romek Wilk, as he styled himself, went into permanent hiding in the spring of 1943. It was hard to say which was worse, the war situation or his own predicament. Either way, he was alone.

At least at first he was still able to move around Krakow, where he passed himself off as a German in order to buy a cheap ticket to the Swit cinema. The twice-daily performances ranged from operettas and westerns to crude propaganda shorts in which murderous and arbitrary purges became a 'triumph over lice and sub-races', the reigning tyrant a 'Father to all Aryans' and heroic founder of the *Volksdeutscher Selbstschutz* (Ethnic German Self-Protection), a militia specifically established to 'nullify' any remaining Jews in Poland. In time Romek's obsession with film led him to fashion a makeshift projector out of a torch and a tin tea-caddy. According to a friend who apparently later heard the story from Polanski himself, he was lugging this device on to the tram one day early in July 1943 when he overheard two German officers enthusing about the death of the Polish prime minister in exile, General Sikorski. 'That's one less yid rat to drown,' they're said to have noted. Feeling understandably vulnerable, the 9-year-old alighted at the next stop and hitched a lift out to his new hosts, the Puteks, a working-class family with a small son, whose somewhat highly strung teenaged aunt took it upon herself to throw Romek's projector out of the nearest window. That ended his current tenancy.

In late summer Romek moved to the remote Polish village of Wysoka, twenty-five miles south of Krakow, on the edge of the blue-capped Tatras mountains, where he boarded with a family named Buchala. It was an almost feudal existence; the area was near exclusively Catholic, anti-Semitic, wretchedly poor and backward. The immediate post-war official census would refer to Wysoka as 'unembellished'. There was one small shop, and even that trafficked solely in string, religious ornaments and copies of the local *Farmer's Almanac*. For many years after the war, the tiny municipal swimming pool in the next village (remembered by one resident as a 'frothing vat') was drained on Monday night and new water was added on Tuesday – Monday was Turks' day. The first Jewish family did not settle in Wysoka until 1992.

In his memoirs, Polanski would describe Mr Buchala, a part-time cobbler, as a 'simple soul, gruffly inarticulate' and his wife as a 'strong, scrawny, energetic woman [with] an amiable, gap-toothed grin.' There were three children: two small sons and a 'retarded, drooling girl' of 12 named Jaga.

Without papers and thus denied schooling, Romek kept to a peasant's routine, rising early and working the Buchalas' small plot of land. The house itself was a hovel, apparently made out of mud, manure and straw, in which he occupied a 'sort of cubbyhole behind the cowshed'. Food was scarce, even by wartime standards, with some of the potato dishes so full of weevils and maggots that they could only be eaten with the eyes closed. When they ran out, the Buchalas experimented with stewed flowers, rat pie and in at least one case the boiled bark of a tree. Romek developed sores on his legs and had to be 'regularly deloused' with paraffin.

★

CHECKING THE TRUTH OF ROMAN POLANSKI'S STORIES, especially about his childhood, is a time-consuming business. The most reliable contemporary accounts of occupied Poland and the *Bundesarchiv* in Berlin both put the total number of non-Jewish Polish citizens killed between March 1943 and the final siege of Warsaw in the autumn of 1944, whether in outrages, forced marches, bombing or shelling at around 6,000, many of them volunteers in the Home Army. Terrible though such atrocities were, relatively few of them occurred in the course of everyday rural life. The brutality of the Nazis' policy of 'repatriation' – ethnic cleansing – with its tragic consequences for Polanski's family is very amply documented (Ryszard's index card from Mauthausen still exists), and the Polish experience as a whole stands out even in the horrific catalogue of Nazi abuses. The events of 1939–45 would have been terrifying for any child. But they weren't always good enough. The roots of Romek's fertile imagination, so adroitly skirting the edges of the truth, may lie in the war, when he was forced quite literally to assume an identity. The 'great fabulist', as one film critic calls him, seems to have begun life in Wysoka.

Speaking to the American TV host Dick Cavett in December 1971, Polanski recalled his time with the Buchalas:

> It was my first contact with the country. I was 7½ and I lived there for a few years . . . Once I was there picking berries and I saw some German soldiers on a horse cart, and I just ignored them. Then I heard the whistle of a bullet. It was the first time I heard such a thing, and then I heard the clap of the explosion. I looked in the direction and saw they were just shooting at nothing to do with me. They just let out a shot.

Actually Romek moved to Wysoka in the summer of 1943, when he was 10, not 7½, and was there for sixteen months, not a few years. Such minor quibbles aside, the 'fabulist' school of events has at least one significant source – Polanski himself, who wrote of the same incident thirteen years later:

> [One] day I was picking blackberries . . . I heard a whistling sound, followed, a split second later, by a sharp crack. I peered around and saw, about 200 yards away, [a] horse and wagon with [two] German soldiers. One of them was lowering his rifle. I dropped my tin mug of blackberries and ran as fast as I could, then hid in the bracken until it was dark. I never discovered why the soldiers took a potshot at me, and I never told anyone.

Now the soldiers, rather than 'just shooting at nothing to do with me', were deliberately taking a potshot – or, rather, 'several shots', a 'prolonged barrage' or 'salvo', using the boy for 'human target practice' as it was variously reported (though not, it should be said, by the subject himself). If the memory was fragile, the story was sturdy, and found its way into all the subsequent Polanski biographies.

★

WHEN THE GERMAN CENSUS-TAKERS CAME TO WYSOKA, Romek took to the hills or, on one occasion, boarded with a 'big and full-bosomed' woman in an outlying village, who took him to bed with her. Between times he learned to ski, using a pair of planks and hazel branches, and swam in the local duck pond. He seems to have been a hard worker, putting in twelve-hour days feeding, milking and 'mucking out' before returning to his rustic billet. Like all their neighbours, the Buchalas were religiously observant, and the most meagre meal began with everyone saying grace and making the sign of the cross.

On 17 July 1944, the first units of the Red Army crossed the river Bug, broke through a fault in the German defence and advanced on Warsaw. Closing in on the city, the Soviets broadcast an appeal in the name of the 'Great Benefactor', Marshal Stalin, for the Home Army to rise up against their 'fascist oppressors', which the underground heroically did – while the Russians sat outside the capital. Hitler ordered that Warsaw be razed, unleashing a shock force of hardened SS fanatics, paroled criminals and lunatics to accomplish the job. Allied transports began dropping supplies on central and southern Poland from early August, a relief operation Stalin not only opposed but actively obstructed. Looking into the summer skies above Wysoka, Romek saw 'hundreds of American planes going east. [It] was one of the most profound moments of my life . . . I was just hoping that none of the planes would explode. They did occasionally and I would see the white parachute, and then I was hoping he would come over this way and I would be able to talk with him. It was a moving experience. It was beautiful.'*

By late October, the Germans, having levelled ninety per cent of Warsaw at the loss of 225,000 lives, were in a phased retreat. The withdrawal brought daily sightings of grizzled, hungry-looking troops in villages like Wysoka, where they raided the local farms for supplies. As well as the pillaging, there were disquieting reports of German units assaulting or murdering Polish civilians who happened to be in their way. After one close encounter with the SS, Romek decided to trek the two days back to Krakow, where, apparently forgiving the vandalism of his projector, he again took refuge with the Puteks. Christmas dinner that year was a freshly slaughtered goose which the family shared in their cellar while an artillery battle raged

---

* According both to official service histories and subsequent accounts by combatants, the enemy 'didn't significantly oppose' 15th US Air Force operations over Poland, although individual cases such as Polanski describes did no doubt occur.

overhead. From time to time direct hits brought lumps of plaster 'crashing down, accompanied [by] terrified cries', reminiscent of the scene in the Polanskis' basement in Warsaw more than five years earlier.

On 27 January 1945, Soviet troops liberated the 7,000 wretched, skeleton-like survivors of the Auschwitz annihilation complex. They subsequently found 830,000 women's dresses, 368,000 men's suits, thousands of pairs of children's shoes and vast quantities of dentures and glasses. According to witnesses there was also a 'procession' of baby carriages, which were pushed five abreast out of the camp into the nearby railway station, and took an hour to pass by. There was no accounting, as yet, for these articles' owners.

Back in their cellar, the Puteks were roused by a loud knocking from their neighbour, a Mr Jozek. He had a bottle of liberated vodka in his hand. 'It's all over,' he shouted hoarsely. The Russians were advancing up Krakowska towards the city centre, quickly raising the hammer and sickle over Wawel Castle, thus beginning the long, ambivalent post-war relationship between Poland and the Soviet Union. For the first several weeks, at least, there was delirious joy at the army's arrival. To Romek and many others, the 'Reds' represented a welcome source of order amid the chaos of shattered tanks, cars, trucks and human corpses lying frozen in the snow. 'They were kind to children,' he notes, efficiently operating a network of soup kitchens without which many more would have starved. (Market conditions, to the extent that they existed, were such that a small bag of flour cost some 2,000 zloty, while a pound of meat of ominously uncertain origin fetched twice as much.) Yet these same troops were to rape an estimated 3,700 local women and girls, some as young as 10, and to display a notably cavalier attitude towards burying both the civilian and enemy dead. Most of Krakow's remaining stocks of liquor soon vanished. This was the 'brutalis[ed] horde of Asiatics, Mongols and Slavs', spiritual descendants of Genghis Khan, that even the battle-hardened SS troops had warned about. The Russians also brought their full propaganda apparatus with them, wheeling out huge plaster busts of Marx, Engels, Lenin and the 'Mountain Eagle' or 'Great Benefactor', Stalin, into the public squares.

The benefactor himself was sitting down just then in the ballroom of Livadia Palace in Yalta, where the fate of Poland was effectively decided in tripartite talks between the Allies. There were vague promises about 'democratisation' and 'free and unfettered elections', the latter of which would take forty-five years to materialise. As Stalin had observed, 'Whoever occupies a territory also imposes on it his own social system.

Everyone imposes his own system as far as his army can reach. It cannot be otherwise.' As a result, Poland became the first model of the Soviet satellite state, with a full set of Eastern Bloc accessories, including a rigorous censorship of films.

ROMEK STILL HAD NO IDEA WHAT HAD BECOME OF HIS PARENTS, or if they were even alive. He spent the first weeks of 1945 effectively living rough on the streets of Krakow, occasionally enjoying a meal with the Puteks, more often applying to a Soviet soup kitchen or simply scavenging. At the same time, the world was coming to learn the full extent of the Nazi genocide. Following their liberation of Buchenwald, Flossenbürg and Dachau, US forces entered Mauthausen on the morning of 5 May. The pathetic survivors who greeted them were described in one soldier's account as 'emaciated beyond all imagination . . . Their legs and arms were sticks with huge bulging joints; their eyes were sunk so deep that they looked blind. If they moved at all, it was with a crawling slowness that made them look like huge, lethargic spiders. Many just lay in their bunks as if dead.' More than 10,000 of those who walked or were helped out of the camp gates would succumb to malnutrition, typhus or other diseases within a month.

In Poland, a nation of Holocaust victims and the children of victims, few families were untouched by the atrocities. The drab Krakow station was the scene of daily pandemonium as trains began arriving to reunite survivors, still dressed in their striped camp uniforms, with those they had left behind two, three or four years earlier. Over the course of the spring and early summer, many more area residents learnt that their loved ones would not be returning.

Running free and wild, and clad in a voluminous pair of Cossack dungarees, Romek turned a corner one day and found himself face to face with his uncle Stefan. Ryszard's youngest brother, it emerged, had spent most of the previous five years hidden in a room outside the ghetto. The middle brother, David, had adjusted to the situation by becoming a camp 'kapo', or trusty, a powerful and frequently sadistic figure assigned by the authorities to oversee each prison block. As noted, Bernard, the eldest, perished in captivity. (He was murdered by a kapo.) Against his protests, Romek would be taken in and domesticated by a succession of uncles and aunts, who were horrified by his vulpine manners and general backwardness. When he ate, he 'shovelled the food down', it was reported. His language was 'ripe'; as to baths, 'he tended not to overdo them'.

Romek was with Stefan and his wife Maria in their Krakow apartment when, on the evening of 8 May, flares and ragged volleys of Russian machine-gun fire lit up the sky. Maria gleefully tore down the blackout curtains. Hitler's war was over.

Dressed in his baggy, hayseed clothes and carrying his latest projector with him wherever he went, Romek at least tried to catch up with some rudimentary education. Such schools as remained in Krakow were basic, and in one graduate's words, 'did not satisfy the most minimal academic or even sanitary requirements.' There was widespread anti-Semitism, with many camp survivors returning only to find that their previous home was occupied by someone else, or that their business had been 'nationalised'. An officially tolerated harassment of Jews, with numerous individual cases of assault or lynchings, lasted well into the Fifties. In an instance of what was described as 'medieval bestiality', forty-two Jews were murdered, among them women and a newborn baby, in a racially motivated riot that broke out one evening in July 1946. Perhaps prudently, Romek would continue not to advertise his true circumstances, even after being partially reunited with his family. While there he helped his uncle David in his plumbers' supply store, and displayed typical ingenuity by hawking plastic identity-card holders on the street as a sideline. It was hard and ill-paid work, bringing him into contact with some unsavoury customers, although Polanski describes himself as having been an 'expert salesman'. In time, he became an enthusiastic member of the Boy Scouts, for whom he registered as 'R. Wilk', an 'observant Catholic'.

After several more weeks of uncertainty, a returning Mauthausen inmate finally brought word of Ryszard. He had survived the camp and was now in an American processing centre. This sensational news was followed, in early August, by confirmation that Bula Polanski was one of the more than six million victims of the Nazis' self-styled 'project' to determine who should inhabit Europe. Her daughter Annette, Roman's half-sister, had endured both Auschwitz and a subsequent forced march, made in midwinter and on starvation rations, which eventually delivered her to the Red Army. Shortly after her liberation, she left Poland forever and settled in Paris.

Ryszard simply appeared in his brother David's apartment one morning, dressed in US Army fatigues and looking astonishingly well after his ordeal. After returning from the shop that evening, Romek was reunited with his father after two-and-a-half years' separation. Nothing speaks so eloquently about Ryszard's essential detachment than the fact that he chose to wait several hours for his son to finish work, just a few streets away, and greeted him even then with a hug and the observation that he 'need[ed] a wash'. Neither of them uttered a word about Bula, preferring to talk in generalities, a routine they followed right up to the end of Ryszard's life.

Although spared the wholesale destruction of Warsaw, Krakow was a wretched spectacle in 1945. House-to-house fighting had reduced much of the ghetto area and its outlying factories to rubble. The Soviet 'Red Hammer' squads were more interested in rounding up and deporting the black-marketeers on the Vistula quays than in rebuilding the city. Ryszard's career, too, never quite recovered its pre-war lustre. After only a few days at home, he left in search of work or other prospects around the mining towns of Katowice and Teschen to the west of Krakow. He returned a month later accompanied by an attractive young redhead named Wanda Zajaczkowska. The couple married in 1946.

Not surprisingly, Romek, still grieving his mother's death, regarded this arrangement as an 'unpardonable betrayal . . . I despised what I saw as Wanda's superficiality, her pretensions, and the way she queened it over the rest of the family.' Bonding with a partner's children is always a challenge, requiring as it does a high degree of tact and at least passing familiarity with the concept of self-denial. It has to be said that Wanda didn't quite conform to this ideal, but did buy her stepson a new bicycle. Since Romek refused to live with his father and his wife, Ryszard found him a series of furnished rooms around Krakow. The 13-year-old fed himself from his earnings as a salesman, or by bartering on the black market. Both backward and stubborn, he did more or less what he wanted. One surviving friend who later followed him to America describes him at the time as 'temperamental – a human time bomb' and 'that weird mix of a small boy and a cynical old man. Never listened to anyone but himself.' Roman Polanski's adult tragedy had begun.

A lot of effort would subsequently go into explaining what happened in 1977 as the result of a warped perspective on childhood. Without descending too far into the briar patch of psychiatry, it does seem reasonable to assume that in later life Polanski might have had trouble appreciating that not everyone necessarily grew up as fast as he had. At any rate, at the age of 43, he ended up in bed with a partner thirty years younger than himself, with whom he had a variety of sexual relations, after which he drove the girl home and went about his normal routine. The journalist Franz-Olivier Giesbert later chided the director in an interview in *Le Nouvel Observateur* for having 'sle[pt] with a 13-year-old.'

'She was about to turn 14,' said Polanski.

MOST AFTERNOONS AFTER WORK OR A DESULTORY FEW HOURS AT SCHOOL, Romek hurried back to Krakow's Swit-Kino cinema. Even in the drenching rain which seeped through the roof there, he could soak up the lushness and grandeur of such Hollywood epics as the censor allowed. A particular favourite was Errol Flynn in the Communist-friendly *Adventures of Robin Hood*, which Romek saw nine times. He and a friend named Piotr Winowski soon took to foraging in the cinema's dustbins for any discarded programmes or stray frames of celluloid. The whole technical process of film-making was fast becoming an obsession quite apart from its artistic qualities. One night at the Swit, Romek sat riveted through Carol Reed's *Odd Man Out*, an emotionally taut chase melodrama with some great Belfast atmosphere; even that sombre backdrop struck him as exotic. Thanks to both the movies and a naturally inquisitive mind, he was already daydreaming about the West. By now there was a formidable Soviet-Polish propaganda machine turning out daily reports about the 'decadence' and imminent decline of their recent allies. Romek thought this a stretch. Compared to the scene he was in, he once commented, the problems of a post-war Paris or London seemed laughable. How could you seriously begin to talk about the British balance of payments crisis with a teenager who dined off rat stew?

Polanski went out of his way in later exchanges to deny that the war, or its aftermath, ever meant that much to him. 'Believe it or not, I had quite a cool childhood,' he assured one actor on *Macbeth*. 'Kids accept life as it is because they don't know anything else,' he insisted elsewhere. 'They can't relate to any other lives . . . The hardships I went through seemed quite normal to me.' Franz-Olivier Giesbert opened proceedings in his *Observateur* interview in 1984 by asking, 'You've gone through hell and high water from the Krakow ghetto [onward]. Are you proud of having survived it all?' 'Not particularly,' said Polanski.

As far as we know, he never specifically referred to the war in his few school essays or in the juvenile film plots he dreamt up in his room. But in the late Forties, Romek was also responsible for a series of highly accomplished drawings, always the first thing that friends like Winowski commented on. The surviving sketches have all the marks of a good draughtsman; and his life-studies are done without a trace of self-consciousness. But a teenager brought up on the spectacle of emaci-ated bodies doesn't have the same instincts as one weaned on floppy bunnies or the products of J. K. Rowling. The figures in Romek's doodles are gaunt, tortured nudes – a man in a crucifixion pose, and disturbing studies of a woman bending forwards, apparently gasping for air. Some of these works are still in circulation today. Almost anything can be read into them, but they wouldn't appear to be the fruits of a particularly 'cool' childhood.

LATE IN THE SUMMER OF 1946, Romek Wilk and the rest of Scout Troop 22 boarded a cattle wagon for a month's camping holiday – 'still my yard-stick for anything memorably enjoyable,' he would note forty years later. Their destination was the village of Bytów, in the Pomeranian hills west of Gdansk, the former Danzig. This rural idyll got off to a poor start when a freight car backed into the Scouts' own stationary train, completely immobilising it. It was in the course of the subsequent two-day truck ride that Romek first came to glory in the name 'Puker'.

Once decanted and under canvas, the troop strung up some lights and staged a concert party, which brought a revelation. Romek was *funny*. If there was a moment when he was at his happiest that month, it was during his show-stopping 'turn' for a delighted audience of 13- and 14-year-old boys. The exact programme of events is difficult to pin down, but most accounts agree that it was divided into three phases. First, Romek improvised a sketch about a gnarled old Polish peasant, two tourists and a carthorse, in which he mimicked all four parts. It got a big hand. From there he shifted gears into a comic tap-dance routine, performed as if suffering from some painful disease in the lower half of his body, which segued naturally into the night's real tour de force. 'I was quite famous for farting,' Polanski, brushing modesty aside, was to allegedly note in later years. According to one well-placed source (not corroborated in Polanski's memoirs), the last part of his act was an 'intestinal oratorio in which he actually played in *tune*. Sensational. One of the kids laughed so hard he had to be taken to hospital.'

From that moment on, Romek was the troop's undisputed entertain-ments officer. He could be 'insanely funny' with his skits and mono-logues, but he could do it 'straight', too, holding his young audience spellbound as he spun stories by the light of the campfire. What's more, he seems to have been a natural organiser, someone who 'came alive when he [had] six or seven kids to assemble in a sketch.' A second audience member remarks that Polanski was 'not an exhibitionist but an entertainer', nowadays the rarer of the two, and had a wonderfully 'quick' face, like that of a 'small forest animal'.

Romek might not, the other Scouts knew, be the easiest boy in the world to deal with. He always did what he wanted and never did anything he didn't. But they were agreed that he was a star. Romek knew how to 'put across' not only a show, but himself. 'It was,' the same friend says of him, 'like he was pulling everyone toward him like a beacon and letting everyone around him know that he was different and special, and that we were all part of the act.'

Summarising this episode in his memoirs, Polanski concludes, 'I had discovered my vocation.'

TWICE A WEEK, MONDAYS AND THURSDAYS, Polish state radio put out a politically correct children's show called *The Merry Gang*. One reason Romek found most of the episodes such a crashing bore was that the bad guys so often turned out to be evil capitalists, corrupt American generals or sinister neo-Nazi hate groups in cahoots with the Catholic Church. The programme was one small part of a disease that afflicted post-war Poland, and in some ways came to define it: the ferocious competition to copyright truth, to square everything with the Party line – as a future Pope wrote, 'to smash opposing versions of events'.

By now, Romek's faith in his own acting skills was already as integral to his make-up as was his proficiency, to quote a girlfriend, 'in the art of offence-taking'. One Saturday afternoon in October 1946, the *Merry Gang* producers held an open day at their ancient studios on Lubicz Street. With nothing better to do, Romek joined the party gathering excitedly in the control room, where he made clear his own disdain for the slow-moving, implausible plots and wooden dialogue so typical, as he saw it, of the programme. The show's director, a Party member named Maria Billizanka, overheard him and asked if he thought he could do any better.

Romek replied that he could. After performing an edited version of his Scout revue at the subsequent audition, he became a regular member of the *Merry Gang* cast, at a token fee of 200 zloty a broadcast.

The ambition to become a 'real performer' grew, whether as something that intrigued a lonely teenager seeking what his girlfriend calls 'fulfilment and revenge' for what he lacked at home, or for the more obvious ego gratification. Romek was on the move again that winter, lodging with an elderly, gout-stricken woman named Sermak. As at Wysoka, it was a deeply religious household. Mrs Sermak began every meal with grace, and crossed herself frequently while in conversation with her tenant; Polanski would later write of it as a 'singularly drab and joyless' place, furnished only by two doilied armchairs, a rickety table and numerous plaster busts of the Pope. In Mrs Sermak's tiny front parlour, a shrine seemed to be operative. Beads, candles and a framed portrait of Cardinal Wyszyński provided the backdrop to the twice-daily services attended by the landlady, her middle-aged, unmarried daughter, an orphaned niece and, on a less fixed basis, Romek himself.

A more enticing prospect emerged when, along with the *Merry Gang*, Maria Billizanka took on the management of a children's workshop group, the Young Spectators Theatre. With little parental encouragement, Romek soon enrolled, and went on to appear in several local productions of such Soviet-friendly spectaculars as *The Workers' Hearts Sing Out Like The Locomotive Whistle* and *Silesia, Silesia, My Dream Is Coming True*.

Romek was the 'court jester', Billizanka reportedly remembered. But, as it developed, he was also 'something of a devil'. Among the 14-year-old's repertoire was a trick he liked to play by slumping down on the bathroom floor, moaning pitiably, having apparently slashed himself with a razor. A retired actress in her seventies named Hanna Parys once visited the theatre, where she's said to have opened a backstage door to find Romek sprawled at her feet, covered in realistic-looking blood which gushed from his wrist. The old lady fled from the scene in hysterics.

SYN POLKA, OR *SON OF THE REGIMENT*, was in a long line of Soviet theatre that harked back to Lenin's 'agitprop' trains that had toured Siberia bringing with them portable stages on which actors performed plays extolling the glory of the October Revolution. The plot was simple, and set in the recent past. A young Russian boy is captured by the Germans, who try and fail to extract information from him before obligingly discussing their own campaign tactics, at some length, in his presence. The boy will freeze to death if he makes a run for it, so he stays put. In the morning, he's rescued by a Red Army unit and reveals the enemy's plans, resulting in a comprehensive defeat for the Nazis. This state-funded work was to receive its premiere in Krakow early in 1948. With a ministry of culture official sitting in the wings taking notes, Maria Billizanka and the playwright Valentin Katayev auditioned eighty-seven young hopefuls for the title role. Romek got the part.

In time, *Son of the Regiment* was awarded the coveted Red Star by a distinguished panel of Soviet judges, although cynics felt that the bauble was bestowed largely for its uplifting message. Later that spring, it was chosen to compete in the prestigious Warsaw Festival. Romek and the rest of the cast lodged at the Bristol Hotel, one of the few pre-war buildings still standing, and while there frequently met the 'rubbler' prostitutes and other entrepreneurs who constituted the city's only real commerce. Representatives of the Soviet special agencies were also on hand, both attending the festival and taking rooms in the same hotel.

This was the start of a mounting file on Polanski that eventually made its way to the 'Specialist Factual' state archive in Moscow. Nothing speaks quite as starkly of Soviet paranoia as the fact that even the most ideologically pristine, if not crudely propagandistic play was considered a potential vehicle for 'unauthorised approach[es] to and from spectators in connection with currency exchanges and other activity', as it was reportedly minuted. The same document would go on to list a Pytor Nikolayevich Shachin as having led the surveillance detail, along with the sorry conclusion that 'only contact with street women' was observed.

Agent Shachin apparently took the occasion to inform his superiors that the 'peasant boy' – Polanski – had been well received. According to less restrained accounts, *Son of the Regiment* played to 'rapturous' audiences, and the male lead was 'mobbed by admirers'. A week later, the play's cast returned to Krakow with a handsome award and their picture in the state *Gazetta*.

Not long after that, a Catholic schoolteacher named Father Grzesiak called at the Sermaks' lodgings. After questioning him in detail about his family background and reviewing his church attendance record, Grzesiak told the young tenant that he didn't care for him. 'You're a little liar,' he noted. 'You've never been baptised at all. You aren't one of us.'

As a result of this confrontation, 'Romek Wilk' renounced the faith formerly adopted as part of his survival plan in Wysoka. What seemed to burn in him most was the feeling that nobody, especially a priest, was ever going to humiliate him again. To reinforce the point, he embarked on bodybuilding classes, rapidly adding fifteen pounds of muscle to his wiry frame. Romek is said to have told a friend from Scout Troop 22 that, because of his looks, he felt that certain individuals had been 'goading' him. 'But I'm going to change all that,' he promised, adding that people would look up to him 'like they do to Errol Flynn.'

Socially, Romek began edging away from the rest of the Merry Gang, who seem to have viewed him with the desired mixture of fear and awe. As well as haunting the gym and the cinema, he joined the Cracovia sporting club, regularly cycling a hundred or more miles a day, up into the foothills of the Carpathian mountains. It not only showed supreme dedication, but made a striking spectacle. 'There was a young boy on his own who went up and down that road to the hills,' reports a local farmer, then himself a teenager, named Josef Masur. 'Sometimes [he] passed by while I was walking to school and the other kids looked at him – curious.'

For all his new-found activities, the summer of 1948 wasn't unduly kind to Polanski. A six-week drought left much of Krakow bone dry, including the filthy well from which Mrs Sermak drew her drinking water. Meanwhile, the onset of puberty effectively ended his brief career as a child actor. His few savings, even when combined with a small allowance from Ryszard, barely covered expenses. Paternal pressure eventually forced Romek to apply, much against his wishes, to the local mining engineers' college, which he entered that autumn. (It's said that Ryszard 'literally prayed' for him to become a welder.) At the age of 15, he was broke, smelly, thirsty, frustrated and angry.

As Polanski later remarked, he dreamt of a different life for himself, a life of fame and adventure not unlike that of his hero Errol Flynn. If not as an actor, he would make it as a professional bicyclist or an Olympic skier. Sport was neither hobby nor relaxation, but lifeline. During that last year before he fully discovered sex, Romek often cut classes, either to disappear up into the hills all day or to spend hours running around town in punishing training exercises, carrying a pillowcase filled with cobblestones on his back.

In the end, people began to wonder if he wasn't becoming a bit touched by it all. 'Romek could never submit to family life,' a relative recalls. 'He was very aggressive, loud and constantly involved in one breakneck sport or another.' The biking, in particular, was 'a real passion – a matter of life and death', Polanski reportedly later noted.

This same obsession would lead, in due course, to his next encounter with a murderer.

CHAPTER 3
STALIN

ARLY ON THURSDAY MORNING, 30 JUNE 1949, Polanski stood waiting near the offices of the state secret police in Krakow's Freedom Square. According to a college friend, the name struck him, as it did many others, as one of those 'great Stalinist jokes'. General Sikorski's successor as prime minister, the inept Stanislaw Mikolajczyk, had fled Warsaw the previous winter, leading to the Soviet-backed creation of the United Polish Workers Party (PUWP), which was fortunate enough to remain in power for the next thirty-three years. As the historian Alfred Bloch has written, the PUWP era was to be one of 'murder, mass arrests, abrogation of personal freedom, denial of privacy and basic human rights [and] the falsification of Poland's history to the point of the absurd.' Almost all Romek's teenage activities took place against a daily backdrop of censorship, snooping and other state-spon-sored indignities. The details varied, but the essence of the PUWP agenda remained the widespread and violent suppression of anyone or anything considered remotely 'different'.

Romek's plan, that summer morning, was to meet a young man named Janusz Dziuba who had promised to sell him a new racing bicycle at a good price. When Dziuba arrived for their rendezvous he was carrying something about the size of a loaf of bread, which he had wrapped in a newspaper. The bike, he announced, was across the park in 'the bunker', a foul-smelling air-raid shelter left behind by the Germans.

Lighting a twist of newspaper and holding it aloft like a torch, Dziuba led the way through the bunker's steel door and down a series of descending passages, mouldy and daubed with graffiti, which levelled off some thirty feet below ground. Along a final corridor, through a vault-like antechamber, and they were into what had obviously been the main refuge. It was a long, T-shaped room about the size of two tennis courts, with a bank of rusted machinery to one side. In that eerie light, even the bunker's huge old generator (once the pride of the Germans' military defence system) was barely visible, half buried among years of accumulated dust, thickly twisted weeds and human debris. The bike was just ahead of them in the corner, Dziuba murmured. At that the newspaper he was holding gave out, leaving them in total darkness.

Romek had taken two steps forward when something caught him, not lightly, on the back of the head. He later compared the sensation, which he could vividly remember after some fifty years, to the jolt of touching a live wire. The sheer suddenness, and murderous force of the blows (there were five of them in all) were staggering. Romek went down on his knees and, as he recalled, seemed to lose consciousness for several seconds. When the haze cleared he was dimly aware of Dziuba standing above him, demanding money. Polanski claimed to have none on him. His assailant then relieved him of his watch and other valuables, before leaving him semi-comatose on the concrete floor, covered in blood.

Dziuba made it into the park, but was spotted and tackled by an alert truck driver whose suspicions were aroused by the sight of a blood-spattered young man emerging from the bunker at a run, while wearing two watches. Romek himself was taken to hospital, where eighteen stitches were inserted in his injured scalp. The wounds had been inflicted by a rock wrapped in newspaper. It later emerged that Dziuba had already assaulted at least eight previous victims, three of whom he had bludgeoned to death. He was tried and hanged for his crimes in December 1949.

Although it was undoubtedly a terrifying and painful experience, the Dziuba episode would become another of those stories that occasionally seemed to improve over the years with the telling. Precisely what happened when Polanski stared death in the face that summer morning has always been notoriously difficult to pin down. Certain facts are common to all versions: namely that there was a ferocious assault, that Romek was robbed of his watch, and that he was subsequently treated in hospital. Speaking to Dick Cavett in December 1971, Polanski remembered that he was 16 at the time, and that immediately after the attack, 'I got out through an escape window.' In an interview with *Der Spiegel* three years later, he recalled being only 8 years old and added that 'when

I woke up, I saw the blood running over my face and eyes. Ever since that day, whenever I'm standing under the shower, I feel the blood running over me' – a vivid new detail seized upon by critics as one of those macabre associations between Polanski's life and his work.

Actually, Romek was neither 16 nor 8 at the time of the attack. Nor did he receive 'twenty blows with a flashlight', suffer a fractured skull, endure 'years of crippling headaches and blackouts' or even give evidence at Dziuba's trial, all of which, though certainly not at his behest, would be endlessly recycled in Polanski press handouts. About all that can be said with absolute certainty is that he was violently mugged when he was 15, and that one of the more arresting scenes in his film *Cul-de-Sac* is of a woman showering in blood.

SURVIVING DZIUBA GAVE ROMEK A CERTAIN CACHET AROUND KRAKOW, particularly after he took to wearing an elaborate, turban-like bandage to conceal his wounds. Even Ryszard abandoned his customary air of mild regret where his son was concerned, and paid for him to convalesce at the fashionable mountain resort of Rabka. The word 'damaged' crops up frequently with Polanski, often in reference to Dziuba. It would be 'almost impossible to miss the connection between the gory assault in *Repulsion* and the damaged 12 year-old [*sic*] left for dead in [the bunker]', ran a typical review in *Look*. The characterisation is both misleading and dated. If anything, it more likely stems from the critical hubris of the late Sixties, when, for the first time, films came to be analysed in terms of their directors' unhappy childhoods. In fact, Romek was to make a full recovery, and was soon able to enjoy a long, fulfilling relationship with his first serious girlfriend. Her name was Krystyna Klodko, a 14-year-old student whose 'small, high breasts' and 'dancer's grace' he could clearly recall forty years later.

Polanski also resumed his acting career, joining the splendidly named Groteska company, a Krakow youth theatre specialising in surrealistic productions combining both puppets and live performers, run by one Wladyslaw Jarema, a vodka-swilling old vaudeville star who 'actively disliked' children. The 16-year-old was to win rave reviews for his role as a street urchin in Jarema's *The Tarabumba Circus*. At the company's New Year party, Romek somehow found himself alone in the upper balcony with a strikingly well endowed, and apparently receptive, teenaged guest. Despite or because of the girl's enthusiasm, he made an excuse and ran back to his lodgings with Mrs Sermak; possibly the last occasion for the next twenty years Polanski passed up on an amenable young woman.

Between times, Romek continued to attend as many plays and operas as were permitted by the Krakow authorities. Although he reportedly later spoke of having 'seen everything within a twenty-mile radius', a sometimes surprisingly varied bill of state-endowed productions, he seems to have largely kept this quiet at the time. Few people, for example, knew that he sat through Polish adaptations of Strindberg, Goldoni and O'Neill, or watched *A Midsummer Night's Dream* every night for a week. These were exceptions; much of the available fare was Soviet 'realism', in which, in a flagrant breach of contemporary fire regulations, the theatre doors would be locked to prevent audiences from leaving within the first few minutes. Of the rare screenings of politically 'sound' foreign films, Polanski perhaps most identified with Carol Reed's *The Third Man*. The moment that seems to have stuck in his memory was how enigmatically the Orson Welles character made his entrance in the movie. A friend notes that Romek spent hours imitating the 'chilly' look on Welles' face in front of the tiny mirror at Mrs Sermak's.

THE EARLY FIFTIES WAS NO TIME TO BE THE TOWN REBEL ANYWHERE IN POLAND. Subservience to the 'maternal' neighbour to the east brought about restrictions not only in films and plays but in the very way people looked and behaved. The boxy Soviet cars, the boiled cabbage smell ground deep into the cheap suits, the red-eyed girls in overalls with scarves over their hair trudging to the Nowa Huta steelworks, and above all the interminable queues outside the few 'meat products' shops, were Romek's chief adolescent memories. Within these restraints, he was considered to have been 'a character – the James Dean of Krakow' and, at least sartorially, among the town's leading *bitniki*. A fellow student named Józef Wolski remembered being startled by the sight of 'Wilk, or Polanski, cycling past me at speed toward the college gates' one day in 1950. In contrast to Wolski's own uniform of starchy white shirt and grey trousers, Romek travelled in dark glasses, a faded corduroy jacket with padded shoulders and pointed winkle-picker shoes. His hair was teased into a greasy DA or 'duck's arse'. Passers-by couldn't help but notice that Romek liked to ride the bike in a zigzag fashion and that he carried a pair of skis slung over the back wheel.

Perhaps unsurprisingly, Polanski wasn't long for engineering college, transferring to Krakow's Institute of Fine Arts shortly after his seventeenth birthday. Run by a foppishly dressed homosexual named

Wlodzimierz Hodys, the school represented a small oasis of sophistica-
tion and freethinking. Compared to most of the authority figures of
Romek's acquaintance, Hodys reportedly struck him as a titan of couth,
'Galicia's own Cary Grant'. In the words of another student, 'the place
was a complete anomaly, some[where] people read Kafka instead of *The
Communist Manifesto*.'

In an intriguing nom de plume, Polanski would sign most of his highly
regarded first-year work at the institute with the name 'Dupa', which
roughly translates as 'arse'. Legend insists that he illustrated the word at
least once by dropping his trousers to 'moon' his amused classmates. Much
of the portfolio itself consisted of cartoons of female and, once or twice,
male nudes; for the most part, they were simple, direct, often very funny,
in the tradition of James Thurber, and almost always offering a rear view.
One might almost say his interest in such things was bottomless, were the
word not so inappropriate. Another of the more striking aspects of Romek's
art was the preponderance of self-portraits, in which he typically distorted
his own face to show a wolf's profile.

He and Krystyna Klodko had parted, but Romek soon took up with
a fellow student named Hanka Lomnicka. That relationship, in turn,
foundered, due to her refusal to go to bed with him. Lomnicka soon transferred her affections to Romek's old cinema-going companion Piotr
Winowski, resulting in a temporary rift between the two boys. When
Winowski resurfaced a few weeks later, it was to announce that his mother
had suddenly died at the age of 40. It was 'tragic, but absurd'. That was
no doubt why the two friends, now reconciled, are remembered as having
run down the main street together laughing hysterically. While Piotr and
his family were out at a May Day parade, Romek managed to get another
14-year-old girl up to the Winowskis' empty flat, where he made love to
her on the floor in front of a large antique mirror propped up against the
wall. Immediately afterwards, he found that he wanted to be alone. 'I've
got to run,' he is said to have announced. Polanski seemed not to understand how cutting this remark was or that leaving so abruptly might hurt
anyone's feelings, because he reportedly did the same thing to a number
of later lovers.

OVER AND ABOVE HIS REPUTATION FOR BEING SPORTS MAD (his latest obsession
was fencing), one trait distinguished Romek Wilk from Winowski and
his other friends: he was more focused, more ambitious and altogether
more serious about improving himself, both for his own satisfaction and

because, even then, he planned to make a better life in the West. The others were quite comfortable within their tight-knit Stalinist world. Many of them, even after they became professional artists, were content to turn out state-commissioned fluff (often specialising in Party recruitment posters), rather than risk their careers. Not Romek. He was 'more eager [to] live life', with himself as 'the hero [of] a great adventure', and his self-fashioning monologues were deployed for this purpose. By December 1950, Polanski had already informed Winowski that he intended to 'get the fuck out of Poland, grow a beard and become a writer' in Paris. They had both laughed. The possibility still seemed quite remote.

All of this prompted a crash course in Western literature, involving everything from Chaucer to the Beats of the Fifties. Within only a year or two, Romek, though lacking almost any formal education, could – and did – offhandedly recommend books for others to read. He was particularly drawn to the Nobel Prize-winning philosopher Bertrand Russell, the central thesis of whose 'logical positivism', boiled down, was that society's ethical conventions were essentially flawed, and that the individual owed it to himself to live for the day. Twenty years later, the journalist Richard Ballad asked Polanski whom, of all the great stars of the past, he would have most liked to meet. 'Bertrand Russell,' was the prompt reply. 'He was my hero for years and years. Somehow, I didn't think that man was going to die.'

Compounding Romek's escape fantasies was a further series of hammer blows falling on both his family and himself. The worsening economic situation, for example, was just one reason among many that he came to despair of his homeland. According to a speech given by the Party chief Boleslaw Bierut in August 1951, official Polish state fiscal policy favoured a 'centralised planning model [with] emphasis on heavy industry, full incomes control and collectivisation of agriculture.' In practice that meant huge new iron and steelworks like Nowa Huta, pitiable wages, and frequent food shortages to rival even the worst wartime austerity. The government then announced that all existing Polish currency was to be 'reformed', or withdrawn, overnight. The result was predictably chaotic: 12,000 angry citizens protested outside the office of economic-administrative affairs, and hundreds of thousands more, including Ryszard Polanski, lost their life savings. That was a national tragedy. What affected Romek even more strongly, if possible, was his abrupt departure from art school. In one of those violent mood swings that characterised his directorship, Wlodzimierz Hodys had ousted a popular student named

Tyszler, apparently for having cut a class, although some felt that there was a sexual motive involved. When Romek loyally sought to intercede on his friend's behalf, he, too, was expelled. 'It was as if an abyss had opened at my feet,' he wrote. 'Art school had been a source of pure joy to me. Now, that paradise was lost. My sense of injustice and deprivation was so keen that I seriously contemplated suicide.'

As a close alternative, Polanski transferred to a school in the mining town of Katowice, where he eventually secured his all-important leaving certificate or *matura*. In a brisk reversal of fortune, he was then summoned by the Lodz National Film School director, Antoni Bohdziewicz, to appear in an unusually literate, if only fitfully inspired propaganda short called *Three Stories*. Bohdziewicz had seen and admired Romek in the Krakow run of *Son of the Regiment*. Because of his short stature, the 19-year-old school leaver was able to play a 12-year-old boy, the first in a series of children's roles he took in the Polish cinema of the period, almost all of them superbly accomplished. *Three Stories* itself proved little more than a recruitment exercise for the local ZMP, or Communist Youth troop. It did, however, bring Romek into contact with several future stars of post-war European film, including the award-winning cameraman Jerzy Lipman and the directing prodigy Andrzej Wajda. They seem to have had few illusions about the quality of their project. At each night's showing of the film's rushes, a dazzling parade of talent sat through a display of stunning underachievement: elegiac set pieces denouncing President Truman, lavishly shot scenes in which young ZMP activists exposed foreign spies and sat around the campfire singing songs to the Great Benefactor. 'Artistically, this is a masterpiece', the *Gazetta* remarked of *Three Stories*. There was praise for the 'thoroughly convincing storyline' and the performance of 'the little lad from Krakow', whom the paper thought was 14.

Fresh from this triumph, the actor – now known as Roman Polanski – set about entering film school. After a lengthy audition, the local Krakow facility turned him down, ironically citing his smallness. A few days later he took the train up to Warsaw and put in for the university's vaudeville section, low if not the absolute dregs of the dramatic arts, which turned him down. In desperation, Polanski then applied for a course in PE at Krakow's state college. They also turned him down. Short of his running away to circus school, which he actively contemplated, his immediate fate seemed to be three years' military service.

Faced by this dire prospect, Polanski decided to make good his escape to the West. His first plan was to build a one-man submarine, to be fashioned out of two modified potato crates (of which there was no shortage) and an old bicycle, which he proposed to sail under cover of night up the Oder into East Germany, and then hitch-hike to Berlin. In those pre-Wall days, it was still possible to obtain a twelve-hour pass and simply walk into the city's western zones in the morning, see the sights, and walk home again in the evening. Over the years, many visitors elected to forgo the return journey. After conducting a number of discreet sea trials for his contraption around Krakow, in one of which he nearly drowned, Polanski decided to abandon the idea in favour of a land crossing.

By studying the timetables and closely observing the security arrangements in place at Katowice station, Polanski eventually settled on a train – specifically the Moscow-Paris express, which stopped for a few minutes each night to take on supplies – as his best bet. He found two teenaged Krakow friends named Adam Fiut and Jerzy Wasiuczynski willing to help him, despite the risk to themselves of lengthy prison sentences if caught. The agreed plan was for the three of them to wait out of sight for the express, then to sidle on to the platform and swiftly board the nearest empty carriage. Once en route, Polanski, who was five foot three, would secrete himself in a tiny crawl-space located in the train's lavatory ceiling. At that stage his two accomplices would screw the compartment's wooden panel back in place and jump off shortly before the last stop on the Polish side of the frontier. Roman would then remain in his quarters throughout the train's westward journey through Czechoslovakia and both Germanies, some 400 miles in all, before alighting when safely past the French border.

On the night chosen for the operation, the train pulled into Katowice station exactly on time – a pleasing feature of Soviet railways. Polanski, Wasiuczynski and Fiut were all able to slip undetected into the lavatory, as planned, and bolt themselves in. There their luck broke. Against the odds, the ceiling panel had been freshly painted, and proved maddeningly stubborn. It took very nearly an hour of muffled hammering and cursing, each of the trio intermittently acting as a lookout, before they eventually prised it off. By balancing precariously on the lavatory sink, Polanski was able to poke his head into the empty space and peer around. It was horribly cramped even for one of his size. For a few moments he stood, apparently undecided, although, Fiut later remarked, still 'impressively cool' under the circumstances. Then, within the space of as many seconds, came three double whistles – the sign of an approaching stop – followed by a wash of light through the window. A voice over the intercom confirmed that they were now 'a minute away' from the station at Opava, the frontier crossing, where the train would be met by customs officers and sniffer dogs. There was a hissed conference between the three friends. The two younger men looked up at Roman, still perched on the sink, with only seconds to make a life-changing decision.

'It's no use,' he said suddenly. In the event, the three barely had time to replace the panel, open the door and jump down from the carriage on the Polish side of the border. Later that night they got comfortably numb on vodka while travelling back on the milk train to Krakow.

AFTER MOSCOW IMPOSED FIRST BOLESLAW BIERUT AND THEN ITS ECONOMIC FIVE Year Plan on Poland, it still had a propaganda war to win. The most obvious weapon remained the cinema, which Lenin himself had declared to be the most important of the arts: the 'great illusion', as he put it in private. While individual Polish studios survived and even flourished in the Fifties, they did so on sufferance. However well written or directed it might be, a film like *Three Stories* never aspired to be anything more than a vehicle to get the Party message across. An entire state apparatus existed to vet scripts and supervise production, and no picture was ever released without a formal screening, or *kolaudacja*, for an audience of hatchet-faced ministry of culture officials. In 1952 alone, this body either rejected outright or referred back for thematic 'reorganisation' forty-eight of the sixty-one full-length features submitted to it. Compared to the Polish model, the Hays Office – which had so thoroughly policed Hollywood's pre-war output – seemed hopelessly laissez-faire.

This was the political backdrop to the 27-year-old Andrzej Wajda's first and best film, *A Generation*, which explored the fate of the director's contemporaries who came of age during and immediately after the war. What distinguished the picture wasn't so much the script, which the ministry completely rewrote, as Wajda's particular visual style. Instead of remaining static, his camera glided in and out of windows and up and down staircases, exploring every inch of the Warsaw tenement building where the action took place, while making extensive use of wide-angle lenses and a range of other optics to put the viewer 'in' the story. Where other directors might have settled for a prefabricated set, Wajda insisted on building an actual house, with bricks and mortar, a lead-coated roof and full interior fittings; when the studio eventually came to dismantle it, they found a large crowd of people waiting outside who wanted to move in.

Some of Wajda's distinctive technique and extreme attention to detail rubbed off on the 20-year-old Polanski, who appeared in the film as a teenage boy named Mundek. As on *Three Stories*, he used the time to learn as much as he could about the whole ritual of film-making. When not actually performing, Polanski would often stand at Wajda's shoulder, notebook in hand, enquiring about matters such as make-up and lighting. It seems to have been at least partly as a result of this experience that he began to seriously consider becoming a director. In later years, Wajda would say that he had never met anyone with more native intelligence, or the will to succeed. Roman 'had only to be shown once, and he never forgot.' Reflecting back on *A Generation* on the fortieth anniversary of its release, Wajda added that Polanski had been an 'insatiable presence' on the set, who was 'passionate' about technical matters but 'with no interest whatever' either in Marxist ideology or Poland's recent national past.

Around the time he was cast in *A Generation*, Polanski was reportedly able to enjoy a three-week working holiday as part of a group of Polish actors touring Vienna. 'I was very, very young and naive,' he recalled of this excursion twenty years later in *Cosmopolitan* magazine. 'I met this mad Viennese promoter who took me out one night . . . We go to night-club, which was once ornate old opera house, the dancing girls were available [and] I find myself with tall girl, upstairs in one of the old theatre boxes, the drapes of it drawn, the orchestra still playing below. She orders champagne, then washes herself with it . . . Incredible!'

While not totally implausible, Polanski's account – always providing it actually refers to the mid-Fifties – does seem curiously at odds with his then ongoing attempts to flee to the West. It would have been relatively straightforward for him to have bought a seat on a train from Vienna to Paris – simpler, certainly, than having to hide in the lavatory ceiling all the way from Katowice.

On the other hand, this may be one of those cases where Polanski's early biographies shouldn't necessarily be trusted as the gospel truth. Although at least one of them insists that the Viennese trip took place in 1953 or 1954, an impression seemingly confirmed by *Cosmopolitan*, the director himself recalls it having occurred a full decade later, by which time he'd already emigrated to London, making the whole question of defection moot. Scouring the cutting files, one further reads that the entire incident happened not in Austria but Australia, and that the tall girl was actually a call girl. This seems to show there is an element of Chinese whispers about Polanski anecdotes, which, often through no fault of his own, become more dramatic, or more farcical, or both, with each telling.

An otherwise plausible woman who was an 'intimately close chum of Roman's' in the mid-Sixties assured me that he had been the hairiest man she had ever seen, and further insisted that when his friend Dino De Laurentiis had later been preparing his remake of *King Kong*, 'he had Roman in mind to play the ape'. Picturesque as it is, it never happened. Polanski had actually been under consideration to direct *King Kong*, not star in it.

In his memoirs, Polanski devotes several hundred words to the story of the ornate Austrian nightclub and the dancing girls, which he dates to 1965 and which undoubtedly happened as he describes. Some of the specific scenario, even so, notably his finding himself upstairs in a theatre with an uninhibited young woman, seems broadly similar to his experience at the Groteska New Year party in Krakow. According to one friend, 'Roman occasionally told different versions of a story as though trying them for use in a screenplay,' although, of course, any of them might well have been true.

IN 1953 STALIN'S EMPIRE BEGAN TO CRACK. The Great Benefactor died on 5 March of that year, an event that triggered a workers' revolt in East Berlin. In a single day of rioting, 267 people were killed and 1,067 were severely injured: many more would be summarily executed or simply 'disappear', including the East German minister of justice, Max Fechner, who had foolishly announced that his state constitution guaranteed the right to strike. Nine days later, Stalin's successor-apparent Lavrenti Beria, the psychotic 'Bloody Dwarf' who had run the Soviet security forces, was himself arrested. (He was murdered in prison.) When Nikita Khrushchev took power on 27 June, he restocked the government in Warsaw with what he termed 'obliging cretins', who in turn introduced yet more measures to protect their citizens from the West. All Poles were issued with new identity cards, and door-to-door searches were initiated for those who had somehow eluded the military draft. Unless he was accepted by an accredited institution, Polanski would be conscripted without further delay.

It was under these compelling circumstances that he applied to the National Film School at Lodz. Founded five years earlier and housed in a textile baron's converted mansion in the one major Polish town not ruined by the war, some 120 miles north of Krakow, the school already enjoyed a reputation for combining the highest technical standards with a uniquely relaxed atmosphere between staff and students. It was also furnished much like a five-star hotel, with extensive grounds, a sweeping central staircase and a well-stocked bar. Unsurprisingly, competition for places on the five-year course at Lodz was fierce. Events had persuaded many thousands of young Poles that the best means of serving their state was in continuing higher education. Encouraged by the school's director Antoni Bohdziewicz, who had cast him in *Three Stories*, Polanski travelled up, at his own expense, for a ten-day round of interviews and tests. He performed indifferently on Marxist-Leninist theory, but was able to boast professional acting experience, as well as to write a polished original screenplay. Overall, Bohdziewicz was to assess him as 'A little wild, but shows promise.' When the results were announced, Roman was one of only nine successful applicants (eight, according to his memoirs) chosen from a field of 312 for the student directors' course.

Ryszard Polanski was delighted when he heard the news, which also merited a small notice in the Krakow papers. He's said to have told Roman, perhaps remembering his own youthful ambitions, that he had a 'God-given opportunity' to 'really make something' of himself. 'In Paris, it took me three years before I was accepted,' Ryszard remarked to friends. 'He's done it in ten days.'

NEWS OF THE FUN-LOVING NEW UNDERGRADUATE TRAVELLED QUICKLY AT LODZ. When Polanski first met Jerzy Kosinski in the autumn of 1954, the trainee director reached over and poured hot tea (apple cider, in some versions) on the future National Book Award winner's best brown suit. 'Why did you do that?' Kosinski asked. 'Because I wanted to see how someone as well organised as you are would react,' Polanski replied. Despite this unpromising start, Kosinski, then studying social science at the University of Lodz, found himself drawn to the elfin 21-year-old with 'the gift of the nose', an innate sense of how to 'win friends [and] entertain people'. Ten years later, Kosinski's novel *The Painted Bird*, a moving story about a young Jewish boy separated from his parents, enjoyed a critical vogue in both Western Europe and America. Many readers took it to be a thinly disguised account of Polanski's life. Possibly aware of the dividend for both their careers, neither party appears to have actively gone out of his way to deny it. Roman's need was to 'constantly be the centre of a hurricane', Kosinski noted in 1979, when discussing his friend's recent flight from America. According to another contemporary, Polanski had been a 'legendary' practical joker, with a particular affinity for explosions in general and fireworks in particular. Once, after a 'long, well-lubricated day' at Lodz's Mermaid bar, Roman had allegedly detonated an 'entire

Fourth of July show' through the open window of a faculty member's office. In some versions, the professor in question was tickled by this display, which he apparently chalked up to youthful exuberance; in others, he emerged singed and ranting, like Hitler after the generals' plot of 1944, and began demanding retribution. Even in those days, Kosinski went on to note, Polanski had had a 'special kind of relationship with women', preferring 'impressionable girls' who hero-worshipped him; girls, that was, occasionally as young as 13. 'Roman', another friend adds, had that 'sort of style, both mental and physical' that was 'catnip to the ladies'.

Polanski also proved himself a gifted and industrious student, who came top of his year in photography exams and second and third, respectively, in editing and sound. 'It was a relaxed and refined environment,' he later told *Cahiers du Cinéma*. 'We were able to keep in touch with Western culture since the censor allowed us "specialists" to see a lot of American, Italian and French films.' A student at Lodz had only to submit a request citing a picture's 'redeeming artistic merit' and the ministry of culture obligingly sent him or her a copy. By filling in a chit, Polanski and his friends were able to enjoy the forbidden fruits of Welles, Kurosawa, Fellini, Wilder, Buñuel and others deemed too decadent for general consumption.

Polanski, recalling this 'unique and totally unprecedented' access, and the mystifying fact that 'we seemed to have had far more freedom than anyone else in the country' was still enthused about the whole *'Brideshead* scene' thirty years later. 'Everything was geared towards a single goal: the efficient schooling of professional film-makers. That was the only criteria, even if it meant savaging the system a little bit.'

It wasn't, even so, that Lodz existed in a vacuum. There were reminders all around of the Bierut regime, which did nothing to disabuse President Eisenhower of his withering description of it as 'hard core even by Red standards'. For years, foreign directors would return from the Soviet Union and Eastern Europe marvelling at the importance of film there, and at how the state 'nurtured' its young talent. Students at Lodz took politicisation lessons, and spent every Wednesday doing military training under the command of a Major Karwiel from the defence ministry, who apparently 'loathed' Polanski both for his practical jokes and his uniform, which is said to have made him look like an amused ferret peeping out of a sack. No self-respecting Polish institution would have been complete without its network of informers and spies, and Lodz was no exception. Among Polanski's circle was a student director named Czarnecki, who took it upon himself to notify the authorities that a mutual colleague, Andrzej Kostenko, was 'unsound'. Kostenko's crime was to have enjoyed a drink, told politically risqué jokes and – as if there could be anything worse – listened to American Forces jazz on the radio. He was expelled. At dinner the next night, Polanski turned on Czarnecki, repeatedly hissing the word 'Traitor' down the table at him. This observation was followed by silence. According to a first-hand witness to the scene, none of the 'eighty or so' other students present defended Czarnecki, not even Czarnecki himself. Seemingly unruffled, he announced merely that he had done his 'job'. An altogether more voluble Party activist named Wieslaw Arct, who often enlivened proceedings by jumping up on a chair to loudly denounce Winston Churchill, would go directly from Lodz to a lunatic asylum. One source adds that a widely disliked faculty member was actually a 'Kremlin stooge', whose sole job was to maintain up-to-date files on the entire student body. Two years later, Polanski and others were able to ransack the office in which these documents were kept, where he learnt that he had been accused of, among other offences, 'cosmopolitanism'.

As part of their course, the trainee directors at Lodz were each given a still camera and told to photograph whatever it was that took their eye. Polanski hit the ground running. His portfolio contained, among various Krakow street scenes, a large number of female nudes. His primary model was his latest girlfriend, a trim, 22-year-old brunette named Kika Lelicinska. The glacially beautiful Kika, an Olympic-class skier, seems to have captivated Roman, whom she affectionately referred to as 'The Brat'. Some years later, Polanski's first wife would tell an interviewer that there had been certain episodes of particularly offensive behaviour in their marriage, 'and I know his first girlfriend Kika [also] suffered it', both claims that have not been adequately sourced. Whatever the truth of the matter (and it would be fair to say that many if not all of the director's later partners were less inclined to make moral judge-ments than to recall his extreme personal generosity), the couple remained an item, on and off, throughout Polanski's time at Lodz. 'Those two were the talk of the town,' Jerzy Kosinski recalled. They were 'devoted' to one another. And they were 'swingers'. Neither party minded if the other had the occasional affair, so long as he or she was brutally honest about it.

By THIS POINT, Polanski had either met or was about to meet a number of his principal future collaborators. Among them was a doctor-turned-jazz pianist and composer named Krzysztof Komeda, who in turn made a fan of 'this thin man who glared at you from under a cloud of black fuzz', whom Roman introduced as Kosinski. It became a kind of chain letter between the more raffish elements of Polish student society. Through Komeda, Polanski met an amateur boxer and author of two locally acclaimed books of Beat poetry named Jerzy Skolimowski, who would be his scriptwriting partner on his first feature film. Another of Komeda's clique was Kuba Goldberg, a sharply dressed bon viveur and cinematographer – and a man who happened to be even shorter than Polanski himself. ('That's how Roman likes all his cameramen,' one of his assistants later confided to the *New Yorker*.) Finally, there was Wojtek Frykowski, whom Roman met at one of Lodz's frequent student dances. Frykowski enjoyed a degree of fame as the only one of his contemporaries to own a car. He had family money, a mysteriously broken nose and a burning ambition, never quite fulfilled, to 'make it' in films. His name would finally become familiar to millions of people some fifteen years later.

IN LATE 1955, Polanski directed his first motion picture, a short he entitled *The Bicycle*. It was based on his encounter of six years earlier with the murderous Janusz Dziuba. Roman played himself, with his friend Adam Fiut, his accomplice in the Katowice station escapade, in the role of the killer. Due to administrative error, the raw footage was lost in transit either to or from the Film Polski lab in Warsaw, and never seen again.

His next effort, a school exercise named *Murder*, was a short lasting eighty seconds in which a man, visible only from the neck down, enters a room, stabs a sleeping figure with a penknife, and leaves again.

His third film, *The Smile* (aka *Teeth Smile*), mixed wit, latent violence and prurience—along with a glancing allusion to his obsession with water—in the perfect Polanskian cocktail. The action consists of a young man peering through a bathroom window at a naked woman. One look at her impossibly beautiful body, and one somehow knows that disappointment will follow. Nearly caught in the act, the peeping Tom leaves the scene. When he returns for another look, all he finds is an ugly but muscular old man brushing his teeth. The man sees him in the bathroom mirror and turns to give him a lecherous grin.

The Smile basically belongs to that brief and not entirely explicable era when the Polish authorities allowed the *Alfred Hitchcock Presents* series to be shown in six-hour marathons on state television, apparently believing it to be a powerful condemnation of the West's obsession with the macabre. Unsurprisingly, Polanski's short homage seems rather dated today. But it has a great twist.

Despite Polanski's loud denials, enquiring critics would find plenty of sport sifting for clues in his earliest films, which even then seemed to reflect his own prior life. There was the obvious thrill of watching, or more accurately anticipating, violence, and the starkly voyeuristic theme of *The Smile*, which would be refined in adult works like *Chinatown* and *The Tenant*. At least some of this fairly invited speculation about whether Polanski was somehow evoking the horrors of the ghetto, many of which he had similarly witnessed from his various hiding places. (We should note, yet again, his impatience with the 'psychobabbling' interpretations of his work.) Like Hitchcock, Polanski would come to be a master at implicating his audience in the acute sense of crisis – what both directors called 'the abyss' – at the heart of everyday life. The most banal of situations, a man asleep in his bed, would be manipulated to achieve the right mood of encroaching danger, that strange mixture of anxiety and fascination so familiar to Polanski's later admirers. All his failings and strengths are on view in those early shorts. On the downside, the necessarily perfunctory storylines are made up of a few broad gestures with, at least in the case of *Murder*, a not terribly surprising surprise ending. Set against that was his obvious technical brillance, a rarer quality in many directors than sometimes imagined. Much of the all-important atmosphere in Polanski's films would come from a camera that, like Andrzej Wajda's, roved constantly from actor to actor, from room to room; some from his unerring choice of supremely gifted assistants, particularly when it came to original music; and, not least, from his practical insights into the whole business of acting, which he characterised as the 'art of know[ing] how to relax and concentrate at the same time'.

Nothing in Polanski's early history had suggested dormant genius. Quite the contrary. The one feature of his childhood on which there's a complete consensus is the lateness with which he learned to read. Even at the age of 13 he wasn't fluent, while reliable accounts of his youth stress hesitancies and the fact that he would reply to certain questions with a 'shifty, vulpine gaze'. At least one family member had feared that he might be subnormal, and it was even thought that he suffered from what would now be called attention deficit disorder. As noted, his kindergarten teacher had gone so far as to use the word 'cretin' in her assessment. Yet at Lodz Polanski not only lost his native shyness, but seems to have impressed even the toughest judges as a rising star. Much to his obvious delight, genuine intellectuals like Skolimowski and Kosinski sat up and talked about him. At 23, Polanski had a glamorous girlfriend and his own small flat on Narutowicra Street, a stone's throw from the coveted ul. Josef Stalin postal district in the centre of Lodz. While not conventionally attractive, he was sourly handsome and built in such a way as to encourage his occasional forays in drag, convincingly dressing up as a woman, not for the last time, in his 1959 short *When Angels Fall*.

It truly was happening, in a poky provincial town whose sole attributes outside the film school were Poland's largest chemical plant and a nearby smallpox hospital. 'At Lodz, Roman went through a kind of metamorphosis,' Kosinski later remarked. 'Just like in the movies. He was sort of the hundred-pound weakling who became the Incredible Hulk once he got his hands on a movie camera.'

Although not exactly a household name, Polanski was occasionally approached in the street for an autograph, surprisingly often by a fan of *Son of the Regiment*. In consequence he was fast discovering that being even a local celebrity had downsides he didn't have to worry about when he was an anonymous schoolboy. One middle-aged female fan he encountered in Lodz rapidly went from fawning on Polanski to abusing him when he declined to join her in her nearby apartment for a drink. 'Little bastard!' she shouted. 'You should get the pox!'

After *The Smile*, Polanski decided to make a film about 'real life', in which he would train the camera on his fellow students while they innocently enjoyed an open-air dance in the grounds. As far as anyone was aware, it was to be a completely benign exercise in newsreel style, and plans were reportedly made by Dean Bohdziewicz to include a copy of the finished product as part of his school's promotional kit. Only Roman and his cameraman knew that there was a twist. By prior arrangement with some of the best-known thugs in Lodz, a gang was to infiltrate the party, help themselves to food, drink and as many of the female guests as possible, smash up the furniture and deposit anyone who complained in the pond.

Polanski's rousing contribution to the Soviet documentary art form and the advancement of understanding between people of diverse backgrounds was only a partial success. A full meeting of the school's disciplinary committee would subsequently reprimand him for his 'poor taste' in subject matter. There was some question about whether he should even be allowed to continue his studies. On the other hand, the director Andrzej Munk, Poland's acknowledged master of *cinéma-vérité* and a part-time faculty member, insisted that Roman's film had been a 'legitimate situationist exercise' and 'proto-realist drama', however crude, and effectively blocked efforts to have him expelled.

From then on, Polanski fairly cultivated the aura of a man who, both by natural force of personality and by hard work, knew how to be the centre of attention in any room he entered. To Jerzy Kosinski, he seemed 'restless and edgy' – always highly strung from the additional pressures to excel that he put on himself, and, the novelist guessed, from the nature of his emotional wiring. Even when he relaxed, he 'seemed to do it flat out'. Polanski was, for instance, 'maniacally passionate' about jazz (then frowned upon by Premier Bierut as a product of 'putrid imperialism'), spending much of his free time with Krzysztof Komeda and his group. Merely being seen in such company was an act of defiance. A small but loyal crowd gathered for Komeda's regular Saturday-night performances in a smoky town-centre basement, where many of the audience came equipped with fake identity cards in the event of a raid by the *Służba Bezpieczeństwa* or SB, the plain-clothes force of the internal affairs ministry. ('Komeda' itself was a well-chosen alias.) Over time, many of these same concerts came to double as de facto protest meetings, broadly demanding a 'Polish road to socialism' more in harmony with national traditions. In Warsaw or Krakow, this would have brought about a violent reaction by the authorities, but the preferred response in Lodz was expulsion and military conscription.

Sporting his new corduroy jacket and a pair of dramatically pointed shoes, Polanski was widely considered 'cool' (sometimes going by the name Elvis), even by the musicians' standards. He also had an energy level Komeda himself thought off the chart. 'Being close to him in those days was like being in the middle of a thunderstorm,' the composer recalled fondly. 'These lightning bolts were all around you.' One day in the summer vacation Roman and Kika went up to Warsaw, where he somehow got into a fight with the bouncer at the door of the theatre featuring the Bim-Bom revue from Gdansk. The stage manager called the law. A short time later, Polanski was released from custody by a sympathetic policeman and spent the rest of the night sprawled on a pile of rubble with Kika and a bottle of vodka. Roman, of course, cut even more of a dash at Lodz on his return. Although he seems not to have actively confirmed (or denied) it, the rumour that somehow went around the student body was that one of their own had survived a night in the SB dungeons, and lived to tell the story.

Polanski stood out, then, in a society where even film-school students were expected to play their part in re-educating the Polish people about their immediate past. The documentary-makers at Lodz dwelt more on the events of the Soviet liberation of 1945 than of the Soviet invasion of 1939. For Polanski, the very idea that one should ever pander to the censor was not only morally reprehensible but artistically absurd. 'I watched some of the most talented students all but commit suicide,' he told a British collaborator some fifteen years later. 'They avoided the well-told story, which is where my interests lay, and instead went in for [propaganda] which, judging from most *kolaudacjas*, was the thing most likely to put a gleam in a bureaucrat's eye. It never worked.'

In February 1956, Nikita Khrushchev spoke to the Twentieth Communist Party Congress in secret session, describing Stalin as a tyrant and a monster. Shocked Stalinists sat in silence as the Soviet leader said, 'The so-called benefactor practised brutal violence, not only towards everything that opposed him but also towards whatever his capricious and despotic nature thought contrary to his belief.' There was no recording of the speech that lasted four hours, but word of it soon spread. There would be particular repercussions for Poland. Boleslaw Bierut was in Moscow, convalescing from pneumonia in the Kremlin hospital, when a copy of the speech reached him. He had a heart attack when he read it, and died on 12 March.

Three months later, hundreds of demonstrators died when troops were called in to quell street riots in Poznań, ninety miles west of Lodz, beginning a long and uniquely distinguished tradition of Polish popular protest against the self-proclaimed workers' state. Apparently realising the need for new leadership, the Party chose a relative moderate, Wladyslaw Gomulka, as first secretary in October 1956.

Gomulka's premiership conspicuously failed to deliver on many of its promises about curbing the police, loosening censorship, reforming the economy and even gradually introducing democratic elections. Early in November, a delegation of workers and students from Lodz was dispatched to Warsaw to lobby the new administration. In a signal honour, Polanski was chosen to represent the film school. Although 'arrangements' had apparently been made, in the event they never did manage to meet Gomulka. After keeping the party waiting for several hours in an anteroom, an assistant came out to address them. A minute of his remarks, and his audience's reaction, is preserved in the national archives. 'Never fear, comrades,' he said. 'We'll do what it takes.' All the Lodz group had achieved, that day at least, was a demonstration of the Party's 'continued [and] almost satirical' contempt for its membership.

Gomulka may have failed to dismantle the fundamentals of the Stalinist system. He did, however, make one concession with dramatic personal consequences for Polanski. For the first time since the war, Polish citizens were to be allowed to visit family members living abroad. This extraordinary development led Roman, who had stayed in touch with his half-sister Annette, to apply for a passport, which eventually arrived six months later, in early May 1957. He was going to Paris.

POLANSKI ARRIVED IN FRANCE WITH HIS USUAL BAGGAGE: style. After landing at Le Bourget he extravagantly took a long sightseeing tour of Paris by taxi, and then deliberately waited until late at night before knocking on the door of Annette's apartment at 100 rue de Charonne, just half a dozen streets from the family's pre-war lodgings at rue Saint-Hubert, in order to make an entrance. It was the first time he had seen his sibling since the Nazis had deported her in 1943. After an emotional reunion, Roman spent the rest of the week haunting the city's cinemas, music halls and other attractions. About 40,000 Polish citizens had, like Annette, settled in Paris immediately after the war, and one could see why. The place was a 'slap in the face of Marxism' as she put it, with its brightly lit streets, its huge shops, its spectacular fashions, its rich and abundant food and its 2,362 licensed places of entertainment. On his last day in France, Polanski would remark that he felt 'like a prisoner [about] to go back to jail' after a furlough.

One of his favourite spots in Paris was the Musée d'Art Moderne, where one spring morning he met a 16-year-old German student named Gesa. She was five foot ten, precociously dressed in a dark Chanel suit, her hair a tumble of copper that, even in his black-and-white photographs of her, has a new-penny glint. The two were inseparable for the rest of the holiday, spending their last night together in Paris at the Grand Hôtel de Lima where, writes Polanski, 'in a room with turquoise walls, azure curtains and a yellow bedspread, we made love till the sky began to pale.' On parting in the morning he told Gesa that he was tempted to move to Hamburg just to be near her, but opted for the Cannes Film Festival instead. There he strolled around on the Croisette carrying his cheap suitcase, attended a screening of Ingmar Bergman's *The Seventh Seal* and even managed to share a taxi with the 68-year-old director Abel Gance, whose *Napoléon* had introduced the whole concept of widescreen photography just now being accepted as an industry standard thirty years later. Gance lived long enough to watch Polanski's first eight feature films, which, in general, he thought 'macabre' but 'well worth the commitment'.

Paris is forever, and Polanski enjoyed even greater fame as a result of his visit once back in Lodz. Most nights found him holding court for a spellbound audience gathered around the bar located at the foot of the school's grand central staircase. His imitation of actors like Marlon Brando or James Dean, which he sometimes enhanced by adopting a French accent, or by rolling around on the floor as if suffering a fit, had his colleagues shouting with laughter. A day or two after his return, he was also called upon to give an account of his trip to an SB policeman, who wanted to know if he had been approached by representatives of any subversive magazines. Polanski said that he hadn't, but carefully made a note of the titles in question so as to be sure to look them up in future.

Midway through his time at Lodz, Polanski was known as a brilliant raconteur and mimic, and as the impish *provocateur* who, eschewing a formal introduction, made the acquaintance of at least one young woman by enquiring serenely, 'Do you fuck?' But it would be churlish not to note that his stellar reputation also owed something to the sheer quality of his films. These included the strange, original and long notorious *Breaking Up the Party* (1957), followed a year later by an experimental short he called *Two Men and a Wardrobe*. Clearly betraying the influence of Samuel Beckett, with a touch of Charlie Chaplin, this dark little fable opens with the two leads, one short, the other tall, emerging from the sea bearing a decorative chest of drawers. Over the course of the next fifteen minutes, they lug their burden from one hostile environment to another. An attractive young woman rebuffs them. The conductor won't allow them on to his tram. They're heckled out of a café and set upon by thugs – one of them played by Polanski himself – who then stone a kitten to death. Apparently disenchanted by their adventures, the two men then turn around and trudge back to the beach, where they carefully avoid a row of sandcastles before again vanishing into the surf.

The making of *Two Men and a Wardrobe* was a perfect miniature of Polanski's more mature work. Even in those collegiate days, there were to be various creative differences on set, some of which weren't so much aired as shouted out. 'Every time Roman couldn't achieve what he wanted,' notes one of the two principals, Henryk Kluba, 'he took it out on his surroundings or even people in the crew – he would beat them up. In that wardrobe that we carried, he smashed the mirror with his fist so many times that in the end we had to carry spares. He was unbearable.' Not for the last time, the director went drastically over both schedule and budget. There were tense scenes back at Lodz when Polanski went to explain himself to Jerzy Bossak, the new dean of the faculty. Despite or because of its production difficulties, *Two Men and a Wardrobe* was extraordinarily accomplished, a tribute both to its director's lightness of touch as well as to the many hours he spent in the editing room. The actual photography was sensational, a collage of fast cuts, innovative camerawork and disturbing close-ups disguising the paucity of the core plot. Komeda's melancholic jazz score seemed to perfectly fit the mood. And there was that maniacal cameo by Polanski, so reminiscent of the one he performed fifteen years later in *Chinatown*.

'Anyone,' said Jerzy Kosinski, 'who thinks Roman calmly sat in his ivory tower, waiting for the fans to find him, never saw him at Lodz. He was always calculating and planning ahead.' Polanski not only ensured that *Two Men* would be entered in a special arts competition held as part of the 1958 Brussels World's Fair, but then coolly informed Dean Bossak that his film would win the Palme d'Or. In the event, it took home the bronze, but that was enough to impress even the ministry of culture in Warsaw. The director not only travelled to Brussels and Paris at their expense to promote the film, but was able to buy a Peugeot scooter – the height of luxury – with his winnings.

At 25, Polanski wasn't only the big man on campus, but one of the few unabashed dandies in central Poland. As well as the Peugeot, he managed to hoard enough government vouchers to buy a dove-coloured suit and a variety of silk shirts, which at the slightest encouragement he wore splayed open to the navel. Those crowds at the school bar lapped up his witty if not, perhaps, always entirely spontaneous descriptions of actors (David Niven, for instance, was like 'a tight, rolled-up umbrella'), and even the imposing Dean Bossak, replying to a concerned letter from the Humane Society enquiring about the fate of the kitten in *Two Men and a Wardrobe*, could only admit that his prize student was 'unorthodox'. In a few short months in 1958, Polanski had developed into one of European cinema's rising young talents; and he fell in love.

Her name was Barbara Kwiatkowska, or 'Basia' as she was known by friends, and when they met she was on the brink of becoming the It Girl of Polish film, by starring in a wildly popular comedy called *Eve Wants to Sleep*. The plot concerned the antics of a country girl, not unlike Basia herself (a former shepherdess) adrift in the big city. Though she mockingly described herself as 'a peasant', Basia's friends recall her as kind, bossy and brisk, 'a character', and the sort of woman who 'lit up a room'. She had gotten her break a year earlier, when she entered a talent contest in a weekly magazine promising to 'Get Beautiful Girls on Film'. Having won first prize, Basia, who had just turned 17, was brought to Lodz for a screen test. Although obviously a gifted actress, hers was an unusually fast rise to stardom, in which, some sniffed, the premium was less on innate talent than on her looks. She was stunning. The so-called 'Polish Sophia Loren' was pert, dark-eyed, with high, Slavic cheekbones, and built to movie-starlet proportions. One friend from those days remembers Basia walking into the Grand Hotel in Lodz, 'a knockout brunette . . . wear[ing] a stylish silk coat studded with tiny silver stars, and a knotted scarf embroidered in lurid colours, [while] on her bosom reposed a gorgeous bouquet of real sagebrush, imported from Szulechow. Her lips were unbelievably full, her eyelashes perfectly curled . . . She was lovely to a fault.'

Polanski, who had been seeing less of Kika in recent months, pursued Basia for several weeks. Then one night, after seeming to consider the matter while out driving around on his scooter, she squeezed up against him and murmured, 'Let's go back to your place.' Her total resolve from that moment on impressed even Polanski, who later recalled, 'Once in my room she stripped and got into bed – just like that.'

Polanski's exhilaration was compounded when, early the next morning, he watched Basia slip out of bed and stand looking down into the street, still au naturel. 'I'd never seen such utter perfection,' he wrote in his memoirs. Thirty-three years later, Polanski directed a scene in *Bitter Moon* in which a young woman – played by his current wife, Emmanuelle Seigner – stares, similarly clad, out of a window, while her lover reads out an only slightly adapted version of Roman's homage to Basia.

What has been authoritatively described as Polanski's 'not inconsiderable talent in bed' would, for now, take its turn among his remaining academic commitments. Sometime between his meeting Basia and asking her to marry him, he shot his two final films at Lodz. The first, a fourteen-minute short entitled *The Lamp*, was about a dollmaker whose shop burns to the ground owing to an electrical fault, possibly caused by the unsettlingly lifelike dolls themselves, in what a critic calls an 'existential prison break'. It seems not to have been a success, and Polanski omits it from his autobiography. The second was his graduation exercise, a compact masterpiece called *When Angels Fall*.

The film's novel, if commercially unpromising premise was to feature an 80-year-old public lavatory attendant as she looks back on her life. Basia (later billed as Barbara Lass) and Polanski himself would play the woman in various flashbacks. As, again, in *Bitter Moon*, the film hops around between present and past while slowly advancing towards a shattering conclusion: literally so, as an angel abruptly crashes through the lavatory skylight.

When Angels Fall enjoyed only a mixed reception by Dean Bossak and his board. According to the note in the archives at Lodz, it was thought 'intriguing and complex [but] with no particular moral value . . . The old woman's predicament seems unconvincing.' There had been 'much to admire in [Polanski's] use of effects and lighting,' one panellist reportedly wrote. The overall stagecraft and set construction was 'meticulous'. But the director had 'possibly overextended himself' as a screenwriter, providing a 'somewhat melodramatic' ending.

Although *When Angels Fall* was eventually accepted by the examining panel, Polanski never formally graduated. There have been various theories floated about this, but the most likely explanation is that he simply failed to turn in the required written thesis and so left without a diploma. In later years, certain Polish film critics became tetchy at Roman's success, and made it a point of honour to show their independence by carping. To them, the rich and fulfilled Hollywood director was still a 'Lodz dropout'.

THE NIGHT BEFORE HE LEFT SCHOOL, Polanski purportedly had one too many in the course of saying his goodbyes and woke up with a 'paralysing' hangover. It didn't stop him from celebrating his departure, an hour or two later, by jumping off a 'dizzyingly high' step (reports vary as to whether it was the seventh, twelfth or even fifteenth) of the building's main staircase, to thus establish a new student record. His climactic address to his colleagues, allegedly a paean to sex, vodka and skiing and the interaction between the three as a model for personal fulfilment, was apparently a tour de force and 'at least on a par' with the official speeches. On his way out the door, an old enemy on the staff is said to have looked him up and down and remarked, 'I don't care much for those red socks, Polanski.'

The reply was blunt. 'I don't care much for your face, Professor. But I can change my socks.'

The story may well have been embroidered by recollection. But it reflects an attitude that juts out during Polanski's youth from beneath the layers of adulation which increased with the years. The description 'a gift for arrogance', coined by Jerzy Kosinski, belongs to this period. According to another Lodz colleague, 'Romek was almost always friendly on the surface, and had a large fan club. I wouldn't have thought him particularly interested in anyone else's problems. You were all there for him, but he wasn't all there for you.'

Polanski remained in Lodz, where he was eventually hired by Kamera Productions, one of the supposedly 'autonomous' film units to have emerged under the Gomulka regime. His first assignment was as assistant director to his old tutor Andrzej Munk, who put him in charge of the crowd scenes for a feature called *Cross-Eyed Luck*. The script revolved around a chronic loser with an unfaithful girlfriend. Roman brought Basia with him on location, insisting that his real-life lover would be perfect as 'the sexy little bitch' who seduces everyone in sight. Basia got the part.

Throughout their courtship, Polanski embarked on several brief affairs, while Basia, in turn, had a more enduring relationship with a Warsaw graphic artist named Zahorski. 'My record was slimmer,' as she later noted. In June, the couple managed to spend a week together at a Spanish film festival, where one of the organisers, Suzanna Ruiz, recorded their arrival in an unpublished memoir:

> As we were all assembling in the foyer, Roman and Basia were seen slowly descending the wide curving staircase. It was the grandest of entrances and, in those Franco days, caused much excitement . . . Basia had a head of silky hair, swept up into an elaborate nest. She wore a thin, diaphanous dress so transparent that it left nothing to the imagination, while he wore a magnificent tight green suit with pointed boots.

After yet another trip to Paris, Polanski went back to Lodz to begin writing the script for his first feature film. Aside from his natural ambition and wanting further insurance against the draft, there was the fact that he needed the money. Roman's letters to friends in Krakow were full of woeful tales of debts, sometimes, purportedly, incurred at the poker table, followed by excited descriptions of his travels around Europe and urgent need of a new Mercedes. Five years earlier, his girlfriend Kika had introduced him to the delights of the Mazury lake district in north-eastern Poland. This, he decided, would be the setting for a 'cramped' thriller about two men and a woman isolated on a yacht. It was called *Nóz w wodzie*, or *Knife in the Water*. Polanski spent three weeks that summer working on the screenplay with his friends Jerzy Skolimowski and Kuba

Goldberg in his rooms on Narutowicra Street, where, existing on fruit juice and bowls of *bigos*, the local cabbage stew, they produced a taut, Hitchcock-like draft with trace elements of Kafka and Genet. Kamera's eventual offer, even after haggling, was far below even the very moderate norm of a 1959 Polish film budget. *Knife*'s creative team would earn just 24,000 zloty between them, or very roughly what a manual labourer took home every three to four months, depending on his productivity. Thirty years later, when the currency finally became convertible, 9,800 zloty equalled one US dollar.

When Basia flew home after attending the International Youth Festival in Vienna, she went back to Warsaw with Zahorski. Polanski followed her there, apparently apologising for his having been 'a bastard' over the summer. Even by Polish theatrical standards, there were some fraught scenes as Basia first rejoined Roman, then returned to Zahorski, and finally reappeared in Lodz in the first week of September 1959. On Wednesday afternoon, the 9th, the couple were married in a small civil ceremony followed by a riotous party. Roman was 26, Basia just 19.

THE SIXTIES. A French film director named Robert Ménégoz spotted a picture of Basia at the Vienna festival and told reporters that he wanted to make her the next Brigitte Bardot. Polanski got in touch with the director's office, who wanted to know whether his wife could speak French. *'Elle parle bien,'* he apparently replied. That was good enough for Ménégoz, who came on the line to announce that he was shooting a film called *The Thousandth Window* in Paris. Could the Polanskis please join him there? Roman told Basia over a bowl of *bigos* that night at their tiny local café on ul. Josef Stalin that she was going to be an international movie star. Basia looked at him. She didn't speak a word of French.

Polanski's new career as Basia's husband came just as his old one, as Poland's most promising young director, seemingly ground to a halt. After *Cross-Eyed Luck*, Kamera had informed him that they had no immediate future need of his services. The ministry of culture gave the script for *Knife in the Water* a frosty reception. Like *When Angels Fall* before it, Polanski's 'three-handed duel' was deemed to be of 'questionable moral value' and 'thematic concern'. The young man's part should be rewritten, the ministry said, in order to make him appear more 'socially committed'. Much of the dialogue between the husband and wife would have to be cut to remove any suggestion of sexual passion, and the censor further insisted on 'adequate dimensions' for all three characters' swimsuits.

Polanski was told that he was free to make the necessary changes and reapply to the state's screenplay committee in a year's time.

The French film's producer, Pierre Roustang, met the Polanskis at Le Bourget and drove them to their well-appointed quarters in the Hotel Napoléon. At intervals during the journey, Roustang turned round to converse with his director's glamorous discovery, only to encounter a glassy smile. Clearly there had been some mistake. Hadn't Polanski assured the office, in answer to their question, that '*Elle parle bien*'? '*Mais non,*' said Roman. Obviously he had been misheard. What he had actually said was, '*Elle parle rien.*'

Despite this unhappy start, Roustang honoured his commitment to Basia, who earned $1,000 for her smaller than expected part in Ménégoz's film. When shooting ended, the portly, middle-aged producer invited the Polanskis to stay with him at his apartment on the Left Bank, where he presented them with a black poodle puppy they named Jules. Basia, in turn, was occasionally known to sit their host down in front of a mirror and make him up as a woman, a ritual he visibly enjoyed. Polanski reportedly came to wonder whether this producing venture was partly a kind of occupational therapy for Roustang (who ended up distributing soft porn), and whether he had designs on either him or his wife.

While *Cinémonde* featured the 'traffic-stoppingly lovely' Basia on their cover, her husband failed roundly in various projects. Apart from subtitling Ménégoz's forgettable film in Polish, Roman was unable to find either work or committed backers for his script. The odds, at this stage, were that he would have gone on to make perhaps one or two more experimental shorts. Then a behind-the-scenes career in Poland, with Kamera or an equivalent unit; the occasional credit for 'additional dialogue' at the end of one of Basia's films; retirement; death; appreciative but not long obituaries, followed by a footnote in the arts reference books – that would have been it. As it was, he and Basia elected to stay on in Paris, moving from Roustang's apartment into a tiny walk-up behind the Gare de l'Est. Without even the price of a Métro ticket, Polanski set off on foot from these modest lodgings one morning for an interview with the Polish ambassador, Stanislaw Gajewski, who had written Basia a friendly note after seeing her photo in *Paris Match*. Seizing the opening, Roman asked the ambassador for his help in obtaining clearance for his wife and him to travel back and forth as they wished. This – the Polish so-called 'consular' passport – was the last word in privilege. With Gajewski's approval, two of the prized documents arrived from Warsaw a week later.

Polanski's double life as 'Mr Kwiatkowska' and the *enfant terrible* of Polish film continued at the Cannes festival in May. There was still no apparent interest in his script, although a French film magazine, *Positif*, came to interview him about *Two Men and a Wardrobe*. Polanski told the reporter that he was already hawking around a new idea for a movie, about 'a girl attracted by the mirage of the cinema, who will do anything to become a star'. Still no takers. Things appeared to be slipping away from him – he was losing at cards, losing at writing and losing at marriage. Basia herself soon attracted the attention of a Cadillac-driving Polish émigré named Leo Lax, the latest of several moguls to take a personal interest in her career. Lax was to offer an advance of $400 for her to star in seven 'exclusive photoplays', the first of which called for her to appear throughout in a bikini. Basia eventually declined to enter into a long-term contract, and Lax passed from the scene. Back in Paris, the Polanskis survived on handouts and sporadic commissions from movie magazines. Roman wrote a short treatment about a hard-drinking circus clown who conducts a doomed affair with a female midget. It, too, failed to find financial support. Then Basia's agent called to say that she had an appointment with René Clément, the celebrated French director who had made a star out of Alain Delon.*

Roman took Basia to the interview at the Hotel Lutétia, and then he and Jules waited for her in a café across the street. The audition was a lengthy one. Eventually Basia appeared, beaming, and announced that she was to star – as Barbara Lass – in Clément's new picture, *Quelle Joie de Vivre*. The upfront fee was $3,000. In due course the couple were able to settle their debts and move into a larger apartment at 5 rue de Bérite, near the Luxembourg gardens. With what was left of Clément's advance, Polanski bought himself a red Mercedes 190 convertible.

A French-Canadian producer of dubious repute then offered to finance the most obviously satiric of Polanski's three or four works-in-progress, a sixteen-minute short called *The Fat and the Lean*. The producer's cheque bounced, but Roman somehow brought in another competent film in the school of Samuel Beckett. A grossly obese man, at least by contemporaneous standards, mistreats his tiny, barefoot servant, subjecting him to various humiliations before awarding him the gift of a goat. The catch is

---

* Quite coincidentally, the film in question, 1960's *Purple Noon*, employed much the same structure as Polanski's *Knife in the Water* some two years later.

that the goat is tied to him, which makes it even harder to do the fat master's bidding. Roman himself played the slave. *Cinémonde* later reported that the writing was 'fresh, erudite, acrobatic', with a touch of what became known as Pinteresque humour. As in *Two Men and a Wardrobe*, there was also a nod in the direction of the classic silent cinema tradition, and more specifically of Buster Keaton. *The Fat and the Lean* won Polanski three prizes in European festivals, but avoided any sales.

On a late October afternoon, Polanski loaded Jules, a friend and himself into the Mercedes and drove to Rome, where Basia was shooting *Quelle Joie de Vivre*. He found his wife installed in a luxurious Via del Po penthouse, rented for her by her director. Roman was able to offer one or two suggestions about the script, but otherwise confined himself to sightseeing. He writes of his meeting a Polish-American woman who had been forced into hiding after having an affair with John F. Kennedy, and of touring the Cinecittà studios 'where the sets from *Cleopatra* were still in place'. The former story would fit the known facts about the late president, but Polanski may be confused about *Cleopatra*, which was in production that very month at Pinewood, outside London.

Back in Lodz for Christmas, Polanski shot his ninth and final short, another variant of the slapstick theme, called *Mammals*. The rather slight plot (two men take turns pulling one another across the snowy tundra, arguing about nothing in particular, until a third party appears and steals their sled) was the sort of thing Polanski could have written if, like Houdini, he were manacled, put into a barrel and dropped into the Thames. It was routine, knockabout stuff, with some mildly surrealistic jokes. None of the state production units expressed any interest in *Mammals*, so Polanski's friend Wojtek Frykowski volunteered to finance the film. It says something for the director's power of persuasion that Henryk Kluba, the actor who had found Polanski 'unbearable' in *Two Men and a Wardrobe*, returned to play one of the main parts. Frykowski himself took the role of the sled thief. Devotees insist that *The Fat and the Lean* and *Mammals* are among the most profound and imaginative achievements in post-war East European film. It's a brave soul who tries to find out for himself. There are flashes of acute and vivid writing in the former, and some neat Harold Lloyd visual gags in the latter, but the treats are sparsely distributed. As a plot, *Mammals* rarely rises above the cartoonish, while at least some of the much vaunted (and often effective) white-on-white photography was done by Orson Welles, twenty years earlier, if admittedly on a higher budget, in *The Magnificent Ambersons*.

Early in 1961, Polanski resubmitted the script of *Knife in the Water*, having inserted seven new lines of 'socially committed' dialogue. While awaiting developments he went back to Paris, often eating at the homes of friends in the large Polish expatriate community, occasionally varying his routine, it's said, by an outing to one of Yves Klein's *Anthropometries*, a striking bit of performance art in which nude women rolled around on the floor covered in blue paint. It was but one of several telling signs that Polanski had finally found the town of his dreams. After a brief stab at remaining faithful to his new wife, he appears to have hosted an impressive number of guests, many of them aspiring actresses, at the apartment on rue de Bérite. Basia herself was already back at work in Rome, shooting an Italian vampire drama entitled *Licantropo*.

As part of his application for a consular passport, Polanski had been asked to take a brief current-events quiz, apparently to ensure that he was up to speed with the latest developments in Marxist-Leninist theory. He allegedly got through the exam with a less than remarkable score, failing and having to repeat a section on the decollectivisation of Polish agriculture and other rural matters. What no one could test for, though, was what he had in spades – a killer instinct and an uncanny ability to size up a situation quickly, particularly as it specifically affected his own interests. Polanski had been a champion fencer in his teens, and is remembered by one adversary for his ability to 'rapidly identify ... [and] exploit' weaknesses in his opponents with 'clinical dexterity'. He would soon be doing something very similar on film sets around the world.

All of that shouldn't, perhaps, have added up to a winning personality, but Polanski, except where they posed a professional threat, was also singularly loyal and generous to his friends. He went out of his way to secure commissions for Krzysztof Komeda, who composed the music for his last six shorts, and spent money, in his father's opinion, 'like a drunken matelot'. Basia would apparently long remember her husband having blown 400 francs, roughly a week's combined salary for the couple, throwing a party for Gdansk's Bim-Bom troupe when they passed through Paris. Cast members were collected in the Mercedes and treated to an evening of champagne and caviar. A guest named Tad Slowacki recalls Basia 'tell[ing] me that her husband was having cash-flow problems. He was down to fifty francs while some script was being sorted out in Warsaw. She and I talked, then Roman came over and asked how I was. "Broke," I said, "in mind, body and pocket." Polanski immediately laughed. "Do you want any dough? I can give you fifty francs."'

In mid-March, as Poland enjoyed a first and decidedly limited relaxation of direct Soviet controls (the so-called 'jazz-playing thaw'), word arrived that the ministry of culture was finally prepared to sanction *Knife in the Water*, with Polanski as director. The casting began immediately. An established stage actor named Leon Niemczyk would play the hopelessly 'bourgeois' husband in the erotic triangle. Polanski proposed himself as the man's handsome young rival. Here some discrepancy exists between Roman's own terse account of events ('I was dissuaded') and that of Jerzy Bossak, his former dean and a director of Kamera, who recalled Polanski having lobbied for the part for many weeks, until the day he had finally burst into the production office – stark naked – to demand, 'Am I not pretty enough?' Notwithstanding this campaign, the role eventually went to a young acting-school graduate named Zygmunt Malanowicz, though, even then, Roman didn't relinquish the field; it would be his voice, dubbed for Malanowicz's, heard in the finished film.

Polanski then devoted several days to auditioning candidates for the bikini-clad female lead, before settling on a Basia lookalike named Jolanta Umecka, whom he discovered at a Warsaw municipal swimming pool. Umecka had never acted before, and was 'very difficult to get emotions out of', the director later told the *Independent*. In one scene in which she was supposed to be surprised, naked, by the Malanowicz character sneaking up on her, Polanski had to resort to firing a flare pistol behind his leading lady's head in order to obtain a reaction.

After ten weeks' preparation in Warsaw, Polanski told the producers in early June – two years after his work on *Knife in the Water* had begun – that he was ready to roll the cameras. The ensuing shoot brought home the many challenges of attempting to fit not only three actors, but the small army of technicians without whom not even a modest feature can exist, on a thirty-five-foot yacht travelling across choppy water. Polanski and his director of photography frequently found themselves hanging perilously over the side of the boat, attached to guy lines, while operating the heavy equipment. Perhaps inevitably, there were one or two mishaps along the way. Trying to light a flaming torch in the cockpit one evening, a gofer managed to set fire to his shorts instead, and had to jump into the lake to extinguish himself. Polanski then got it into his head to film a particular scene on deck, in a high wind, without the safety harnesses, and dutifully joined in the subsequent search party for scraps of camera and lighting equipment. The cast and crew spent the summer living in close quarters on an ancient houseboat, and are said to have conspicuously avoided the 'luvvy' atmosphere associated with certain film sets. Polanski grew increasingly frustrated at Jolanta Umecka, the woman he discovered at a swimming pool – who, he now learnt, couldn't swim. After observing the effect of the flare gun being fired behind her back, Roman enquired, 'Well, did that help, you bitch?' Jolanta replied that it had, but that perhaps it was a tad excessive. Soon the two forsook subtle sarcasm and began hurling demure eff-yous at one another. By the second week on location, Umecka was stuffing herself with rich foods and popping out of her bikini, prompting Polanski to take her out jogging. When the young actress lagged behind, he tugged her along by a rope tied round her wrist.

In July, a reporter from *Ecran* magazine came calling, returning Polanski's hospitality by filing a piece entitled 'For Whom and for What?' This seems to have been the starting point of the director's long continuing love-hate relationship with the media. According to *Ecran*, *Knife in the Water* was little more than a floating orgy, and thus a 'colossal waste of Polish taxpayers' money'. Wojtek Frykowski remembered that his friend had to be 'hosed down' after reading the article, which also brought an unwelcome visit from the ministry of culture. As a gesture towards economy, Polanski reluctantly changed his prop car from a Mercedes to a Peugeot. Not long after that, he and his principal co-screenwriter spent the night in jail, for having made some tactless remarks to a policeman while sitting in a bar mourning the sudden death of their friend Andrzej Munk. A day or two later, Polanski opened an Italian film weekly to see a photograph of his wife out on the town with her director Gillo Pontecorvo. Soon a letter arrived from Basia herself, announcing that she needed 'time to think' about her situation.

On 11 September, things, already apparently at their darkest, quite literally turned black. The cameraman Jerzy Lipman was driving Polanski and Kuba Goldberg back to the houseboat late at night when the Peugeot skidded on some leaves and hit a tree. Polanski woke up in hospital with a fractured skull. Later that morning, after taking a few unsteady steps down the corridor, he passed out and remained unconscious for seventy-two hours. When Ryszard and Wanda Polanski arrived to visit, they found Roman swathed in bandages, much like the scene following Dziuba's attack on him twelve years earlier. To the director's embarrassment, his stepmother took a room nearby and brought him freshly cooked meals every day for the next fortnight.

Polanski was to describe *Knife*, which he managed to wrap shortly thereafter, as a film that 'uses a holiday atmosphere tinged with a generous amount of irony.' In practice, that meant propelling a young hitch-hiker into the path of a car taking the middle-aged Andrzej and his wife Krystyna to a weekend cruise. Andrzej throws down the gauntlet, not only giving the stranger a lift but inviting him to join them on the boat. Polanski then sees to it that the three engage in various progressively more kinky power games, primarily involving Andrzej squabbling with Krystyna while their guest, separated from them by age, class and experience, demonstrates his prowess with a pocketknife. American critics, in particular, later made much of the Freudian imagery. Andrzej, an experienced sailor, concludes one exchange with some remarks on nautical etiquette. 'If two men are on board, one is the skipper.' This observation leads him to physically confront his rival, who swiftly topples into the lake, presumed drowned. All will end inconclusively, with Andrzej on his way to the police, uncertain as to whether the mysterious drifter is dead or alive, or whether his wife has been unfaithful to him.

But to summarise the plot of *Knife in the Water* is to concentrate on the mechanics of a beautifully constructed thriller to the exclusion of its style. Seen today, it still seems as fresh as the moment it was released forty-five years ago. Among other charms, *Knife* has some of the most convincing examples of the kind of pure and honest personal hatred that can pass for conversation in a marriage since *Who's Afraid of Virginia Woolf?* Polanski relies not on special effects or spectacular scenery, but on his script's gift for the vernacular. All cult black and white Polish films should be shot on a shoestring, in an increasingly mutinous atmosphere – that way they might be half as good as this one. Most of us enjoy a story about sexual tension now and again, especially when it also tells us something about human nature. This Polanski does supremely well, if, thanks to the censor, a bit more elliptically than necessary.

The *kolaudacja* for *Knife in the Water* was predictably intense, with an impressive number of niggling official complaints. The ministry app2-ratchiks objected to everything from the amount of cleavage to the deliberately ambiguous ending, which Bossak was able to 'tidy up' over Polanski's protest. Taking their lead from Premier Gomulka, most of the domestic critics savaged the film. The correspondent from the Young Communist organ commented on its lack of 'seriousness', virtually a criminal offence in post-war Poland. 'Nothing particularly moves us,' the paper said, in phrases possibly supplied by an adult hand, in its review of *Knife*'s opening in March 1962. 'The director has nothing of interest to say about contemporary man, and we don't identify with any of his characters.'

Eighteen months later, *Knife in the Water* was eventually released in America, where it enjoyed every critical reaction except indifference. *Life* was unkind: 'Not much seems to happen, and we wouldn't much care if it did.' No one in the press talked about Polanski's past, or spotted the film's parallel with *Purple Noon*. The anonymous correspondent in *The New Republic* objected that since Umecka (when clothed) was rather plain, it was difficult to take the film's premise seriously. But the *Republic* and many others conceded that a 'bold new talent' was at large.

Polanski arrived in New York on 8 September 1963, by which time some of his habitual cool seemed to have wilted. After a year-and-a-half's subsistence in Paris, he was down to one good suit, and that was ruined in his luggage on the flight over. *Knife in the Water* was first shown as part of the New York Film Festival on Wednesday 11 September. (Things frequently seemed to happen to Polanski on this date, the anniversary of his car crash, long before it became engrained for other reasons.) Nine days later, *Time* put a still from the movie on its cover. Although Roman affected not to care, it was the ultimate media accolade. Back in Lodz, even his old adversaries on the film-school faculty admiringly referred to him as 'Time Cover' from now on. Most friends were stunned. 'It was like someone walking on Mars; there [was] no precedent,' said Jerzy Kosinski. Andrzej Wajda had come closest to it with *A Generation*, and that wasn't very close.

There was more. Four months later, the Academy of Motion Picture Arts and Sciences nominated *Knife in the Water* (already a European festival award-winner) for an Oscar in the Best Foreign Film category. Polanski flew in for the occasion. On the afternoon of 13 April 1964, a black stretch limousine with a Polish flag took him to the Santa Monica Civic Auditorium, where he was seated next to one of his heroes, Federico Fellini. Fellini himself won the Oscar. Immediately after the ceremony, Polanski moved out of his complementary suite and into a basement room in the same hotel. The car similarly disappeared, and the director was left to make his way around town by bus or taxi. A friend in London eventually wired him $400 in order to pay his bills.

POLANSKI'S ENSUING REUNION WITH HIS WIFE TURNED OUT TO BE A FRAUGHT affair. Basia had ended her relationship with Gillo Pontecorvo, who was said to have attempted suicide as a result, and taken up with the suave stage and screen actor Karl Heinz Böhm. By a strange twist, Böhm had been the star of one of Polanski's favourite films, 1960's *Peeping Tom*. Basia made a high-profile appearance in Warsaw at about the time of *Knife in the Water*'s release, where her practice of strolling around with her German lover, both dressed in the height of fashion, caused something of a stir among the Polanskis' old friends. Roman seems to have initially resisted any suggestion of divorce, and arranged at least one further meeting with Basia in Paris. A witness to this remembers the couple having locked themselves in the Mercedes for what appeared to be a quite animated discussion. Sometimes the sheer depth of Polanski's misery seemed to stir his wife, who, it's said, even at this stage went nowhere without his photograph in a silver frame. Although a few embers continued to smoulder, Basia eventually served papers on Roman and married Böhm. 'It was all a question of dominance,' she later informed the press. 'From the moment I became a public figure, I held an advantage over Romek. I ran away. I was too proud to say it then, but I was afraid of him.'

After Basia's defection, one of Polanski's friends was to publicly review their marriage. 'I had a feeling,' he remarked, 'that Romek was deeply humiliated by her. I mean by the divorce and the movie star and his being a short man and Basia's being tall and young and beautiful.' The armchair psychological theory insists that Polanski's entire subsequent career was a sort of artistic revenge on women. Over time, that simplification seemed to draw strength from the endlessly recycled memoirs, both published and private, of various actresses with direct experience of working for him. Words such as 'childish', 'bullying' and 'volatile' went round like stops on the Circle Line. While not completely ruling out a touch of misogyny in, say, *Cul-de-Sac*, Polanski's many admirers would point to a number of other redeeming qualities, among them the director's sense of fun. In *Rosemary's Baby*, for example, events go from already pretty hideous to even worse, and then still more awful. For all that, as the critic Pauline Kael says, 'Polanski remains generally sympathetic to [the] Mia Farrow [character], while enjoying the in-joke of casting John Cassavetes to play a ham actor. Like all of his films, it's full of humour. Black humour, necessarily, but there it is all the same.'

After *Knife in the Water* received its initial mauling, Polanski loaded up his Mercedes, drove to Krakow, said goodbye to his father and stepmother, and then headed back to France. He would not return to work in Poland for another nineteen years. Once across the West German border he evidently began to feel more like his old self, peeling off the kilometres to the tune of 'Hit the Road, Jack' (then all the rage), and in one account 'fairly sizzling' down the rue Belgrand into Paris. Basia's ultimate desertion left him 'weightless – free as a bird', he insists. Overnight, it seemed, the abandoned husband and spurned artist had been converted into a happy-go-lucky bachelor and merry prankster. And yet the next two years were often not happy, and the atmosphere was rarely merry. It was an uncertain future Polanski was heading to, as well as a sorry past he was fleeing that spring.

CHAPTER 4

'BOLSHEVISM'S BOY WONDER'

T HE MONTH OF MAY 1962 – WITH HIS VARIOUS GLOSSY appearances around Paris and the Riviera – saw Polanski in apparently rare form. Having given up the lease on rue de Bérite, he initially stayed at the flat of a friendly Polish émigré on the boulevard de Ménilmontant, once again close to his childhood home on rue Saint-Hubert. He was a conspicuous presence at the Cannes festival, and subsequently cut a slick dash at various discos in the then ultra-hip resort of Saint-Tropez. The high spirits proved relatively short-lived, however. After the festivities had ended, Polanski and several friends reportedly found themselves, in the early hours of the morning, sitting in the lobby of their cheap seaside hotel. None of them had any immediate plans. Roman, it's remembered, tried telling one or two jokes, but mostly they just sat there, looking tired and grizzled, in silence. There was a heavy, end-of-holiday atmosphere. Eventually, Polanski turned to the others and asked the question that everyone had on his mind: 'What are we going to do now?'

THROUGH PIERRE ROUSTANG, the producer who befriended the Polanskis at the time of *The Thousandth Window*, Roman met Gérard Brach, a writer for whom the word 'struggling' barely conveys the precariousness of his daily existence. Brach struck some in Roustang's circle as a faintly comic figure: small and gnarled, with his dented forehead, he would never be entirely comfortable in café society, much less in Hollywood, due in part, it's said, to a morbid fear of germs. Despite or because of that, Brach was to prove an accomplished screenwriter, with a particular gift for distilling the most convoluted plot down to the three- or four-line summary required by most producers.

Shortly after meeting Brach, Polanski was tempted to Munich by the promise of directing a 'major international motion picture' about wartime Yugoslav partisans, apparently to be financed by a Byzantine consortium of Franco-German-Bosnian backers. In the event, the deal, to the extent that there ever was one, revolved around the seduction of a local garment-factory owner named Rifka Shapiro (described by Polanski, a trifle ungallantly, as a 'short, dumpy, inexpressibly ugly Jewish girl with bow legs') who had drip-dry money to invest. This real-life version of the plot of *The Producers* then moved to a restaurant on the Adriatic coast, where the aspiring film-makers and their patron met with the author of the book they intended to adapt. The occasion was rather spoilt when one of the party christened the author 'Dupa', or 'arsehole', but eventually proceeded to the negotiating stage. Polanski could have his source material, he was told, in exchange for a small cash sum and a second-hand car. Rifka Shapiro made the payment, and in a brilliantly pragmatic move offered their own ancient Mercedes sedan. The vehicle then either failed to start, or started and broke down immediately thereafter, leading the author to withdraw his property, and Polanski to endure a long ride home in the back of a passing truck.

Once in Paris, Polanski entered into an informal but long-running alliance with Gérard Brach, the first result of which was their screenplay *If Katelbach Comes*. (The title was a homage to Roman's co-star in *The Fat and the Lean* and current landlord, Andrzej Katelbach, and more allusively to *Waiting for Godot*.) This was a ghastly story, powerfully told. The partners made for a nearly perfect creative team: according to one well-placed source, 'Polanski was Mr Outside, the big-picture guy with a vivid imagination, and Brach was Mr Inside, the details guy with an ear for dialogue. Roman came up with some truly inspired sequences in [*Katelbach*] . . . I remember he insisted it should start with two wounded gangsters in a car. This was thirty years before *Reservoir Dogs*. In my recollection, Polanski was responsible for most of the smart plot twists. Brach gave them definition.'

In September 1962, it seemed as though the partnership had found a backer for their project: one Hans Reitz, a travelling representative of the Munich-based Atlas Productions and a leading proponent of the *Junger Deutscher Film*, as the new wave of West German cinema became known.

Reitz would offer Polanski a combined screenwriter-director's fee of $10,000, more money than he had made from all his previous films combined, for *Katelbach*. If modest by Hollywood standards it struck Polanski, then still living in a variety of furnished rooms, as more than acceptable. 'I can't believe I'm actually getting paid for this,' he's said to have remarked to Brach. As it happened, he wasn't; Atlas apparently reconsidered matters at boardroom level, and shortly thereafter withdrew the contract.

There was better news to come on the European festival circuit: *Knife in the Water* won the Critics' Prize at Venice, and *Mammals* took the gold at Tours. But neither film ever found an audience, and even French reviews of *Knife* were largely negative. *Le Monde* conceded that it showed one or two 'visionary touches', though even these had to be set against a perfor-mance by Jolanta Umecka that resembled that of a department-store dummy that had somehow wandered away from its window. For the rest of the year, Polanski was effectively kept afloat by Pierre Roustang, the producer who had so taken to both Basia and him on their arrival in Paris. At lunch at Maxim's, a friend of Roustang asked him the same question that had intrigued a number of mutual colleagues over the past three years: What exactly did he see in Polanski? Roustang asked him to repeat the question. Then he silently stood up and walked out of the restaurant.

AT THIS FINANCIAL NADIR, Polanski accepted a commission to adapt a novel called *Aimez-vous les femmes?* for the screen. The plot concerns a neces-sarily exclusive culinary society devoted to eating young women. Of the finished product it's perhaps kindest to be silent, although it did later enjoy a brief cult in France's second-run cinemas.

As well as the professional challenges, Polanski was also wrestling with his personal relationships. While lodging at Roustang's elegant new apart-ment on the rue Jacob, he played the part of the kid in the candy store. Polanski's success in enticing various young women up to the flat at the weekend was perhaps not impaired by their logical, though mistaken assumption that he personally owned the place. Back in his more modest digs, the director was intrigued to notice an attractive neighbour who was in the habit of walking around naked without first drawing her curtains. This experience became the basis of a script that he and Brach wrote though never submitted, entitled *The Girl Opposite*. There were also occasional excur-sions to Les Halles, traditionally a meeting place for the city's prostitutes, though these seem to have been more out of passing curiosity than anything else, and a more extended affair with a model and aspiring actress named Nicole Hilartain. But, for Polanski, none of these women seemed to quite compensate for the loss of Basia, who, in one later Polish magazine profile, was described by a 'close friend' as the 'most obvious, enduring [and] painful failure' of his life. The source of the analysis wasn't named.

Back in the eleventh arrondissement, Polanski found a small arts cinema where he reportedly sat through several repeat screenings of Alfred Hitchcock's *Psycho*. As a movie it seemed to distil Roman's own propensity for sex, violence and voyeurism, as well as for telling a good story. He was less impressed with the so-called *nouvelle vague*, the loose conglomerate of French film-makers who, with one or two exceptions, he wrote, 'dismayed me by their amateurism and appalling technique.' Polanski happened to speak to the British director Lindsay Anderson (who, on their first meeting a year earlier, had thought 'the kid' to be 'overconscious of his own cleverness, [with] a need to be the centre of attention', but for all that, 'brilliantly inventive') shortly after they both endured Jean-Luc Godard's *Une femme est une femme*. Polanski told Anderson that he thought Godard's film 'unbelievably dreary'. Back at his arts cinema that night, he watched *Psycho* again.

In January 1963, Pierre Roustang commissioned Polanski and Brach to write a sketch for an omnibus film he was producing called *Les Plus Belles Escroqueries du Monde*, or *The World's Most Beautiful Swindles*. Polanski was to be paid a further $5,000 plus expenses for directing the thirty-three-minute episode, which he shot on location in Amsterdam. His girlfriend Nicole turned in a polished performance as a young woman who pretends to fall for a Dutch businessman and instead relieves him of a diamond necklace. Polanski prepared for the assignment with typical diligence, making several visits to the Cartier company to learn about jewel frauds. Although his segment showed flashes of class, along with some gauzy tourist footage of canals, *Les Plus Belles Escroqueries* was only a mixed success. Roustang perfunctorily sent it on its way through the second-run circuit, where it disappeared completely a few weeks later. Roman's fee similarly vanished when his producer-benefactor, faced with a cash-flow crisis, suddenly called in all his loans.

One British film producer who encountered Polanski at the time (although the specific anecdote would seem to belong a year later) remembers a 'rather sad' individual, who, through no fault of his own, 'clearly wasn't comfortable when speak[ing] English.' This seemed to the producer to be more of a 'cultural' than 'strictly linguistic' shortcoming. 'Roman would chug along all right, but then suddenly go hopelessly over the top by making a taste-less joke about "women's plumbing". You'd correct him, and Polanski would look puzzled and fascinated, like a Martian making a mental note: "Plumbing not funny."' Meanwhile, Pierre Roustang had taken a suite at the Carlton Hotel in Cannes, where he eventually managed to unload *Les Plus Belles Escroqueries* on an American distributor. Flushed with this relative (and fleeting) success, the producer put Polanski and Brach on retainer to write a script about the adventures of a wealthy US businessman seeking a foreign bride. Their treatment, which hinted more at farce than satire, was called *Cherchez la femme*. Although the project soon went into turnaround, the film industry equivalent of a coma, Roman, having lost his Mercedes in the divorce, was able to part-exchange a second-hand Triumph for that defining symbol of Swinging Sixties mobility, a Mini Cooper.

Somehow, Polanski made it all seem so easy. Despite his unconventional looks, thick accent and occasional gaffes, he was able to use his feline charm to win over some of the entertainment industry's toughest customers. While table-hopping across the Carlton terrace at Cannes, the director met Victor Lownes, the *soigné*, 35-year-old Chicagoan who was the circulation and advertising brain behind Hugh Hefner's publishing empire. Lownes happened to be in the throes of moving to London, where in due course he opened the Playboy Club on Park Lane. This legendary edifice would provide safe haven to virtually everyone who would ever be famous, from the Prince of Wales to Bob Dylan to the Muppets, over the next fifteen years. Lownes himself was one of those seemingly paradoxical figures who managed to combine laissez-faire morality with a keen entrepreneurial spirit. He had a nearly infallible nose for an investment, and was known to be particularly drawn to projects concerning the Holocaust and the Second World War generally; some time later, he was a principal backer of Rolf Hochhuth's play *Soldiers*, about the Free Polish leader General Sikorski. After watching *Knife in the Water*, Lownes, too, became a paid-up member of the small but intensely loyal Polanski fan club. If and more pertinently when Roman ever came to London, he was to be sure to look him up. It was an offer the director accepted, and one with ultimately dramatic results for both men. Even at low moments for Polanski, there always seemed to be some new saviour in the wings.

IN THE FIRST WEEK OF AUGUST 1963, Polanski was a guest at the Montreal Film Festival. His lavish suite in the Hotel Windsor was in sharp contrast to his latest bachelor pad in Paris, a cold-water flat he was sharing with his dog Jules. Roman and Nicole had parted, by mutual agreement, shortly after completing *Les Plus Belles Escroqueries*. Later that month Polanski turned 30, the age by which, he once assured friends in Lodz, he would 'make it'. There was another tantalising glimpse of fame that autumn in New York, culminating in the *Time* cover story entitled 'Cinema as an International Art'. The American film industry, like much of the country, would then go into a tailspin as a result of events eight weeks later in Dallas. Having seen their young president assassinated on the very day Kanawha attempted to officially launch *Knife in the Water*, the US was in no very good mood to embrace a moody Polish black-and-white psychodrama with subtitles.

When Polanski was asked to introduce *Knife in the Water* at the Lincoln Center, he responded with a single, self-deprecatory sentence, stating in Polish that he was no good at making speeches – which he then repeated in French and English. 'That need to impress was part of his charm,' says Judy Flanders, who had watched him repeatedly rehearse the performance in front of a mirror. Like most of those who encountered the director in New York, she remembers him with amused affection. Once in Paris, Polanski bought a set of linguaphone records and spent ten hours a day, six days a week, teaching himself to speak fluent English. It was the same ferocious discipline he'd shown when bicycling up into the Carpathian foothills or running around with a pillowcase filled with cobblestones on his back. As he was reportedly later to remark, in reply to suggestions that he led a charmed life, 'The harder I worked, the luckier I got.' One morning that December, he picked up the phone to hear a Polish-born producer named Sam Waynberg offer him $2,000 out of the blue for an option on *Katelbach*. Polanski used the windfall to pay off some outstanding debts, and print a new batch of business cards. With the balance of the money, he bought himself a tailored Italian suit, which he ruined by slipping on a wet driveway on his first night in Los Angeles.

Early in 1964, Polanski was contacted by yet another would-be benefactor: a 40-year-old, London-based, Polish-American producer named Gene Gutowski, then in the throes of making a briefly acclaimed sex melodrama called *Station Six-Sahara*. Gutowski, who was bowled over by the script for *Katelbach*, invited his compatriot to stay with him in his flat in Belgravia's fashionable Eaton Place. He would even provide him with a first-class air ticket. Polanski, who had been living a hand-to-mouth existence since returning from New York, was on the next plane over.

Looking back years later, Polanski would reflect that his semi-permanent residence in London throughout the Sixties was the happiest time of his life. 'In France I wasn't *nouvelle vague* enough and really didn't know what was expected of me,' he told *Cahiers du Cinéma*. 'But in England I felt truly free . . . It was a very exciting place, an environment I needed to experience. I wanted to be able to meet lots of different people. There was a cultural renaissance with English and European artists, graphic designers, and also many Americans – all the film-makers, screenwriters and actors who'd fled from Hollywood.'

Polanski was, indeed, not only in the right place but there at the right time. Within a few months, he was on the fast track to social success as a member of the 'Ad Lib' set, a collective of Swinging London's most beautiful people. Located in a cramped, smoky room in a building behind Leicester Square, the Ad Lib itself somehow regularly packed in three or four hundred guests, throbbing, sweating, dancing the conga and crashing into the laps of strangers. Then it was typically on to the Playboy Club, where Polanski would renew his acquaintance with Victor Lownes, who offered him both female companionship and his first taste of LSD. The director didn't need a subpoena. Always a sharp dresser when circumstances allowed, Polanski would soon be fitted out for a navy-blue blazer and several pairs of bulbous flares, which flapped madly around his too-high boot heels. Even among such achingly hip peers as Mick Jagger and Keith Richards, ten years his junior, Roman would be known for his youthful elan.

Meanwhile, for all the friendly patronage of men like Lownes, Waynberg and Gutowski, there was still no serious studio interest in *If Katelbach Comes*. Twentieth Century Fox did contact Polanski with a 'great idea' – a remake of *Knife in the Water* with Richard Burton, Liz Taylor and Warren Beatty playing the three leads. He rejected the offer. Gutowski, to his growing frustration, was thus obliged to hawk his protégé around a series of small, increasingly dubious shops, all of whom similarly declined to commission *Katelbach*. The script that had so electrified Hans Reitz, among others, was judged by even the Hammer company to be 'rather macabre'. Eventually Gutowski was able to secure an appointment with the Compton Group, a Soho-based concern specialising in soft-core porn films like *Gutter Girls* and *London in the Raw*. So lucrative was this venture, which had recently swung to a zenith with *My Bare Lady*, that Compton's owners, two East End entrepreneurs named Michael Klinger and Tony Tenser, were keen to expand. The company's principals listened politely to Gutowski's claim that Polanski would one day be bigger than Alfred Hitchcock. Having read the script of *Katelbach*, they could understand why a story about a young French woman and her middle-aged, transvestite husband living in an eleventh-century castle might not have been considered an instantly commercial property. But, unlike everyone else, they actually agreed to make a film with Polanski: not *Katelbach*, but a horror story he called *Repulsion*.

THE FAINTLY COMIC-OPERA PAIR OF KLINGER AND TENSER DROVE A HARD bargain. Representing the barest of investments by Compton, *Repulsion* would notionally be shot for £40,000, with Polanski, Brach and Gutowski sharing a fee of $5,000, or just over £1,000, plus expenses. Negotiations were brisk, as was the writing process: Polanski and Brach drafted their initial idea, about a seemingly innocent young woman who goes berserk, inside five days, Roman enlivening proceedings by miming the scenes as they went along. On the sixth day, they began to tackle the question of structure. After seventeen days, they submitted their final script.

Terror is within and without in *Repulsion*: the woman's drab apartment (constructed in a corner of Twickenham studios), where a rabbit dinner sits rotting on the kitchen table, is mirrored by Polanski's unique vision of Swinging London, inhabited not so much by pop stars and dolly birds as by grotesque old codgers and lecherous navvies. It's this atmosphere and attention to the texture of 'ordinary' life that helps make *Repulsion* so evocative. There had already been plenty of other Sixties films about love and sex and politics and football and God and drugs and abortion, but relatively few about what it was like to be simply living and working in a rather shabby-looking central London. The flat itself starts off as merely grim and ends up as a crucible of homicidal delirium, with an obvious nod to *Psycho*'s Bates Motel. At least one critic has compared the set of *Repulsion* to the Krakow ghetto, a very broadly similar, self-contained world with its background glimpses of the macabre and horrific.

The 21-year-old Catherine Deneuve plays Carol, a withdrawn if not clinically repressed blonde who lives with her sister Helen on the top floor of a seedy South Kensington mansion block. Since the atmosphere in *Repulsion* is all-important, it's worth repeating that, unlike the usual heavy-handed representation of a London pad, the detail and observation of the place are exactly right; you can believe that two foreign girls would end up there. Beneath Carol's dreamy facade evidently lurks a schizophrenic chaos, which boils over into the climactic rampage. More deliberately paced (among numerous other distinctions) than today's standard slasher flick, *Repulsion* lets us know how susceptible its heroine is, not just to criminal insanity, but to the full spectrum of neuroses. Things begin to go awry when we see Carol lying rigid in bed, listening to Helen and her married lover Michael (Ian Hendry) consummating their relationship in the next room. In a coup that had previously eluded even the Compton Group, this would be the first ever depiction of a female orgasm (sound only) to be passed by the British censor. The happy couple then go off on holiday to Italy. Left alone, Carol starts to suffer hallucinations, a mental disintegration Polanski captures by bleaching Deneuve's face and filming her with a distorting wide-angle lens. Her mild-mannered suitor Colin (John Fraser) comes calling, to enquire whether they still have a future together. Carol bludgeons him to death in response. The sisters' landlord follows, after ill-advisedly making a pass at his tenant, who slashes him with a razor. When Helen and Michael return they find two corpses on the premises and their catatonic killer hiding under the bed. Along the way, Polanski indulges in a miscalculated if not faintly ludicrous plot twist, in which Carol apparently sees several pairs of hands groping her from inside the flat's walls. This contrived and visibly low-budget effect comes off as both shlocky and bland, the one scene to do so, and may have been included to appease Polanski's producers. *Repulsion* has its occasional shortcomings, but still shows an originality and lightness of touch well beyond the stock Hammer-horror genre that Compton had apparently had in mind. The gradual crack-up of what Polanski calls 'an angelic-looking girl with a soiled halo' is what seems really shocking: both pitiable and ugly.

As usual on a Polanski film, the shoot for *Repulsion* had its full quota of behind-the-scenes drama. There was constant creative strife with, in particular, Michael Klinger (a former sausage salesman, said by one associate to be 'only partly successful at learning to make films as an alternative'), who repeatedly complained about the rather inordinate amount of time that the script took to get going – or, as he protested formally in a memo, 'Fuck all happens in the first fifteen minutes.' Then there was the inevitable, and linked debate about Polanski's meticulous approach to his craft. Klinger watched his director shoot one scene, a simple close-up of a hand that could have been done in a minute, twenty-seven times. As a result of such compulsive perfectionism, *Repulsion* came in at £95,000, or roughly 130 per cent over budget.

A second source of tension lay in Polanski's relationship with the British film unions, whose rules insisted that they stop work promptly at 5.20 p.m.

each weekday, and that they earn triple-time on the weekends. The director, who often liked to compare himself to a doctor performing delicate brain surgery, perhaps understandably chafed at having to ask permission in order to shoot beyond the specified hour. Polanski's opinion on the subject hardened steadily over the years; his sometime admirer Margaret Thatcher might not have completely disowned, for example, his comments to *Cahiers du Cinéma* in late 1979:

> How can you improve the quality of an organisation if the management doesn't have the right to sack useless employees? And most of them *are* useless. They arrive late without an excuse, climb up the scaffolding to go to sleep, and afterwards climb back down to discuss their next strike. The people who are interested and motivated – those who actually want to do some real work – are stifled by the others. They're scared of being branded a fascist or a scab.

Some of the same uncompromising attitude inevitably coloured Polanski's relations with his cast, even if tinged with a personal empathy that came from his being an 'old ham' himself. To judge by Catherine Deneuve's account, his chief concern was the same as hers, indeed that of most self-respecting actors: to make a serious, emotionally mature film, and, if need be, to fight off the producers to do so. The 32-year-old, Scottish-born actor John Fraser, a veteran of epics like *The Dam Busters*, remembers taking the part of Colin, the Deneuve character's lover, 'for a fraction of my usual fee; it was sold to me by my agent as a prestige film, and I loved what Roman had done in *Knife in the Water*.'

When Fraser, having already signed his contract, then read the script for *Repulsion*, he was 'momentarily speechless ... I rang Polanski and asked him, "Have you been analysed?"

'"Why?" he enquired.

'"Because the film is sick."

'"But, John," he said, "it's meant to be *funny*."'

Despite this inauspicious start, Fraser found Polanski a 'wonderful' director. 'As far as I'm concerned, he was remarkably patient and inspiring – he could always show you a fresh way of doing something – although he and I weren't exactly on the same wavelength socially. I was an in-the-closet gay and Roman was into Swinging London, particularly the girls, with a vengeance. I seem to remember going to one party at his place with dozens of young birds in miniskirts, all the Stones and at least a Beatle or two in attendance. He absolutely loved that.'

Other sources insist that, at times, Polanski resorted to shock tactics in order to extract the best possible performances from his cast. The actor Hugh Futcher, who appears with Fraser in several scenes shot in the Hoop and Toy pub in Kensington, remembers the director having been 'short-tempered and intimidating'. To Futcher's colleague James Villiers, he was the archetypal 'Napoleon'. Michael Klinger would recall how Polanski 'clinically' turned the voluptuous Deneuve into the sexually frustrated Carol. 'He made sure that, in the whole eight weeks or so when we filmed, Catherine didn't get next to a man.' When, eventually, the actress' distress stirred even Klinger, he asked that Polanski allow her to fly to Paris for a conjugal visit with the father of her child, Roger Vadim. '"I'll let her do it next weekend," Roman said, "because she'll be having her period. Then I don't mind her going."'

When it came to filming the inevitable semi-nude scene, Deneuve and Polanski debated at length what, if anything, she should be allowed to wear under her diaphanous nightgown. 'I objected to panties,' Polanski notes, eventually leading them to compromise on a body stocking. To ensure coverage in the British press, the director later persuaded his leading lady to do a nude *Repulsion* spread in *Playboy*, a decision she ruefully calls one of the worst moves of her career.

In the same spirit of thorough perfectionism, Polanski occasionally clashed both with the unassuming Yvonne Furneaux and the British character actor Ian Hendry, the latter of whom enjoyed a lunchtime drink. The general idea seems to have been to get his cast in part by getting them angry. Klinger once remonstrated with Polanski over his seemingly harsh treatment of Furneaux. 'Michael,' the director replied, 'I know she's a nice girl. She's too bloody nice. She's supposed to be playing a bitch. Every day I have to make her into a bitch.' Almost certainly exaggerating at a private dinner some years later, Klinger claimed that Hendry had been 'impossible' to direct some afternoons after returning from the pub. 'According to Michael, Ian sat down and drifted off into a sound sleep from which he would awake very suddenly reciting speeches from *Hamlet*,' one guest says. 'Klinger said he had to tell him repeatedly that it was a very fine performance, but that it wasn't the subject under discussion.'

Klinger eventually warmed to *Repulsion*, which would go on to make him and his partner a tidy profit, but his praise for the 'boy wonder', as he called Polanski, remained at best grudging and at times sarcastic. Most of the critics were respectful, if somewhat puzzled by a film that, however technically accomplished, didn't give up its secrets without a fight. ('You could literally fall asleep in the first reel' was the *Evening News'* ungenerous view.) Reviewers and audiences alike agreed that they were in the hands of an expert craftsman, whose camerawork deftly drew the viewer into the action. Even in 1965 films about psycho killers were already a cottage industry, but *Repulsion* had a disturbing and rare look of authenticity to it, one that made it occasionally difficult to watch. In the scene in which Carol batters her suitor with a candlestick, Polanski swings his camera around to show not the orthodox view of the crime but, chillingly, the victim's own perspective, panning down from the blood-spattered wall to the floor as he collapses. For the subsequent scene in which the killer dumps the corpse in a full bathtub, John Fraser remembers 'Roman hav[ing] me do take after take in order to get the exact look a dead man's eyes would have submerged in water. He had clinically precise views on the subject.'

Even Michael Klinger thought this particular shot masterly. 'Roman,' he was to recall, 'had an expert comprehension of both madness and death.'

Although Polanski himself insisted that *Repulsion* was a 'potboiler', little more than a holding device before he made *Katelbach*, many of his peers agreed with Lindsay Anderson that, while 'superficially boring', the film 'conceal[ed] real depth, sophistication and insight' – and, in general, 'marked the arrival of a major talent.' Speaking in 1967, Alfred Hitchcock ruefully recalled 'the terrible panning we got when *Psycho* opened. It was a disaster. One critic called it "a blot on an honourable career", and then the same man reviewed *Repulsion* by saying it was "a psychological thriller in the classic style of *Psycho*."' As the sorcerer's apprentice, Polanski was fast learning to out-Hitchcock Hitchcock. Within a year or two, the initial curiosity of many well-established directors had given way to a professional respect that led to their own Polanski-like flourishes. *Repulsion* opens with a close-up of an eyeball, recalling the notorious pupil-slicing scene in Luis Buñuel's 1929 *Un chien andalou*. Repaying the compliment, Buñuel later admitted that some of the much admired voyeurism sequence in his 1967 *Belle de Jour* (also with Catherine Deneuve) 'was a nod in Roman's direction'.

Deneuve herself speaks of the 'incredible power' exuded by the physically diminutive Polanski, who thought nothing of snapping out directions in a mixture of English and French, before briskly shinning up a rope ladder to the lights, or rolling around on the floor to demonstrate the proper way to die. Altogether, he enjoyed a remarkable personal and professional triumph thanks to *Repulsion*. Seemingly overnight, Polanski had made a name for himself as a master of both atmosphere and detail, and a self-styled 'crusader against cliché'. He'd also learned that the only alternative to long-term unemployment was an at least tenuous alliance with his producers. Further, he had an outstanding reputation as someone who actually understood actors and acting. '"Ask Roman about it",' reported *Life* several years later, was 'a byword among his casts'. Once work was over he was also charming, generous and affable – such a pleasant party-goer that some of his critics, like Michael Klinger, wondered if this was the same man who 'drove you nuts on set'.

Some of the cast of *Repulsion* fared less well than their director over the years. One or two of their lives, much like the film, often proved unhappy, macabre, obscure and downright bleak. Ian Hendry's career suffered a steep decline in the Seventies, ending in bankruptcy and ill health, before his premature death aged 53. Patrick Wymark, who gave a spirited perfor-mance as the sisters' sweaty, frog-faced landlord, died at just 44. Both John Fraser and Yvonne Furneaux chose to appear in only a handful of further films after *Repulsion*. Even Catherine Deneuve, while enjoying international acclaim playing a variety of exquisite, if often frigid beauties, never quite recovered from the indignity of her *Playboy* layout. 'It was a terrible mistake,' she says, 'and I would never do anything like it again.' (Deneuve did, however, proceed to marry the photographer in question, David Bailey.)

Repulsion opened in London on 10 June 1965, and electrified its first-night audience. The crowd rose when Polanski appeared in his box, and chanted his name at the end. It wasn't just all the 'exclusive T-shirts' and other accessories on sale in the lobby that carried a whiff of a rock concert.

Repulsion gained traction in the weeks ahead, not only through word of mouth and reviews but also the much rarer endorsement of the British psychiatric profession. Before clearing it for release with the inevitable X certificate, the Board of Film Censors had shown a print to Dr Steven Blake, a Harley Street specialist to whom they always referred 'difficult' pictures. Dr Blake pronounced it a masterpiece, a view publicly shared by several of his colleagues in London and New York. When the doctor subsequently met the film's two authors, he asked them how it was that they came to know so much about schizophrenic frenzy. 'We made it up,' said Polanski.

While mental-health professionals on both sides of the Atlantic competed to heap praise on *Repulsion* for the acuity of its psychological insights, Polanski himself insisted that he was just a director with a particularly vivid imagination. 'The whole "art" cinema thing and the philosophical depth don't interest me at all,' he later told the German magazine *Die Woche*. 'I just like to play with the camera, the lights, the actors. To me, film-making is what a train set is to a child.' Among his other observations at the time of *Repulsion*'s release was one insisting that 'the more fantastic you are, the more real you become.' It was a quip that seemed to apply as much to Polanski himself as to his work.

When *Time* magazine came to officially dub London the Style Capital of Europe, they concentrated on a few, photogenic locations and eye-catching developments like miniskirts and the rise of the Rolling Stones. Unbeknownst to *Time*, a more general revolution was also underway against the Britain of *Hancock's Half Hour*, with its grinding conformity and identical redbrick semis furnished just like grandmother's. After the drab years of rationing and austerity, Terence Conran's brightly coloured, brilliantly packaged Habitat became a flagship of hip, formally declaring the three-piece suite 'grotty' and 'far too boring' a concept. Instead customers would be buying a basic cotton-covered Larnaca sofa with a couple of related beanbags. Although rock music and drugs took their place against a normal existence, for millions of people, of knitting, cricket and pottering about the garden, thanks to a few enterprising artists and retailers, most Britons, as Harold Macmillan said, had 'never had it so good'. Put simply, there was less deference and more choice around. Gone were the days when a night at *The Sound of Music* followed by the Berni Inn Family Platter was the height of aspiration. It was in this relatively freewheeling atmosphere that a macabre, bizarre and brilliant Polish film director could feel at home.

Polanski both looked and acted the part, whether tottering up the King's Road in his Beatle boots and velvet flares, or expertly rolling a joint at one of the legendary parties he threw at his London mews home. Speculation about his 'gladiatorial' love life soon grew in the months following *Repulsion*, and Polanski didn't actively disown it. One day shortly after the film's release, friends took the affectionately known 'Krakow shagger' to a department store to choose a new bed. After testing the springs of several models, Polanski asked the uniformed salesman whether a particular brand was sufficiently well built. The salesman assured him that the bed in question was quite adequate for two adults.

'Yes,' said Polanski, 'but how about three?'

It was with something of this same elan that the director graced the 1965 Berlin Film Festival, where his restless shuttling between his hotel, the cinema and the Kurfürstendamm nightclubs whilst dressed in a loud check shirt struck Klinger as 'like a carnivorous fish darting around'. *Repulsion* took the festival's second highest award, the Silver Bear. Klinger himself accepted the statuette, which he then never surrendered to Polanski. The Compton Group did, however, approve a £120,000 budget – including a director's fee of £10,000 – for *Cul-de-Sac*, as *If Katelbach Comes* was now called.

When asked by Klinger and Tenser to explain the script, Polanski told them that it was the 'story of a married couple. He is approximately 46 or 48, and she is 22 or 23. They live in a decaying seaside house. He is very rich, but she is ruining him by her extravagance. She is crazy, but he's in love with her. A wounded gangster falls into the house, where he holds them hostage overnight while waiting for his boss, Mr Katelbach – who, like Godot, never comes'. That would be for starters. The husband, George, in this 'skewed thriller' is a recently divorced businessman and serial cuckold with a taste for cross-dressing. His new wife, Teresa, is played as a nymphomaniac tease who wedges pieces of paper between the gangster's toes and lights them while he's asleep. At this the gangster removes his belt, bends her over and, not wholly to George's distaste, tans her with it. While waiting for the mysterious Katelbach, both husband and wife undergo various other humiliations, some of them pleasurably, until the three-handed drama (reminiscent of *Knife in the Water*) ends in a somewhat incongruous shoot-up. The mild-mannered George finally confronts his unwanted guest, drilling him with a sub-machine gun, which causes the petrol tank of his car to explode. In the ensuing confusion, Teresa runs off with her lover Cecil, who happens to be passing, leaving George perched in the fetal position atop a large rock, crying maniacally and calling out for his first wife. A typically wrought Polanski film, in other words.

The obvious starting points for *Cul-de-Sac* were such hard-boiled Humphrey Bogart sagas as *The Desperate Hours*, William Wyler's classic version of the novel about escaped convicts terrorising a family, along with slyly allusive references to the works of Samuel Beckett and Harold Pinter. Polanski made no bones about his admiration of Pinter, the film of whose *The Caretaker*, about a more insidious sort of home invasion, had been shown to great acclaim at Berlin the year before. Much of Polanski's and Brach's script had a distinctly allegorical and surreal, if not 'Pinteresque' flavour, for instance in the scene where George first greets his captor while fetchingly clad in his wife's negligee. Although the transvestism was pure Polanski, the same sort of identity breakdown was very much *The Caretaker*'s stock-in-trade. Faced with a work of such overpowering authority – compounded, perhaps, by Pinter's recent triumph in Berlin – Polanski and Gérard Brach seemed to have experienced the cinematic equivalent of the *Führer Kontakt*. At their director's insistence, the Compton Group would go to great lengths to hire Donald Pleasence, one of the stars of Pinter's film, as their leading man. Pleasence would surprise everyone by reporting for work with his head shaved, a look he believed 'added to the character'.

Rounding out the cast were Catherine Deneuve's sister Françoise Dorléac as the swinger wife, who got the part after Polanski had personally screen-tested 'more than 200' aspiring starlets and models. The director wanted her to play the role as a 'little girl' – as illustrated by the spanking scene – who was nonetheless sexually precocious, broadly in the tradition of Vladimir Nabokov's *Lolita*. Beckett's great favourite Jack MacGowran, a charming but troubled Irishman who turned to pills and liquor when his frequent depressions struck, put in a memorable performance as the gangster's mortally wounded sidekick. Twenty years later, Polanski cast David Kelly, a gifted television actor but shamefully unknown in Hollywood until 1998's *Waking Ned Devine*, in his swashbuckler *Pirates*. Kelly modestly insists that he got the job 'largely because I reminded Roman of Jack, whom he'd loved.' Polanski also found a walk-on part for the 21-year-old Jacqueline Bisset. Bisset recalls that 'It was a fascinating experience [and] I spent every second of my free time – I had lots as it turned out – watching, watching, watching. Roman directed and I'd sit nearby learning.' Although Polanski refers to 'Jackie Bisset's consoling presence' while on location, she declines to confirm whether or not they had an affair.

For the part of Dicky, the cocksure gangster, Polanski took a risk on 57-year-old Lionel Stander, a gravel-voiced New York comedian who, long blacklisted by the House Un-American Activities Committee, would eke out work in London before making a belated comeback as the co-star of various spaghetti westerns, as well as of the inexplicably popular TV series *Hart to Hart*. Stander's self-styled 'no bullshit' persona was first revealed when he appeared explosively in the foyer of the cinema in which *Repulsion* was being premiered, bellowing out 'Polanski!' at the top of his lungs while the director was across the room exchanging small talk with some European royalty. A week or two later, Stander accompanied Polanski and Gene Gutowski to a cast meeting in the Connaught

Hotel. The front desk, unimpressed by Stander's attire of pink linen suit, blue suede shoes and cravat – these were the days of the ties-only rule – discreetly suggested that he and his friends reconvene elsewhere.

'Perhaps Sir might wish to consider his position.'

Sir might. Stander gave it a second, then told the Connaught to go fuck themselves.

Topping off the crew for *Cul-de-Sac* were the cameraman Gil Taylor, whose innovative use of reflected light bounced off the ceiling and walls had so contributed to *Repulsion*'s success, and Polanski's old friend Krzysztof Komeda, who composed the score. Principal photography began on Holy Island, a speck of rock off England's extreme north-east coast, in August 1965. Matching the mood of the film, it happened to be the gloomiest summer month in even Northumbria's recent history, with the cast sitting out frequent rain delays in the pub while Michael Klinger paced up and down, once again fretting about costs.

For most of those who have worked with him in recent years, Polanski is a grand old man of wisdom, generosity, seraphic good nature and an inexhaustible interest in other people. Forty years ago, reaction to him, while never less than professionally respectful, was rather different. Back from the *Cul-de-Sac* shoot, Donald Pleasence, for one, remembered how he kept being asked the same question about his famous director. 'Was he nice?'

'Not especially,' Pleasence replied to one writer. 'At least not to me. But yes, as he prowled around the set, it was clear that he knew most of the crew personally and, what's more, understood their jobs: which lens to use and how exactly a certain light would look. It's a rarer skill in directors than you'd think. But then he'd abruptly bollock Stander or me, and the whole thing would come to a halt.

'So, on balance, Roman wasn't nice. He was an average, Hollywood-type megalomaniac, an unsentimental, restless young man. He was also about twenty IQ points brighter than most directors. You were always conscious of being in the hands of an absolute master of his trade.'

Whether out of jealousy or because Polanski still occasionally spoke in mangled English and was self-conscious around strangers, a certain sport was made of his perceived social shortcomings. Lionel Stander, in particular, was known to do a cruel, if wittily accurate impersonation in which he barked out instructions 'like an enraged seal.' Another crew member, who prefers anonymity, recalls with amusement that when everyone settled down in the large wooden chairs in the local pub, 'little Romek's' feet barely grazed the floor. Yet even Stander conceded that, once at work, Polanski was a 'natural leader ... He'd shin up a sheer cliff or jump in and stand half immersed in freezing cold water to get a shot. Roman never asked you to do anything that he didn't do himself. His impulse to active leadership and his instinct to always be on the attack were phenomenal, and it was a genuinely inspiring sight to see the little brat right there at the head of his troops.'

Françoise Dorléac had arrived on Holy Island with twenty mono-grammed suitcases, her incontinent chihuahua Jaderane and a particu-larly acute case of PMT or its immediate aftermath, which, Polanski noted ruefully, 'rendered her incapable of working' for several days. She and the dog made a striking pair as they were periodically ferried around the island in the back seat of Donald Pleasence's shiny Lincoln Continental, itself the source of some local excitement. Pleasence would remember a 'small crowd of islanders gathering to look in through the window, quailing a bit as Jaderane hurled herself at it.' About halfway through the shoot, Dorléac somehow chipped a tooth and insisted on flying to her dentist in Paris, taking her pet with her. When, passing through Heathrow, she attempted to smuggle the animal through immigration in her handbag, Jaderane emerged to bite a customs officer on the hand, and was promptly placed in quarantine for six months.

When Dorléac returned, Polanski announced that they were to shoot a particularly long and technically complex scene in which the Pleasence and Stander characters engage in a drunken argument on the beach while the actress walks past them, nude, and stands in the icy water. To compound the challenge, which also involved synchronising a light aircraft, possibly piloted by the elusive Katelbach, flying overhead, the whole seven-and-a-half-minute sequence was to be filmed in one contin-uous take. Everything seemed to go perfectly the first time around. Nonetheless, Polanski, announcing himself dissatisfied, snapped out, 'We go again!' and actors, crew and plane duly repeated the performance. Midway through the third take, it was noticed that Dorléac had fainted. Pleasence and Stander waded into the surf to rescue the young actress, who had apparently begun to menstruate, in addition to suffering from the early stages of hypothermia. Before Polanski could call for a fourth take, the crew's shop steward lodged a formal protest. 'There was even talk of a strike,' the director notes sanguinely, although the crisis was averted when Michael Klinger intervened. The actual sequence used in the film was a tour de force, all sides agreed.

Dorléac's ordeal continued in the scene in which Stander was called on to beat her for setting fire to his foot. The actress, not unreasonably, flinched in pain at this genuinely violent assault, causing Stander in turn to wince and yell out, 'You stupid cunt! You hurt my knee!'

Stander's limp in time gave way to acute chest pains, which led him to be airlifted to Newcastle's Royal Victoria Infirmary. On his release, the insurance company insisted that he work only six hours a day, roughly half Polanski's preferred quota. A bit later on, the director happened to enquire whether Stander thought that he could drink a pint of milk in one gulp. Stander assured him he could. Polanski then filmed the scene – sixteen times. 'Look!' the director exclaimed. 'Lionel can swig a gallon of milk and not even wrinkle his nose!' In time, Polanski came to quite respect Stander, apparently insisting that he planned to make him the star of his next film, the long-stalled *Cherchez la femme*.

After several weeks filming on a windswept rock, even the most equable of crew members was suffering from island fever, a claustrophobic malaise that mirrored that of the fictional characters. Particularly in its last few days, the *Cul-de-Sac* shoot was marked by a disastrous series of bad 'vibes' and mysterious accidents. Polanski's normally unflappable cameraman Gil Taylor took exception to the actor Iain Quarrier one night and punched him in the face. Gene Gutowski and his young son then drove up to visit the cast, but their truck was cut off by the tide and sank in the North Sea. Michael Klinger went down with a respiratory infection, or, as he put it, 'Polish flu'. Lionel Stander knocked back a bottle of dynamite-strength local spirit and promptly went blind for a day. As a result of his various woes on *Cul-de-Sac* and other sets, the veteran actor was moved to repeatedly announce that he 'wasn't long for the world'. Only Françoise Dorléac seemed to actively rally the longer the shoot went on. 'She eventually found solace in the arms of Roy Ford, Gil Taylor's assistant, and became much more relaxed,' notes Polanski, consistent with his theory that all young women want, if not pathologically need sex for their emotional well-being.

The director faced his own professional and personal trials on Holy Island, among them his accommodations – a rather basic trailer, which one visitor thought 'more like a gypsy caravan', infested by earwigs, which he parked next to the local cemetery. Speaking to the journalist Philippe Haudiquet, Polanski summarised his overall experience on *Cul-de-Sac* as 'exhausting . . . The weather was terrible, the food was disgusting, and the actors turned out to be very difficult and aloof.' As usual, too, the director and his executive producer fought like ferrets in a sack. Michael Klinger is reported to have appeared in the makeshift projection room one evening in order to look at the day's rushes 'and see where all the money is going'. This was the signal for Polanski to storm in, announcing, 'Never in all my experience have I been treated like this!' 'What experience?' Klinger enquired. 'You've made three films in your whole life, and two of them have been for me!' Polanski then left the room, announcing, 'I quit!' 'Good,' Klinger retorted. 'Piss off! And remember, there's a director in London waiting to come out and finish the film, and you'd better pray he's good, because when it goes out, it's gonna say "Directed by Roman Polanski".'

Polanski drove off at speed in his Mini, but seems to have reappraised matters overnight. He and Klinger shook hands on set the next morning, although the relationship, at least professionally speaking, was beyond repair. Halfway into the editing of *Cul-de-Sac*, Polanski, by now stepping out with the buxom American actress Jill St John, took a skiing holiday with friends in the Austrian Alps, leaving behind a long spool of raw film at the production office in London. Klinger, who had wanted to release the picture before Christmas, was reportedly furious that 'Roman [would] push off, leaving me literally holding the can.' As a result of this misunderstanding, the Compton Group withheld Polanski's fee for five weeks.

Cul-de-Sac was finally released in Britain in February 1966, and in America nine months later. There's barely an unflawed character or a moral certainty in the film, which features a generous quota of leaden, Pinteresque pauses and non sequiturs, and once again demonstrates its director's familiarity with themes such as claustrophobia, terror and the erotic triangle. The astonishing thing is that it all works so well. Polanski may not quite have woven together 'an epochal hit' that 'truly breaks new ground', as Klinger buoyantly contended, but it did manage to be dark, funny and provocative, quite often all at once. Much the same sort of taut character study was then all the rage in British theatre, but few film-makers had even tried to pull off anything remotely as adventurous. It is arguably Polanski's greatest extreme work. In the best ballyhoo tradition, the producers sold out the opening week in New York by advertising their property as the 'Top London Smash', with the strapline 'Sometimes There's Nothing Left To Do But Laugh!' The critics were unmoved. Brendan Gill in the *New Yorker* found *Cul-de-Sac* an 'odious freak show' that would entertain only those 'who can laugh off nausea and/or sheer amazement at the prodigious waste of talent on tripe'. The next day, the line formed early at the box office, not to buy tickets, but to demand refunds. In time, many of these same reviewers would come to reassess *Cul-de-Sac*, which went from being a flop to an absurdist classic without ever quite being a success.

As with *Repulsion*, the film's cast enjoyed mixed fortunes over the years. Françoise Dorléac appeared to be on the brink of international stardom when she was killed in a car crash in June 1967, aged 25. Lionel Stander and his young Cherokee wife moved from London to Rome, where he became a cult figure after playing a grizzled bartender in Sergio Leone's *Once Upon a Time in the West*. He lived to be 86. Donald Pleasence enjoyed a comparable late success as James Bond's nemesis Blofeld (retaining his shaved dome) in *You Only Live Twice*. Jacqueline Bisset went on to co-star with some of the industry's big names, and even survived becoming an erotic poster pin-up in a wet T-shirt advertising 1977's *The Deep*. Polanski and Michael Klinger never worked together again.

The Compton Group executive later called *Cul-de-Sac* the most 'memorable' of his nearly three dozen productions, which would go on to include both *Confessions of a Window Cleaner* and, perhaps striking a higher artistic note, *Get Carter*. Furthermore, Klinger noted, the company had done everything possible to 'aggressively market' Polanski around the world, with some tangible success. While belatedly promoting *Repulsion* on one junket to California, the director enjoyed a layover at Jill St John's home in Bel Air, a stone bungalow tucked away on a steep canyon road, at the top of which lay a cul-de-sac named Cielo Drive. One night Polanski noticed what he took to be a prop pistol lying on the bedside table. His hostess assured him that the gun was not only real, but loaded. It was a 'routine precaution'. The news surprised Polanski, who had logically assumed that that particular area, with its knoll of Spanish villas and sprawling, mock-Tudor follies set behind high security gates, was one of the safest in Los Angeles. Jill St John told him that, as a whole, he was right. 'But, you know, once you delve into it, it can be a pretty crazy world. You have no idea.'

IT ENDED, as it began, with a rather strained meeting in Soho. Polanski had what the minutes refer to as a 'frank encounter' with Michael Klinger, in which they debated among other topics the Compton Group's bookkeeping. The director was curious to learn, for instance, that whereas *Repulsion* had made a healthy £425 profit in Ceylon, its entire box-office revenue from France and the Low Countries amounted to £364 15s. Apart from a few such residuals, the two men had little more to discuss and apparently even less in common. While Klinger habitually paced around with a calculator, Polanski's preferred props were a joint and a succession of pneumatic young women. With his Jaggeresque haircut, Carnaby Street gear and souped-up Mini, he struck the visiting *Time* stringer as a 'Renaissance Man; the pop star as auteur.' This was precisely the decadent West that Polanski had dreamt about in Krakow, and he did whatever it took to make his mark there, whether leaping up to deliver impromptu speeches at the Cannes festival, or agreeing to appear on a British television chat show flanked by two witches. John Lennon once said, not unaffectionately, that 'Roman was a kind of mascot for us: the kid who runs on in front of the team at the Cup Final.'

After three films, Polanski had established not only a professional style, but himself. Along with many people in the lively arts, he seems to have been afflicted by both nerves and vanity. The former caused him to lose several nights' sleep whenever starting a project, and the latter was expressed in his sometimes impressively abrasive manner. An English actor whom he later cast in *Macbeth* remembers complimenting the director on having made the best film adaptation of Shakespeare 'since Orson Welles in the Forties'. 'What made Welles better?' Polanski shot back, apparently deeply miffed. Terence Bayler, whom Polanski would cast as Macduff in the same production, similarly recalls 'Roman's thirtysomething birthday party, when he seemed to spend most of the evening scowling around the room, hissing, "Who the fuck *are* these people?"' (As Bayler adds, 'He had a point. It was crawling with freeloaders.')

On 14 April 1966, Kenneth Tynan, the renowned critic and latterly artistic czar of the National Theatre, wrote to his co-director Laurence Olivier proposing they offer a short-term contract to the 'brilliant young Pole who directed *Knife in the Water* and *Repulsion*. He's also worked in the theatre and Peter Hall is after him to direct a play at the Aldwych. He has exactly the right combination of fantasy and violence [for] us.' Olivier enquired merely whether Polanski spoke English. 'He's a genius,' Tynan assured him.

That particular project foundered, but two months later Tynan invited Polanski to direct a film which the critic described as 'a sort of sexy *Batman*'. This, too, went into turnaround, as did yet another project whose would-be producer recalls their first and only meeting, in which he greeted

'Roman's screw-you air' with a 'kind of mute fear' that at least got them through the allotted half-hour.

'Due respect, I found, was one of the ingredients for dealing with Polanski,' the producer says.

Sometime that summer, four of the five directors of the Compton Group, who seem to have been simultaneously impressed and appalled by their 'boy wonder', reportedly wrote him an unusually long, conciliatory letter, noting that, for all their financial woes, both *Repulsion* and *Cul-de-Sac* had been a pleasure to make. (Polanski may very reasonably have had his reservations on this point.) They concluded that a lot had happened since the day Gene Gutowski had brought them together, and that they sincerely hoped that they might yet meet somewhere, over a meal, for a discussion of those 'few issues' that lay between them.

Polanski declined the offer.

MOST RETROSPECTIVES TAKE THE SUMMER OF LOVE (loosely agreed as being the period from about the time England won the World Cup in July 1966 to the Beatles' ill-fated retreat with the Maharishi Yogi, during the course of which their manager, Brian Epstein, died, thirteen months later) on its own terms. 'Society was shaken to its foundations!' a recent BBC documentary on the subject shouted. 'All the rules came off, all the brakes came off . . . the floodgates were unlocked . . . a youthquake hit Britain', and so on. For most people what this mainly seems to have meant was some very silly shirts, better furniture and a slight increase in the use of soft drugs. The contraceptive pill also meant that a few more young women spent the night together with their boyfriends.

As noted, the Polanski of this period was both socially and sartorially ambitious. (One party refers to him archly as a 'brightly painted gnome'.) His friend Victor Lownes remembers that he liked to practise his newly acquired vocabulary at parties by 'telling jokes and watching the reaction of his audience to see if they were forcing laughter, or if they genuinely understood the humour. [If necessary] I would patiently explain to him where the joke went wrong in translation.' One example of this was the occasion when Polanski reportedly provoked a degree of mirth by innocently using the word 'harass' with a break between the two syllables, while, another night, he had brought his audience up short by loudly proclaiming his desire for 'a penis'; one of Lownes' guests had gently explained to him that in England the word was pronounced 'happiness'. In another concession to the times, Polanski steadily increased his chemical intake, which, though relatively modest compared to many of his peers, came to include champagne, vodka, marijuana and the occasional hit of acid. The still-legal LSD-25 was billed as the door to a new consciousness by such apostles as Lennon and McCartney, the former of whom, at least, wrote some of his best songs on it. Under Lownes' supervision, Polanski took five drops of the drug one night and then unwisely climbed into his Mini, where, in the first sign that something unusual was happening, he felt the steering wheel suddenly alter shape. Once back in his house, Polanski was curious to note that his hair colour had changed to a mixture of fluorescent green and pink. Meanwhile, the eyes of the girl who had accompanied him became, in what can hardly have been a random image, two bulging swastikas. After a further hallucination or two, Polanski then suddenly discovered the meaning of life, which he had the presence of mind to later jot down on paper. The formula read, 'First love, then sex, then work.'

His home now was a small but elegant villa at 95 West Eaton Place Mews, a cobbled lane modestly squeezed in behind Sloane Square. There were quaint Victorian coaching lamps by the door and, within, red carpets, several large oil paintings, the latest TV and video gear, and a spiral staircase that led to a sunken, all-black bathroom, the whole bathed by special 'trippy' lighting. Among subsequent furnishings were two busts, one of Napoleon, the other of Polanski himself, and a downstairs coffee table consisting of a nude female mannequin on all fours supporting a sheet of glass. The overall impression was of a Sixties art gallery with submerged Olde English charm. Polanski seems to have taken a justifiable pride in the house, which he bought for a reported £40,000 on a low-interest loan arranged by Gene Gutowski. The place hummed with activity, 'like Heathrow, arrivals from everywhere' whenever the director was in residence. Nor was there ever a shortage of overnight guests. Ken Tynan would later recall, for the benefit of numerous journalists, 'Roman leaf[ing] through his address book, asking, "Who shall I gratify tonight?"' 'All I was interested in,' Polanski said in a police polygraph exam in 1969, reflecting back on the period, 'was to fuck a girl and move on. I had a very bad marriage, you know . . . My wife dumped me, so I was a success with women again and I just liked fucking around. I was a swinger, uh?'

All three of the ex-partners interviewed for this book agree that Polanski was a generous host, but that it was perhaps rash to depend on him for anything remotely resembling a long-term commitment. One of the three recalls him fondly as a 'wine and roses at night, pat on the bum in the morning' type. Another woman confesses that she once sent Polanski a note saying, 'Remember how much I adore you all the time.' This, she now concedes, was like 'someone signing their own death warrant'. Polanski's third lover went into long-term therapy when he left her, and now believes that he had a 'permanent apparatus of self-containment'.

PARTLY AS A RESULT OF THEIR AUSTRIAN SKIING HOLIDAY, Polanski and Gérard Brach wrote a script, billed as an 'affectionate Hammer spoof with contemporary values' (meaning sex), that they set in a snowbound Rumanian village flanked by mountains. Despite the unusual theme, Polanski confidently predicted that he and his partner would sell their property to a major Hollywood studio within a month. Actually, it took two.

The Dance of the Vampires duly emerged as a mixture of humour and horror which its producers, desperate for a laugh, eventually renamed *The Fearless Vampire Killers* and subtitled *Pardon Me, But Your Teeth are in My Neck*. It was bought, and awarded a $1.7 million budget by Filmways, a Los Angeles-based company where Gene Gutowski had a contact, and which proved to be better connected, thanks to a multipicture distribution deal with MGM, if no more philanthropic, than the Compton Group. Polanski told Filmways' two principals, Martin Ransohoff and John Calley, that he wanted his friend Jill St John to play the female lead. They told him that they had their own talent in mind.

Even so, in a few short weeks in the summer of 1966, Polanski had a lucrative new job with the sort of fringe benefits the Compton Group could never aspire to, among them a publicist who got his client splashed over everything from the *New York Times* to *Playboy*. (The latter's piece, introducing readers to 'Bolshevism's boy wonder', carried with it a faint ring of Michael Klinger.) Aged 33, Polanski was doing better than any member of his family ever had, drawing £200 or £250 a week in salary from his company Cadre Films. After some forty years' back-breaking work, his father Ryszard was earning, at best, half as much. Now, with the Filmways project, Polanski was poised on the verge of his 'commercial breakthrough', in the Hollywood sense of the phrase; and he fell in love.

Her name was Sharon Tate, and when he met her she was in London playing opposite Donald Pleasence in a movie about the occult and human sacrifice called *Eye of the Devil*. The 23-year-old starlet was under an exclusive seven-year contract to Filmways, who announced that they were keeping their discovery, the 'Texas firecracker', under wraps until the right parts appeared. Among these was apparently Polanski's Dracula skit, because Filmways' top brass insisted that Tate, not Jill St John, take the role of Sarah, a compulsive bather who, early in the proceedings, falls prey to Krolock the vampire and disappears with him through a bathroom skylight (the opposite premise to Polanski's 1959 short, *When Angels Fall*).

Tate was born in Dallas on 24 January 1943, the eldest of three daughters of a military family who moved frequently around the US and Western Europe. She won several beauty contests as a teenager, was the victim of a date rape at high school and subsequently lived with her parents in Verona, where the actor Eli Wallach, shooting some 'pretentious junk' called *Adventures of a Young Man*, recalls 'this gorgeous, wide-eyed blonde visiting the set with her father, and appearing as an extra in one or two scenes.' As a result, Sharon got the acting bug and, once back in the States, hitched her way from her family's new posting in San Pedro, California, to Hollywood, where she was signed by an agent named Harold Gefsky. The *Hollywood Reporter* refers to her 'dazzling smile' when subsequently advertising a brand of cigarettes. After a few undistinguished modelling jobs, Tate was spotted by 36-year-old Marty Ransohoff, who put her in a black wig and cast her in a variety of frothy TV shows like *The Beverly Hillbillies, Petticoat Junction* and *Mr Ed*, a saga about a talking horse. Ransohoff also personally selected the actress' dresses, which tended to be short, tight and cut to accentuate her breasts. *Eye of the Devil* was to have been her last apprenticeship role before Filmways launched her on the world.

With her particular combination of wholesome, all-American looks and European sophistication – she spoke passable French and Italian – Tate had enjoyed a brisk social life since moving to Hollywood. 'She was very bohemian,' recalls a friend named Jessica Flint, 'listening to Janis Joplin, burning incense, wearing Bob Dylan T-shirts. A bit later on, there was a red Ferrari. But she also had this lost little girl thing going on as well. She was emotionally vulnerable.' Tate is said to have had one affair with a visiting foreign film star, who beat her up so badly that she required hospital treatment. She was then apparently close to the 45-year-old actor Jack Palance, before undergoing that ritual for almost any starlet, a personal audition with Steve McQueen. Late in 1964, Tate had tested for a role in the Filmways adaptation of Dick Jessup's novel *The Cincinnatti Kid*. McQueen, the film's lead, came back from the first day's rehearsal and enthused to his wife, Neile, that 'Sharon was being shot wearing a silk shirt and no bra, [so] you could see her nipples . . . Ohh, that set was wild.' (In a move that did little to check the production's emotional voltage, Tate was later replaced by the actress Tuesday Weld.) A number of brief romantic interludes followed in the professionally frustrating period in which, at Ransohoff's insistence, his protégée appeared under an assumed name.

Tate then saw something of her *Eye of the Devil* co-star David Hemmings before embarking on a rather more serious affair, tentatively launched some years earlier, with the celebrity hairdresser Jay Sebring. Anyone familiar with the 1975 comedy-drama *Shampoo*, with Warren Beatty in the role of a priapic crimper, has only to think of that same character in a wide-lapelled suit and a paisley tie to get a bit of the flavour. Born Thomas John Kummer in Alabama (but raised in Detroit), the 32-year-old Sebring boasted a client list including McQueen, Frank Sinatra, Paul Newman, Peter Lawford and George Peppard, many of whom had invested, or promised to invest, in his successful chain of salons eventually to be known as Sebring International. He lived in a 'haunted' Beverly Hills mansion once belonging to Jean Harlow, employed a full-time butler and threw lavish parties where cocaine circulated in silver salt-shakers. Although a gentle, somewhat diffident man, there was an exotic side to Sebring's love life. According to the official police report in August 1969, 'He was considered a ladies man and took numerous women to his residence. He would tie the women up with a small sash cord and, if they agreed, would whip them, after which they would have sexual relations.'

When Marty Ransohoff flew to London to finalise arrangements for *The Fearless Vampire Killers*, he threw a party for the director and cast at the Dorchester Hotel. It was there that Polanski apparently met Tate, reportedly jumping several inches into the air in order to reach her with an introductory kiss. (Victor Lownes puts the event at his house a mile or so away, in Montpelier Square.) The subsequent courtship was unorthodox, even by Hollywood standards. Polanski initially made two dates with Tate, both of which she broke. 'I wanted to take her out,' he told the Los Angeles police, 'and she was being difficult, wanting to go out, not wanting to go out, so I said "Fuck you," and I hung up.' Tate later confided that this was the 'very moment' she fell in love with Polanski.*

---

* Some apparent discrepancy exists about the timing of what precisely happened next. Polanski told the police, speaking of the interval between his first meeting Tate and their working together, that 'I remember I spent a night – I lost a key – and I spent a night in her house . . . And I knew there was no question of making love with her. That's the type of girl she was.' In his autobiography, written fifteen years later, he recalls a night during the same general period in which he and Tate took LSD and 'went to bed together [as] dawn was breaking'. As to the trip itself, Polanski would tell the police that 'in the morning. Sharon [had] started flipping out and screaming, and I was scared to death'. His memoirs paint a rather different picture of the whole episode, which was 'not at all scary'.

The perfectionist director, for his part, remembered as 'sighing with frustration' for Jill St John, was no pushover. Polanski stubbornly resisted Ransohoff's attempts to sell him on Tate (whom he thought, not unreasonably, 'didn't look Jewish enough') but eventually bowed to the pressure, put her in a red wig and screen-tested her. She got the part. With Polanski himself taking the role of Alfred, the assistant vampire slayer, the crew and cast left for an extended shoot in Ortisei, about an hour's drive up a mountain pass from where it all began for Tate, in Verona.

'LEAVE YOUR EYES AT HOME!' said one of the reviewers of *Vampire Killers*, praising the film's 'literate' script over its 'clichéd' visuals. That was hard to do when actors of the calibre of Jack MacGowran, Alfie Bass and Polanski himself (playing against type, as a sweet but naive putz) are all on display, and Sharon Tate takes a series of picturesque baths. There's also, it's true, a certain amount of *shtick* involved. *Vampires* occasionally stoops to the level of a freak show, one that lacks real pathos or humour; the mincing portrayal of the vampire's 'sensitive' son Herbert, to give one often quoted example, is straight out of the John Inman school of caricature. With a Shagal, an Abronsius and sundry Von Krolocks and Koukols, the movie shamelessly adopts a *Carry On*-like formula of silly names and knock-kneed gags, such as the one in which a monster takes one look at the crucifix thrust under his nose and says in a richly Yiddish accent, 'Oy, have you got the wrong vampire!' The sheer slapstick elements of the film were much discussed, not always favourably, by the cast themselves. The distinguished British character actor Ronald Lacey would recall his initial excitement at being summoned to meet Polanski, 'whose work I thought absolutely brilliant', to discuss the prospect of his playing a 'substantial role' in this 'major new international feature'. But the eventual outcome proved something of a disappointment, Lacey's character being billed in the script as the 'Village Idiot' and hardly auguring well for the 'Oscar-worthy turn' he'd had in mind.

With everyone on location in the Italian Dolomites, Polanski once again found himself playing 'half director, half nursemaid' to his crew. The former world middleweight boxing champion Terry Downes, playing Koukol the hunchback, was known to enjoy a drink with dinner, after which he might demonstrate his impromptu striptease act and, perhaps no less alarming, his profound dislike of all Germans. As luck would have it, there were several coachloads of tourists from Frankfurt in Ortisei, staying in the same hotel as the cast. Downes (career record: 34–9, with 27 knockouts) duly picked a fight his first night on location, and everyone got hauled down to the *prigione* by the tough Italian cops and threatened with deportation. Thereafter, Polanski saw to it that Downes was never left unchaperoned in the evenings.

Polanski and Sharon Tate officially became an item whilst staying in that same snowbound hotel. Their relationship seems to have co-existed, at least initially, with Tate's continuing fondness for Jay Sebring. Indeed, all three parties would become friends back in London, meeting at least once over a civilised meal at Alvaro's, or enjoying a drink at the Antelope, just around the corner from West Eaton Place Mews. In time, the cynics among their group began snickering, quite groundlessly, about a *ménage à trois*. Although their physical affair was over, Sebring confirmed to a number of friends that he 'still adored Sharon', whose ring he would wear on a chain around his neck for the rest of his life.

Tate was both a serious and talented actress, but from now on she preferred spending time with Polanski to furthering her own career, in so far as there was a distinction between the two. She devoted her life to fulfilling his every need, from cooking him huge, Texas-style meals, to cutting his hair (a skill learnt from Sebring), to packing and unpacking his bags whenever he went anywhere. 'She was *beautiful*,' Polanski recalled. 'She was fantastic. She loved me . . . She would say, "I don't want to smother you. I only want to be with you," etc. And I said, "You know how I am; I screw around." And she said, "I don't want to change you." She was ready to do everything, just to be with me. She was a *fucking angel*.'

THE FEARLESS VAMPIRE KILLERS IS, in its director's cut, something close to a greatest-hits collection of Polanski themes. There's violence, nudity, a touch of both homosexuality and sadomasochism, among other, darker corners of the human psyche, and of course voyeurism, notably when Alfred (Polanski himself) peers at Tate through a keyhole as she takes a bath. As in *Cul-de-Sac*, he and Brach also introduced a scene in which their leading lady is spanked. The film starts, like 1962's *Mammals*, with two characters travelling across the snowy landscape. A batty old professor (MacGowran) and his sidekick are on their way to Dracula country, where they conspicuously fail to protect Sarah (Tate) from the wily vampire (a very plausible Ferdy Mayne). After a variety of mishaps and sight-gags, the whole thing ends in a Chaplin-style chase and an elaborately choreographed Monster Ball. The two vampire hunters manage to infiltrate this and rescue the undead (but still radiant) Sarah. Yet another chase ensues, the professor and his party fleeing from the cripple Koukol, who sleds after them on a coffin. This shouldn't, perhaps, add up to much of a film, but with the sweeping alpine views, some typically deft, gravity defying camerawork and another haunting score by Krzysztof Komeda, it makes it to the top of Polanski's second division. (His own extreme affection for *Vampires* might partly be due to the 'great memories it conjures up' of his life at the time.) Oddly enough, Polanski's real contribution to the film may have been less as a director than an actor. His Alfred is both an endearing and ridiculous character, the sort of loveable-klutz role Woody Allen came to patent in later years.

POLANSKI WAS A HAPPY MAN when he landed back in London with the raw footage of *Vampire Killers* packed into eight cans in his luggage. As far as he was concerned, he'd all but completed the best film of his career to date. The final interior shots were done on a soundstage at Elstree, where, thanks to time and money pressures, exacerbated by the film unions' work-to-rule, most of the goodwill soon evaporated. Filmways, like the Compton Group before them, expressed their concern about Polanski's habit of shooting repeated takes of each scene, leading to eventual production costs of $2.1 million, or $400,000 over budget. Scheduling conflicts at Elstree meant that the whole crew then had to move to Pinewood. At that stage, Marty Ransohoff sent Polanski a memo informing him that he had exactly five days to wrap it up, and that MGM were worried about the amount of Tate's 'unduly exposed' cleavage.

That was tame compared to the nude *Playboy* layout Tate, like Catherine Deneuve before her, underwent to promote her film. This time Polanski himself was the photographer. A variety of his shots and stills from the movie ran in the magazine's March 1967 issue with captions depicting Sharon as 'a very tasty dish indeed', under the heading 'The Tate Gallery'. In Britain that spring, the actress received nearly as much attention as Marianne Faithfull and her allegedly unorthodox technique with a Mars Bar. Polanski remarked happily to Marty Ransohoff that Tate seemed to be growing in self-confidence, and had 'shaken off some of her hang-ups'. 'She's shaken off some, and she's acquiring others,' the producer growled, an apparent reference to her affair with Polanski. Shortly after completing *Vampire Killers*, Tate flew back to Hollywood, where Ransohoff cast her in a generic Tony Curtis comedy called *Don't Make Waves*. Not long after that, she was able to buy her way out of her seven-year contract with Filmways.

Polanski himself soon followed to Los Angeles, where in early October he showed Ransohoff the rough cut of *Vampire Killers*. Ransohoff is reported to have 'fucking hated' it. The end result was that the film appeared in two distinct versions: Polanski's in Europe, where it was a huge hit, and Ransohoff's in America, where it bombed. The latter featured several striking departures from the director's cut. Some thirteen minutes (twenty, according to Polanski) were lopped off and replaced by an interminable cartoon trailer. The actors' voices were redubbed to make them sound more American, and Komeda's soundtrack was rendered all but inaudible. Finally, worried lest the original prove insufficiently potent at the box office, Ransohoff gave the film its 'kooky' new name and subtitle, having apparently narrowly rejected *Love at First Bite* as an alternative.

Those who witnessed Polanski's subsequent fury would long marvel at the scene, speaking of it like old salts recalling a historic hurricane. After raging at Ransohoff (impotently, as Filmways had the 'right of final veto' in the western hemisphere), the director first tried to take his name off the credits, and then gave an interview to *Variety*, complaining that 'What I made was a funny, spook fairy tale, and this is a sort of Transylvanian *Beverly Hillbillies*.'

The Fearless Vampire Killers was released in Britain in February 1967, and in the US nine months later. Like audiences, the critics divided largely according to which version they saw. *Time* spoke for many in North America when it called *Vampires* 'neither spooky nor spoofy; it never manages to get out of the coffin.' Compounding Polanski's anger, perhaps, was his own investment in the film, which, in its original form, he continues to call one of his favourites. By the same token, he revelled in the fact that his cut of *Vampires* eventually penetrated American art houses and university campuses, where it enjoyed much the same midnight-cult status later conferred on *Night of the Living Dead*. A certain well-known actor saw the picture twelve times and would pay homage in 1968 by announcing in the middle of shooting his own film that his crew were to emulate Polanski's 'cool' point-of-view camerawork for a particular scene. 'I want that same feeling of racing downhill, leaving your guts behind, only on a road instead of a mountain,' he said. The film was called *Bullitt*; the actor was Steve McQueen.

FOR A MAN SUPPOSEDLY DISTRAUGHT at having to leave his girlfriend behind in LA, Polanski showed every sign of enjoying life at home in London.

A businessman calling by appointment at West Eaton Place Mews around nine one morning was struck by meeting a young brunette dressed in what appeared to be a leotard 'sitting demurely on a chair in the hall, [like] a job applicant'. Polanski himself soon appeared, descending the spiral staircase, sporting a red silk shirt 'splayed open to reveal an impressively hairy chest', with a 'ravishing blonde' in tow. Another individual who had occasion to visit the mews house recalls that 'Roman set about a programme of screwings that would have been enough to construct an entire office block . . . His practice was basically to invite every pretty face he met to go to bed with him, and one by one they took him up on the offer.' *Repulsion*'s Hugh Futcher remembers standing in a long line outside the Odeon Leicester Square, at around the same time, 'when Roman came by in high spirits with three or four good-looking friends, saw me, and asked what on earth I was doing waiting in a queue. I told him that that's what one did in England. "Not me," he said. At that Roman led me straight to the front door of the cinema and said something to the commissionaire, who promptly ushered me to my seat while Polanski disappeared with his entourage.'

An air of sexual possibility also charged the set of *Don't Make Waves*, where both Tony Curtis and his co-stars are remembered by one of the film's writers as 'swaggering around giving interviews and entertaining their fans', while also managing to make a quite creditable film which enjoyed a snappy title song by the Byrds. Tate reportedly sent Polanski long letters from the set, telling him all the news, including that of her recent purchase of a vibrator. 'You should get one, it's really funny,' she wrote. 'Mine can't plug in on English current, but I must try it on you. It's also good for stiff necks!'

Don't Make Waves came and went in June 1967, earning Tate mixed reviews. After breaking from Ransohoff she went on to co-star in Twentieth Century Fox's *Valley of the Dolls*, which she and the critics alike dismissed as 'exploitation junk'. Tate's main commitment was clearly to Polanski, even if theirs continued to be a non-exclusive arrangement. Just as she still occasionally saw something of her old friends, so he still squired a prodigious number of women around London. The glamorous couple did, however, manage a secluded Easter break in, of all places, Eastbourne. Polanski would remember this as an 'horrific experience'. Tate added that, while the sign above their seaside hotel room had said 'Captain's cabin', it might as well have read 'Steerage'. With two narrow iron beds, each furnished with a chamber pot, and a black and white television set that showed a solitary channel, this wasn't exactly an environment conducive to their lifestyle; cutting the stay short, Polanski and Tate drove back in the Mini to West Eaton Place Mews, where they spent the rest of the week 'listening to records, talking and making love'.

Some of Polanski's old friends from Lodz had followed him to London, where in time a sort of commune developed around Krzysztof Komeda's large flat in the Edgware Road. Among the semi-permanent exiles was Wojtek Frykowski, the comparatively wealthy student (allegedly the beneficiary of his father's illicit currency-exchange business) who financed *Mammals*. The gregarious 'Fryko' enjoyed only mixed fortunes on finally moving to the West. After a period as an unemployed actor in Paris, he would take to calling himself an author, although no one could ever recall having read anything he wrote, at least in published form. 'Wojtek', Polanski would later recall, 'was a man of little talent but immense charm.' Although Frykowski's money ran out, he maintained a busy social life. An inveterate playboy, he's remembered as having once thrown a party in a London hotel room for several male friends. Midway through the proceedings, the door opened to admit a group of scantily clad women who briskly fanned out, draped themselves in the guests' laps and lit cigarettes. 'Go ahead, boys,' Fryko had announced, rather unnecessarily.

One or two of the old crowd appeared somewhat ambivalent about Polanski, whom Jerzy Kosinski, then enjoying his early success with *The Painted Bird*, before allegations of plagiarism blighted his later career, described as 'the socialist brat'. When Kosinski first met Sharon Tate he thought she was '13 or 14', and didn't bother to talk to her. He was astonished when Polanski told him that Tate was 25.

'Roman was rather wary of Fryko and that lot,' says an English-born actress who knew them through Komeda. 'It wasn't so much that he was worried of being ripped off. I know he gave [Frykowski] money and helped him get started when he moved to New York. But it had to be done quietly. Roman would never have wanted to get a reputation as a soft touch.' Polanski, as noted, was also a conspicuously good host. Though not a big drinker himself, his house was permanently stocked like a 'luxury bar', Frykowski recalled, and guests were plied with champagne and caviar. Another Polish visitor dropped in to the mews house on his last day in London, 'where Romek asked if I was busy that evening. As I wasn't we had the most fantastic dinner together, which lasted most of the night and caused me to breakfast off aspirins in the jet flying back to Warsaw in the morning.'

HAD POLANSKI SOMEHOW DIED IN 1967 he would probably be remembered today as a talented underachiever. The reviewers of *Repulsion*, at least, had unanimously acclaimed him as the most original, most intelligent and perhaps most important film-maker of the day. He enjoyed the prestige of a major cult. On the other hand, Polanski's first and only Hollywood feature was yet to show a profit, and he'd found a way to exasperate most of his backers. Michael Klinger, in particular, thought Polanski 'a genius' behind a camera but a 'human grenade' around the office table. 'In film there's a consultation process, and with Roman it worked like this: "Do as I say." He wanted it done his way or not at all.' One or two of Polanski's peers, like Jean-Luc Godard, also had their doubts about him on purely artistic grounds. One leading French critic wrote at the time of *Vampire Killers* that, whereas 'Polanski always panders to the average audience member, the action in Godard's films takes second place to the development of character and mood. Most of the significant [reviewers] are agreed that, to be successful, a picture must explore social issues and be of relevance to the wider political community.'

How terribly true much of this was in 1967. That same summer saw the release of Godard's *La Chinoise*, an interminable documentary-style account, enlivened by glimpses of the lighting and sound crews at their work, of five middle-class students who spend their holiday discussing Maoist ideology before returning, suitably refreshed, to the Sorbonne. Noting the film's 'stark' plot, one devoid of anything sordidly commercial, the Paris *Tribune* gave it a rave review. The same paper, and for that matter Godard himself, would regularly denounce Polanski for 'going Hollywood'. Meanwhile, Hollywood, in the form of Martin Ransohoff and Filmways, wanted nothing to do with him. Only the public, it seemed, could hold in its head simultaneously the ideas that Polanski was right on the cusp of the old and new; that he was technically innovative; that his attention to detail, while a cause of prolonged vexation on set, gave his films their distinctive atmosphere; and that he told a great story.

POLANSKI AND HIS COMPANY CADRE FILMS were at a low point in the early summer of 1967. After the director's creative differences with Marty Ransohoff, Filmways had agreed to dissolve their three-picture contract together. Unfortunately for Polanski, there was little else on the horizon, except a curious satellite project, written by Gérard Brach, and directed by one Joe Massot, called *Wonderwall*. In a strangely familiar plot twist, this concerned the antics of an elderly professor, played by Jack MacGowran, who spies through a peephole at a young girl. With nothing more pressing to do, Polanski was on his way to a late-season skiing trip in Vermont when he took a call from Robert Evans, the 36-year-old vice president in charge of production at Paramount. Evans asked Polanski to meet him to discuss a script called *Downhill Racer*. Polanski replied that he preferred to do some actual skiing first, but ten days later was on a plane to Los Angeles. When he arrived, Evans told him that *Downhill Racer* had just been an excuse to get him there. What he really wanted Polanski to read was an unpublished novel called *Rosemary's Baby*.

Evans' career might (and later did) make a good movie in itself, having touched every facet of the entertainment industry. He started on stage at the age of 11, becoming, like Polanski, a successful juvenile radio actor before graduating into television and a role opposite Errol Flynn and Ava Gardner in 1957's *The Sun Also Rises*. With his share of the sale of his family's garment business in New York (the very firm responsible for, as Evans put it, the 'revolution in women's pants') he went on to set himself up as an independent producer. Over the next forty years, plenty of people would have fun at Evans' expense – his marriages, his ego, his unfeasibly luxuriant hair, his old-style movie-mogul posturing, his Sinatra-like series of comebacks. Those omnipresent tinted shades. Dustin Hoffman enjoyed something of a career impersonating the producer (and particularly his slurred mumble) at parties, an act he successfully reprised in 1997's *Wag the Dog*. But Evans was also able to boast an impressive stable of landmark hits, such as *Barefoot in the Park*, *The Odd Couple*, *Goodbye, Columbus*, *Love Story*, *Serpico* and *The Godfather* saga, among many others. He was gearing up production on a then mildly scandalous homosexual police drama starring Sinatra, called *The Detective*, when Charles Bluhdorn, the Austrian-born chairman of Gulf+Western, rather whimsically bought Paramount Pictures. (The conglomerate's origins were in metal plating and stamping.)

With Paramount close to bankruptcy, and ranked ninth of the nine major studios, Bluhdorn quickly sought out Evans, of whom he'd read a glowing profile by Peter Bart in the *New York Times*. Evans' first move at Paramount was to hire Bart as his right-hand man. The two of them then spent several weeks doing nothing but reading scripts, most of which had already been rejected by the more well-heeled studios. Nothing appealed to them until the day Bill Castle, a contract producer of horror B-movies, who occasionally bought the screen rights to a property that happened to take him, walked in the door with the proofs of Ira Levin's satanic thriller.

Evans not only loved *Rosemary's Baby*, but insists he immediately had only one man in mind for it – the 'little Polack' whose first two films, in particular, had so impressed him. The 53-year-old Castle, something of a pioneer of such effects as special 'spook viewer' glasses which he personally distributed to audiences for his 1960 feature *13 Ghosts* (along with a written disclaimer warning of the risks of a heart attack brought on by 'excessive terror'), had plans both to shoot *Rosemary's Baby* in his own 'Illusion-O' (3-D) format and to cast his friend Vincent Price in the lead, but eventually settled for $250,000 and a percentage of profits to act as the film's producer. Although the cigar-chewing Castle appears to have had his doubts about the 'arty kid' who spent most of their first meeting together looking at himself in the mirror, Evans himself was instantly won over. 'Roman [was] some character,' he recalls. 'Within five minutes, this Polack's acting out crazy stories. They're somewhere between Shakespeare and theatre of the absurd. Maybe that's why we clicked so well; we both came out of the same school of drama.'

Polanski was also able to charm the choleric but brilliant Bluhdorn, who wanted to know merely how much this picture about 'the girl who gets shtupped by the devil' was going to cost him. The parties agreed on a budget of $1.9 million, of which Polanski, via his Cadre Films, was paid $150,000. With this relative windfall, more money than he made for his first four films combined, he was able to hire a lawyer and an agent, and to rent a waterfront villa in Santa Monica. While the lease for the property was being negotiated, the director flew back to the mews house in London, where, pacing around the small upstairs study and dictating to a secretary, he completed a 272-page screenplay for *Rosemary's Baby* in just over three weeks. Although largely true to his promise to 'stick right to the book', there was one particularly inspired departure from Levin's novel. In Polanski's version, it was left deliberately open as to whether Rosemary's impregnation was real, or all a figment of her neurotic imagination. According to one well-placed friend, 'Roman chiefly used the early films to hold forth on a bigger platform on a variety of subjects close to his heart, such as the female psyche. That's better than talking to yourself in the bathroom.'

What emerged was the tale of a young woman whose world, like that of the heroine in *Repulsion*, spirals into a living hell. After moving into an apartment in New York's venerable Dakota Building (rechristened the

Bramford) Rosemary and her actor husband Guy, a seemingly normal, self-obsessed American couple, go about making a baby. It being a Polanski film, the mood soon darkens. The neighbours take an unusual interest in Guy's career, which takes off when a rival candidate for a choice part suddenly goes blind. Weird chanting can be heard through the apartment walls at night. Another neighbour commits suicide by jumping out of a window. Rosemary duly gets pregnant, after a nightmare in which somebody, or something, penetrates her on an altar-like bed apparently located below decks in the late President Kennedy's yacht. (Polanski's treatment of this scene suggests more than passing familiarity with LSD.) So enters what must be the worst recommended obstetrician of all time, the demonic Dr Sapirstein, who's in on the plot. The doctor will tell Rosemary that her child has died at birth, even though she can hear its cries from the next-door apartment. Confronting Guy and the witches' cabal, she finally locates her baby, which, it appears, has highly unusual eyes, causing Rosemary to clap a hand over her mouth to stifle a scream.

As usual, much would be made of the autobiographical clues in Polanski's film, where these embellished the source novel, especially when he vehemently denied them. While not even the *National Enquirer* could reasonably accuse him of siring the Antichrist, there was something in the scene in which a pregnant Rosemary is dragged away, kicking and screaming, that resonated horribly with Bula Polanski's fate. Rosemary herself was very much in the woman-child tradition, right down to her schoolgirlish dresses, of Polanski's previous three heroines. On a lighter note, there was the fact that the generally unappealing Guy was an actor. 'Paramount's within an inch of where we want them!' he crows, in an obvious self-referential joke. Nor would it go unnoticed that Rosemary's and Guy's next-door neighbour was a worlock named Roman.

In the late summer of 1967, the euphoria of the $150,000 dissipated and Polanski had to focus on casting, as well as hiring a crew of some sixty technicians. He and Tate moved into the Santa Monica house and, as he reportedly put it, 'inspected every filly in the stable', though, curiously, apparently not Tate herself, for the part of Rosemary. The name of Jane Fonda was mentioned. Tuesday Weld, Patty Duke and Goldie Hawn came and went as the summer wore on. After several more weeks' frustration, Bob Evans brought a reel of *Peyton Place* TV episodes to Polanski's home and asked him what he thought of the pioneering soap opera about the secrets, scandals and hypocrisies of a fictional New Hampshire town. The director thought it was lousy. However, he did agree to screen-test the show's 22-year-old waiflike star Mia Farrow who, though far from Levin's description of his 'strapping, all-American' woman, exuded a fey charm that got her the part. At the time Farrow happened to be married to Frank Sinatra, who was thirty years her senior.

Among the many auditions for the role of Guy, Polanski would see Jack Nicholson, Warren Beatty and Robert Redford, all of whom were rejected, in Redford's case because, in a spectacular example of a studio being at cross-purposes with itself, the Paramount legal department happened to be suing him for an earlier breach of contract. Laurence Harvey was tested, as was a 36-year-old star of light, family-oriented fare (most recently *Monkeys, Go Home!*) named Dean Jones. Jones found the atmosphere on Paramount sound-stage 12 markedly different to the one he was used to at the Disney studio. 'I hated it,' he recalls. 'I went in to read, and it wasn't my scene at all. Polanski just stood there watching and didn't say anything for the entire thirty or forty minutes. He literally didn't speak. After the reading I shook hands with Bill Castle and told him that, while I had one or two reservations about the part, I was certainly interested. Polanski, again, just stood there staring at me. He never revealed what was going on in his head, if anything, although by then I'd pretty well accepted that I wasn't going to star in *Rosemary's Baby*.'

With Jones duly excluded, Polanski settled on John Cassavetes, an actor whom he had met in London. Cassavetes was then 37, and divided his time between starring in conventional, studio-mould productions like *The Dirty Dozen* and directing his own, semi-improvised workshop pieces, typically touching on marital issues, and often starring his wife Gena Rowlands, which did well with the critics but rarely at the box office. He and Polanski conspicuously failed to hit it off. To one observer, Cassavetes appeared to be both 'opinionated and listless' (though still undiagnosed, he was suffering from the early stages of the infectious hepatitis that would kill him, aged 59), and, as a rule, Polanski had no use for the 'whole "art" cinema thing' he seemed to represent.

At the end of 1968, Michel Ciment of *Positif* magazine conducted a lengthy interview with Polanski about *Rosemary's Baby*. He was particularly fascinated by the casting process, and wanted to know how much the director felt he had benefitted from having a 'fellow film-maker' of the calibre of Cassavetes on set.

This wasn't to be one of those Sixties outpourings of peace, love and mutual respect. 'He's no film-maker,' Polanski snapped. 'He's made some films, that's all. Anyone could take a camera and do what he did with *Shadows*. He got the chance to work within the studio system and showed he was completely incapable of doing so, whatever he might say about it being Hollywood's fault. I went to Hollywood and it worked OK for me.'

Another party later asked Polanski if, like, say, Hitchcock, he thought certain actors should be treated as animals. 'I used to give my cast bananas in the morning,' the director conceded. 'They liked them very much. I had my prop man bring them in. After a while, whenever they didn't get their bananas, they became very upset.'

Polanski cast his secondary actors and actresses by drawing sketches of what he wanted, which Paramount's scouts then set about matching. A somewhat unlikely series of elderly Broadway stars like Ralph Bellamy, Sidney Blackmer and Ruth Gordon (the last of whom won an Oscar) were mustered to play the witches, with Charles Grodin as Rosemary's original, soon departed doctor. Krzysztof Komeda again supplied the score, which would be his last for Polanski. Tate's friend Tony Curtis was recruited to lend his voice for a phone conversation. A focal character in the film was the Dakota Building itself, whose 'formal', gloomy interior was painstakingly recreated by Polanski and his designer Richard Sylbert on a sound-stage in Los Angeles.

September 1967. A 'wired' Polanski woke early on the Tuesday morning after the Labor Day holiday, threw up, and drove in to the Paramount lot in his rented Mustang convertible. Although nervous, he followed the same, simple motivational routine that he had developed at Lodz. A friend from those days explains, 'Romek changed on set, completely. He became sort of like an ogre, which was his way of getting it done.' Polanski himself expounded on the 'ogre' school (as distinct from the collaborative, Cassavetes school) in a 1986 interview with the journalist Pierre-André Boutang. 'I pep myself up by telling myself I'm the greatest,' he said. 'The most talented, a genius. When I'm working on a film, I truly believe it's going to be a success, and that's why I ask the people I'm working with to do all sorts of things I'd never usually ask of them.'

Certainly Polanski worked both himself and his crew to the bone on *Rosemary's Baby*. As Ruth Gordon, who 'adored' her director (whom she awarded the affectionate title 'the little bastard') recalled, 'Roman brought new meaning to the word "rushes", doing all the parts in rehearsal, setting everything up . . . calling "Action" and then going into his sort of crouching run behind the camera as it tracked up and down the apartment.' The sheer energy of Polanski's directing style was such that another actress present 'fully expected to see dust and newspapers eddying around in the air when he went by, much like what happens when the Long Island Express passes through.' Though Polanski still spoke imperfect English, sometimes skipping a word in his impatience, no one ever doubted what it was he was saying to them. 'We go again' became the operative phrase. As usual, Polanski shot an impressive number of takes. He generally liked to allow the camera to show his protagonist's, Rosemary's, point of view, panning in and out, sometimes lingering on a seemingly trivial object, and to give himself the greatest number of choices in the editing room. According to one source, it was as though Polanski felt that the killer shot was always just around the corner. 'It was exhausting. Instead of calling "Cut," he'd just say, "We go again." "We go again." "We go again."' But Polanski was also capable of inspired, improvisational touches that even Cassavetes admired. Mia Farrow shared much the same mix as her co-star of 'generally very positive vibes' and occasional doubts about their director. One morning, shooting exteriors in New York, Polanski told his leading lady, padded as though about to give birth, that he wanted her to walk straight across six lanes of busy traffic. Farrow reportedly enquired, 'Are you out of your mind?' Polanski just smiled and said, 'I may be, but please do it. Nobody will run down a pregnant woman.'

Farrow was unscathed, though there was a material price for Polanski's distinctive style, as Bob Evans observed. 'By the end of the first week's shooting, we were a week behind schedule,' he recalls. '"Fire the Polack" were the words from [Bluhdorn] . . . I grabbed Polanski aside. "Listen to me carefully, Roman. My ass ain't on the line. My ass is out the door, and so are you. Now pick up the fucking pace or we'll both end up in Warsaw."'

While the familiar, threatening memos began issuing from Bluhdorn's office, one morning on the lot Polanski happened to pass the legendary Otto Preminger (*Laura*; *The Man with the Golden Arm*), then reduced to shooting a feature called *Skidoo*. They exchanged shop talk. A rare example of a director with the personality of a producer, Preminger was famous for his extreme cost-consciousness. Bluhdorn, his fellow Austrian, was among his best friends. Even so, after listening to Polanski's 'litany' of problems, he was unequivocal in his advice. 'Fuck Charlie B. No one in this town is ever fired if their film is any good.' The early footage of *Rosemary's Baby* was, as Bluhdorn acknowledged, very good indeed. Although the memos continued, Polanski proceeded at his preferred pace. The picture, like its predecessor, went $400,000 over budget, eventually costing Paramount $2.3 million. Over the next forty years it would gross an estimated $87 million in total sales in the US, and half as much again overseas.

Frank Sinatra, too, was vocally unhappy about Polanski's policy of shooting up to fifty takes, with the inevitable scheduling problems that resulted. Everyone on the crew of *Rosemary's Baby* knew that the singer and sometime actor had wanted his wife to join him on the set of *The Detective*, and that this meant her leaving the 'dumb Polack' who 'couldn't find his own ass with both hands', and instead flying immediately to New York. The designer Richard Sylbert would remember being present at a dinner when 'Frank and Mia argued non-stop about the matter', although, it seemed to him, they were really debating the proper role a wife should play in her husband's life. After reaching an apparent impasse, Sinatra first complained to Bluhdorn and Evans and then dispatched his lawyer, Mickey Rudin, to serve divorce papers on Farrow as she was about to step on stage to film one of the last scenes in *Rosemary's Baby*. Some time later, Polanski knocked on the door of his star's trailer, decorated (somewhat incongruously, for a satanic-cult film) with pictures of daisies and butterflies, and found her sobbing in a corner.

In March the following year, some three months behind schedule, Polanski went into the editing room with an assistant and cut his picture from six hours to two hours sixteen minutes. As famous for his supervision of the post-production stage as of the actual filming, he then doggedly followed it through to completion, startling the technicians at the Paramount laboratory by arriving early one morning to thrust a thermometer into the vats in which his 'baby' was about to be developed. There was then a protracted wrangle both with the British censor and the two principal UK leisure chains, all of whom voiced doubts about the film's rape scene, leading the director to fume that he would leave England and move full-time to California, 'where the money-men don't control the creative process and the unions let you get on with making good pictures.' After adding Komeda's soundtrack, Polanski and Evans held a private screening of the rough cut for Charles Bluhdorn's benefit. Bluhdorn, who was jet-lagged, slept soundly throughout it.

Rosemary's Baby was released commercially on 12 June 1968, and provoked what *Time* called a 'commotion'. Long queues promptly formed outside cinemas everywhere from London to Los Angeles, enticed by both glowing reviews and a round-the-clock radio and print advertising campaign with the strapline 'Pray for Rosemary's Baby!'* The movie also had the morbid good luck to appear at a time when much of America was in a state of mind midway between depression and hysteria, and thus, perhaps, unusually receptive to its saturnine charms – the latest Vietnam War protests having been followed, just six days before the film's premiere, by the assassination of Robert Kennedy. (Polanski and Tate had attended a dinner party in the senator's honour the night beforehand.) Almost uniquely, the public, the studio and the critics were as one in hailing *Rosemary's Baby* as a genuine masterpiece. The consensus was that it successfully established its own 'fluid' and 'highly credible' imaginative world, always a hallmark of a great film-maker.

With the benefit of hindsight, *Rosemary's Baby* would seem to be one of those pivotal moments, like *Bonnie and Clyde* and *Easy Rider*, in the evolution of 'the New Hollywood' – a term loosely applied to the industry's output between 1967 and 1976. Academics debate to this day the chicken-and-egg dilemma of which came first, the audiences' taste for freewheeling, taboo-busting movies like Polanski's, or a sudden awakening on the part of the studios. The answer, at least in *Rosemary's Baby*'s case, was a bit of both. The sort of bolshie, youth-led cultural radicalism of America in the late Sixties, largely a reaction to Vietnam, provided a new market for pictures with idiosyncratic heroes and unconventional themes. But the US has always had a particular genius for absorbing any new trend that appears on the horizon, however deviant, and turning it into a commercial property. (Think of rap music.) Faced with the reality of the civil-rights movement, the peace movement, the women's movement and other phenomena then in the throes of changing America from a stable, traditional society into a political and cultural war zone, Hollywood could hardly have avoided dismantling a 'quality control' apparatus that, as late as 1967, was still busy turning out films like *Monkeys, Go Home!* An old-fashioned respect for the bottom line was enough to persuade even a man like Charles Bluhdorn that it was high time to slough off the past and join the Age of Aquarius, or else risk losing a significant proportion of his audience to television or other alternatives. All it took, from then on, were a few, socially alert producers like Bob Evans to infiltrate the system, which was simultaneously shaken by a series of corporate takeovers, such as Bluhdorn's of Paramount, where the emphasis would henceforth be

---

* The comments of both the National Catholic Office for Motion Pictures and the League of Decency, which gave *Rosemary's Baby* its 'C' (condemned) rating, and of the British Board of Film Censors, denouncing the film's 'elements of kinky sex', undoubtedly helped.

on giving the public what it wanted rather than on moral niceties. The ensuing revolution brought about the abrupt scrapping of the Production Code, a pre-war set of principles that had included such regulations as 'The sanctity of the institution of marriage and the home shall be upheld', 'Excessive and lustful kissing, lustful embracing, suggestive postures and gestures, are not to be shown' and, it's said, Polanski's own favourite, 'Pictures shall never infer that low forms of sex relationships are the accepted or common thing.'

Rosemary's Baby, then, appeared, like its director, right on the cusp of the old and new. It also saved Paramount from near-certain bankruptcy, and made a star of Mia Farrow into the bargain. Frank Sinatra duly terminated his young wife with as much dispatch as if a guillotine had been erected in the divorce court. But Farrow, who thought Polanski 'the world's best director ... He inspired awe because he always seemed to know exactly what he was doing', was undaunted. This supposedly 'sweet little flower child', as she once characterised herself, showed a rather different side of her personality when she requested that Bob Evans take out a double-page advertisement in both the *Hollywood Reporter* and *Variety*. On one side of the ad, Farrow said, she wanted Evans to list the box-office figures for *Rosemary's Baby*, and, on the other, those for *The Detective*.

Within a week of his film's premiere, Polanski had reportedly received $2 million-worth of commercial offers – movies and TV, books, interviews and articles. At 35, twelve years after he directed his first short, and more than six years after his first full-length feature, he was an overnight success. He also enjoyed a crash course in the realities of Hollywood. Polanski found himself in the quandary of nearly every director and actor other than the biggest stars. The proposals rolled in, but mostly from producers who lacked financing for their dubious scripts (still exclusively concerned with the occult, and witches' covens) and who were counting on Polanski's fame to get their projects made. Meanwhile, a beaming Bill Castle approached his director one afternoon at a friend's wedding reception and assured him that he could look forward to a 'real big' slice of *Rosemary's Baby*'s profits. That was the last Polanski ever heard of the matter.

PARAMOUNT ALSO DIFFERED WITH THEIR 'HOT NEW TALENT' (as *Variety* dubbed him) over *Downhill Racer*, the picture which Bob Evans had used as a pretext to get Polanski to Hollywood. After debating budgets for several weeks, the studio suddenly tired of the negotiations and hired a novice director named Michael Ritchie for the project, which starred one Robert Redford. Polanski's agent Bill Tennant tried to explain the workings of the 'mental ward' in which his client now found himself, wisely advising him to take time off before even considering his next move. When the lease expired on their Santa Monica home, Polanski and Tate moved first into Patty Duke's house at 1600 Summit Ridge Drive in Bel Air, and then to West Hollywood's Sunset Marquis Hotel. It was a sanctuary where Roman could escape to explore the rhumba bikinis around the pool, while Sharon dutifully read scripts in their seventh-floor suite. In time, Tate tired of the place's 'early Jewish' decor, and the couple relocated to the mock-Victorian Château Marmont, where their Friday-night parties became a fixture for guests like Jack Nicholson, Warren Beatty, Peter Sellers, Jay Sebring and *Rosemary's Baby*'s designer Richard Sylbert, the last of whom found 'Ro's scene [to be] more sexual than psychedelic'. Seeming to confirm the impression, Polanski presented his friend Victor Lownes with an unusual fortieth birthday gift on a flying visit back to London: a rather generously sized phallus, cast in gold.*

There remained only a few discordant notes among all the festivities of the *Rosemary's Baby* launch. One or two of the auteurs personified by Jean-Luc Godard never quite reconciled to Polanski's commercial success, and he cordially returned their misgivings. This set the scene for an unseemly spat involving Robert Merle's book *Un animal doué de raison*, which was at the centre of a brief but lively bidding war among the major studios early in 1969. United Artists emerged with the prize, which they then asked Polanski to develop into an inadvertently comic script about some dolphins trying to assassinate the president of the United States. Godard, of all people, had also wanted the job, noting bitterly to a journalist that 'those rights were stolen from me'. He later flippantly remarked that some film students had made a pilgrimage 'to gaze upon the vast asylum where Mr Polanski is currently reported to be confined.'

Meanwhile, Tate, who made no bones about her ambition to be a wife and, more pertinently, mother, had taken the opportunity of the Christmas holidays of 1967 to begin gently talking to Polanski about their getting married. She was to report in a card back to her friend Jessie Flint, who quotes from memory, that 'Roman had certain reservations' on the subject, and a not illogical fear of commitment based on what had happened to him in the war. Still, she thought she might resume the plan next year, under 'better auspices'.

---

* Sylbert, who had a 'professionally warm' but 'personally mixed' relationship with Polanski, also long remembered 'Roman's incredible monologues, which went on for twenty or thirty minutes at a time. You couldn't get a word in edgeways . . . He was like one of those guys who gets up at a bar mitzvah to dance and sing.'

CHAPTER 5
MANSON

F. SCOTT FITZGERALD WAS RIGHT: THE RICH *ARE* different. And the very rich are *very* different. This was perhaps particularly true in the London of the late Sixties, where a relatively small number of conspicuously well off, or raffishly aristocratic, swingers took their place alongside millions of others for whom interminable queues, strikes and black-and-white television remained the norm. For the successful few, and, more pertinently, their managers, the word 'millionaire' became commonplace, and psychedelic cars like John Lennon's, stately homes, Chelsea crash-pads and villas in foreign parts were little cause for excitement. Occasionally, however, a particular 'scene' caught the public imagination more than just the latest celebrity drug bust, and became one of those defining moments of the times. Such an event was Polanski's wedding to Sharon Tate on 20 January 1968.

Although Tate had encountered some initial resistance on the subject, Polanski was sensitive enough to appreciate that her Catholic upbringing and basic instinct both made a 'proper do' important to her. The eventual arrangements were nonetheless brisk, the couple settling at the last moment on London rather than Los Angeles, for the simple reason that most of their friends lived there. The stag night was a typically robust affair hosted by Victor Lownes in his new Connaught Square home, attended by Sean Connery, Michael Caine and sundry Rolling Stones, as well as numerous female friends and a solitary butler fearful, as well he might have been, for the house's decor. (Most of Lownes' expensive furniture and carpets, it's said, were subsequently replaced.) Polanski and Tate were married at eleven the next morning at Chelsea Register

Office, Swinging London's most fashionable venue for such events. Although several hundred photographers, reporters and fans enlivened the occasion, there were a relatively few invited guests. Polanski's father and stepmother flew in from Krakow, and soon found themselves mingling with the likes of Keith Richards, Vidal Sassoon and David Bailey. Gene Gutowski and the Polanskis' doctor Tony Greenburgh were the witnesses, and Barbara Parkins from *Valley of the Dolls* the maid of honour. The bride wore a cream-coloured tafetta miniskirt, and the groom an off-green Edwardian jacket with a frilled ascot at his neck. 'We were a grotesque sight,' Polanski admits.

The numerous parties that followed would enjoy near-iconographic status in the years ahead. Lownes' Playboy Club was the scene of the 'official' wedding lunch, which lasted until 5 a.m. Running in parallel to it were a series of less formal receptions and other ad hoc events thronged with creative, medallion-clad types, from Rudolf Nureyev to the lowliest crew member on *Rosemary's Baby*, and reminding John Mills, also in attendance, of nothing so much as the 'cattle call for some transvestite Broadway revue'. Polanski and Tate slipped away early and spent the night at West Eaton Place Mews, before honeymooning in Cortina.

1968 would prove a difficult year to recall, both for Swinging London in general and Polanski specifically, as anyone who reads his autobiography will find. He writes that 'there was a revival – almost a continuation – of the wedding jamboree when *Rosemary's Baby* opened in Paris shortly afterwards.' In fact, not even Victor Lownes' hospitality extended quite that far: the film debuted in France on 17 October 1968, some nine months after the confetti had been swept up at Chelsea Register Office. The confusion is perhaps understandable, given the fact that the Polanskis spent much of the year commuting almost weekly between Britain, France and America, and that Sharon, at least, enjoyed a steady diet of self-baked hash brownies. After returning from the movie's New York premiere that June, the couple divided their summer between their London mews house and a suite at L'Hôtel, a small but beautifully proportioned establishment with a central spiral staircase onto which sunlight pours through a domed glass ceiling, and by some distance the best appointed of Polanski's Paris residences to date. Tate somehow managed to break her ankle while getting out of bed there one morning. Not long afterwards, there was an unpleasant incident when Polanski was helping his wife hobble down the avenue Wagram on their way home from the cinema. Turning down a dark side road to their car, the couple passed a crowd of rowdy young

Spaniards leaving a bar. Tate took their eye and there was a bit of wolf-whistling along with other lewd endearments, one of the gang pinching the helpless woman's bottom. Polanski retaliated, knocking down the main offender but taking a beating from his friends. When the normally glamorous Hollywood couple attended a *Rosemary's Baby* preview later that week, she was on crutches, he had a mouthful of stitches.

POLANSKI'S WEDDING HAD BROUGHT ABOUT A TENTATIVE RECONCILIATION WITH his immediate family, with some of whom he had exchanged no more than a few words in six years. What exactly happened between him and his father in the winter of 1967–8 is unclear, as is much about their relationship. By Roman's account, he invited Ryszard and his wife Wanda to visit him in Los Angeles, and that once there both had been duly 'proud of Sharon, the house and my new lifestyle'. Most of the solid evidence, however, suggests that Ryszard, while indeed appreciative of Roman's success, found the 'whole Hollywood scene' distasteful, and worried, not without good reason, that his son was being used by his recently acquired friends. Most of these tended to be young, vaguely artistic and insolvent. There was evidently one party that gave Ryszard particular cause for concern. He was later to refer to a roomful of 'loud, unattractive guests, [with] people tugging at Romek's arm every few seconds.' It was the previously hostile Wanda who seems to have most enjoyed the occasion, charmed by Tate's hash cakes.

Sharon's parents had also been visitors to the Santa Monica house, and later the Château Marmont. Colonel Paul Tate had openly fretted about his daughter getting mixed up with 'the Soddom crowd', but appears to have taken immediately to his son-in-law (only nine years his junior), with whom he shared a fondness for spy stories. Tate's mother Doris, thrilled just to be in the proximity of movie stars, was reported to be 'delighted' by the whole arrangement. Some time later, she presented Sharon and Roman with a Yorkshire terrier puppy, which he named Dr Sapirstein, after the devil's physician in *Rosemary's Baby*.

Being young, successful and open to experiment, Polanski and Tate also found themselves at the heart of the 'Peter Sellers set', a dangerously combustible place to be. The 42-year-old actor, then deep into his caftan and beads phase, was stepping out with Mia Farrow, one of those slightly dazed, pixieish women whose company he sought. For a few pot-fuelled months, the two couples were virtually inseparable, often taking off around sunset to the desert, one of the rare perks of Los Angeles, to stretch out on blankets, light a communal cigarette and tell stories. On one such trip, Sellers and Farrow wandered off to 'find God' and were secretly tailed by Polanski, who hid behind a rock and threw sticks at their feet. 'Did you hear that?' Sellers whispered. 'What was it?' cooed Farrow. 'I don't know, but it was fantastic. *Fantastic!*'

Back in London that Christmas (Polanski records it as a year earlier, in December 1967), the director invited some friends to a Chinese restaurant so that they could plan a skiing trip together. At some stage Sellers began to debate medical ethics with Tony Greenburgh. The latter noted, reasonably enough, that, in the event a patient went about destroying himself with drink and drugs, then there was little he, as a GP, could do about it. In a terrifying shift, the two men were suddenly in the midst of a violent argument. 'You're wrong, Doctor!' Sellers bawled hysterically. 'You're wrong! You're *fucking wrong*!' Peace was restored only when Polanski physically prised Sellers' hands from Greenburgh's throat. Although the host tactfully tried to laugh the whole thing off for the benefit of his guests, he was forced to concede that the evening was 'a downer'.

On weekends when not free-associating among the Mojave rocks, Polanski arranged to take martial-arts lessons from a neighbour and would-be actor named Bruce Lee. Much like Sellers in his Inspector Clouseau role, though with very different results, Lee was always urging his famous student to attack him while off guard. A visiting kung fu enthusiast was a witness to the first and apparently only occasion Polanski did so. 'Bruce shot out a hand and Roman ended up upside down on the front lawn.'

Tate, meanwhile, told friends that marriage and the prospect of motherhood meant more to her than her once 'burning' professional ambitions, and added that, at 25, her best days were behind her. *Valley of the Dolls* was followed by a project originally entitled *The House of Seven Joys*, which became a leaden *Goldfinger* spoof, starring Dean Martin and Elke Sommer, called *The Wrecking Crew*. Here Dino was hopelessly miscast as a boozy, skirt-chasing journalist who, presumably as a form of relaxation, moonlights as a boozy, skirt-chasing spy. Sharon's role was summarised by one reviewer as that of the 'house bimbo'. Public and critics alike greeted the picture with restraint on its release in February 1969. Later that winter, Tate was awarded top billing, over the likes of Orson Welles, in an Italian-made farce called *12+1*. Although she gave a creditable performance, the film was described as 'a crock', 'hollow' and 'absurd'.

Tate's marriage was none of those things. Some fifteen years later, Polanski would write, a shade tartly, of his first wife Basia that 'she was no housekeeper [and] didn't cook'. Tate, by contrast, thought nothing of coming home from twelve hours on the set of *The Wrecking Crew* to the couple's newly rented home across from the Beverly Hills Country Club and serving a full, Southern-style dinner to Roman and his myriad guests. Ken Tynan's wife Kathleen would long cherish a memory of just such an evening, in which 'Sharon, a gentle, raw-boned girl, [sat] cross-legged doling out a hash-brownie cake she'd just baked.' It seemed to Jerzy Kosinski that Tate 'devoted her entire life to a single cause – pleasing Roman'. When Polanski happened to mention that he liked a particular dress of his wife's, she immediately bought twelve more of them in the same style. A 'ragingly feminist' English friend once accompanied Tate on her way back in the Ferrari from Harrods to the mews house, where she could only watch in dismay as the glamorous actress promptly strapped on an apron and 'scurried around the kitchen [in] frenzied antic-ipation of Roman and the gang'.

Tate had known all about Polanski's other appetites (his so-called 'away fixtures'), which she was apparently happy to accept up to and perhaps even past the moment they got married. 'Don't worry,' she had once told him, allaying his fears of monogamy, 'I won't swallow you up like some ladies do.' Tate is said to have confided to one girlfriend that she and Polanski 'have a good arrangement. Roman lies to me, and I pretend to believe him.' There were limits, even so, and by early 1969 Sharon was to admit to a degree of impatience as her husband continued to travel around the world and, as she put it, 'not maintain our marriage vows'. Tate's indulgence had already been put to a severe test in the period, some weeks before their wedding, when she and Polanski were living together in Santa Monica. During a weekend when Tate was away relaxing at a spa some 300 miles up the coast in Big Sur, the director had invited a young Balinese model over for the night. Gene Gutowski and his wife Judy also happened to be staying at the house for several weeks. Polanski had apparently thought nothing of it – the girl was gone again by Sunday evening, in good time for him to welcome Sharon back at the airport. Besides, Judy Gutowski was having an affair of her own, with a Broadway producer named Hilly Elkins; she knew how it was; Polanski, he writes, 'thought [he] could rely on [the Gutowskis'] discretion'.

Judy told Sharon about the model as soon as she got back.

Tate had heard such things before, and would hear them again in the future, reasoning that they were 'what made Roman Roman'. With one or two notable exceptions, she seems to have been heroically tolerant of his lapses, strengthened, perhaps, by the conviction that none of them 'meant' anything. As a close mutual friend of the couple observes, 'Sharon knew that she had nothing to fear from any of the women. She intended to be Roman's lawful wedded wife until death should them part, and she wasn't about to jeopardise that in the event that he shtupped some starlet.'

With both a beautiful wife and a successful film to his credit, Polanski appears to have been at his happiest in the second part of 1968. The afore-mentioned Hilly Elkins met him at the time and recalls 'a charming and totally self-made man, the kind [of] intuitive genius who could flip through the most complex script and distill it down to a few, well-chosen words,' a skill Elkins had encountered only once before, in his former client Steve McQueen.

Although certain friends offer different interpretations of the director's 'away fixtures', and their effect on his wife, it's agreed by all parties both that Polanski loved Tate, and that the eighteen months of their marriage represented his first real exposure to anything resembling a stable home life. When in the right mood, 'Roman was the best company in the world', Ken Tynan wrote, a 'semi-hippie' who enjoyed crooning 'If You're Going To San Francisco' while padding barefoot around the house. At any given moment, the Polanskis' California home would typically include three or four Polish expatriates, along with stray friends passing through from London or Paris, and putative colleagues including a young screenwriter named Simon Hessera and his singing brother Henri, all of whom enjoyed their hosts' extended hospitality. Brian Morris, the owner of the original London Ad Lib, recently closed by fire damage, arrived in Los Angeles with few resources but determined to open an American version of the club; Polanski gave him $7,000. Another friend remembers 'leaving a bar with Roman, and a tramp coming up to him and saying: "You know, that's a fine coat you're wearing, a lovely coat."' Polanski immediately took off the coat (actually a new suede jacket) and handed it to the tramp: 'Without emptying his pockets either,' the friend adds.

Among the long-term Polish visitors to Los Angeles was Krzysztof Komeda, whose music for *Rosemary's Baby* had enhanced the picture and won him a Golden Globe nomination into the bargain. In great demand as a result, the composer and his wife Zofia had stayed on in California. There appears to have been some marital tension between the couple, exacerbated by the presence of a young Israeli actress, and quite possibly tainting Zofia's view of Hollywood as a whole. At Komeda's thirty-seventh birthday party in April 1968, a lively affair attended by most of the local Polish community, Polanski had jumped up on a table to recite lines from *Pan Tadeusz*, a popular ballad about their homeland, and then to make a gracious speech paying tribute to Krzysztof, saying he owed everything to him and to the selfless devotion of others too numerous to mention. The composer went on to enjoy some success for his score to the violent, Bill Castle-produced film *Riot*, while regularly drinking, Castle ruefully noted, 'about a gallon' of vodka. After a late-night binge the following December (not, as Polanski writes, a year earlier) Komeda somehow found himself wandering around with some friends in the Hollywood hills, where he fell and hit his head. One of his companions picked him up but dropped him again, causing him to hit his head a second time. Komeda had revived to assure everyone that he was fine and had been driven home, where he collapsed after having developed flu-like symptoms and experienced difficulty breathing. The composer was belatedly hospitalised and diagnosed with a clot on his brain. Shortly thereafter he sank into a coma and underwent emergency surgery, in the course of which he was said to have clinically 'died' and been resuscitated by the medical team. Polanski recalls his having raced to the hospital and, in a wrenching scene, sitting at his friend's bedside, speaking to him in Polish and gently squeezing his hand. Komeda's by then estranged wife, however, would give interviewers a different and perhaps subjective view of events. 'When I arrived,' she notes, 'Krzys was already dying but I did not hear from Polanski, not in the next three months I was there. I did not exchange a single sentence with him . . . Once, when I came to visit Krzys in hospital, there was Romek and his rabble. He was very loud and noisy and I could see it upset Krzys, so I asked the hospital to ensure that Mr Polanski should not be let in to see him ever again.'

Zofia Komeda flew her husband home to Warsaw, where he died on 23 April 1969. 'Only then,' she says, 'did Romek telephone me and uttered one sentence: "How can I help?" I replied, "It is *I* who can help you. Try and become a human being again, because now you are an animal."'

Polanski and Tate had, meanwhile, been guests at the annual Cannes festival, where he was to be a juror and she was to promote *Valley of the Dolls*. Almost every attendee would have their own favourite Cannes moment from over the years, whether it be Jean-Paul Sartre strolling the Croisette in a bathing suit in 1947 or Brigitte Bardot doing the same, to rather different effect, in 1953. For sheer ostentation, however, nothing would quite match the Polanskis' electrifying arrival at the Hôtel de la

Figuière on the evening of Sunday 12 May 1968. The couple swept up around seven o'clock in their bright red, California-registered Ferrari, which was furnished with op-art cushions, joss sticks and a concert-volume sound system, which happened just then to be blasting out a pre-release tape of the Stones' 'Jumpin' Jack Flash'. The car's two doll-like occupants, dressed in matching Rodeo Drive suede suits with added beads and medallions, were ushered to their suite by half a dozen porters who strained under the weight of various monogrammed bags, a perhaps overstocked travelling library and Sharon's extensive spring wardrobe, the whole caravan watched by an admiring audience of fellow guests, tourists and reporters. Polanski distributed a generous tip.

Although by no means the best-paid director in the business, *Rosemary's Baby* had been 'a step up for Roman', Sharon acknowledged, allowing him to 'set [him]self new standards' of wealth, fame and glamour. These standards were the very stuff of Hollywood fantasy, creating, in turn, a degree of resentment from those denied, for any variety of reasons, the same level of material success. Some of this professional hostility perhaps helps explain what happened next.

On the morning of 16 May, Polanski was woken by a phone call from François Truffaut, who had an unusual request. He wanted his fellow director to join him immediately at the Palais du Festival, where an animated discussion was under way as to how to respond to the student riots erupting in Paris, and, more specifically, to the government's dismissal of Henri Langlois, head of the state-funded Cinémathèque, or film school-cum-archive, a body currently in its Maoist phase. There was a general consensus among the assembled film-makers that they should refrain from awarding themselves prizes and instead somehow 'demonstrate their solidarity'. Polanski arrived to find himself in the midst of a debate that might have been taking place in Krakow, or any other Eastern Bloc community, in the years immediately after the war. 'Comrades,' cried one of the orators, 'down with the festival of decadence! Down with the festival of stars! What we need is a *festival of dialogue*!'

It was into this already charged atmosphere that Polanski strode, decked out in his Beverly Hills attire, with a pair of sunglasses propped up on his hair. His speech, broadly defending Cannes in its established format, was only a mixed success. Although some applauded when he reminded them that 'None of us would even be here but for Hollywood stars like Cary Grant', there were ill-mannered boos and catcalls from among those seated behind him on the stage, including his old foe Jean-Luc Godard.

'I wanted to make myself clear,' Polanski subsequently complained, reflecting on his experience at the festival, 'but whenever I'd open my mouth to say anything, Godard would interrupt me.'

At the heart of the debate seemed to lie the question of whether or not, as proposed by the radical directors' group, the États Generaux, French cinema should be under 'worker control'. For some, like Godard, the Cannes festival embodied a superficial, profit-driven industry deep into a mire of frivolity and decadence. From the very windows of the Palais du Festival, the speakers could look across the palm-lined Croisette, thronged with scantily clad starlets, and enjoy the spectacle of some of the world's most luxurious yachts anchored in the bay. To Polanski, there was nothing remotely wrong with making films that set out to entertain as well as to educate their audiences. What's more, unlike most of his ideologically pristine peers, he actually had some experience of living in a Communist state. 'People like Truffaut and Godard are like little kids playing at being revolutionaries,' he noted later. 'I've passed through this stage. I was raised in a country where these things happened seriously.'

With several of its jurors and guests engaging in a boycott, the festival carried on in a rather haphazard manner. The premiere of Carlos Saura's *Peppermint Frappé* was enlivened when Saura himself, a devoted Marxist, attempted to disrupt the screening. In the ensuing melee rival factions of filmgoers ran amok through the aisles, screaming slogans, ripping up seats and hurling one another to the floor. The cinema's red and gold velvet curtains, embossed with the festival's crest, were torn to shreds. Saura and his companion Geraldine Chaplin both managed to climb a safety rope and thence swing, apelike, from the rigging. Chaplin's own father might not have been disappointed by the comedic potential of the scene, which ended when the curtains and their occupants crashed to the floor. When he could make himself heard, Polanski calmly informed Godard that attempting to nationalise the French cinema was problematic, and that an artist's only obligations were to himself and his audience. Godard told Polanski to 'fuck off back to Hollywood'.

With France then in the grip of a general strike, the Polanskis elected to leave Cannes and enjoy a week's unscheduled holiday in Rome. Although without Italian visas, a combination of the red Ferrari, its American licence plate and the couple's own impressive argumentative skills overcame the border guards' objections. On 1 June Polanski returned to London and flew to California just ahead of the *Rosemary's Baby* premiere on the 12th, arranging for the car to be shipped back to meet him in Los Angeles.

By mid-1968 the gap between how Polanski was seen in private and how he was viewed in the press wasn't just unusually wide, but yawningly so. The 'rather soft-spoken young boy' whom Kathleen Tynan knew had his own uniquely lurid and louche public image, one he didn't always conspicuously go out of his way to disown. As a result, Polanski wasn't short of character witnesses of a certain kind when he least needed them, just over a year later. A bit cocky, if not (as *The Facts* put it) a 'clinical megalomaniac', proverbially vain, bloody-minded, combative and pushy, with freaky friends, and 'into' the occult, were the messages that kept being recycled in the media. The sort of director almost certainly with a pair of jodhpurs and a riding crop somewhere in his wardrobe.

Polanski, then, was something of a mixture. Beneath what Truffaut called the 'peacock facade' and an obvious affinity for the macabre was a surprisingly gentle, well read and intensely sensitive orphan – a born actor who knew how to put up a front. Jerzy Kosinski, one of his closest friends for thirty-seven years and with whom he fell out and made up 'almost annually', left the best description of this 'rare bird': he was a 'different man at different times . . . I knew at least four or five Polanskis.'

For the vast majority of those who read about him in connection with *Rosemary's Baby*, it was as though Polanski himself had sold his soul to the devil, as some real-life equivalent of the Faustian pact entered into by Rosemary's tormentors. One reporter who interviewed him in mid-1968 recalls that for the occasion, the director converted his room into a candlelit grotto, 'with blackout curtains, dozens of blood-red roses and an apparently human skull' (which later turned out to be an innocent replica) as the chief decor. A sort of 'chanting music' hung in the air. Apart from the subject in hand there was also an 'extremely animated' discussion about the life of the violinist Niccolo Paganini, another artist whose knowledge of the black arts was allegedly far from cursory. Elsewhere, a newly opinionated Polanski held forth on a wide range of subjects. 'I enjoy female nudity,' he confirmed. 'I even enjoy male nudity. Even very limited brains, sometimes, have beautiful bodies.' Among his other artistic tenets, broadcast either now or in the near future, was that 'You have to show violence the way it is. If you don't show it realistically, then that's immoral and harmful. If you don't upset people, that's obscenity.' And, 'Normal love isn't interesting. I assure you that it's incredibly boring.' No wonder, perhaps, that one often-quoted headline at the time, parodying the advertising for *Rosemary's Baby*, ran 'Pray for Roman Polanski'.

The press coverage was mild stuff compared to Polanski's anonymous critics, some of whom took to writing to him in their blood, complaining that his film had been, if anything, insufficiently reverent to the Evil One. The director now got his very own first death threats, including one, which a friend read, 'promising that he or she would cut off Roman's and his family's heads', among other remarks of an unappreciative nature. Polanski himself would acknowledge his 'extremely negative' public image when discussing the horrific events of August 1969 with Lieutenant Earl Deemer of the Los Angeles police department. As part of a polygraph test, Deemer asked his subject if any hate mail had come in as a result of *Rosemary's Baby*. Polanski admitted it had, surmising, 'It could all be some type of witchcraft, you know. A maniac or something. This execution, this tragedy, indicates to me it must be some kind of nut, you know.

'I wouldn't be surprised if I were the target. Absolutely. In spite of all this drug thing, the narcotics. I think the police like to jump too hastily on that type of lead.'

For several million more genteel readers of mainstream publications like *Time* and *Life*, Polanski was a self-advertising showman whose most recent film had had a touch of genius. Typically, a few reviewers had bridled, making it a point of honour to show their independence by knocking him. Polanski earned himself some of the critical yappings and shin-bitings that inevitably greet true class, and he was more or less used to being 'savaged by pygmies'. But what he was hardened to was the ill will of the comfortably paid hacks and second-raters who wrote, like *The Facts*, about his having an 'unwholesome [and] un-American view of motherhood'. Such censure was easily brushed aside. Polanski had gently caricatured such people wherever he could, and payback was fair play. But the contempt of the moral majority was one thing, threats to actually decapitate him and his wife and 'then piss in the skulls' something else again. By one account Polanski was the 'most hated director in Hollywood [since] Elia Kazan' – the man who had named names to the House Un-American Activities Committee, and gone in fear of his life as a result.

WITHIN SIX WEEKS OF *ROSEMARY'S BABY*'S TRIUMPHANT PREMIERE, Paramount effectively dropped Polanski. The studio not only assigned *Downhill Racer* to a rival director but rejected his idea for a 'bawdy cowboy spoof', some five years before Mel Brooks defined the genre with *Blazing Saddles*. Polanski seemed to be in danger of ending the Sixties as he began them, trailing his more successful actress wife around Europe. His only immediate prospect, other than the film about the American president and the dolphins, was to write the screenplay for a curiosity called *A Day at the Beach*. This short tale about an alcoholic stumbling around a seaside town, featuring some of the cast of *Vampire Killers* and a memorable cameo by Peter Sellers as a homosexual stallholder, enjoyed a limited release in 1970. Polanski also agreed to write two brief inserts for Ken Tynan's erotic revue *Oh! Calcutta!*, which the director called collectively 'The Voyeur'. In the first, a girl would appear and strip, but her breasts and crotch remain concealed by the strategically positioned furniture, a gag used to good effect by Austin Powers thirty years later. Another girl then enters, also strips and makes similarly veiled love to her friend. In the second sketch, Polanski's script opened with a man and a woman sitting opposite one another in a train compartment. Each character in turn would expose themselves, an act suggested solely by their partner's facial expression, before they dive below the window frame, and thus decorously out of shot, apparently screwing. Tynan thought the two pieces classic 'cock-teasing' Polanski films, but in the end, for budgetary reasons, never used them.

IN THE WEEK BEFORE CHRISTMAS 1968, Tate told her friend Mia Farrow that she was expecting a baby. It was an unplanned pregnancy, and she was concerned at Polanski's likely reaction. Although one source insists that the director had duly 'jumped up on a chair, shouting "Abandon ship! Abandon ship!"' in his shock, Polanski admits only to having been 'rather thrown' by the news. Apart from the whole matter of his commitment issues, the one living thing to which he'd ever abandoned himself in an 'uninhibited effusion of irresponsibility, happiness and love' being his dog Jules, there was the fact that Tate had just signed to make the Italian folly *12+1*, which would involve her being away on location in London and Rome.

Polanski himself was still at a professional standstill, dividing his time between dealing with 'dim, philistine producers' and 'mentally deranged screenwriters' who both continued to ply him with their satanic-cult projects, few of which would ever get close to being made. For lack of anything better to do, he spent several days in February 1969 at Twickenham studios, repaying the favour to Peter Sellers by taking an unpaid cameo role in *The Magic Christian*. Polanski played the part of a solitary drinker propping up the bar in a gay nightclub, being serenaded by Yul Brynner in drag. Early in March he collaborated with the British writer Ivan Moffat on a script based on the life of Paganini, only to abandon it again, unconvinced that the film 'would ever avail [in] the land of Disney'. Paganini was followed in turn by an only slightly more accessible project called *Donner's Pass*, sometimes known as *The Donner Party*. This was the true story of a group of early Californian settlers who fell prey to cannibalism, a subject Polanski had visited seven years earlier in *Aimez-vous les femmes?*, his adaptation of the dark little fable about a Parisian society serving female flesh.

As part of the research process, Polanski corresponded with Charles Champlin, entertainment editor of the *Los Angeles Times* and one of the relatively few professional film critics he admired. Champlin, for his part, speaks fondly of 'Roman [as] a force of nature . . . He was inescapable after *Rosemary's Baby*, and I always looked forward eagerly to my next meeting with him . . . Apart from his pronounced gallows humour, he was one of the best-informed men in Hollywood, passing trenchant opinions on pretty much everything, and occasionally break[ing] off to jot down ideas and jokes for later use.'

On 19 February 1969, Polanski wrote to Champlin about his cannibalism script, outlining some of the salient facts of the story:

> The 4th of January, 1847, Fosdick died, and the body was left about a mile back from where they camped that night. In the morning, Mrs Fosdick, feeling that she must kiss once more the cold lips of her dead, started back for that purpose. Two individuals accompanied her; and when they arrived at the body, they, notwithstanding the remonstrances, entreaties and tears of the afflicted widow, cut out the heart and liver, and severed the arms and legs of her departed husband . . . Mrs Fosdick took up a little bundle she had left, and returned with these two persons to one of the camps, where she saw an emigrant thrust the heart through with a stick, and hold it in the fire to roast . . . The party had now all but consumed four bodies, and the children were sitting upon a log, with their faces stained with blood, devouring the half-roasted liver of their father.

The letter concludes, 'Best regards, Charles, and bon appétit! Roman.'

By Easter 1969, with *The Donner Party* shelved, Polanski invested in a British-Italian-Swiss farce entitled *The Adventures of Gerard*, directed by his *Knife in the Water* co-author Jerzy Skolimowski. This was such a debacle that no reputable distributor would even release it. As a result of these disappointments Cadre Films, the profit-sharing entity launched by Polanski and Gene Gutowski on the back of *Repulsion* in 1965, had all but ceased to exist. That April, the partnership was formally wound up. Polanski was still able to enjoy a paid trip to the Rio Film Festival, though this too ended badly when the Brazilian authorities somehow lost his coveted passport. It was at this point that another man, similarly undocumented, might have reconsidered his plan to pay a surprise flying visit on his wife in Rome. Once on Italian soil, Polanski quickly found the immigration officials less accommodating than in May 1968, and he was detained in a 'cell-like office' for a day before being put on a plane back to London, not having managed to even catch a glimpse of Tate, who had been filming a scene elsewhere in the airport.

Later that week, Polanski finally agreed on his next project – not Paganini or cannibalism, but the script about the killer dolphins. To sweeten the deal, Sandy Whitelaw, the vice president of United Artists, wrote a note to say that he was thrilled to be working with the world's best director, and that he would personally guarantee the studio's 'full' and 'unstinting' support, whatever the cost. '"Ro Ro"' – Roman – 'is a visionary, and should be treated as such,' counselled the accompanying memo.

Meanwhile, Polanski and Tate had signed the lease on a new Hollywood home, a secluded ranch-style estate at 10050 Cielo Drive, which they rented, for $1,200 per month, from a theatrical agent named Rudi Altobelli. Located at the dead end of a narrow canyon road, the house featured a flower-filled English garden complete with both a swimming pool and a wishing well. The interior was open-plan: whitewashed walls, exposed beams and what the prospectus called a 'minstrels gallery', or small loft, reached by a wooden ladder, at one end of the living room. Beyond the French doors was a sweeping, panoramic view that looked straight down on to the ocean and, to the east, the red smudge of Beverly Hills. To reach the front door a caller had to press a button to operate an electric gate, although this was often left open. At the back of the property there was also a small guest house, occupied by a 19-year-old caretaker named William Garretson and Altobelli's three dogs. Running around the estate was a rustic, split-rail fence which the previous tenants, the actress Candice Bergen and her fiancé, a record producer named Terry Melcher, had strung with Christmas-tree lights. The Polanskis turned the lights on every night, adding a permanent festive touch and acting as a beacon for anyone driving up to the property from Sunset Boulevard, a mile and a half below.

The Polanskis took over the tenancy of Cielo Drive, which Tate would call her 'love nest', on 12 February 1969. Just over a month later they threw a housewarming party for more than a hundred friends. It was a characteristic Hollywood affair – large, loud, chaotic, with several complete strangers mingling with the invited guests. One of the gatecrashers got into a row with Bill Tennant, Polanski's agent, and the director had the man thrown out. Tennant would later tell the police that this individual and his friends had returned to the residence at regular intervals over the next four months, apparently in a bid to sell drugs.

On Sunday 23 March, Tate had been in the house with some friends, Polanski himself having flown to London two days earlier. Around eight that evening a small, slightly stooped figure with long brown hair and a straggly half-beard had walked through the open gate and knocked on the door, asking for Terry Melcher. A photographer friend of Tate's had brusquely informed the man that 'the people you want are down the alley' – meaning the guest house – a turn of phrase that the visitor would later remark had made him feel like 'a bum'. Continuing past the expensive sports cars parked in the driveway, the caller had encountered Rudi Altobelli, in the process of doing some maintenance around the property, who had spoken to him for a moment or two and then asked him to leave. The next morning, Altobelli and Tate were on the same plane to Rome. Halfway into the flight, Sharon leant over and asked him, 'Did you see that creepy-looking guy at the house yesterday?' Altobelli had actually met the 'creepy-looking guy' once before in Melcher's company, and knew him as Charles Manson.

Manson, then 34, had been in and out of institutions since the age of 12, when his unmarried mother had declared him 'incorrigible' and had him committed to a reformatory in Terre Haute, Indiana. After eleven months there he ran away and returned to his mother. That reunion had failed, and Manson embarked on a full-time career as a petty criminal, whose range of offences, among them car theft, housebreaking, assault, credit-card fraud and cheque forgery, as well as a sideline in sexual felonies including sodomy and pimping, was matched only by his incompetence. Long before he came to wider international attention, Manson enjoyed a virtual season ticket to the southern California court system. Sentenced to ten years in June 1960 for breaking the terms of his latest probation order, he was due for early release in March 1967. The night before he was to be freed, Manson got down on his knees and literally begged the warden to let him remain in prison. It was his 'only home', he insisted; by then he had spent seventeen of his thirty-two years in various correctional facilities. His request for sanctuary was denied, and Manson instead made his way to the Haight-Ashbury section of San Francisco, where he attempted, like many of his immediate neighbours, to establish himself as a songwriter. Although Manson's compositional skills proved modest, his credo of drugs, free love and pseudo-Scientology would attract the company of twenty-five or thirty fellow drifters, chiefly middle class teenage girls in rebellion against their parents, whom he fondly called his 'Family'.

One evening in May 1968, Dennis Wilson, the singing drummer of the Beach Boys, picked up a pair of attractive female hitch-hikers and obligingly took them back to his palatial home on Sunset Boulevard. The girls, named Ella Jo Bailey and Patricia Krenwinkel, favoured their host 'with the full *Kama Sutra*' of erotic arts before telling him about this 'fantastic guy, Charlie', also a musician, who had recently relocated to Los Angeles. Manson himself appeared at Wilson's home in the middle of the following night, talked his way in, and eventually stayed for three months. Wilson later calculated that his hospitality had cost him about $100,000. Manson, whose 'spontaneity' the rock star professed to admire, accounted for perhaps half of the total in personal loans, while members of his Family also took full advantage of the facilities. A fellow musician named Victor Tomei happened to visit Wilson one evening in July 1968, and remembers that the house had, at first glance, the air of 'a dilapidated farm rather than a luxury pad'. A large pig, tethered by one hind trotter, lay squarely across the driveway, while assorted sheep and goats roamed freely on the front lawn. There was also a three-legged dog, which snarled at visitors as they edged past, and other pets and friends of Manson's sprawled around the house itself. Wilson's living room, bedroom and home studio had all been 'demolished'. His new $20,000 Mercedes-Benz, recently smashed into a cliff by one of Manson's associates, sat, beyond repair, in the garage.

Through Wilson, Manson came to meet a number of people in and around the music business, including Terry Melcher. The 26-year-old producer, the son of the actress Doris Day, had enjoyed some early professional success with groups like the Byrds, but had recently taken to auditioning, he later admitted, 'more or less anyone own[ing] a guitar'. Among them was Manson. Melcher would eventually twice drive out to the

Family's new residence, a derelict cowboy-movie set called Spahn Ranch, in order to hear Manson and his friends perform. He later described his reaction as 'not enthused'. On the second occasion, Wilson had given Melcher a lift back to the house on Cielo Drive, and Manson had gone along, singing and strumming his guitar throughout the forty-minute journey. Wilson had let Melcher out at the gate and then driven Manson back downtown. Shortly after that, Melcher and Candice Bergen had abruptly decided to leave their secluded hillside property and move into an oceanfront villa owned by his mother. None of this was thought worthy of mention at the time the Polanskis signed their lease in February 1969, and even Wilson at that stage thought 'Charlie [was] just another of those fringe guys' who abound in Los Angeles. Five weeks later, Sharon Tate came face to face with Manson when he drove back to Cielo Drive looking for Melcher. Despite being evicted by the landlord, Manson would appear at the front gate of the property at least twice more in the following months, racing his dune buggy up and down the hill, while Tate was away in Rome. Victor Tomei recalls that by then, 'Terry was acting distinctly paranoid about Charlie', and perhaps with reason. On 30 July, Melcher received a note at his beach house saying that Manson had been in the neighbourhood, and was hurt that his 'favourite producer' was avoiding him. The next morning, Los Angeles police went to an address on Old Topanga Road, a few blocks from Melcher's home in Malibu. They found the decomposing body of Gary Hinman, a 34-year-old hippie and occasional music teacher, who was known to have visited Spahn Ranch. He had been stabbed to death.

WHILE THE POLANSKIS WERE AWAY IN EUROPE, they arranged for Roman's old friend Wojtek Frykowski to stay at their house. The perennially struggling artist, now 32, had moved to New York in early 1968 and conspicuously failed to make it as either an actor or a writer. He struck one member of the local Polish expatriate community, Josef Oziecka, as a 'slightly cartoonish' figure who wanted to be 'more American than the Americans', customarily wearing a pair of bell-bottoms, an open shirt and a cap pushed back at a rakish angle, while 'adopting the latest slang [without] ever quite mastering it'. Fryko's only real professional prospect remained Polanski himself, who showed commendable loyalty, a year later, by apparently commissioning him to carry out various research projects on behalf of his killer-dolphins movie. The police report on Frykowski would note that 'He had no means of support . . . He used cocaine, mescaline, LSD, marijuana, hashish in large amounts . . . He was an extrovert and gave invitations to almost everyone he met to come visit him at his residence. Narcotic parties were the order of the day.'

While in New York, Frykowski had met a 24-year-old social worker named Abigail ('Gibby') Folger, heiress to the Folger coffee fortune. Theirs was not to be the smoothest relationship, in large part thanks to the drugs, although Fryko did, at least once, propose marriage. In August 1968, the couple drove across America and rented a small house at 2774 Woodstock Road, in the uppermost reaches of Beverly Hills. The residence could be reached only by a 'narrow and sharply serpentine road', and would later strike one visitor as a 'sort of mini version of Cielo Drive' in its craggy isolation. Although rather plain-looking, particularly compared to the Polanskis' movie-star friends whose company she 'adored', Folger was very far from a mere Hollywood groupie. While in Los Angeles she continued to volunteer for the county welfare department, rising before dawn each weekday to drive out into the city's worst ghettos. She also seems to have been genuinely fond of both Tate and Jay Sebring, in the latter of whose salon business she invested $3,700. Several friends felt that Folger was tiring of Frykowski by the summer of 1969, and that she was particularly concerned by their mutual coke habit.

Polanski himself appears to have warmed to the idea of his impending fatherhood, although, as he remarks in one of those candid asides to his memoirs, 'the love and tenderness I felt for [the pregnant Tate] went hand in hand with a total inability to make love to her.' To fill the void, he continued to seek out an impressive variety of young women, as social companions if nothing more serious. For the most part, these starlets and models from the Whisky a Go-Go or the pages of *Spotlight* magazine knew exactly what was wanted from them, and they were more than happy to oblige. They needed no courting or foreplay. Among Polanski's short-lived affairs was one with an aspiring actress recalled only as Lola, and another with Michelle Phillips, estranged wife of the Mamas & the Papas singer John Phillips. Neither appears to have been a completely isolated lapse of the director's marital vows that spring, although, it should be stressed, this would in no way necessarily reflect on his broader commitment to his wife, or on an arrangement that evidently worked to their mutual satisfaction. Tate herself often told a story, always with exceptional good humour, of how Polanski had been driving his Ferrari along Sunset Boulevard when, spotting a pretty girl walking ahead of him, he hollered, 'Miss, you have a bea-u-ti-ful ass.' Only when the girl turned did he recognise his wife.

While rehearsing *Rosemary's Baby*, Polanski had talked Paramount into loaning him one of the first commercially available videotape decks, so that he could record scenes and play them back for the cast. When the shoot ended, the studio agreed to sell him the machine at a discount. Polanski installed his new toy at Cielo Drive, where, with the participants' full knowledge and consent, he shot a number of fly-on-the-wall home movies, along with one rather more striking feature. When the police eventually came to search the property, they found an unmarked metal canister partly concealed under some cushions in the living-room gallery. The officers took the canister downtown, where they discovered it contained a spool of film showing Polanski and a pre-pregnant Tate making love. Despite subsequent reports that the authorities also seized a 'vast collection of porn' on the premises, depicting 'well known Hollywood figures at play', the only other mildly unusual photographs found were a set of wedding pictures from January 1968, on which Polanski had scrawled some unflattering remarks about his own appearance.

The director's professional and personal frustrations aside, he was, he reportedly wrote home to a relative in Krakow, *spokojny* – 'on an even keel'. Every first-hand account of the Polanskis' marriage depicts it as the happiest time of their lives. Sharon appears to have been consumed by the prospect of motherhood and notably relaxed about her husband's extracurricular affairs. She also enjoyed keeping in touch socially with a number of her own ex-flames, among them David Hemmings and Jay Sebring, and may even have slept with the British actor Christopher Jones, the star of *Ryan's Daughter,* or so Jones insisted some 38 years later. Roman, for his part, told friends that he was getting over his old fear of commitment, as well as his 'Polish hang-up' that 'Whenever things go well, [I] have a terrible feeling'. 'Rock and *roll!*' he used to shout in his more buoyant moments in the summer of 1969; or, alternatively, 'Yeah, baby!'

AFTER BEING EFFECTIVELY DEPORTED FROM ROME, Polanski had settled down to several weeks' work on *The Day of the Dolphin*, as it was now called, at his London mews house. The at least temporary loss of his Polish passport also forced him to consider the question of his nationality. Although the director had now lived in Britain, on and off, for five years, it seemed that he would have to prove himself 'of good character', among other qualifications, before becoming a subject. At some stage that summer it occured to him that, having been born in Paris, French citizenship might be the better bet. This 'purely convenient' step (which he chose not to pursue for several more years) was later to prove one of the luckiest breaks of Polanski's life.

Meanwhile, the numerous challenges of making the dolphins talk to one another about their presidential assassination plot dragged on throughout June and July. Polanski's interest in directing the picture waned appreciably when he sat down in Wardour Street one morning to listen to a sound-archive recording of the creatures communicating in their native tongue. Some ten minutes later, he slowly removed his headphones, shrugged in despair and finally muttered, 'Well, I'll do my best.' (Summarising the problem later to a colleague, he mused, 'Squeaks, grunts, what the fuck? We'll be laughed out of town.') Polanski also didn't particularly like the first draft of the screenplay. Nor did United Artists. The studio was already busy pre-selling the film as a 'sexy suspense thriller' and, in what would have been a breakneck schedule, was determined to release it by Christmas, 'whatever it takes'. With a budget estimated at over $4 million in the balance, someone at head office contacted Robert Towne, the script doctor whom Warren Beatty had called in at a similar stage on *Bonnie and Clyde*. When Towne wasn't available, Polanski enlisted a young American author named Michael Braun, who moved into the small upstairs study at West Eaton Place Mews throughout some of the hottest July days on record.

Back in Los Angeles, Frykowski was constantly on the phone, doing what he insisted was 'production work' for Polanski's film. When, from time to time, a particular call stirred Fryko to action, he thought nothing of jumping in his car and disappearing to unspecified points downtown for ten or twelve hours on end. On one such morning, he accidentally ran over and killed Tate's beloved puppy, Dr Sapirstein. Polanski tactfully told his wife in Rome only that the dog had 'disappeared', and quickly acquired a replacement. A month later, the pet would accompany its new owner on a sea and land crossing to Cielo Drive, where it joined a ménage of fifteen or twenty cats – no one had done a full inventory – left behind by Terry Melcher. With a generosity and a sensitivity that might have surprised his critics, Polanski also bought Tate a second gift: a vintage Rolls-Royce Dawn which he could hardly afford, but which he insisted she deserved as either (reports vary) a belated first wedding anniversary gift or a 'maternity bonus'.*

---

* At this stage in their careers, Polanski, despite being one of the most sought-after directors on the market, was still earning significantly less than his young wife. By most accounts, Tate was to be paid between $110,000 and $120,000 for her role in *12+1*, roughly the equivalent of $2 million today.

As John Phillips saw it, 'Roman and Sharon had a great marriage, and often told us so.' Every time Polanski took a break from the *Day of the Dolphin* script, he seemed to be enthusing to friends about his 'beautiful' and 'exuberantly pregnant' wife. The director even found time for lunch with his old adversary Michael Klinger, who thought him a changed man from the 'talented shit' who directed *Repulsion* and *Cul-de-Sac*. In the second week of July, Tate finally completed sound-dubbing on *12+1* and joined her husband in London. She was due to give birth in mid-August, close to Polanski's own birthday on the 18th, and no airline would fly her across the Atlantic. After several heated exchanges on the subject with his British travel agent, Polanski decided to book Tate a cabin on the *QE2*, promising to join her in Los Angeles early in August, the second *The Day of the Dolphin* allowed.

On a perfect summer morning, Polanski drove the couple down to Southampton and walked his wife on to the ship. Despite or because of his glorious happiness, he says that he had the feeling he would never see her again. After 'hugging her tightly, [Sharon] pressing her belly against me in a way she'd never done before', Polanski drove back to a party at Victor Lownes' house in London, where he listlessly chatted up several girls, 'while Victor banged some chick in his bedroom'.

On Monday 21 July, for the first time, man walked on the moon. Polanski watched the event on television at West Eaton Place Mews and spent the remainder of the week in continual script meetings with Michael Braun and the designer Richard Sylbert. On the 25th he learned that the American embassy was 'minded to accept' his work permit application on behalf of Marie Lee, an English nanny whom Tate had hired to look after the baby. The final approval of Lee's visa was contingent on Polanski himself satisfying the embassy as to his 'current and future residency status'. The ensuing interview, three-quarters of an hour in length, was apparently conducted as an official and he stood beneath a portrait of President Nixon in the hallway. Polanski seems not to have taken the opportunity to obtain a renewal of his own visa for entry into the US. Meanwhile, Tate and her dog Prudence had arrived safely at Cielo Drive, which was in the grip of a Californian heatwave. Sharon would make a number of phone calls to London in the first week of August, half-seriously protesting about Roman leaving her alone in the house with Frykowski and Folger. Fryko and his drug connection were frequently up at one end of the home while a decorator named Frank Guerrero was at the other, painting the baby's nursery. William Garretson, the caretaker, would walk out to the pool early one morning to find Frykowski and two other men taking photographs of an unfamiliar nude woman. After listening to her complaints, Polanski quite truthfully reminded his wife that he was under an obligation to finish his screenplay. In one of their last calls, Tate announced that she had enrolled him in a course for expectant fathers, beginning on 18 August, which happened to be his thirty-sixth birthday. Polanski rightly suspected that this was a deadline for his return.

On 8 August, a Friday, Polanski rang and spoke to Tate for between thirty and forty minutes. A housekeeper named Winifred Chapman was working at Cielo Drive and overheard one side of the conversation. Sharon was still concerned about her husband's 'due date', as she put it, and emphatically told him that she wanted Frykowski and Folger out of the house, 'but without any[one] hurting their feelings'. Polanski apparently decided then and there that he would apply for his US visa when the embassy opened on Monday morning and fly home later that week, probably on the 12th or 13th of August. A 'delighted' Tate told Winifred Chapman the news. It was by then noon in Los Angeles.

About half an hour later two of Tate's friends, Joanna Pettet and Barbara Lewis, arrived at Cielo Drive for lunch. Sharon was reportedly to take the better part of an hour in vehemently bemoaning her husband's absence over the previous three weeks. The party broke up at about 3.30 p.m. Winifred Chapman, the decorator Frank Guerrero and two gardeners employed by Rudi Altobelli all left the premises in the course of the afternoon. Contrary to many published reports, there was no party planned at Cielo that night, and thus the likes of Frank Sinatra, Kirk Douglas, Steve McQueen, Peter Sellers, Bruce Lee and Jerzy Kosinski never mysteriously declined their invitations at the last moment, although Tate's 16-year-old sister Debra did ask whether she could drop by with some friends. Sharon, who said she was feeling 'tired' and 'fat', asked that they do it another time. Around 7.30 that night, Tate, Frykowski and Gibby Folger joined Jay Sebring for dinner at the El Coyote restaurant on Beverly Boulevard. Fryko was in the ninth day of a continuous mescaline trip and squabbled with Gibby throughout the meal. The four of them then drove up the winding canyon road to Cielo Drive. At ten, Mrs Folger called the house and spoke to her daughter, whom she thought sounded lucid but 'a little high'. At some stage over the next two hours, Tate appears to have stripped down to her underwear, the twin ordeal of the heat and her pregnancy loosening any inhibitions, and gone about some household chores before retiring to her bedroom, where she was joined by Jay Sebring. Sebring sat fully clothed on the side of the bed, smoking a joint. The small, rather spartan room contained a wooden chair, a television and a wardrobe, on top of which was a baby's bassinet. Abigail Folger was sitting in her own bedroom reading a book. Frykowski had passed out on the living-room sofa, where he lay partly covered by a large American flag.

TWENTY MILES TO THE NORTH-WEST, at Spahn Ranch, Manson and his clan had developed a new game, which they called 'creepy-crawl'. Five or six Family members would select a house at random, anywhere in a wealthy neighbourhood, break in while the occupants were asleep, and silently rearrange the furniture, so that, for instance, the television set would be in the bathtub. Everyone carried knives on these excursions. Terry Melcher had recently been creepy-crawled at his house in Malibu, and woke up to find that a telescope and several gold records had been moved around in his upstairs den.

At around ten o'clock on the night of 8 August, Manson walked out of the swing doors of the ranch's old movie-set saloon, looked up and down at his Family assembled under the glare of a klieg light, and slowly pointed at four of them in turn. They were Charles 'Tex' Watson, 23, Patricia Krenwinkel (one of the two women Dennis Wilson had picked up in his car fifteen months earlier), 21, Susan Atkins, 21, and Linda Kasabian, 20. Manson drew each of them aside on to the boardwalk where, pacing up and down in his scuffed cowboy boots, he repeated his announcement of earlier in the day that 'Helter Skelter is here', before telling them to fetch a change of clothing and a knife. The 'chicks' were to do exactly as Watson, a burly former football star, ordered them. Convinced by then that Charles Manson was Jesus Christ, none of the three girls objected. All four climbed into a rusty yellow and white Ford, where Susan Atkins noticed that there was a pair of bolt cutters, some rope and a long-barrelled revolver on the back seat. As Watson started to drive off, Manson suddenly appeared immediately in front of them, fixed in the car's headlights, and yelled 'Wait.' He then leaned in the front window on the passenger side and said, 'Leave a sign. You know what to write, girls. Something witchy.' At that Manson waved them on their way. Not until they were some distance down Benedict Canyon did Watson tell the women, to quote Atkins, that 'they were going to a house up on the hill that used to belong to Terry Melcher' and that he, Tex, had not only 'scoped' the property with Manson, the two of them racing a moon buggy up and down the neighbouring roads, but had even been inside the main house on an unsuccessful mission to borrow money from Melcher. According to Linda Kasabian, Watson never actually stated their destination, which she presumed was to be the scene of another creepy-crawl sortie. He did, however, repeat that he and Manson had been up to the place, and that he 'knew the scene' there. Despite his assurances, Watson had then gotten lost somewhere in the dark maze of streets around Cielo Drive. The hillside eyrie was 'a fucker' to locate. It was already midnight by the time he finally found the turn-off and parked the car in front of the Christmas-tree lights at number 10050. Without speaking, Watson then took the shears from the back seat, got out, shinned up the telephone pole and cut the wires, which clattered down on to the front of the car. There was no noise, or reaction of any kind from inside the house. A minute later, all four Family members made their way down a bushy embankment to the side of the gate and on to the property, their knives in their teeth.

As they ran crouching, one behind the other, towards the house, Watson saw the headlights of a car coming up the driveway in their direction. He could make out that it was a 'boxy piece of junk' (actually a 1965 Rambler), which struck him as incongruous among all the Ferraris and Porsches parked nearby. The car was driven by one Steven Parent, a bespectacled, 18-year-old school leaver, who had had the great misfortune to be visiting the caretaker, William Garretson, in his guest cottage at the back of the property. He had no connection at all with the Polanskis. Watson approached the car and shouted 'Halt,' after which Atkins heard 'another voice, male, say "Please don't hurt me" and "I won't say anything."' Watson reached in the open driver's-side window and slashed Parent across his left arm, then shot him four times. He died instantly. There was still no reaction of any kind from inside the house, although Linda Kasabian would later insist that Parent's murder, the first intimation of the night's slaughter, left her 'numb'. When they reached the house, Watson slit a screen over the dining-room window, climbed in and opened the front door for Krenwinkel and Atkins. He told Kasabian, by now shaking violently, to wait for them in the car. Making her way past the Rambler in which Steven Parent's body could be seen slumped over, covered in blood, she locked herself in the back seat of the Ford. A minute or two later, Krenwinkel came bounding out and asked Kasabian if she could borrow her knife, and told her, with a broad smile, to 'Listen for sounds.'

Watson, Krenwinkel and Atkins then made their way to the living-room, where they found the supine form of Wojtek Frykowski. With the notable exception of Parent's murder, the evening to then had proceeded much like one of the Family's creepy-crawl missions. Watson woke Frykowski up by jabbing him with the barrel of his revolver. Frykowski stretched his arms, opened his eyes, and, not yet aware what was happening to him, asked lazily, 'What time is it?' Watson thrust the gun in front of his face and said, 'Don't move or you're dead.' At that Frykowski started awake and asked Watson, 'Who are you and what are you doing?'

Watson's reply was chilling. 'I'm the devil, and I'm here to do the devil's business.'

On Watson's orders, Krenwinkel and Atkins went to check the rest of the house, though, providentially for William Garretson, they ignored the guest cottage. Atkins put a knife to Abigail Folger's throat and marched her into the living room. There Watson and Krenwinkel had tied up Frykowski, who asked them, with diminishing hope, 'This is some game of Roman's, no?' Atkins then walked back down the corridor and returned with Tate and Sebring, who appear not to have seen or heard anything amiss to that point. None of the four offered any resistance. Atkins would later describe the expression on their faces as 'shock'.

Watson looked over the three arrivals, a heavily pregnant woman in her underwear, a second young woman in her nightgown and the slight figure of Jay Sebring, and ordered them to lie on their stomachs in front of the fireplace. Sebring protested that Tate be allowed to sit down. At that, Watson stepped around the sofa and shot him once in the back. Tate and Folger began screaming and Watson, in something of an emotional shift, calmly asked them if they had any money. Folger recovered herself sufficiently to return to her bedroom with Atkins, where she shook out her purse and found $72, or the equivalent of just over $14 for each victim. Atkins and her associates managed to overlook the party's jewellery, including Sebring's $1,500 Cartier watch and Sharon Tate's 22-carat gold wedding ring.

On their return to the living room, Watson told Atkins to retie Frykowski's hands with a towel; as she did so, Watson himself took the rope, tied it around Tate's and Folger's necks, then coiled it round Sebring's body, threw the end of the rope over an exposed beam and pulled on it, dragging Tate and Folger to their feet. Atkins was later to observe that the two women had 'gone through some changes' while struggling to avoid strangulation. After a few moments, Tate was able to gasp, 'What are you going to do with us?' 'You're all going to die,' said Watson. The women's subsequent cries were stifled as he pulled tighter on the nooses around their throats.

Amid an 'unearthly' mixture of sniggering and screaming all around him, Frykowski began struggling on the sofa, trying to work his hands loose from the towel. Watson ordered Atkins to kill him. As she wound up with her knife, Frykowski, to quote Atkins, 'knocked me down, and I grabbed him as best I could. Then it was a fight for my life as well as him fighting for his life . . . Somehow he got ahold of my hair and pulled it very hard and I was screaming for Tex to help me . . . Somehow [Frykowski] got behind me, and I had the knife in my right hand and I was – I was – I don't know where I was at but I was just swinging with the knife, and I remember hitting something four, five times repeatedly behind me.'

Frykowski was able to break free and stagger towards the front door, where he was intercepted by Watson. By now both men were shouting hoarsely, in an atmosphere Atkins would compare to a slaughterhouse. Watson's eyes bulged over a thick coating of blood spattered around his face. He shot Frykowski twice, hit him over the head with sufficient force to break the butt of his gun, and then began repeatedly stabbing him. Assuming his victim was dead, Watson broke off and ran back into the living room. Frykowski, however, managed to crawl across the porch and lurch a few yards further on to the lawn, where he came face to face with Linda Kasabian.

Kasabian, in an apparent fit of remorse, had left the car and run back to the house in order to plead with Watson and the two women 'to stop what was happening'. As she reached the front porch, 'there was a man, a tall man, just coming out of the door, staggering, and he had blood all over his head, and he was standing by a post, and we looked into each other's eyes for a minute, I don't know however long, and I said, "Oh, God, I'm sorry"'; Frykowski then collapsed. In the nightmarish events that followed, Kasabian saw a woman in a white nightgown stumbling across the lawn a few yards to her left. Krenwinkel was chasing her, an upraised knife in her hand. Abigail Folger, already mortally wounded, had found the strength to break free from the living room and take a few faltering steps into the garden. Krenwinkel and Watson caught up with her by the swimming pool. Watson then grabbed Folger by the hair, and began slashing at her with his knife. She was stabbed a total of twenty-eight times. Folger's last words were, 'I give up. I'm already dead. Take me.'

Somehow, Wojtek Frykowski managed to haul himself to his feet and stagger through a small hedge that ran in front of the house, where he again collapsed. He lay there on the warm grass for some moments, weakly mumbling a phrase in Polish. Watson moved across the lawn and fell on Frykowski with his broken gun in one hand and his knife in the other. At the conclusion of the frenzied attack that followed, Watson stood up and kicked his victim in the face. As well as being shot twice, Frykowski had been struck over the head thirteen times and stabbed a total of fifty-one times.

Sharon Tate was the last to die. In the chaos of Frykowski's and Folger's flight from the living room, Jay Sebring, whom the killers had assumed dead, had stirred and crawled a few inches to his right, towards the back door of the house. Returning inside, Watson, according to Susan Atkins, 'bent down [and] viciously did Jay in the back'. Sebring suffered seven stab wounds, at least three of them fatal, and haemorrhaged to death. In later years, a ghoulish public debate would take place between Watson and Atkins as to whom, exactly, had committed the final murder. The most generally accepted version is that Atkins locked her arm around Tate's neck, dragging her on to the bloodstained sofa, and that Tate began begging for her life. To again quote Atkins, 'I looked at her and said, "Woman, I have no mercy for you."'

Watson then ordered Atkins to kill Tate, who was screaming, 'Please don't. I don't want to die. I want to live. I want to have my baby. I want to have my baby.' Atkins, in a confession she later partly recanted, stated that she then drove her knife directly into Tate's belly. (The coroner would determine that the main blows had actually been aimed at the ribcage, where they penetrated Tate's heart and lungs.) 'It felt so good the first time I stabbed her, and when she screamed at me it did something to me – sent a rush through me – and I stabbed her again,' Atkins recalled. Watson then fell on Tate, bringing his knife down into her chest and back approximately a dozen times. At that Atkins stabbed Tate again in the midriff, the macabre thought occurring to her to cut out the unborn baby and bring it back as a trophy to Manson. Atkins' knife had jammed, however, and Watson, in the doorway, yelled 'Let's go.' Tate was stabbed a total of sixteen times. Her final words were to call, 'Mother, mother.'

Watson and his two blood-soaked accessories then strolled out into the garden, where they were rejoined by Linda Kasabian. The three of them were smiling and giggling, Kasabian reportedly recalled, 'as though it were all a game'. As they were leaving the premises, Watson remembered what Manson had said and told Atkins to go back in the house and write 'something witchy' on the door. Atkins returned to the living room, where she picked up the towel that had been used to bind Frykowski, and walked over to Tate, who lay on her left side in front of the fireplace, her legs tucked up towards her stomach in a fetal position. As she leant down over the body, Atkins heard 'gurgling sounds'. She again considered exsecting the baby, but instead smeared the towel in Tate's blood, walked back to the front door and daubed the word 'PIG' on it. Atkins then threw the towel over her shoulder into the living room, where it fell on Jay Sebring's face, and walked back through the now open gate to the car.

The four stopped several times in the course of their light-hearted return to Spahn Ranch. Having changed clothes on the way, one of the girls holding the wheel for Watson, they parked the car on a conveniently dark stretch of road two miles along Benedict Canyon, where Kasabian got out and 'threw everyone's stuff, all drippy with blood' down a ravine, where it was found by a television news crew four months later. The gun and the knives were similarly dumped at two or three different locations on the way north through the suburbs of Sherman Oaks and Van Nuys. The Family members then pulled off on a residential street and used a garden hose to wash off the remaining blood. A man and a woman had emerged from the house to challenge them but Watson and the three girls, amid great hilarity, had jumped back in the car and driven off at high speed before they could be reprimanded. The four made a final stop at an all-night service station, where they again checked for bloodstains, before finally reaching their desert fastness at around 2 a.m.

A celebratory mood also prevailed at Spahn Ranch, where they found Charles Manson dancing naked in front of the boardwalk with a female acolyte. Dismissing the woman, Manson walked over to the car, leaned inside and, after listening to a brief report, asked each of the four in turn a question familiar to him from his own numerous court appearances. 'Do you have any remorse?' They assured him that they didn't. Manson then told the three girls to go to bed and to 'say nothing about it to the others'. Susan Atkins later described her emotions as 'so elated . . . at peace with myself', although she remained indignant that Frykowski, in his death struggle, had 'hurt my hair'. When they were alone, Manson asked Watson for a more detailed account of what had happened. Watson told him that, although there was 'a lot of panic', everything 'went perfectly' and, as he summarised it, 'Boy, it sure was Helter Skelter.'

★

THE PHRASE, a ghastly misappropriation of a song title on the Beatles' White Album, was Manson's house name for a campaign of 'urban guerilla terror'. Some of the specifics varied, but the gist of the idea was that 'the black man [would] rise up and attack whitey'. The 'black man' being reluctant to start proceedings on his own initiative, Manson at some stage in the early summer of 1969 decided to ignite the race war himself. A cohort named Danny DeCarlo 'heard Charlie preach [this] incessantly . . . "The karma is turning, it's blackie's turn to be on top."' According to a former Family member called Brooks Poston, 'Helter Skelter was what [Manson] called the Negro revolt . . . He said the Negroes were going to revolt and kill all the white men except the ones that [were] hiding in the desert . . .' Some time earlier Manson had told Poston, 'When Helter Skelter comes down, the cities are going to be mass hysteria and the piggies [police] won't know what to do, and the [system] will fall and the black man will take over . . . then the battle of Armageddon will be at hand.' Manson and his clan would merely wait out events at Spahn Ranch while the Beast – 'He who will wreak the final conflagration and darkness, and cause a great stench to emanate from the earth' – brought His chaos to the streets of greater Los Angeles. Not that Manson was primarily concerned with the redress of any racial inequality per se. As another Family member, Paul Watkins, puts it: 'According to Charlie, blackie then would come and say, you know, "I did my thing. I killed them all and, you know, I am tired of killing now. It's all over . . ." And then Charlie would scratch blackie's fuzzy head and kick him in the butt and tell him to go pick cotton and go be a good nigger . . . It would be our world then. There would be no one else, except for us and the black servants.'

As far as could be gleaned, the three primary sources of Manson's philosophy were Scientology, the Bible and the Beatles, all of which he quoted extensively, if on a selective basis. He also had some passing interest in history, and specifically in the years 1933–45. Brooks Poston would remember that 'Charlie said that Hitler was a tuned-in guy who had levelled the karma of the Jews.' Perhaps unsurprisingly, Manson and his followers also enjoyed an extensive knowledge of drugs – grass, peyote and LSD were in wide circulation at Spahn Ranch – although the theory that the Tate murders were committed by a 'cult of satanists wild on acid', as the *Herald Examiner* put it, is well off the mark. In her sworn affidavit, Susan Atkins was adamant that 'none of us were under the influence of LSD or any other drug', a claim later corroborated by both

Watson and Kasabian. Some time before she met Manson, Atkins had, however, been a devotee of one Anton LaVey, founder of the San Francisco-based First Church of Satan. As such, she had taken part in one Black Mass in front of LaVey's congregation, in which she 'dropped some acid' and then 'lay down in a coffin while tripping'. Atkins was supposed to re-emerge after only a minute or two, but later stated that she 'didn't want to come out', and that the service ran 'badly late' as a result. She had drifted away from LaVey's church early in 1968 and worked in a bar as a topless dancer, her profession at the time she joined Manson's Family.

There was a secondary, more routine motive for the massacre at Cielo Drive. Both Manson and Watson were familiar with the layout of the property from their dealings with Terry Melcher. The house's isolation at the dead end of a canyon road made it a 'sweet' location, Watson noted. Contrary to most reports, Manson had, however, known full well that Melcher himself had moved out some months before the murders. Shahrokh Hatami, the photographer who had answered the knock on the door at Cielo Drive on the evening of 23 March, was positive that 'Sharon had been standing on the porch' while the 'small, thin man [with] long hair' was on the walkway, at most six or seven feet away, with 'nothing but air' between them. Tate had looked directly at the man who had subsequently ordered her death. A minute or two later, Rudi Altobelli had intercepted the visitor whom he 'recognised immediately' and asked him what he wanted. Manson told him that he was looking for Terry Melcher. Altobelli said that Melcher had moved away to 'somewhere in Malibu' and that his tenancy had been taken over by 'some entertainment business celebrities' who 'shouldn't be bothered'. Manson, even so, appears not to have known the identities of the house's new residents. No one at Spahn Ranch had ever heard the names 'Polanski' or 'Tate' until they were read out by a television newscaster on the evening of 9 August, raising a loud cheer among the watching Family members. It was enough that the intended victims were white and rich – Manson also needing bail money (hence the $72) on behalf of a jailed associate.*

The murder of the Buddha-worshipping music teacher Gary Hinman, shortly before that of Tate and her guests, showed the full extent of the

---

* Legend insists that Charles Manson, an avid reader of movie magazines, may have seen *Rosemary's Baby* in the summer of 1968 and somehow become enraged as a result, although no one can be sure. I put this point, among others, to Manson in a letter in June 2006. He declined to answer.

Family's homicidal derangement for the first time. Susan Atkins and two confederates named Bobby Beausoleil and Mary Brunner had called in on Hinman, an old friend, on or around 26 July. A dispute had quickly arisen about money, and Beausoleil had begun hitting Hinman about the head and face with a gun. Beausoleil then rang Manson at Spahn Ranch and told him, 'You'd better get up here, Charlie. Gary ain't co-operating.' Manson had arrived a short time later and 'promptly whacked off Gary's ear with a sword', sufficient for Hinman to sign over the deeds to two of his cars. When further pistol-whipping failed to extract any cash, Beausoleil had stabbed Hinman to death. On the wall in the living room, he wrote the words 'POLITICAL PIGGY' in the victim's blood.

The almost incalculably cretinous murderers thus successfully launched Helter Skelter, but signally failed to wipe any of their finger-prints from the crime scene. In lieu of any money, they removed Hinman's two vehicles and a set of his bagpipes. Beausoleil took this distinctive instrument back to Spahn Ranch, and blithely continued to carry the bloodstained knife around with him. The police found it when they arrested him on 6 August, two days before the Tate killings, driving Hinman's car.

On the night of Saturday 9 August, Manson, Watson, Atkins, Krenwinkel, Kasabian and two Family members named Leslie Van Houten and 'Clem' Grogan crowded into the yellow and white Ford and drove randomly around Los Angeles, eventually pulling up at a property at 3301 Waverly Drive, not far below the 'Hollywood' sign in Griffith Park. According to Kasabian, Manson himself walked inside and returned to the car some ten minutes later, telling Watson, Krenwinkel and Van Houten that 'there were two people there, and that he had tied them up.' The three myrmi-dons strolled in and stabbed the owner, Leno LaBianca, 44, and his wife Rosemary, 38, to death. The husband had twelve knife wounds and a further fourteen wounds made by a carving fork; his wife was stabbed a total of forty-one times and left lying face down on the bedroom floor, her nightgown rucked up around her waist, exposing her legs and buttocks. Both victims had a pillowcase over their heads. After butchering the LaBiancas, their killers took a shower together. Following that, they helped themselves to some watermelon in the kitchen. After their snack, and before finally quitting the premises, they left no fewer than four messages. Someone carved the word 'WAR' in Leno LaBianca's naked abdomen, and the words 'DEATH TO PIGS', 'RISE' and 'HEALTER SKELTER' [sic] were variously found on the walls and the refrigerator door, written in blood.

★

WINIFRED CHAPMAN, the maid, had discovered the bodies at Cielo Drive shortly after eight o'clock in the morning of 9 August. When the immediate neighbours didn't answer her cries, she'd run to the next house down the hill, screaming *'Murder, death, bodies, blood!'* The police arrived around 9 a.m., soon to be followed by the press. Around noon the authorities eventually located Bill Tennant, Polanski's agent, who arrived dressed in his tennis clothes. Tennant identified the victims, went outside to be sick, and then drove home to make 'the most difficult call of my life'.

In London, it was already nine o'clock on Saturday night. Polanski had reportedly spent the previous evening at a discotheque called the Revolution, before passing the early hours in the company of a more select group of friends at West Eaton Place Mews. He appears to have been working on the troublesome *The Day of the Dolphin* script with Michael Braun and the film's producer Andy Braunsberg throughout the afternoon, and planned to have dinner with Victor Lownes that night. In a small discrepancy, Polanski says that his meal with Lownes was to have been a 'reconciliation' after some weeks' estrangement, while Lownes remembers their having been to the disco together the previous night.

As Polanski was setting out for the restaurant, the phone rang.

'Roman,' said Tennant, 'there's been a disaster at the house.'

'Whose house?'

'Yours.' Tennant said the rest as simply as he could. 'Sharon's dead, and Wojtek and Gibby and Jay. They're all dead.'

'No, no, no!' Polanski immediately assumed that the home must have been buried in a mudslide, or subject to some other natural cataclysm. Tennant, now sobbing loudly, told him that everyone had been murdered.

Polanski dropped the phone and began walking around in circles, crying and slamming his head and fists against the wall. A small group of friends including Lownes, Warren Beatty and Richard Sylbert quickly arrived at the mews house, followed by a doctor who shot the 'hysterical' director, apparently brokenly repeating the words *'Why . . .'* and *'Again . . .'* full of sedatives. Unspeakably savage in and of itself, the Family's rampage at Cielo Drive had created a hideous symmetry: Polanski's mother and wife had now both been brutally murdered while pregnant.

Early the next afternoon, Lownes and the others accompanied Polanski on a flight to Los Angeles. A full-scale media frenzy greeted them on arrival. From the airport, Polanski was driven straight to a 'courtesy suite' at Paramount studios, who later charged him $400 for his three nights' tenancy there. Several friends appeared to pay their condolences, while others found their way barred at the studio gate. Polanski was convinced that the killer or killers were among his acquaintances, and an early police theory was that he himself had been the intended target.

On 13 August, Polanski moved out of his quarters at Paramount and into the Malibu beach home of his friend Michael Sarne, who was away directing *Myra Breckinridge*. Overnight, Sarne's neighbours sent him a petition protesting that 'The presence in your house of Mr Polanski endangers our lives' and asking that 'this person immediately leave our community'. Sarne declined the request. Sharon Tate's funeral, and that of her unborn son, took place later that same Wednesday afternoon. Polanski, wearing dark glasses and leaning on the arm of his doctor, appeared to break down several times during the ceremony. Colonel and Mrs Tate and their two surviving daughters came to Holy Cross Cemetery, as did Hollywood luminaries like Warren Beatty, Yul Brynner, Kirk Douglas, Lee Marvin and Peter Sellers, as well as several dozen bystanders with cameras. Polanski was later to write that 'the only absentee was Steve McQueen, one of Sharon's oldest friends. I never forgave him for that.'* Although the coffin was closed, it was reported that Tate was buried in a 'Pucci minidress personally selected by Victor Lownes'. Polanski would recall that in his shock all he could think about was the small scar on his wife's knee, the result of a skiing injury, that he would now never see again. In death, the Polanskis' son was given the names Paul Richard, after his two grandfathers.

That same day, Twentieth Century Fox re-released *Valley of the Dolls*, with Tate's name given star billing on the marquee. The emphasis of the press coverage as a whole was hyperbolic, sometimes cruel and often hysterical. 'i drank sharon's blood!' was one prime example from the tabloid end of the spectrum. By 10 August, all three national television networks had begun broadcasting live from outside the crime scenes at Cielo and Waverly Drives. A satellite-uplink truck was similarly stationed in the parking lot outside the El Coyote restaurant, where Sharon and

---

* Polanski may have been understandably confused on this point, since McQueen's wife Neile seems to recall their having been at the service together, and an associate of the actor's named Jim Hoven told me, 'Steve wasn't only there – he was packing a gun in the event, as he put it, "Some honcho tries to off *me*."' It's possible, even so, that McQueen (who had a low tolerance for funerals) may have only 'looked in' to pay his respects to Tate, before driving immediately to the ceremony for Jay Sebring.

her friends ate their last meal, while within, a reporter from the *Star* – which would deploy its twenty-four point size headline, most recently used on the moon-landing story, for the occasion – brandished a cheque-book. For its part, the *Examiner* brought off the difficult feat of criticising the 'crass profiteering' that followed Tate's death while printing an eye-catching advertisement, two pages later, for '*Vampire Killers* collectibles'. At least one press photographer had had to be evicted from the medical examiner's office over the weekend of 9–10 August while trying to locate one or more of the victims' bodies. The account of a young American woman who eventually emerged claiming to be the child that Tate had been carrying at the time of her murder, and who subsequently launched herself on the talk-show circuit under the name 'Tate-Polanski', best belongs in fairyland.

Polanski and many of his friends attended Jay Sebring's funeral, which was held later on the same afternoon as Tate's, and which also attracted Sebring's former clients Paul Newman, Henry Fonda and James Coburn. Abigail Folger would be buried on a hillside near where she had grown up on the San Francisco peninsula. There were no celebrities present when Steven Parent was laid to rest by his immediate family and six of his high-school classmates at a small church in the Los Angeles suburb of El Monte. Wojtek Frykowski's body remained in police custody until his mother and brother were given permission by the Polish authorities to fly to America and claim it.

On 17 August, Polanski accompanied a *Life* magazine reporter named Tommy Thompson and a photographer to Cielo Drive. As they approached the gate of the house, a burly, wavy-haired man in his fifties pushed his way out of a small crowd of onlookers and introduced himself as Peter Hurkos, 'the well-known psychic'. Polanski, who was still heavily sedated and thus perhaps not at his most astute, invited Hurkos to join them inside.

Once through the gate, Polanski allowed himself to be photographed sitting on the front porch of the house, immediately in front of the white door still clearly daubed with the word 'PIG' in his wife's blood. He then walked around the murder scene, silently touching various objects of Tate's and opening a bedroom closet to stare at the supply of baby clothes neatly folded on the shelves. In the kitchen he found a small kitten cowering behind some old boxes, apparently unfed for the past week and spotted in blood. According to Thompson, when Polanski spoke, 'each word came out with difficulty ... "Why?" he said, and he said it again and again and again. And, after a long while, "Sharon ... was ... the supreme moment ... of my life ... I knew it would not ... last."' Thompson asked Polanski how long Frykowski and Folger had been staying in the house. 'Too long, I guess,' he answered. 'I should have thrown him out when he ran over Sharon's dog.' Before leaving the premises, Polanski climbed the ladder to the living-room loft, found the film canister that the police had tactfully replaced, and drove off with it in his pocket.

The *Life* feature, headlined 'A Tragic Trip to the House on the Hill' appeared on 29 August, and quickly became one of the magazine's most sought-after issues. Peter Hurkos proved an only modestly gifted psychic, assuring the press that 'Three men killed Sharon Tate, and I know who they are. I have identified the killers to the police and told them that these men must be stopped.' The murderers, he added, were friends of the Polanskis, turned into 'frenzied homicidal maniacs' by vast quantities of LSD. Hurkos did, however, demonstrate dazzling entrepreneurial skills, selling a number of Polaroid pictures of the home to the media and taking out a full-page advertisement in the *Citizen News* announcing that, in between his 'consult[ing] in murder cases, including the current Sharon Tate massacre' he would be 'opening Friday night at the Huntingdon Hartford, appearing through August 30'.

Polanski returned, unaccompanied, to Cielo Drive several times over the next few days, before formally returning the property to its owner Rudi Altobelli on 31 August. Altobelli in turn sent his ex-tenant a bill for cleaning the bloodstains out of his carpets and upholstery. Contrary to legend, *Life* never paid Polanski $5,000, or a fee of any kind, to pose on the house's front porch. Material gain was the 'very last thing on Roman's mind' when his agent, Bill Tennant, gently raised the question with him of Tate's estate. Polanski told him simply to 'give it all away'. Tennant himself got the white Rolls-Royce that was apparently to have celebrated the birth of the Polanskis' son.

On 19 August, Polanski gave a press conference, in which he denounced those who 'for a selfish reason' wrote 'horrible things about my wife', specifically that there had been a marital rift of some kind. ('Were Sharon and Jay lovers, Roman?' a reporter then promptly shouted.) Tate had been 'beautiful' and 'a good person ... The last few years I spent with her were the only time of true happiness in my life.'

That same week, Polanski submitted to a police polygraph test, which revealed that he felt 'responsible' for the murders in the sense that 'I feel responsible that I wasn't there.' This was perhaps akin to the survivor's guilt that his father Ryszard, and others from the camps, had experienced after the war. The director was able to offer the police the advice that 'If you're looking for a motive, look for something which doesn't fit your habitual standard, with where you use to work [sic] as police – something much more far out.' What was most striking about this was how much closer Polanski was to the truth than the professional investigators, who had provisionally ruled out any connection between the Tate and LaBianca homicides and assured reporters that 'Sharon was the victim of a violent burglary, possibly drug-related.'

Shortly after the polygraph test, which formally absolved him of any involvement in the slayings, Polanski flew to the Caribbean to scout locations for *The Day of the Dolphin*, which, reasonably enough, he found it impossible to focus on. The whole project was finally dropped that winter, only to be picked up four years later by the director Mike Nichols. On the plane back to Los Angeles, Polanski told his friend John Phillips that the film was 'spooked' for him.

'Bad vibes,' he elaborated. Too many memories.

From Malibu, Polanski first moved into a room on Robert Evans' estate before flying to New York, where he took a suite at the Essex House on Central Park South, his home during the *Rosemary's Baby* shoot. Thanks to the recent publicity, he was rarely left alone – photographers waited in the lobby, passers-by stared at him in the street, fans asked for autographs and organisations wanted to send him their 'demented' literature on everything from satanism to baby adoption. Richard Sylbert, who joined him in Manhattan, would later point out that 'Roman was undoubtedly the only living film director who could literally stop traffic when he walked down Fifth Avenue.' Mia Farrow was to observe some of Polanski's 'unwanted fame' when she accompanied him to a dinner at the restaurant Elaine's. 'We were waiting for a table and I remember there were two women who seemed to be trying to flirt with him,' she says. 'I remember because I remember thinking how inappropriate it was.' Farrow also recalls that Polanski was 'a wreck' at the time, telling her of his discovery of the ensanguinated cat, among other stories, and that after ordering their dinner 'we just left the restaurant. He was that upset, and I was, too.'*

On 10 September, Polanski took out an advertisement in several Los Angeles-area newspapers, offering a $25,000 reward for information 'leading to the arrest and conviction of the murderer or murderers of Sharon Tate, her unborn child and the other four victims.' The police were furious at this well-meaning appeal, which they rightly feared, to quote one Sheriff's Department retired officer, would only 'double the already large number of crackpots . . . The Black Panthers did it. The Polish secret police did it. Little green men from Mars did it. Downtown, we had two trays for those calls: one was marked "Crank" and the other was marked "Psycho".'

At a slightly more exalted level in the press, the Tate murders would become the biggest single 'human interest' event since the kidnapping and murder of the Lindbergh baby in 1932. Within hours, the carnage on Cielo Drive was front-page news across the nation and the world. The story elbowed aside the triumphant return of the Apollo 11 astronauts and the investigation into Senator Kennedy's mysterious accident at Chappaquiddick, in which a young woman drowned while trapped in the front seat of his car. In France, 'L'Affaire Tate' dominated the print and broadcast media for the remainder of the year, offering as it did the potent ingredients of glamour, scandal and the opportunity to sneer, not for the last time, at American barbarism. Polanski took particular exception to the 'hyena newspaper writers' and 'jackal photographers' who besieged him on his eventual return to London. 'Have you ever,' he asked a friend, 'tried ignoring a cockroach on your food when you're eating, or a bee caught in your ear?' He apparently added that when people told him 'That's the price of fame', he felt physically sick at their stupidity.

---

* This was the same night on which *Vanity Fair* magazine would falsely claim Polanski had made sexual advances toward a 'Swedish beauty', allegedly telling her, 'I will make another Sharon Tate of you.' Although nothing of the sort happened, a blonde Norwegian model named Beatte Telle, who was dining at Elaine's that evening, recalls that 'Polanski came over to the table. He just stared at me for ages . . . Perhaps I reminded him of Sharon Tate.' Telle is at pains to point out that Polanski neither spoke to her nor 'slid his hand inside her thigh', as the magazine alleged. As part of his post-traumatic therapy, the director did, he notes, start having 'casual sex' again about a month after Tate's death.

Tate, Polanski complained, had effectively been assassinated a second time in the weeks immediately following the murders. To mainstream American publications like *Time* and *Newsweek*, the director and by association his family had come to represent something 'faintly off-colour' with a personal and professional affinity for the 'lurid and occult'. Thus the slayings were an opportunity to blame the victims on the basis that they 'brought it on themselves' ('LIVE FREAKY, DIE FREAKY' was one unforgettable headline), while simultaneously dwelling on the choicest details and making the heavy-handed comparison between Polanski's life and work.

To *Newsweek*, 'The scene could hardly have been more bizarre had it appeared in one of the Pole's own peculiarly nightmarish motion pictures. There, on the sun-drenched lawn of a mansion overlooking Hollywood, lay the bodies of a beautiful brunette in a nightgown and a modishly dressed man – both horribly slashed and smeared with blood . . . Had there been cameras rolling, they would have captured the most chilling sight of all. A gorgeous blonde, clad only in panties and a bra, lay brutally knifed on the giant living-room floor . . . In the end the bosomy Miss Tate . . . took the lead in a murder mystery far more tragic and twisted than Polanski could ever have crafted for her on the screen. "Man," gasped one detective, "this is weirder than *Rosemary's Baby*."'

Even this was a model of journalistic accuracy and restraint compared to the report in *Time*, America's self-styled 'magazine of record':

What the police found when summoned to the Benedict Canyon home of Roman Polanski was far bloodier and grimmer than they had let on, *Time* learned last week . . . Sharon Tate's body was found nude, not clad in bikini pants and bra . . . Sebring was wearing only the torn remnants of a pair of boxer shorts. One of Miss Tate's breasts had been cut off . . . She was nine months pregnant, and there was an X cut on her stomach . . . Sebring had been sexually mutilated, and his body also bore X marks . . . Frokowoski's [*sic*] trousers were down around his ankles . . . No fingerprints were found anywhere . . . Theories of sex, drugs and witchcraft cults spread quickly in Hollywood, fed by the fact that Sharon and Polanski circulated in one of the film world's more offbeat crowds . . . They habitually picked up odd and unsavory people indiscriminately, and invited them home for parties. 'Roman and Sharon had as much idea about security as idiots,' says publicist Don Prince. 'They lived like gypsies. You were likely to find anyone sleeping there . . .'

There are a minimum of nine factual errors in *Time*'s 'exclusive' account of the murders, notably the condition of Tate's, Sebring's and Frykowski's bodies.* Aside from that, several fingerprints were found on the scene, including those of the killers Watson and Krenwinkel, notwithstanding various other procedural lapses on the part of the investigators. Don Prince, a British-born author and, briefly, unit publicist on *Myra Breckinridge,* was one of those who came forward that August to vaunt his supposed intimacy with the Polanskis.

The police, for their part, may not have established a link between the Tate and LaBianca murders, but many ordinary Los Angelans, reading of the tell-tale identical multiple stab wounds and words written in blood, were able to make the connection instantly. Someone still out there was responsible for seven particularly vicious homicides and, presumably, could be expected to strike again. In the week beginning 11 August 1969, with newspapers running leads like 'LOCAL COUPLE SLAIN IN SECOND BLOOD ORGY', the city experienced something akin to a municipal nervous breakdown. There was a reported 25-fold increase in the already impressive daily number of local firearm sales, from approximately 70 to 1,750. The going price for a trained guard dog rose overnight from $200 to $1,500, with a six-week delay on 'non-essential orders'. Area locksmiths found themselves in similar demand. Meanwhile, the rumours kept up a relentless drumbeat. Had some sort of 'kinky sex party' turned violent? Or had a contract killer executed both sets of victims for reasons buried in their pasts, which in Leno LaBianca's case included hefty gambling debts? It being California, the police were soon inundated with tip-offs implicating everyone from President Nixon to agents of the extraterrestrial-masonic conspiracy engulfing the world, the latter complete with flow-diagrams to Armageddon, typically composed in red ink and apparently written in short bursts of manic energy around the edges of the note, so that one had to turn the paper through 360 degrees to read all of it. Both the police and local news organisations later played host to a number of callers, among them a fair few 'state-certified lunatics', who attempted to claim part or all of Polanski's reward money.

---

* It was also widely reported that Jay Sebring's corpse had been found 'shrouded in a hood', lending weight to the theory that the 'Cielo five' had been the victims of a cult. In fact, the only 'hood' was the bloody towel Susan Atkins had tossed randomly into the living room, where it fell on Sebring's face.

Among those theories plausible enough to be actively investigated was that a 'dope orgy', possibly with a sexual component, had been in progress at Cielo Drive. When the police arrived on 9 August, they found a gram of cocaine in the glove compartment of Sebring's Porsche, thirty grams of marijuana in Frykowski's and Folger's bedroom, and a number of other controlled substances in cupboards and ashtrays around the living room. According to this thesis, someone had 'freaked out' either while halluci-nating or negotiating a sale and slaughtered everyone present. The author-ities went to the trouble of arresting William Garretson, the young caretaker and recreational pot user who had been in the guest house twenty yards behind the main residence on the night of 8 August, and had 'heard nothing'. Garretson took and passed a lie-detector test, and was released. Meanwhile, a nationwide search produced the four men who had gatecrashed the Polanskis' housewarming party five months earlier, at least one of whom had publicly threatened to kill Frykowski in the course of a subsequent drug deal. They, too, had cast-iron alibis for the night in question.

In the absence of any more obvious suspects, the police turned their attention to Polanski himself. Was it all something to do with his films, the most famous of which concerned the grisly mistreatment of a preg-nant woman? Or, alternatively, there was Tate's own role in 1967's *Eye of the Devil*, whose dramatis personae had included a hooded gang who practised ritual sacrifice. It was shortly after the film's release that she and Polanski had appeared on a British chat show with two witches in their ceremonial robes, one of whom had noted that Polanski would make a good recruit to the coven. Was the director, as was rumoured, 'hip' to the black arts, and conceivably in two minds about his marriage? Had he even arranged, as one prominent American film critic privately alleged, for the 'wholesale extirpation' of his wife and friends, to somehow ingra-tiate himself to his fellow cultists? Polanski's polygraph test (among a wealth of other evidence) soon put an end to all such fanciful bunkum, at least as far as the police were concerned, although even then a few of Hollywood's most notorious fantasists continued to spuriously insist that 'Roman did it'.

The Tate murders marked both the apex of Polanski's public fame and the onset of his fall from official grace. Henceforth his own disillusion with the Hollywood 'system', not least its press corps, would proceed in tandem with his exclusion from it.

While the official investigators continued to favour the 'dope orgy' theory, Polanski himself, back in Los Angeles, remained convinced that one of his own circle – possibly a jealous husband – was responsible. The first police on the scene of the crime had found a pair of horn-rimmed glasses that no one could identify on the floor not far from Tate's and Sebring's bodies. Had the killer or killers dropped them? As part of his private investigations, Polanski went to an optician's outlet on Beverly Drive and bought a Vigor lens-measuring gauge, which he carried around in his pocket for the next four months. Although he managed to furtively examine the glasses of several friends and colleagues, including Bruce Lee, nothing matched the pair found at Cielo Drive.

Convinced that the culprits must have left a trail of blood in their car, Polanski then acquired a box of Q-tips and a jar of a white, salt-like substance called Luminol, which becomes a powerful reactive agent when dissolved in water. The idea was to dip a Q-tip into the solution, then to surreptitiously swab the seats of his friends' Lamborghinis and Porsches. Much like a home pregnancy test, blue meant a 'positive' result, in this case indicating the presence of blood. Dressing entirely in black, and sometimes adding a balaclava for good effect, Polanski took to creeping around Los Angeles with this kit under cover of dark. One night, two armed sheriff's deputies interrupted the director in the course of letting himself into his friend John Phillips' garage on such a mission. Thinking quickly, he made up a story about having left a bag in Phillips' car, and the sympathetic police let him go.

In time, Polanski also allegedly equipped himself with several powerful 'pin' microphones and transmitters, which, it's said, he left strategically positioned around certain of his friends' homes. As the story goes, various well-known actors or producers would sit down to dinner with their families, occasionally even discussing Polanski, not realising that the director himself was listening to them from his tracking post in a nearby hotel room. One day, the *Rosemary's Baby* producer Bill Castle dropped by to 'offer support and see how Roman was doing'. Polanski met him at the door with a piece of paper and asked him to write 'PIG' on it. This and samples from other friends were then sent to a handwriting analyst in New York, who charged Polanski $2,500 and never conclusively identified a suspect. The net spread as far as the author Jerzy Kosinski, whose 1968 novel *Steps* recounted a particularly barbaric and senseless murder. Whether acting independently or at Polanski's request, Victor Lownes sent a letter to the Los Angeles homicide division, suggesting that they investigate Kosinski. The letter ended by asking, 'Is it just remotely possible that the author of such weird material might himself be a very weird person indeed?' A variant of the same question was still being posed daily in the Los Angeles press, applied to Polanski himself. Kosinski was duly interviewed and cleared, whereupon he publicly criticised 'Roman's attempt to "direct" the *Life* magazine [layout] on Cielo Drive', which he thought grotesque.

The most charitable explanation is that Polanski was temporarily deranged by shock at the murders, and a sense of guilt at his somehow not having prevented them. There remained the nagging belief, too, that the male victims, at least, should not have been, as one Hollywood friend put it, 'sheep to the slaughter'. Wojtek Frykowski, in particular, had been a nationally recognised athlete and an accomplished brawler, who once casually picked up a heavy wooden chair and smashed it over a stranger's head while at a party. According to several sources, he had subsequently even knocked out two members of the Polish secret police, an event which may have accelerated his decision to emigrate. Before the facts of the murders were fully established, Polanski, quite understandably, some-times wondered aloud why his old friend hadn't 'done something' to resist. As was subsequently proven, Frykowski had fought heroically for his life; but for the drugs and alcohol, it's arguable that he might have got the better of his assailants.

Polanski wasn't the only bereaved family member to conduct his own investigations into the atrocities at Cielo Drive. Colonel Paul Tate had never been entirely comfortable with his eldest daughter's choice of career, although not even he could have forseen the horrific ultimate result. After taking early retirement from the army, Tate, 46, grew his hair, donned a pair of beads and took to frequenting various 'hippie pads' in the vicinity of Sunset Strip, convinced that someone there knew the truth about Sharon's death. The former military-intelligence specialist went armed with his old service revolver, but, like Polanski's, nothing concrete came of his enquiries.

On 10 October 1969, Inyo County sheriff's officers began a series of co-ordinated raids on Barker ranch, a ghost town on the southern edge of Death Valley, to which Manson and most of his Family had migrated the month before. The dragnet accounted for twenty-four suspects, who were charged with a variety of offences ranging from car theft to arson. Among the last individuals seized was Manson himself, who was found squatting in a small cupboard underneath a bathroom sink. One of the arresting offi-cers speaks of the unexpected timidity of the 'stooped, shuffling' figure, who remarked only that he was 'glad to stretch [his] legs again' and 'wouldn't give anyone any trouble'.

While in custody three weeks later, Susan Atkins strolled over to the bunk of a fellow inmate named Virginia Graham and, after some preliminaries, told her that the police were such idiots, 'there's a case right now, they're so far off track they don't even know what's happening.'

'What are you talking about?' Graham asked.

'That one on Benedict Canyon.'

'Benedict Canyon? You don't mean Sharon Tate?'

'Yeah,' said Atkins, who then seemed to get 'very excited'. 'You know who did it, don't you?'

'No.'

'You're looking at her.'

As a result of this, a subsequent confession and other developments including the discovery by a 10-year-old boy of Charles Watson's discarded gun, the Los Angeles police chief Edward Davis was able to announce on 1 December that his force had 'solved' the Tate case. Davis praised the 'magnificent performance' of his investigators over the previous four months. He added that the same suspects were involved in the LaBianca killings, which, as reporters noted, was at odds with the chief's official statements up until then.

At her preliminary grand jury hearing on 5 December, Atkins was asked if she recognised a police photograph of Steven Parent's body.

'Yes,' she replied cheerfully. 'That is the thing I saw in the car.'

The trial of Charles Manson, Susan Atkins, Patricia Krenwinkel and Leslie Van Houten opened in Los Angeles on 24 July 1970. Manson appeared in court with an 'X' carved into his forehead. Six months later, the jury found the defendants guilty on all twenty-seven charges of murder and conspiracy to commit murder. They were sentenced to die in the gas chamber. On 12 October 1971, a separate jury found Charles Watson guilty of seven counts of first-degree murder; he, too, was sentenced to death. 'Clem' Grogan was found guilty of murder, although the trial judge, remarking that 'Grogan was too stupid and too hopped up on drugs to decide anything on his own', imposed a sentence of life imprisonment. Linda Kasabian was given immunity in return for her testimony about her fellow Family members.

On 18 February 1972, the California Supreme Court voted 6–1 to abolish the death penalty in the state, based on the constitutional clause forbidding 'cruel or unusual punishment'. In the event, a modified version of the statute was re-enacted just five years later, making specific provision for execution in cases of 'exceptional concern' to public safety, for instance 'those involv[ing] particular brutality, or the homicide of multiple victims.' The murderers of Sharon Tate and her friends, and of Leno and Rosemary LaBianca, were exquisitely lucky in the timing of these events. Following the Supreme Court's original decision, the sentences of Manson, Watson, Atkins, Krenwinkel and Van Houten were automatically commuted to life imprisonment, with the potential of parole after seven years. Doris Tate, Sharon's mother, proved a tenacious campaigner against her daughter's killers and a pioneer of victims' rights generally until her death from cancer in 1992. Manson and most of his Family members remain incarcerated today. It is estimated that they may have been responsible for up to forty murders.

Polanski had no public comment on either the original sentences or their subsequent reduction. Nearly forty years later, the virtually random nature of the killings apparently remains difficult to grasp. 'Bullshit! Bullshit!' Polanski told the New Yorker in response to various theories about the Family's motives. 'Manson was targeting Melcher – that's all there is to it. He was an artist spurned, and it can be a very, very dangerous thing to spurn a certain kind of artist. Think of Hitler.'

Unsurprisingly, the ordeal did little for Polanski's overall state of mind, which one friend characterises as 'not untouched by shadow' well before August 1969. In middle age he suffered from melancholy and depression, assuming, he wrote in his autobiography, a number of his father Ryszard's characteristics – 'his ingrained pessimism, his eternal dissatisfaction with life, his profoundly Judaic sense of guilt, his conviction that every joyous experience has its price.' (In the usual course of events there are few things to lower the spirits like a Polish memoir, but, it should be said, Polanski's also shows the sensitivity, invention and wit of a born story-teller.) In 1974, the director told an interviewer that 'Sharon's murder was the final blow to any belief that remained in me at that time.' Ten years later, he confirmed, 'I can't enjoy myself as freely as I used to. I feel [that] sense of Jewish guilt, and Sharon's death increases my belief in the absurd.'

Polanski came to particularly dislike the media, or the elements of it which had as good as accused him of being one of Manson's accomplices. 'I don't read it,' he told the talk-show host Dick Cavett. 'But . . . in general, I despise the press tremendously for inaccuracy, for its irresponsibility, for its often even deliberate cruelty. And all this for lucrative purposes.' Yet this distaste for the 'hyenas' wasn't the whole story. 'There was something of an awful drama about everything you did with Roman,' the director and actor John Huston recalled, after co-starring in Chinatown. 'His films, you soon found out, were his real sustaining passion.' Huston came to believe that, other than his 'immediate tribe', people were in some sense unimportant to him, 'except as subjects for movies'. Polanski was impartial, Huston noted ruefully: 'everyone was equally redundant'.

The Tate murders changed not only Polanski and the other victims' families, but arguably America itself. Thanks to Vietnam, a degree of self-doubt had crept in earlier in the Sixties, but the process seemed to gather pace on an almost daily basis in the period between the grisly discoveries of 9 August 1969 and Richard Nixon's resignation in disgrace exactly five years to the hour later. It would make a strong bid to be the most traumatic era in post-Civil War American history, not excluding the present one. The conservative maverick and presidential candidate Barry Goldwater, a gifted social critic whatever one thinks of his politics, dated the 'end of our national innocence' to the night when a 'carload of kids went berserk' in a secluded hillside home in Hollywood.*

IN THE SAME WEEK THAT CHARGES WERE FILED AGAINST MANSON AND HIS GANG, Polanski packed his belongings, handed the keys of his Ferrari to Paul Tate and left America with no plans ever to return. He spent some time in Paris, never the ideal place for a celebrity to enjoy the 'total peace and quiet' he insisted he wanted; one night Polanski and Gérard Brach reportedly got into a brawl with a photographer, who protected his roll of film from them by removing it from his camera and swallowing it. The director spent Christmas of 1969 with Victor Lownes at a rented chalet in the Swiss Alps, an opportunity both to lose himself on the slopes as well as to become acquainted with the other members of Lownes' party, among them two identical twins who went on to grace a *Playboy* 'Double Trouble' centrefold. Polanski also availed himself of a number of comely students at the various nearby finishing schools. At a prearranged time most evenings he would be waiting in his car at a discreet distance from the academy's gates in order to collect his 16- or 17-year-old date, hurriedly clad in a nightgown, before returning her safely to her dormitory in the early hours of the following morning. Polanski found these brief, and entirely consensual liaisons (which didn't necessarily lead to sex, he says,

* In 1984, Polanski told the journalist Franz-Olivier Giesbert of *Le Nouvel Observateur* that the murders 'sounded the death knell of the flailing hippie movement. Along with the moon landings it's one of the events that marks the transition from the Sixties to the Seventies. Rather symbolic, don't you think?'

'though some of them did') therapeutic, and it seems to have been mutual. Certainly there was no shortage of young volunteers willing to oblige, even at the twin risks of frostbite and expulsion; ready to drop everything to accompany Polanski back to his villa, servicing the famed director at least a change from deportment lessons.

Ten years earlier, Polanski had rung in the Sixties with his new wife Barbara Kwiatkowska in a French hotel room, though their home remained a tiny, cold-water flat on Narutowicra Street in Lodz. Now he commuted between Gstaad, Paris and London for a series of meetings with his friend Warren Beatty, whom he wanted to direct in the big-budget feature *Papillon*. That Polanski had enriched the decade with the moody charm of his films – infinitely superior to any his leaden imitators could manage – was beyond debate. But, for him, success and power were balanced by the 'crippling' price of fame. A psychiatrist whom Polanski had met in late August 1969 had warned him that it would take fully 'four years of mourning' to get over the grief of recent events.

'It has taken far more than that,' Polanski notes.

CHAPTER 6

SHAKESPEARE, SEX AND SURREALISM

'H E'S A GENIUS. HE'S A FREAK. HE'S A LITTLE BIT OF both,' one newspaper profile said of Polanski, which may explain why the major studios kept a well-disposed eye on him without necessarily committing to his every whim. Early in the new decade, *Papillon*'s author Henri Charrière flew to Gstaad and was suitably impressed by 'Roman and his whole set-up ... He [was] a benign dictator. He'd say, "Well what do you think about 'X' as the star?" and you'd say "Well, how about 'Y'?" and then in a few days it would be back to "X" ... You listened to him talk about a particular actor and that was collaboration. But basically he was a plotter [who] did everything himself.'

In the event, Polanski got as far as a script reading with Warren Beatty (whom Charrière had never heard of), although only after a biblical-seeming period encompassing 'six non-stop days [of] parties, discos and girls'. On the seventh day, Beatty paused long enough to finish the script, and rang Polanski to say that he was 'definitely interested', though disinclined to appear on screen 'bare-assed'. Shortly afterwards, the whole project collapsed through lack of funding. Three years later, Allied Artists managed to get *Papillon* into production with an exotic consortium of Franco-American backers (subsequently the target of assorted lawsuits) and Steve McQueen in the title role. McQueen's friend Don Gordon, a co-star in the film, would long remember the hot tropical days spent on location in Jamaica. 'None of us were getting paid,' he says. 'As I heard it, the suits were taking cans of film, getting on the night flight to Paris, showing the backers the raw footage and coming back with just enough cash to at least keep the cameras rolling.' *Papillon*, which cost an estimated $12 million, has so far grossed $145 million around the world.

Although Polanski was a 'plotter' who 'did everything himself', his career path never excluded its moments of inspired spontaneity. One day on the ski slopes, he appears to have suddenly remembered his youthful ambition to make a film of one of Shakespeare's plays. Brushing aside both Bill Tennant's objections and the lack of obvious investors, the director approached Kenneth Tynan, the white-suited dramaturg at the National Theatre, and proposed that they co-adapt *Macbeth* for the screen. Tynan, then 43, had had Polanski on his radar for the previous four years, when, as noted, he had praised him as having 'exactly the right combination of fantasy and violence'. They were both qualities that put him in good stead for *Macbeth*. As a critic on the *Observer*, Tynan had delighted his readers with witty descriptions of stage and screen personalities ('Anthony Quinn', he wrote, 'always acts as if he were wearing a suit for the first time') while becoming something of a public figure – his habit of effetely holding a cigarette between his middle and ring fingers was parodied by Alec Guinness in *The Ladykillers*. Like Polanski, he was known, as well, as a connoisseur of wine and women, with a particular fondness, in Tynan's case, for sexual spanking. Towards the end of his life, he cancelled his subscriptions to the daily newspapers and took to reading the *Fetishist Times*. More to the point, Tynan had pronounced views on Shakespeare, and later admitted to being 'highly cagey' when the 'notorious Pole' first appeared to explain his 'vision' of the project. 'I see Macbeth as a young, open-faced guy, who is gradually sucked into a whirlpool of events because of his ambition,' Polanski said. 'He's a man who hopes to win a million, a gambler for high stakes.' Tynan thought this interpretation 'masterly'. Though in no doubt of his intelligence, he was less immediately impressed by Polanski personally. According to Tynan's wife Kathleen, 'Ken thought of Roman as an "imposer", someone about whom you worried whether his response to your next remark [would be] a smile or a snarl. You shrank from his scorn and cherished his praise.'

While he was busy adapting Shakespeare, Tynan was also toiling on a screenplay of his own. Entitled *Alex and Sophie*, it concerned a middle-aged man and his wife who meet and sexually coerce two nubile girls, who in the course of the story undergo initiation into bondage, flagellation, bestiality and other, less easily classified debauches. Polanski was unenthused by the result. On reading the final script, he told Tynan that he wanted to make a film 'about love as well as sex' and, perhaps wisely, moved on to other projects. *Alex and Sophie* eventually passed to *Macbeth*'s co-producer Andy Braunsberg, who apparently offered Tynan an advance of £500. Tynan later went back to pitch the idea a second time to Polanski, who, no doubt to be kind, reportedly agreed to reconsider the script in two or three years' time. 'I shan't be alive then,' Tynan said.

Macbeth proved a hard sell to the big-name studios, few of whom deemed a 364-year-old Scottish melodrama as being on a par with a *Rosemary's Baby* 2. An increasingly dog-eared copy of the proposal circulated between Paramount, Universal and MGM, where the president, a former TV sales executive named Jim Aubrey, in turn passed it down to his production staff in a bulky internal file marked, a trifle condescendingly, 'MACBETH (by Shakespeare)'. They all rejected it. Polanski kept the project alive thanks to a small personal loan from Victor Lownes and the infectious enthusiasm of Ken Tynan. One of Tynan's friends was with him at his home in London's Thurloe Square when, having agreed on their mutual vision for the film, Polanski rang to ask if they could meet to consummate their deal by drawing up a 'firm schedule'. 'My memory of it was one of those cartoon cuts,' the friend says. 'I have this image of Ken skidding out of the room, going sideways he was trying to run so fast. He literally flung himself into a taxi to get to Roman's place.'

Polanski recalls that in short order he and Tynan then found themselves stripped to the waist, acting out scenes from the play in the cramped upstairs study at West Eaton Place Mews. Colourful as it sounds, this would have been in keeping with both men's hands-on directing style, even though Tynan, painfully thin at the best of times, was already suffering from the early stages of terminal emphysema. When it came to Macbeth's murder of Duncan, Polanski writes that 'I made Ken stretch out on a bed . . . I crept up with a paper knife, and started stabbing him . . . We repeated the scene a number of times, with variations, when Ken caught sight of some people watching us from the balcony across the street. A group of middle-aged Belgravia residents were gazing at us, transfixed, sherry glasses frozen in mid-air . . . They doubtless assumed that our antics were all part of the Swinging London scene.' Although something of the sort undoubtedly happened, the only balcony in the mews at that time was set almost flush to Polanski's second floor, rather than opposite it, which would have required the bystanders to lean perilously forwards and sideways in order to enjoy the show. It's a small point, but perhaps another example of how certain Polanski anecdotes become more amusing, or dramatic, over the years.

According to Tynan, there were two 'immutable' ground rules when working with Polanski. 'We agreed never to discuss either politics – Roman being a shade or two to the right of me – or the murders. I [was] glad to comply.' To others in the media, many of them tabloid reporters obliged to hurriedly brush up their Shakespeare, it seemed that Polanski's choice of *Macbeth* was a macabre commentary on the events of the previous August. There was the scene, for instance, where Lady Macduff and her son are brutally stabbed, as well as a general abundance of violence, guile and dark incantations, culminating in Macduff's disclosure that he was 'from his mother's womb/Untimely ript'. As a score of rather heavy-handed articles pointed out, there were more than enough 'painful allusions' in the play as a whole to the horrors on Cielo Drive.

Tynan added that, as a result, he had 'certain qualms' when it came to writing the scene in which the murderers surprise Lady Macduff and her family. 'And a difficult moment arrived when I queried the amount of blood that would be shed by a small boy stabbed in the back. Polanski replied bleakly, "You didn't see my house last summer. I know about bleeding."'

In the meantime, Bill Tennant's best efforts on behalf of *Macbeth* had drawn a blank with even the smaller, or allegedly independent Hollywood studios. In early July, Polanski told Tynan that 'nobody else is biting', and turned to Victor Lownes and the Playboy organisation to get the project off the ground. Although not previously known for its support of the arts, Playboy was awash in profits from its UK casino operations and eager to invest; Polanski thought its brisk response 'a . . . welcome relief in an industry where bovine inertia [was] the rule, and speed the exception.' This was the same Lownes, of course, who had offered to help the director in any way he could on their first meeting at Cannes seven years earlier. Tynan, too, had been a 'contributing editor' at *Playboy*, even though the magazine had once spiked one of his stories, to his lasting indignation, because of its 'profusion of buttocks and masturbation'. Lownes in turn put in a good word for *Macbeth* with his boss Hugh Hefner, 44, who flew in for a meeting at the Malaga Hilton accompanied by three recent centrefolds on his personal black DC-9, the *Bunny*, and quickly agreed to advance Polanski $1.5 million. Columbia, who were to distribute the film, added a further $925,000. As the pyjama-clad Hefner was leaving the room, he looked over his shoulder and casually asked Polanski if he minded signing a completion guarantee, which meant that if he went over schedule or budget he would be removed as director. 'I hope you spend our money wisely,' he added benignly. Polanski agreed to do so.

With the first instalment of the advance, Polanski and Andy Braunsberg went out and bought a Rolls Royce Phantom VI. To go with the car, they engaged a chauffeur by the striking name of Armand de Saint Herpin. The two partners then formed a limited company called Caliban Films. Their associate producers on *Macbeth* were one Hercules Bellville ('Belville', in Polanski's memoirs), a young Oxford graduate who had worked as a gofer on *Repulsion* and *Cul-de-Sac*, and an urbane 39-year-old Old Etonian named Timothy Burrill. Burrill's own production company, incorporated on 6 February 1968, would flourish as a result of his long-term association with Polanski and others, eventually allowing him to entrust all ten of its issued shares to an asset-management firm based in Zurich.

On 24 July 1970, the trade press announced that 'Roman Polanski's *Macbeth*' was in production.* The news happened to coincide with the opening day of the trial of Manson and his accomplices in Los Angeles. The first witness called to the stand was Paul Tate, who described his last meeting with Sharon and identified police photographs of her body. In London, the *Daily Telegraph* falsely claimed that Polanski had declined to fly back to testify unless the state of California reimbursed him. As Vincent Bugliosi, the successful prosecuting attorney, says, 'There was no need for Roman to be here, and to this day I've never met him.' Polanski sued the newspaper for libel and won an undisclosed settlement.

AS IN PREVIOUS POLANSKI FILMS, the cast of *Macbeth* were extremely able performers whose reputations were not of the first magnitude. Martin Shaw, fresh from the TV series *Doctor in the House*, was signed to play Banquo, and Nicholas Selby (*Softly Softly*) was Duncan. John Stride, the storyteller from *Jackanory*, played Ross, Stephan Chase of *Crossroads* was Malcolm and a young Keith Chegwin, some years before his acclaimed tenure on *Multi-Coloured Swap Shop*, was Fleance. The New Zealand-born

---

* Sean Connery, who had been toying with the idea of filming his own version of *Macbeth*, abandoned his plans and made a reluctant comeback as James Bond in *Diamonds Are Forever*.

character actor Terence Bayler took the part of Macduff. Bayler was on location for 'six wrenching months', and was paid 'in the hundreds of pounds' (with expenses).

As Macbeth, Polanski wanted Albert Finney, who turned him down. Tynan then suggested Nicol Williamson, who had the benefit of having just starred in a film version of *Hamlet*. 'The guy has to be sexually attractive, and Williamson isn't,' Polanski said, adding that he wanted someone who would 'speak Shakespeare naturally' rather than 'declaiming'. He eventually settled on Jon Finch, the 29-year-old star of *Z Cars*, whom he met on a plane. Finch, as several papers pointed out, bore a faint physical resemblance to Charles Manson. Lady Macbeth was played by Francesca Annis, 26, who had once auditioned for the Catherine Deneuve role in *Repulsion*. According to Michael Klinger, Polanski had made an unflattering remark about her nose. 'Michael,' he asked, 'why do you bring me this Cyrano de Bergerac?'

Wherever possible, Polanski insisted that the characters 'look and behave exactly as they would have done' in the eleventh century, which, on occasion, involved a certain degree of nudity. The actress Tuesday Weld had turned down the part of Lady Macbeth for this reason. Polanski decided to increase the quota of witches from the traditional three to a coven of fifteen or twenty, whom he wanted to be similarly 'bare-assed'. As many of them were recruited from the Playboy Club, there was no problem. Eighteen months later, the witches, like Catherine Deneuve and Sharon Tate before them, became a *Playboy* centrefold.

Principal photography of *Macbeth* began in the first week of October 1970 in the heavily wooded hills above Portmeirion, the Italianate resort village on the coast of Snowdonia, and the setting to Patrick McGoohan's enigmatic TV series *The Prisoner* a year or two earlier. As on Holy Island for the shooting of *Cul-de-Sac*, it happened to be the worst autumn and winter in recent local history. The cast and crew spent much of the next six months performing in a sea of thick, Welsh mud, with Polanski shouting directions as best he could in the teeth of a howling gale.

Thanks to the weather and other issues there were to be various stresses involved in the production of *Macbeth*, one senior cast member referring to the director's 'petulance' and 'frequent evacuation [of] toys from his pram'. The traditional perception of Polanski as a temperamental *enfant terrible* burdened with genius was one that he occasionally found useful. As Tynan said, 'You were never quite sure which Roman you would be dealing with, [which] kept one nicely off balance.' But, Tynan added,

Polanski was 'never Queen Victoria'. He was an instinctive collaborator as well as an inspiring leader, actively considering suggestions from any quarter. 'Anywhere, anytime. Absolutely. It's all for the good of the bloody film,' he remarked. William Hobbs, the fight director on the production, remembers that 'Roman was a stickler for rehearsal. We went on and on in the rain, getting the actors fit enough to simultaneously wield their swords, charge their horses and recite lines from Shakespeare . . . It was like training for the decathlon. But Roman himself was always the first on set in the morning and the last to leave at night. I must say I liked and admired the man . . . I mean, Roman Polanski looking you in the eye and asking you, "How can we make this scene better?", as if he valued your opinion. It's very motivating.'

Hobbs and several others on *Macbeth* recall Polanski as being on top of the smallest detail, always riding the horses or testing the latest props before anyone else did. When it came time to smear various actors with blood, the director took a personal interest in mixing up a 'fetid' brew of equal parts Nescafé, glycerene and gravy. 'I have some experience,' he remarked. In more than one scene, Polanski found himself standing ankle deep in manure while choreographing a cast of goats, sheep, pigs and other farm animals. Martin Shaw quickly came to realise that 'for Roman, making a film wasn't for people who want to swan around in Winnebagos and come out when everything's ready, say a few lines and then go back into the jacuzzi . . . As far as he was concerned, acting was a job for a jobbing actor who was very serious about it. As with his conversation and the rest of his personality, there was no room for bullshit. It's just, "Get it done."

'Time after time,' says Shaw, 'when it was a hand-held shot for instance, Roman would take the camera out of the hands of his operator and do it himself. He just could not contain himself . . .' One morning, after a 'forensic' discussion of eleventh-century infantry tactics, Polanski turned to Ken Tynan and said, 'Should the soldiers move right to left across the frame, or left to right?' 'Does it matter?' Tynan asked rashly. 'Of course it matters,' Polanski said. 'To the Western eye easy or successful move- ment is left to right, difficult or failed movement is right to left.' Before even rehearsing the scene, Polanski told Tynan that they should read some of the text leading up to that point, in order to 'get the flavour of the action'. Tynan went back a few lines and began reading, and Polanski said, 'No, Ken – I meant the beginning of the Act.' So the two men read for something like twenty minutes before Polanski decided on how to direct the dozens of actors and scores of extras waiting patiently in the rain. After the first run-through, which Tynan thought 'magnificent', Polanski picked up his loudhailer and asked everyone to do the same thing again, this time with the cameras rolling. They repeated the manoeuvre, with no obvious variations. 'Once more, please,' said Polanski. The whole company turned around and trudged back to their places. After five or six further takes, Polanski looked up and announced in his widely mimicked accent, 'That's mudge bedder. Fandastic, fandastic . . .' As everyone prematurely relaxed, he added, 'We go again.'

One day a young member of the cast got up the nerve to ask Polanski the 'secret to great acting'. The director told him that 'you could forget about the classical training. All you needed, instead, was to relax and focus at the same time.'

It wasn't all heavy weather and artistic struggle, however. Most of the film's interiors were shot, like *Cul-de-Sac*'s, on a sound-stage at Shepperton. Once or twice, the top brass from Playboy flew in on a tour of inspection. To mark the occasions, a 'bunny' flag was hurriedly raised at the studio gate, and in their own obscure tribute various cast members taped centre-folds from the magazine on their dressing-room doors. The following spring, as *Macbeth* wound up, Tynan mentioned to Polanski that Hugh Hefner was about to celebrate his forty-fifth birthday. The director took time away from the concluding scenes to assemble a group of elderly female extras (described in the script, a touch ungenerously, as 'hags') and film them in the nude singing 'Happy Birthday, Hef'. The footage was then sent to the Playboy Mansion in Chicago, where it was 'well received'.

Back on the beach at Portmeirion, Polanski began to rehearse the phys-ically demanding fight sequence between Macbeth and Terence Bayler's Macduff. Due to the 'mad geography' and other constraints of the shooting schedule, the scene would be completed 200 miles away, at Shepperton. Like Martin Shaw, Bayler was struck by his director's '"no bullshit" approach . . . If I did a good rehearsal, it was "Terry, you're a samurai." If I did a bad one, it was "Terry, you're a sissy." None of your typical British understatement. Most directors will season even the mildest criticism with oodles of love and appreciation. You could forget about that with Roman.'

Towards the end of the shoot, Bayler went up to Polanski's villa half a dozen times to read through the scene in which Ross arrives to tell Macduff of the wholesale murder of his family. The operative lines were, 'Your castle is surprised; your wife and babes savagely slaughter'd.' Even as Bayler rehearsed in Polanski's living room, 'the ongoing trial of Charles

Manson was being daily reported in the British press, so I was very much aware of the relevance of Macduff's bereavement to Roman . . . On one reading, walking across the room with bowed head, I asked Polanski if, having just learnt of the brutal killing of my wife and children, I should keep walking in a daze. He said that I should, and added simply that he knew about this situation.' Although it was later reported that the director 'blew up' at the question, Bayler and several others present recall it as a 'quiet and sad' moment, with its obvious allusion to Polanski's own reaction to the news of Tate's death.

The actual scene was shot on the last day on location. As Bayler notes, 'It was fortunate that Roman had taken such trouble in rehearsing a sequence that clearly meant so much to him . . . As it was, we did the full four-minute scene in one take in rapidly fading light. The performers had time for a quick walk-through the action with Polanski, who was also manning the camera. With dusk falling we knew there was no possibility of a second take, or any pick-ups or cutaways. So we had one chance to nail the scene, being aware of the hand-held camera, hitting our marks in the mud, and remembering Shakespeare's lines. I had the additional responsibility of beginning to weep when appropriate. A magazine later claimed that I "differed with Polanski over a fine point of interpretation during the shooting of this scene." There was no time for fine points – we were pleased to get the bloody thing shot at all.'

Bayler remains a 'firm Polanski fan', although others in the cast came to weigh their professional respect against certain personal reservations about his maverick behaviour. John Stride had arrived on set and apparently piqued the director by asking him to 'Shoot me from my good side, please.' A certain mutual coolness developed as a result. Polanski once looked at the compact *Jackanory* star, turned to the crew and loudly requested 'A box for little Mr Stride to stand on.' Stephan Chase, as Malcolm, also came in for some occasionally sharp direction. Meanwhile, Polanski enjoyed a 'very spirited' relationship with his leading lady, Francesca Annis. At her audition, Annis had read her lines, Tynan recalled admiringly, 'like a little girl'. When her subsequent performance proved insufficiently robust, Polanski was seen to snap an amyl nitrate capsule under her nostrils to achieve the necessary zip. Annis performed her 'Out, damned spot! out, I say!' sleepwalking sequence in the nude. It was a closed set. Polanski preserved at least a degree of Annis' modesty by the use of strategically positioned props (among them the actress' cascading hair), a gag he had introduced in his aborted 'Voyeur' sketch for Tynan's *Oh! Calcutta!*

The climactic scene in which Terence Bayler's Macduff duels with Macbeth occurs offstage in the play, but provided a gory resolution to the film. Both actors used real swords. In an unscripted moment, Bayler was gashed under his eye and keeled over, followed by the assistant director's mildly unfortunate cry of 'Cut!' Cast, crew and medical assistants frantically made their way to their fallen comrade, who, he notes, was 'haemorrhaging at an alarming rate'. Someone ran to find an ambulance. Then, suddenly, through the crowd, came Polanski's voice. 'Well, Terry,' he announced calmly, 'this will make you *very* attractive to women.'

Above all, everything on *Macbeth* was to be 'authentic', which necessarily proved a consistent challenge to the cast. The English had by that time in history emerged as the most fearsome fighting force in northern Europe while wearing polished steel boots, tights, brightly coloured tunics and chain-mail hairnets, worryingly close to the fashions sported in a Seventies disco. Bayler recalls his having 'suffered mightily' in this gear, which he wore for up to twelve hours at a time, occasionally even 'clanking down to the pub' in full Macduff regalia. It was part of Polanski's particular artistic vision that he wanted his cast to stay in character, and even to address each other when off duty by their names in the film. As another actor confirms, 'Roman bestrode that set like Napoleon', a comparison the director himself might not have disowned. As well as the cast and crew, there were no less than three separate tiers of extras to marshal. Some 1,200 'derelicts' were recruited from the local labour exchange, for £5 each a day, to act as the English army marching on Dunsinane. At a slightly more august level, a number of professional athletes and dancers were engaged to run or ride around the countryside in the role of Macbeth's messengers. Finally, there were several small children, some of whom played Macduff's slaughtered family. Polanski explained to one sweet-looking young blonde girl that she should lie down and pretend to be dead while he daubed his special 'blood' over her body. 'What's your name?' he asked, in the midst of the operation. 'Sharon,' she replied.

IF POLANSKI THE DIRECTOR WAS WIDELY ADMIRED ON THE SET OF *MACBETH*, Polanski the man earned mixed reviews. In addition, apparently, to John Stride, one or two of the secondary cast thought him high-handed, and awarded him the nickname 'the raging Pole'. To Tynan, Polanski referred to such people as 'comics' and 'monkeys'. In similar vein, a local Welsh landowner who demanded and got a substantial cash compensation for film-induced 'stress' was 'One of those parasites . . . Fucking leeches. I hate them.' Polanski even ridiculed a potent symbol of the Seventies British landscape, the Amalgamated Engineering and Electrical Union. In the week preceding Christmas, the union's organisers called a one-day national strike which disrupted Polanski's film, among many other activities. 'What's this fucking nonsense all about?' he asked his co-screenwriter. Tynan, who said later that he 'recognised that enquiry as a signal for trouble starting', explained patiently that 'Some people aren't as lucky as us, Roman. They have to work in factories.' Polanski laughed derisively. 'If I worked in a factory,' he said, 'I'd be running it inside six months.' A day or two later, while shooting some 'castle footage' in Northumbria, one of the technical crew looked up and saw Polanski and the well-padded figure of Timothy Burrill walking side by side on a hilltop in the mid-distance. 'There go Pooh and Piglet,' he remarked, to general merriment. The character actor Richard Pearson played the doctor in *Macbeth*, and went on to appear in two further Polanski films. 'Roman,' in his measured description, 'was a man of uneven temper.'

That was mild compared to the Playboy organisation's reaction to Polanski as *Macbeth* drifted serenely over its agreed budget and schedule. Victor Lownes grew increasingly exasperated on his visits to the elaborate sets built on two adjacent sound-stages at Shepperton. 'Roman,' he writes in his memoirs, 'was acting like a small child.' Among other foibles, Polanski was said to have spent three hours filming a candle because it wouldn't flicker as he wanted it to. Yet more farmers had had to be paid 'hundreds of pounds' apiece in order to temporarily remove swing gates, electrical wire and other twentieth-century devices from their fields, all for a few seconds of film. Then there was the long, tragicomic saga of the bear-baiting sequence. Polanski wanted to show a 'real animal fight' in *Macbeth*, because, as he frequently argued on other points, it was 'true to the times'. After several alarming rehearsals, he settled, instead, on having a stuntman named Reg dress up in a bear suit. According to the script, Reg was to 'roll around on the floor, grappl[ing] with three wild dogs.' At the first run-through, the dogs went 'fucking berserk', individually attaching themselves to Reg's neck, arm and crotch, leading to genuine fears for his life. 'Good, good!' Polanski yelled from behind the camera. 'Keep going, Reg!' After peace was restored and the unit nurse had departed, Reg told Polanski that the most he felt he could handle was one dog. The director nodded, seemingly sympathetic. Once Reg was out of earshot, Polanski summoned the dogs' trainer. 'We let all three loose on him,' he muttered. 'If it doesn't work, I cut the shot.'

Although the bear-fighting sequence was eventually scrapped, it had its real-life equivalent in the crisis meeting between Hefner and the senior staff at Playboy Productions on one hand and Polanski on the other. For their part, Film Finances, the underwriters involved, were aggressively pressing for a change of director. To that end, Peter Collinson of *The Italian Job* was put on a retainer and, in Polanski's absence, 'shot several crowd scenes' at Shepperton. Andy Braunsberg was fired and replaced by one of Film Finances' efficiency experts, who duly produced a new, streamlined timetable for completing *Macbeth*. When all parties met in Hefner's penthouse suite at the London Hilton, Polanski insisted that he was doing the very best he could, given the 'shitty weather' and other problems. In a dramatic summation, he offered to forgo the remaining third of his fee, which was accepted, and to 'give you a pint of my blood', which was thought excessive. After all the arguments had been presented, Hefner generously agreed to advance a further $500,000, which was enough to finish the film. In the course of the next few months, relations between Victor Lownes and Polanski would reach an all-time low, the American ending one meeting with the observation, it's said, that his director was 'a selfish cunt'.

A note in the Columbia Pictures archive records that '*Macbeth* [was] successfully resolved' in April 1971, although this was to prove premature. In some ways, the film's life was only just beginning. There were to be nine further months of editing and sound-dubbing, much of the original dialogue having been lost in the wind, followed by a protracted squabble about the film's rating, the American censors taking exception to the rare glimpses of Francesca Annis' bottom. Here some discrepancy exists between Polanski's account of the post-production process – 'I flung myself into the work in an attempt to make up for lost time and meet the [release] deadline'; and Tynan's, in a letter of 5 August 1971 – 'Roman grows a little bored with *Macbeth* and keeps flying off to Saint-Tropez, leaving me to look after [it].' Polanski was, however, more than willing to assist with the aggressive promotion and marketing campaign for the film. Although he complained, with good reason, that 'Most journalists review only my life', he was happy to accommodate them if simultaneously their 'tabloid crap' served to sell the movie. In an interview with *Positif* magazine in February 1969, Polanski had remarked drily that 'scandal always helps with commerce'. He was speaking of *Rosemary's Baby*, but it applied equally or more so to *Macbeth*.

In a notable coup, Victor Lownes was able to turn the film's premiere into a Royal Command Performance, scheduled for 9 December 1971 in the Odeon Leicester Square. No less a dignitary than the Queen Mother was to attend, Her Highness, it was widely reported, having been born in Macbeth's castle, and also being a 'huge fan' of Polanski's work. A preview of the final cut for the senior Columbia management apparently put paid to this plan; in something of an understatement, the archive refers to the audience's 'diversity' of reaction, which seems to have run the gamut between indifference and revulsion. The scene in which Macduff's family is slaughtered (featuring both the core violence, and some brief child nudity) was so potent that an executive's wife vomited at the screening, and the film's release was subsequently rearranged for January 1972 at Hefner's newly opened Playboy Theater in New York.*

Opening a two-and-a-quarter-hour film adaptation of Shakespeare in a New Year blizzard was, as Polanski notes, 'cinematic suicide'. Many of the first-night critics, who laughed loudly as the words 'A Playboy Production' appeared on screen, quite clearly came to scoff. One scribe referred in print to the 'proverbial witches' teats', which were 'all too apt for a Hefner presentation'. There was more in similar vein. For the broadsheets and trade press, meanwhile, the inevitable comparison was to Polanski's private life.

To *Newsweek*, 'The parallels between the Manson murders and the mad, bloody acts of these beautiful, lost Macbeths keep pressing themselves upon the viewer . . . All that is good here seems but a pretext for close-ups of knives drawing geysers of blood from the flesh of men, women and children. No chance to revel in gore is passed up.' To 'America's leading critic' and Pulitzer Prize-winner Roger Ebert, of the Chicago *Sun-Times*, 'It's hard to watch a film directed by Roman Polanski and not react on more than one level to such images as a baby being "untimely ripped from his mother's womb" . . . Polanski's characters all resemble Manson.' According to one Kevin Lyons of the *Encyclopaedia of Fantastic Film and TV*, 'It's a bitter film, full of hatred and passion, and it's almost impossible to see it as anything but an exorcism for Polanski . . . The appalling events of 8 August 1969 inform [*Macbeth*] much more vividly than the Bard.'

---

* *Macbeth* was also shown as a 'gala New York exclusive' to an invited audience of distributors and selected reviewers on 20 December 1971.

The few, mostly British critics who reviewed *Macbeth* on its own merits rather than as a cathartic exercise by its director agreed about the violence. 'It makes *The Wild Bunch* look like *Brigadoon*,' one wrote, with perhaps a touch of hyperbole. (Responding to specific criticisms about Macduff's decapitation of Macbeth, Polanski observed, 'When you tell the story of a guy who's beheaded, you have to show how they cut off his head. If you don't, it's like telling a dirty joke and leaving out the punchline.') But there was praise, too, for Polanski's 'dark, enthralling' vision, with its 'finely judged details' and 'escalating horror'. Thirty-five years later, the film still has a shocking and moving virtuosity, streaked with what would come to be called 'Romanesque' humour: the scene, for example, when Duncan and Macbeth embrace fondly, shaking a cloud of dust sprinkled with flies off Macbeth's well-worn cloak. The cast are uniformly excellent, even if Francesca Annis, at times, seems oddly diffident in a role traditionally played as a cross between Margaret Thatcher and Sharon Stone in *Basic Instinct* mode. At the moment when, hesitating whether or not to kill Duncan, Macbeth remarks, 'We will proceed no further in this business; He hath honour'd me of late', some particularly crisp spousal response would seem to be in order. Francesca Annis breaks into tears. There are one or two only fair special effects – notably the ludicrous 'floating dagger', and some under-cranked camerawork on fight sequences, which look dementedly fast as a result – while the music by the Third Ear Band, in the words of the press release 'achiev[ing] a degree of ethnic fusion of Indian, medieval, gypsy, Middle Eastern, electronic, jazz, trance and folk' (if not all in the same song) was the sort of thing Mike Oldfield did better. But these few quibbles aside, Polanski's *Macbeth* remains deft, well paced and a solid piece of work.

After the Royal Command Performance was dropped, *Macbeth*'s British premiere was moved to the less glamorous surroundings of the Plaza Cinema 2 in London's Piccadilly Circus. It was attended by Victor Lownes and sundry Playboy bunnies, as well as a large number of press. At the last moment Princess Anne agreed to appear, reportedly because of 'all the riding sequences' involved. 'I hated them,' Polanski told her in the receiving line. 'I'll never make another film with horses in it.'

In a characteristic bit of promotion, Polanski had shown Sydney Edwards of the London *Evening Standard* a cut of *Macbeth* and then taken him to a lavish dinner in Lownes' VIP room. Edwards loved the film, but was surprised when the director told him that 'I don't really like it here,' referring to the Playboy Club. Asked why he had accepted Playboy financing,

Polanski responded, 'Pecunia non olet – money doesn't smell.' When he read the interview in the next day's paper, Lownes 'hit the roof ... Not only was this not the way to talk about a friend, but it was lousy business as far as the film itself was concerned. We deserved better, and Roman's reference to our money smelling was totally undeserved.' Lownes wouldn't speak to Polanski again for another ten years. In a letter to Hefner, he wrote that 'Gene Gutowski analyses Roman's attitude as being the result of his "not having anything more that he can get out of you and Playboy" ... The thing that's so distressing to me is that for years I did everything I possibly could to be helpful to the son of a bitch and only recently have I come to realise that I was merely being exploited by him ... It was as if I had a blind spot where Roman is concerned.' Lownes concluded by returning Polanski's gift of a solid gold phallus. The accompanying card read, 'In view of recent developments, I no longer care to have this full-length, life-size portrait of you around the house. I'm sure you'll have no difficulty finding some "friend" you can shove it up.' Polanski forwarded the letter to his handwriting expert in New York, to ask him if he thought Lownes was deranged.

Ken Tynan, meanwhile, made a second, desultory stab at selling Polanski his masturbatory fantasy Alex and Sophie. It remained mercifully unproduced. From the few surviving notes, this self-styled 'upmarket spank movie' was unworthy of the facilitator of modern British theatre. In increasingly poor health, Tynan moved from London to Los Angeles, where he wrote a number of scintillating film-star profiles, as well as a long, melancholy list of 'many friends, including those who, for one reason or another have turned into enemies' that included Polanski. The director had apparently managed to offend even Tynan's sensibilities by once casually allowing in the course of a spirited discussion on the female anatomy that 'Sharon's ass wasn't bad.' A Los Angeles colleague recalls that 'towards the end, Ken was in the truest sense of the word a pathetic figure. When I visited him he was sitting in a little hut in his back yard, trying valiantly to write and breathing through an oxygen mask.' Tynan died on 26 July 1980, aged 53.

POLANSKI DIDN'T SEEM PARTICULARLY BOTHERED BY THE REVIEWERS, since, as one of them factually noted, he was not only the 'world's best-known director, but better known than any movie star.' Such celebrity cut both ways. One hugely important Hollywood figure and liberal activist found himself appearing as a guest on the same talk show as Polanski. 'No one even glanced at me,' he notes ruefully. 'To have been sitting opposite

Roman Polanski . . . In terms of being overlooked, that must be roughly what it feels like to be the uncarved side of Mount Rushmore.' Less agreeable were the 'cuckoo scripts' that still poured in to Bill Tennant's office, offering Polanski endless variations of the 'same basic satanic-killer crap', and the fallout from the Manson murders generally. Thanks to the continuing front-page coverage of the killers' trials and subsequent events, there was no escaping the story, even thousands of miles from Los Angeles. Polanski was tainted by association. While skiing together in Gstaad the previous winter, a well connected Swiss businessman named Peter Notz had put the director up for membership of the exclusive Eagle Club. The elderly club manager, noting the name on the application, had asked him whether he wasn't 'in some way involved in that crime in Hollywood?' Polanski had replied that he was a victim of it. Such distinctions were lost on the committee of the Eagle Club, who blackballed him.

'I never have any problems going to sleep anymore,' Polanski remarked three years after the murders. As a rule, he rounded off his evenings with an expensive dinner and some dancing, after which his chauffeur Armand would return 'Mr P and his party' to West Eaton Place Mews. Not only was Polanski one of the most sought after (if not always gainfully employed) directors throughout the early Seventies, but his love life was manna to the gossip sheets. 'These things are unknowable,' a friend concedes, 'but one would guess at a total of two to three hundred "pulls" a year.' Kenneth Tynan would call Polanski's attitude to women 'tribal . . . he beguiles them into submission with his urchin charm, but if they presume to engage him in argument, he soon grows bored and petulant. Women's lib arouses him to a high pitch of bewildered fury.' After a day's scriptwriting at West Eaton Place Mews, Polanski would 'fling himself exhausted into the back seat of his Rolls with smoked-glass windows and, murmuring, "Who shall I gratify tonight?", thumb through a constantly amended list of candidates.' On the way to Shepperton one morning a few days into production, Polanski picked Tynan up in the Rolls with the words: 'You had garlic for dinner last night, my friend. Open the window. How you like my new tape? Elton John. Fantastic, huh? Listen, I screwed a Chinese lawyer last night. She's a barrister from Hong Kong. Beautiful! . . . I'm going to Gstaad this weekend with those two chicks I scored at the party that Victor gave for Warren . . . You remember there was one in drastic hot pants? Sure you know the type, sort of between a starlet and a secretary . . . Hey, look at that one over there . . . What a great ass *she's* got . . .'

The journalist Neil Norman recalls sitting in the Open Space Theatre in London around the time of *Macbeth*'s release, 'watch[ing] a rare production of Picasso's play *Four Little Girls*. The fact that all four young actresses performed the entire play naked is neither here nor there . . . Fifteen minutes after the play began there was a kerfuffle at the door and a diminutive man in a camel coat with a fur collar swept in with three blonde girls in tow . . . Fifteen minutes later, having had his fill of Picasso, he got up and swept out again with his glamorous entourage. It was my first sighting of Roman Polanski and it left an indelible and not altogether favourable impression. In plain English, I thought he was an arrogant prick.'

The 'restless widower', in another contemporaneous assessment, was 'just this side of a sex addict'. According to this source, Polanski was a gastronome whose love of a good meal 'rather mirrored his libido'. Just as no dinner was complete with less than three courses, so 'some of Roman's nights were like a menu, with an entrée, a meat dish and a dessert' in the form of a blonde, a brunette and a redhead. *Macbeth*'s Richard Pearson adds that Polanski 'had an eye for the girls, to put it mildly', although this 'never, to my knowledge, interfered with the film'.

In between his editing *Macbeth*, Polanski had managed both to produce a documentary about the Formula 1 racing driver Jackie Stewart, with the title *Weekend of Champions*, and to co-write a screenplay called *The Boat on the Grass*. The latter was produced by a young film enthusiast and dangerous-sports fanatic, later to fall prey to a debilitating drug addiction, named Jean-Pierre Rassam. Rassam and his partner subsequently issued a formal invitation to the 'chairman and board of Caliban Films' – in reality, Polanski, Braunsberg and their runner Hercules – to a development meeting in Paris. Various ideas were discussed, the most promising apparently being a lesbian-oriented drama to be made in 3-D. With Rassam footing the bills, Polanski shot a number of tests of young actresses, but reluctantly abandoned the project when it became clear that the 'optical technology' wasn't yet up to the challenge.

Back on their recurrent holiday in Gstaad, Polanski and Gérard Brach began writing a screenplay they called *The Magic Finger*. This, too, inclined toward the erotic: a priapic Hollywood producer and his sex-mad entourage submit a young starlet to various unorthodox auditions. Jack Nicholson was to have played the lead. In the 'new Hollywood' that Polanski had helped invent, adult films ran the gamut from big-studio releases like *Carnal Knowledge*, which won an Oscar nomination and a Golden Globe, all the way down to triple-X rated 'speciality' features, typically concentrating more on their vivid action sequences than on any plot subtleties or production values. From the surviving notes, *The Magic Finger* fell fairly low down the scale, although no doubt Polanski would have polished the script had it come to fruition. As it was, Nicholson reportedly read the first draft and passed on it. Jean-Pierre Rassam contented himself with 'skimming through' the three-page synopsis. He, too, declined to proceed with *The Magic Finger*, but recommended Polanski and Brach to his friend, the 60-year-old mogul Carlo Ponti, producer of *Doctor Zhivago* among some forty other films and long since happily married to Sophia Loren (although, technically, the Italian authorities had refused to recognise Ponti's prior divorce until 1964).

By the spring of 1972, Caliban Films, launched with such expectations two years earlier, was all but bankrupt. Thanks to the cost overruns, Polanski had lost his equity in *Macbeth*, not that it would have done him any good once the final figures were added up, and it had been four years since the success of *Rosemary's Baby*. One writer familiar with him in the early Seventies remembers 'Roman shuttl[ing] around somewhat forlornly between London and Paris. It was him, Andy and that slightly absurd chauffeur, who always stood to attention and held the door open for you ... Although Roman habitually travelled in style, appearances were deceptive. The Rolls was second-hand, and in my memory also doubled up as a mobile office and even a bedroom on the odd occasion. Roman told me that he liked to ride around in the back seat and take notes.' The author and critic Iain Johnstone tells the story of Polanski peering out of the window of a car, if not the Rolls, and remarking, '"London is such a red city" ... He was a master of the subliminal detail. A postbox or a phone booth was just the sort of thing he noticed.'

On 13 May 1972, Polanski made an appearance at the Cannes festival where, along with Jon Finch, he tried to revive the public's flagging interest in *Macbeth*. Later in the proceedings, they were joined by Francesca Annis. The three linked arms and strode up and down the Croisette for the photographers, Polanski, in particular, throwing himself into a subsequent round of interviews and public lectures. Despite his best efforts, *Macbeth* soon disappeared into the obscurity of the film-reference books (with a reported gross of less than $1 million), only to be rediscovered as a 'lost classic' some thirty years later.

In the meantime, Polanski wasn't only without a major Hollywood studio, or any significant source of financing; he had even contrived to lose his own agent. Bill Tennant had driven off in his client's old car one day and wouldn't come back for ten years. He was said to have been 'bored with it all', and had succumbed to cocaine addiction. At one point in the late Seventies, Tennant was to be found selling sandwiches off a catering truck in the less salubrious parts of Los Angeles. Polanski's own claim to have been a Hollywood 'non-person' at the time may be close to the truth. Jack Nicholson, among others, insists that there was an unofficial industry boycott of the director following his wife's murder and that 'Roman was down for the count'. As usual, he would beat it: even then, Polanski's old benefactor Bob Evans at Paramount was talking to the screenwriter Robert Towne about his adapting *The Great Gatsby* for a reported salary of $175,000. Towne said no, but mentioned that he was working on a script of his own, which Evans eventually optioned for a fraction of the *Gatsby* fee. It was called *Chinatown*.

When Polanski assured Ken Tynan on the set of *Macbeth* that he would be running any factory in which he found himself working 'inside six months', he hadn't overstated his case. As well as his prodigious intelligence and drive, the director was consistently lucky in his choice of well-connected patrons. The meeting with Carlo Ponti in the producer's elegant offices on Rome's Piazza Aracoeli went so well that Polanski and Brach walked out again half an hour later with $1.2 million, to be paid in six monthly instalments, in order to finance a new film. It was to be called *What?* Jean-Pierre Rassam's latest offshore company, Cinequanon, was the prospective distributor. Polanski and Brach were also given eight weeks' generous expense allowance while they worked on the script. After banking Ponti's first cheque, Andy Braunsberg was able to rent Caliban Films its own estate on the outskirts of Rome, the Villa Mandorli, set in a well manicured seven-acre park planted with palm and cypress trees. There were sweeping views of the Quirinale hills, and the neighbours included a distinguished aspiring actress, the former Queen Soraya of Iran.

That summer of 1972, Polanski's home was a luxurious commune as he and Brach wrote by day and entertained the likes of Franco Zeffirelli, Warren Beatty and Andy Warhol and their respective entourages by night. Warhol in particular loved the place, with its cool, tiled floors, frescoed ceilings and 'sweet young kids'. Another guest would remember the Villa Mandorli as 'a Scott Fitzgerald fantasy, ten people for lunch . . . fifteen for dinner.' Hired chefs served up exquisite cordon bleu meals at odd hours, accompanied by the finest wines. Sitting with Brach in the villa's formal salon decorated with antique brocade chairs, Polanski turned the screenplay into a postmodern version of *Candide*, crossed with *Alice in Wonderland*. In a wild leap of imagination, *What?*'s young heroine would find herself trapped in a secluded seaside palazzo, inhabited by sex maniacs.

Over the coming years, Polanski's 'Roman holiday' would enjoy iconographic status amongst biographers and fans alike as a golden era in which art and culture were combined with *la dolce vita*. As well as Warhol and company, the villa would be home to a constantly shifting cast of friends, actors and displaced European royalty. One evening, a fashion designer from London was dining with Polanski, Brach and 'some ruined Polish count' at Mandorli, where she watched the two authors of *What?* acting out scenes from the prospective film. Brach took the part of Alex, an apparently impotent retired pimp who, perhaps in veiled homage to Kenneth Tynan, enjoyed flagellation. Meanwhile, Polanski 'fluttered around the living room' imitating the young ingénue. The additional presence of Hercules, the runner, and Armand, the chauffeur, gave the proceedings 'some of the surreal properties of a Lewis Carroll story'. The designer's assessment of Polanski's nocturnal habits is that he wanted something to happen every night: 'I don't think he cared that much for parties as such, but there had to be some kind of adventure . . . He usually had his own gay little scene – he'd mimic people or tell stories – and while it was great fun, you were conscious of being in the presence of a highly gifted but temperamental child.' This 'Peter Pan-like host' of the Villa Mandorli was then just over a year short of his fortieth birthday.

On 9 June 1972, Jean-Pierre Rassam declined to participate in *What?* His long letter – not a form rejection – explained that while he 'sincerely enjoyed' the script, he was 'currently overextended' in producing a film coincidentally called *Me, I want to have Dough*. Fortunately, Carlo Ponti remained fully committed both to the project and Polanski, whom he appears to have seen as a protégé, issuing further cheques at monthly intervals throughout the summer. Since Ponti himself was heavily in debt, this was notable generosity on his part. One associate revealed that 'Carlo always treated Roman with deference and respect. In the early Seventies, big movie stars waited for weeks for an audience at Piazza Aracoeli; Polanski could go in whenever he wanted.' During negotiations to agree a final budget for *What?*, one of Ponti's conversations with Polanski was transcribed. The legendary mogul's replies consisted of little more than *'Bene, bene!'*

Unlike some of his predecessors as Polanski's producer, Ponti would remain a close friend even after their business together was concluded. Elsewhere there was a more mixed response. As many people testify to Polanski's arrogance as to his charm; often it's the same people who testify to both. The actor Damien Thomas, for instance, later to star in *Pirates*, remembers the director 'stomping around a reception somewhere in London, asking people, "Who the fuck are you?"', very similar to Terence Bayler's account of Polanski's birthday party a year or two earlier. Thomas also recalls 'visiting Roman's flat in Paris in the mid-Eighties, where, breaking off from a script conference, he announced that he had a "new toy" to show his guests and strode over to a corner of the room. Everyone experienced several moments' mild anxiety before, with a great flourish, Polanski pushed a button which, it transpired, automatically opened and closed his curtains ... He was absolutely chuffed by the device, and demonstrated it several times with a wide grin. Roman was in his fifties at the time, and I thought it was rather endearing that he was that fired up by a curtain machine.' One of *Macbeth*'s cast similarly remembers Polanski 'picking me up in the Rolls, whereupon he asked me if I was too hot. As it was North Wales in the depth of winter, I said that no, I wasn't. Ignoring my reply, Roman proceeded to operate the car's electric windows, raising and lowering them half a dozen times with such obvious enjoyment that you could only laugh. He was like a 10-year-old kid at Christmas.'

For Polanski, the casting of *What?*, and more particularly its female lead, proved to be another protracted exercise, to which he applied himself with selfless zeal. After an extensive search both of 'name' actresses and aspiring starlets in London and Paris, he eventually gave the job to the 21-year-old novice Sydne Rome, who had recently left her home in Upper Sandusky, Ohio, determined, like ex-Queen Soraya, to 'make it [in] Italian film'. Polanski found her living a few streets away from the Villa Mandorli. The director explained to her, with some understatement, that *What?* was to be a 'very different' concept to *Macbeth*. Instead of the traditional beginning, middle and end, there would be only 'feeling'. Rome herself would be required to shed most of her clothes, ending the proceedings sitting stark naked in a truckload of farm animals, while shouting the film's title as she disappears from view. Polanski played the small but obnoxious part of Mosquito (one of his less flattering nicknames), which, despite his denials, seemed to offer the familiar autobiographical allusions. A difficult childhood, Mosquito announces at one stage, is 'no excuse for being a pain in the ass'.

Just before the filming began, Polanski and Brach moved out of Mandorli and into one of Carlo Ponti's villas a hundred miles down the coast at Naples. It was another strikingly generous act by the producer, who was currently embroiled in a disastrous spaghetti kung-fu film called *Hercules Against Karate*. As a result, *What?*'s two authors were able to make some much needed revisions while living together under the roof of the very building they would use as their main set.

They weren't there alone, of course. The usual retinue of aides, cooks, valets and chauffeurs whom Polanski had come increasingly to depend on at the Villa Mandorli came south, to be joined by various members of *What?*'s forty-strong crew. 'Roman,' as one of the latter explains, 'would rehearse all afternoon, host an incredible dinner, spend the night with one or other (and perhaps both) of his current girlfriends, and rise at six the next morning to call a story conference.' To round out his time, Polanski was reading 'half a dozen French novels', running 'several miles daily' up and down the nearby mountain roads, and taking flying lessons.

Andy Warhol was increasingly a part of Polanski's court, and vice versa, and was said to have read and loved the script of *What?* Carlo Ponti was simultaneously exploring a 'multi-picture relationship' with the pop artist, who appears to have harboured acting ambitions. Thus, when Warhol appeared in Naples just as Polanski was casting his film, he 'hoped [he] would be the first name considered for the part of Alex', and he was – the first considered and the first rejected. The job went, instead, to the 48-year-old Marcello Mastroianni, who presumably took the role of the impotent, cross-dressing sadist as an antidote to his standard 'Latin lover' screen persona. In an even more incongruous match-up, the British character actor Hugh Griffith played Noblart, the elderly Italian grandee, and one Guido Alberti, the scholarly founder of Italy's Premio Strega annual literary award, gave a somewhat laboured performance as a priest. The supporting cast were excellent in their various roles as obnoxious American art dealers and sexual deviants, many of them playing from life. With a 'Naked Girl (uncredited)' and a 'Naked Girl with Hat (uncredited)' also on hand, *What?* was clearly destined to be something other than all-round family entertainment. Polanski himself would note wryly that, in a further departure from *Macbeth*, the film would present few if any challenges in terms of wardrobe, most of the cast appearing in their pyjamas, or less.

And the plot. Much like *Cul-de-Sac*, *What?* took the potentially interesting idea of sending an outsider into a hostile and morally perverse world, and ran with it. Along the way, Polanski would revisit the scene of both *The Fat and the Lean* and *Mammals*, specifically in what he called the 'eternal riddle of the master-slave relationship' – addressed here by having the Rome and Mastroianni characters take it in turns to flog one another. The other occupants of the house barely impinge on the story, such as it is, and pass their time listening to Mozart, playing ping-pong and having sex. For the most part, *What?* would be impeccably acted but hopelessly contrived, with every characterisation and plot twist visible a mile off. Mastroianni is so unattractive, especially when clad solely in a pair of briefs and a tiger skin, that it's hard to see what anyone would find so compelling about him. As it is, the S&M action comes dangerously close to the anal-erotic rompings of Tynan's lost oeuvre, *Alex and Sophie*. Even then, *What?*'s livelier moments are badly outnumbered by its relentless gags and ever more strained efforts to shock: to watch this film followed by *Rosemary's Baby* is like drinking a glass of cold spring water after gorging on heavily salted crisps. There's also some possibly deliberate awkwardness of dialogue, much of it on loan from Harold Pinter, and at least one scene straight out of the *Carry On* series. As the Griffith character lies mortally ill, he asks Sydne Rome to stand spreadeagled over him and let him peek between her legs. Rome complies with this unorthodox dying wish, whereupon Griffith expires. The heroine, clutching only her diary, then makes good her escape in a convoy of pigs, a satirical comment, perhaps, on her recent human companions.

While principal photography of *What?* got underway at Carlo Ponti's villa, Polanski and the cast moved a few miles south and took up residence as Ponti's guests at the San Pietro di Positano, one of the best-appointed hotels in Italy, if not Europe. The main building was hewn out of the jagged cliffs overlooking this idyllic stretch of the Amalfi coast. Hugh Griffith would remember 'incredible evenings . . . out on the terrace with Polanski', who would sit at the head of a long, elegantly set table 'with the sea crashing below and the sun setting, talking about the great film we were all going to make.' Griffith and his co-stars were repeatedly exhorted by the 'dashing Roman' to 'excel, be superior, be the best.' After a long night of dining and sipping the local wines, Polanski would rise at dawn, take the lift to the hotel's boathouse at the foot of the cliff and waterski at breakneck speed to the set, pulling up at the jetty in a plume of spray. For Griffith, whose last role had been in the campy Vincent Price vehicle *Dr Phibes Rises Again* ('so low-budget, I bought my own tea in the canteen'), it was all an unheard-of luxury. 'One never really realises how special these moments are until they're gone,' he noted wistfully. 'We were presumptuous to assume this magic would somehow rub off on the film.'

But Griffith's subsequent 'shock and disappointment' at *What?* didn't entirely dispel his professional respect for Polanski. 'Given the script, I thought he did a remarkable job. If you look at the scene where the old man begs to be allowed to feast on this beautiful girl's body and then dies, it's actually very moving. What a lesser director would have treated as porn, turns out in Roman's hands to be visually creative – that final shot of the old boy through Sydne's legs – poetic and sad.' (One respects his opinion.) Rome's performance in the film as a whole would be better than some had feared, but without a jot of star quality. To fulfil her purposes as *What?*'s heroine, it was enough that she appear in the nude.

With an enthusiastic cast and, belying their reputation, a singularly energetic Italian film crew, Polanski was able to bring in *What?* on budget and ahead of schedule. It enjoyed a mixed reception at its pre-release screenings. At least one of Carlo Ponti's associates felt that Mastroianni gave a rather overstated performance as a 'sex pervert with a whip'. The same critic, while admiring the fluidity of the film overall, worried that there were certain scenes where Polanski's 'formal technique' appeared to desert him, leaving the camera to 'flop around [like] a newly hooked fish'. The most frequent criticism was that Polanski's and Brach's screenplay failed to achieve a strong single effect: because the girl wasn't convincing as a character, her various trials didn't elicit much, if any reaction from the viewer. Other advance critics cited the script's 'faulty organisation' and 'lack of unity'. It was 'aptly named . . . The whole thing calls out for an editor.' *What?* was eventually published in hardcover by the Third Press in New York. One noted literary reviewer remarked that 'the book [was] so bad, I set fire to it in the garden.' The film got a similar mauling, perhaps because people knew Polanski could do so much better.

After a hurried edit and with the addition of some largely perfunctory music, *What?* was rush-released in December 1972. One of the myths is that it was an unmitigated commercial failure. It was a flop in terms of Polanski's expectations; otherwise it did respectable business for an art-house release. There was one notable exception, however. *What?* was a Christmas blockbuster in Italy, with long lines initially forming outside every cinema showing it, one of the principal reasons Polanski decided to settle in Rome for the next three years.

The voluntary exile certainly didn't 'ruin' him in Hollywood, as *Time* thought it might, but it didn't help his cause either. Into many of the reviews there crept a new and more aspersive note, the gist of which was that Polanski had 'flipped'. Quite apart from the damning evidence of *What?*, there was a widely held perception that there was now a 'daytime Roman' and a 'night-time Roman'. The former was a hard-working, resourceful, somewhat austere and utterly dedicated artist who could be relied on to finish the job, if not always strictly on schedule. The latter was a gregarious and generous host who also happened to be 'just this side of a sex addict'. His appetites in this particular area are worth mentioning once again, if only because they so obviously defined him at all times when he wasn't actually on a film set, and once or twice even then. Hugh Griffith would recall 'Roman's tendency to leer at every girl that went by on the terrace' at San Pietro, quite often followed by an appreciative remark about her 'great ass'. In Griffith's vivid account, the director once appeared for dinner with two attractive guests, both in transparent blouses – 'breasts bobbing like melons under cellophane' – and '*still* ogled every woman who walked past'.

Back at his new Roman villa on the via Appia Antica, rented from the Countess of Warwick, Polanski had a fat old housekeeper named Olga, a valet, Guiseppe, a live-in maid, two full-time gardeners and a cleaning lady. With his staff's assistance, he entertained at occasional large parties. To one of these came not only Warhol and his entourage, but also, visiting from Paris, one of the few former leading lights of the *nouvelle vague* with whom Polanski had maintained an at least civil relationship. A mildly curious thing apparently happened after this particular dinner. Everyone had gone but Polanski, his house guests and the distinguished visitor from Paris, the last of whom allegedly noticed 'among all the glittering decanters and punchbowls' on the sideboard 'several opened bottles of Polish plum brandy'. He had long had an old recipe that called for just this ingredient, but could 'never find any of the stuff back home', and so asked Polanski whether he could have these remnants. 'Take them,' he said. The Frenchman was not a little surprised, a day or two later, to receive a bill for the brandy, although, as he conceded, it may well have been submitted not by Polanski, who was rarely if ever less than a gracious host, but by his housekeeper, in the visitor's assessment 'a dragon [who] ran the place like a Jewish mama'.

Yet against Polanski's alleged parsimony, which may have been isolated to this one guest, there was his almost eccentric lack of interest in money. An English actor employed on *What?* remembers that 'Roman blithely admitted how he hadn't a clue about stocks and shares, could just about balance a chequebook, and had to be forced to attend business meetings of any kind.' While cash continued to rain down from rentals of *Rosemary's Baby*, Polanski himself had collected and spent the final instalment of his $150,000 fee four years earlier, and 'hadn't the least interest' in attempting to sue for a better deal. Even with Carlo Ponti's regular financial transfusions, Caliban Films was barely breaking even. Another colleague on *What?* once 'heard Roman note cheerfully that he had $5,000 cash and a further $5,000 in personal "guarantee payments"' from Ponti's Compagnia Cinematografica, and that this had to get him from June to September. Because it was impossible to listen to Polanski for long without wanting to impart financial advice, his friend had said something responsible about how he had $10,000 to last him a quarter. 'I don't know whether it's going to last me until Monday,' Polanski said. Every available cast and crew member on *What?* speaks of their director's personal generosity, and willingness to sign the biggest bill without a second glance.

What? was formally released in North America on 3 October 1973, although it had escaped on to a few college campuses and other select venues in the course of the previous summer. Robert Evans watched it with some friends in his lavishly furnished home cinema, which also featured the world's largest seamless screen, at 21 feet wide, to enjoy the full majesty of the subsequent 'horror . . . the worst film I [had] ever seen'. One of those present at Evans' preview remembers that '*What?* eventually seemed to lose interest in its story, though not before we did . . . The general consensus was that the movie had nothing to say, and was a bit too cleverly titled for its own good.'

When *What?* opened commercially, the critics, some or all of whom seem to have come out of morbid curiosity, were as one with Evans. 'The decline of any talent is painful to watch,' wrote Rex Reed, a friend of Tate and another of those said to have narrowly missed Manson's assassins in August 1969. 'But the decline of Roman Polanski is doubly excruciating because it has been accomplished with so much glee, so much pomposity, and so much public nose-thumbing that it seems almost like a calculated exercise in self-destruction.' After a lengthy and factually flawed retelling of Polanski's 'Holocaust and Manson double whammy', the Los Angeles *Review* noted perfunctorily that 'the film stinks. The acting is ghastly, and the much-vaunted nudity was better in *Macbeth*.' Because *What?* was directed by Polanski, it wasn't completely without interest, however. There was grudging acknowledgement of the movie's one real twist, the Sydne Rome character waking up to find herself trapped in a replay of the previous twenty-four hours, which would wittily anticipate the much-praised plot of *Groundhog Day* twenty years later. But without word of mouth or the organisational machine of a major studio behind the film, audiences stayed away: there was a 'volley of clanging seats [and] derisive glee' at the West Coast premiere, after which *What?* quickly transferred to the 'speciality', or porn circuit, where, retitled *Roman Polanski's Forbidden Dreams*, it would appear on a double bill with *Eager Beavers*.

It's worth dwelling on *What?*'s disastrous reception in the US and to a lesser degree Britain, if only to show how close Polanski came to being washed up in 1973. Most filmgoers and reviewers still thought of him, to the extent that they did so at all, in terms of the Manson saga. Neither of Polanski's projects since then had set the box office alight, and he was generally considered difficult, if not, as Victor Lownes said, a 'son of a bitch' to work with. He was also fast approaching 40, an age at which his friend and hero Orson Welles had already made not only *Citizen Kane*, but *The Magnificent Ambersons*, *The Stranger*, *Macbeth* and *Othello*, among many others. While some of these had been less than enthusiastically received by the critics, each had had an impact as great as *Rosemary's Baby*, Polanski's one and only film so far to enjoy a sustained sale outside of Los Angeles and New York. As Welles himself observed, 'In our business, not to have made it by 40 is to be remembered as a certified moron.'

So one can see how much in the balance Polanski found himself in the first week of May 1973, when Jack Nicholson rang to say that there was a script he 'simply had to read', and in which Paramount was investing $6 million. This was followed by a call from Robert Evans himself, who confirmed that the project, *Chinatown*, was his for the asking. It's not clear to what degree Evans balanced his aversion to *What?* with his sympathy for Polanski personally, or whether he simply felt the director of *Rosemary's Baby* was the best man for the job. On the surface of it, the two films would seem to have little in common except for their quasi-rape scenes (offstage in *Chinatown*) and pervasive nihilism, the 'bad guys' prevailing in both cases. Nor was Polanski in any particular hurry to return to Los Angeles, which he had left amid some acrimony in December 1969. On the other hand, there was the long-awaited challenge of working with

Jack Nicholson, and someone had to pay for the villa on the via Appia Antica, which was costing Caliban Films $3,000 a month.

Reviewing Ingmar Bergman's 1957 *The Seventh Seal*, Polanski wrote admiringly that it had 'levels of complication . . . Bergman seemed to follow the principle that anything too easy to grasp is flat and boring. His remarkable talent was that he could leave his audience with the feeling that if they hadn't fully grasped the complications, it was their fault. Whatever one didn't understand, one gave the director credit for.' It was a maxim Polanski applied sixteen years later when he sat down with Robert Towne at a booth in Nate 'n Al's, the Beverly Hills delicatessen, to discuss the script for *Chinatown*.

Towne was then 38, and specialised in turning out long, densely plotted screenplays that touched on the moral ambiguities of the times, most recently the navy drama *The Last Detail*, whose tart dialogue (the movie sailors for once cussing like their real-life counterparts) contributed to a quintessential Jack Nicholson performance. The writer had been at work for two years on *Chinatown*, which he regarded as the best thing he'd ever done, if a touch on the 'layered' side. To cut to the heart of its intricacy, the story basically follows the misfortunes of Evelyn Mulwray, a mystery blonde with a past, and the modestly prosperous private eye J. J. Gittes (Nicholson) in Thirties Los Angeles. Their mutual adversary is Noah Cross, Evelyn's father and rapist and the head of a labyrinthine scheme to divert water from agricultural areas to the city's burgeoning real-estate development. *Chinatown* is Raymond Chandler's penchant for complex high-low conspiracies writ large. What takes it beyond the level of a routine homage is the ending, in which, instead of a stock resolution, Evelyn, trying to escape with her child, is shot through the back of the head. Cross then wraps his tentacles around his screaming daughter-granddaughter and carries her off, with Gittes impotently standing by, in what the *New York Times* calls 'one of the more unregenerate moments in American film'. (This part of the screenplay was all Polanski's.) A baffling plot and an incomprehensible lingo seem to be de rigueur in a film like this, but *Chinatown* is no mere exercise in style, and manages to break free of much of the noir convention. It has startling, funny and brutal moments, sometimes all in the same scene. For a supposedly 'dark' film, it's gorgeously photographed. It's long, deliberately paced, but never boring. The characters are never too busy playing hard-boiled to be thoroughly believable. *Chinatown* deals with events that supposedly happened some thirty-five years in the past.

Nearly as much time again has gone by since the film's original release, but it remains as fresh and vivid today as ever.

When he sat down for lunch in the delicatessen, Polanski told Towne that, while 'all for a bit of obscurity', his screenplay was both an hour too long and needlessly convoluted. It was also in need of a new 'moral'. In the original version, of which Towne was fond, Evelyn shoots and kills Cross and makes her escape with their incestuous child while Gittes diverts the police. Polanski pronounced the script as a whole 'undisciplined' and requested that a 'shorter, simpler' rewrite be ready by the time he returned from Rome a month later. That meeting proved only a partial success. Towne's next draft was even longer than his previous one. At that stage, Polanski took the lease on a millionaire bachelor's pad on Sierra Mar Place, roughly a ten-minute journey across Benedict Canyon from Cielo Drive. The futuristic, split-level house, craning out over Beverly Hills like a hippie Berghof, had a waterfall, a swimming pool and a spacious, glass-walled living room where Polanski and Towne worked together eight hours a day for the next eight weeks. On some days, there would be a 'full' and 'mutually rewarding' meeting of minds; on others Polanski would mutter, 'Just fucking *do* it, Bob,' and that concluded the creative exchange. Towne was said to have taken umbrage on occasion at the director's 'superior' attitude and particular 'vision' of *Chinatown*, which led him to question not only the core plot structure, but individual lines, words and – more than once – punctuation. As well as changing the ending, Polanski also wanted to have the Gittes and Mulwray characters go to bed together. Then, to 'give [the] whole thing focus', he insisted that they discard the script's 'sideshows and subplots' and instead limit the action to the detective's point of view. When, as a result, tempers sometimes frayed at Sierra Mar Place, Towne took to disappearing down the canyon road for long walks with his sheepdog. Polanski resumed his flying lessons at Santa Monica airport.

Despite such occasional artistic differences, Towne was reportedly impressed by Polanski's talent, in particular his ability to cut through to the heart of any given scene. 'This woman is drowning between two men,' he once remarked of the Mulwray character, in a typically deft precis. He would also entertain his audience, when this included visitors from Paramount, by suddenly breaking off from the script in hand to deliver a monologue on the current Watergate crisis, or to perform 'side-splitting' impersonations of Hollywood bigwigs. According to a studio executive named Bud Crowe, 'You couldn't spend an hour with Polanski without learning something new, or laughing yourself hoarse.' With a characteristic combination of scholar, philosopher, raconteur and night-club comedian, 'Roman and his script conferences were among the hottest tickets in town.' Crowe's response to Polanski wasn't unusual. 'He really had the ability to charm and dominate, and in the end you forgave him the rest.' Towne, for his part, continues to call his uncredited co-writer on *Chinatown* 'my very good friend Roman'.

With the script agreed and Orson Welles' old cameraman Stanley Cortez on board, Paramount asked a casting director named Mike Fenton to go up to Sierra Mar Place and 'see what the crazy Pole had in mind'. Fenton found the director 'delicately wired' and 'temperamental', but nonetheless 'fun to work with'. Jane Fonda turned down the part of Evelyn Mulwray, so they settled on Faye Dunaway, 32, hot off her supporting role as Lady de Winter in Dick Lester's slapstick interpretation of *The Three Musketeers*. Dunaway appeared for the comparatively modest fee of $50,000. Polanski had once played host to the actress at the Villa Mandorli and notes ruefully that 'I knew her well, or thought I did.' With Nicholson signed as the male lead, the grand old Hollywood titan John Huston agreed to play Cross, and Burt Young, the future omnipresent brother-in-law in the *Rocky* series, was Nicholson's client and sidekick Curly. Polanski himself was hopelessly miscast as a thug with a knife.

According to Mike Fenton, 'When shooting began, that part still hadn't been cast . . . I remember one night the production van brought a dozen hopefuls out on location to meet Polanski. Roman didn't even read them. Ten minutes later, the van turned around and took them back home again . . . Polanski looked at me and said, "Let's have some fun with it. *I'll* be the guy with the knife," which one somehow gathered had been his plan all along.' The subsequent cameo, reminiscent of Polanski's role in *Two Men and a Wardrobe*, provided one of the most notorious scenes in the film, and another milestone down the road to his becoming, in the *Review*'s words, 'Hollywood's favourite psychopath'. Confronting the Nicholson character as he clambers over a fence, a familiar-sounding voice yells, 'Hold it!' Nicholson turns, and a moment later finds an elfin man in a white suit shoving a switchblade up his nostril. There is a spurt of blood. As Nicholson collapses, Polanski informs him, 'Next time you lose the whole thing. I cut it off and feed it to my goldfish.'

Principal photography of *Chinatown* began on 28 September 1973, the hottest early autumn day on local record. It was ninety-six degrees when the cast assembled in an orange grove outside Pasadena for the first set-up. A 'jittery' Polanski emerged from his chauffeured car, vomited, and set to work. Although the temperature dropped appreciably over the next week the production was to prove agonisingly slow, even for a film that consciously paced itself. Polanski eventually concluded that the fault lay with Stanley Cortez, the 64-year-old cinematographer whom he found 'full of old-fashioned charm' but 'completely out of touch' with post-war technological developments. On the ninth day of the production, Cortez was fired. In his place Polanski hired John Alonzo, a supremely self-confident individual and a comparably brisk cameraman and bit actor who had played a memorable cameo in 1960's *The Magnificent Seven*. With Alonzo's help, *Chinatown* would be the second film running that Polanski brought in ahead of schedule.

Cortez's abrupt departure appears to have aggravated certain members of *Chinatown*'s crew, who were already labouring under Polanski's regimen of early starts and long, arduous workdays. One particular technician, who prefers anonymity, admits to his having been a 'boat rocker' who subsequently tried to organise a petition against the director, specifically his habit of calling for continual takes, if necessary 'well past official hours'. Such a protest seemed to strike at the heart of the question, common to many film sets, of who exactly was in charge. When Robert Evans heard of this, he allegedly called the disgruntled employee into his office one evening and offered him a choice. 'Do you want to tear up your contract, and take a hike,' he was asked, 'or make up with Roman?'

Confronted by the alternative, the man asked how he could frame his apology.

'Just go up to him and say, "Mr Polanski, I'm sorry. I'm an asshole."'

That seemed to work.

BURT YOUNG NOTICED how 'Polanski always directed you with the Big Picture in mind. For instance, you might say, "My character should lose it and break down in tears here," and Roman would say, "No, that's not consistent with what he does a week down the road."' The opening shots of *Chinatown* call for Young to shuffle through some photographs of his wife caught in flagrante with another man, a delicate scene made even more challenging by the logistics of 'organising guys with cameras and mikes running around, getting, with incredible difficulty, the exact amount of light to show through the blinds, lining up the props and cuing in Nicholson, and here I am, basically saying, "What's my motivation?" ... And Roman, in the midst of this war zone, didn't only sit down and explain it to me – he could already see how it related to the end of the movie, weeks in the future.' Polanski could always do two things at once, and was in his element. Back on location one day, Young watched as 'Roman entertained my 4-year-old daughter, posed for photos and generally behaved like the sweetest guy in the world. He was a regular Santa Claus.' Still 'smil[ing] like a neon sign', the director leant over to John Alonzo so that nobody else could hear him. 'Let's fucking roll 'em,' he instructed his cameraman. 'I'm on a schedule here.' Alonzo remembered being 'struck' by the deftness of the performance; 'Roman was so tough [and] yet could keep up that act.'

Robert Evans was the ideal producer for Polanski, a man to talk with hours at a time about the most minute and technical aspects of filmmaking, and then unwind with 'champagne and blondes', their other mutual passion, at the weekend. Evans' associate producer 'Doc' Erickson was present for many of these sessions. 'Working with Polanski wasn't easy,' he confirms. 'You were always exhausted and, like Bob, he didn't suffer fools gladly.' But, for Erickson, 'Roman was also the consummate professional. Although there were God knows how many – thirty-five? forty? – takes of some shots, you always felt that Polanski was closing in on what he wanted rather than just flailing around. There were no extravagances. If anything, he was trying to atone for some of the excesses of *Rosemary's Baby*.' The great character actor Roy Jenson plays the oafish Mulvihill, the 'fat' to Polanski's 'lean' in *Chinatown*, and as such the man who subdues Nicholson during the nose-slitting scene. Jenson similarly speaks of his director as a 'taskmaster' who 'did everything for the film'. In his account, 'John Alonzo was a great cameraman, and an asset to the movie. He was also an arrogant SOB who called everyone, "Hey, you." The second or third time he tried it on me, Roman cut the action, got up from his monitor, walked across the set to a spot immediately in front of Alonzo and said, "Do you realise this man has to stand here and *act* now? For a living? Please do him the courtesy of learning his name."'

After such minor teething problems, everyone settled down to a prolonged shoot that eventually involved nine separate southern Californian locations as well as extensive use of the Paramount lot. Back in his home cinema, Bob Evans watched the first few days' rushes and fired off a memo to his boss Charles Bluhdorn, promising him that they had a 'hot one'. What was more, it was 'original'. *Chinatown* may have started out like a technicolour remake of a Thirties melodrama, but, as

Evans noted, it 'took the clichés of detective movies and applied them to something real'. For one thing, Polanski wasn't afraid to strategically slow the action, which, like good sex, 'savoured the build-up' and 'delayed the outcome'. Some of Jack Nicholson's best scenes are those in which 'nothing' happens: when he's forced to sit and wait for an interview with a city bureaucrat, for instance, we wait with him; there's not a wasted second. From time to time, Polanski returns to *Chinatown*'s opening device and freezes the screen into a still photograph. And, in a refreshing break from Hollywood artifice, Nicholson agreed to play more than half the movie with a bandage clamped on his nose 'like a sanitary pad', because, as Polanski convincingly argued, 'that's what would happen in real life'.

Chinatown also just conceivably benefitted from a series of in-jokes and related visual puns. 'One of the secrets of the movie,' Nicholson says, 'is that there was a kind of triangular offstage situation. I had just started going out with John Huston's daughter, which the world might not have been aware of, but it actively fed the moment-to-moment reality of my scenes with John.' Polanski ensured that the one day on which Anjelica Huston visited the set was the day on which her father's character asks the detective, 'Mr Gittes, are you sleeping with my daughter?' After a suitable pause, Huston continues, 'Oh, come on. You don't have to think about that to remember, do you?'

In another personal connection to the material, Polanski cast a Hollywood boutique owner named Jack Vernon, the man who had sold him the green Teddy-boy jacket he wore at his wedding, in a supporting role. Although only briefly on screen, he would be on the receiving end of the film's most quoted line, later said to have 'cost it the Oscar'. Vernon plays the warden of an old people's home, where Nicholson appears on the pretext of enquiring about a place for his father. He has just one question about their admissions policy. 'Do you accept people of the Jewish persuasion?' 'I'm sorry, but we don't,' Vernon replies. 'Don't be sorry,' Nicholson says. 'Neither does Dad' – not only 'good for a belly laugh', Vernon recalled, but 'actually saying something pertinent'. There appears to be a running joke, too, foreshadowing what will happen to Evelyn Mulwray at the film's climax. The camera follows a car's broken left-rear light; Polanski shows a pair of watches, the left one crushed; the left lens of a murder victim's glasses is smashed. Robert Towne recalls that it was 'something Roman and I consciously played with as the movie went along', culminating in the scene in which Evelyn's left eye is shot out by the police. At least one observer concluded that this represented Polanski's 'final artistic revenge' on his leading lady, who had 'drive[n] him nuts' over the previous three months. In his memoir, the director captions a particularly gruesome photograph of the scene with the words, 'Farewell to Faye Dunaway'.

Many column inches have been devoted to Polanski's own cameo as the impish, knife-wielding tough. According to Roy Jenson, who played opposite him in the scene, 'Roman did it explicitly because of Sharon Tate. He wouldn't let another actor handle a shiv if he could help it. No one else was ever going to play that part.' In the final credits, Polanski's role would be listed as 'Man with knife', a sly allusion, apparently, to his first feature film. Some time after *Chinatown* wrapped, Jenson 'bumped into Roman and jokingly asked, "I wonder what's become of that punk with the knife?" Polanski smiled and said, "Oh, he's off screwing virgins somewhere in Mexico."'

Jack Nicholson at his most svelte was perfectly cast as Gittes, his gable-arched eyebrows and smirking grin bringing the lightest touch to the heaviest material, and doing his own stunts to boot. But even he occasionally chafed under Polanski's regimen, described by a crew member on *Chinatown* as 'combin[ing] amazing technical ability and psychological insight with a wee bit of sadism'. One evening there was a particular basketball game that Nicholson, a long-time fanatic for the sport, wanted to watch on television. It also happened to be a night when Polanski was trying to film a complex scene that required the actor's undivided attention. Nicholson kept sidling back and forth between his trailer and the set, all the while cursing 'the little bastard' who, true to form, continued to enthuse 'Fandastic, fandastic' at the conclusion of each take, followed by the inevitable 'We go again.' Eventually Nicholson walked off to his mobile dressing room and simply refused to return. Polanski ran after him and, in a distressing scene, 'grabb[ed] a heavy mop and tried to smash the TV set . . . The trailer was so small, I couldn't get a good swing at it. The set went dead, but the spectacular implosion I'd hoped for didn't occur. I clouted it again, smashing it beyond hope of repair. "Know what you are?" I yelled as I swung at it. "You're a fucking asshole!" Then I took what was left of the set and hurled it out of his dressing room.' Although Nicholson replied with some choice words of his own, peace was restored when, later that night, the two men found themselves waiting in their cars immediately adjacent to one another at a light. Nicholson glanced over and muttered the words,

'Fucking Polack.' 'Struck by the comedy of the situation', Polanski laughed; Nicholson laughed back and they drove off again the best of friends.

Or did they? Although some sort of scene certainly occurred, it may be another of those anecdotes in the director's memoirs that seemingly expand to fit the space available. Given that he was writing more than ten years after the events in question, Polanski also shows commendable powers of recall for the smallest detail. He writes, for instance, that the traffic light in question was on Marathon Street, which runs immediately south and east of Paramount studios, whereas his and Nicholson's houses were both to the north-west. While by no means impossible, it would have been an unorthodox route by which to start their journeys, always presuming that they were driving home. Polanski also notes that the contentious basketball game was between the Los Angeles Lakers and the New York Knicks, that it took place on a Friday, and that it was so finely balanced it went into overtime, a key factor in detaining Nicholson from the set. The two teams played twice in the autumn of 1973, at the time *Chinatown* was being shot. The first game was on 2 November, a Friday, and the second on 20 November, a Tuesday. The former ended in a 106–91 win by the Knicks, who went on to take the latter by 105–89. Neither game went into overtime. It's possible that Nicholson's bad mood was as much a result of his home team's performance as it was of Polanski's behaviour.

Whatever the truth of Polanski's relationship with Nicholson, it was to seem idyllic compared to the director's war of attrition with Faye Dunaway. After eight feature films, this was his first real experience of the sort of Hollywood superstar for whom 'roads are straightened [and] petals strewn at their feet', to quote a *Chinatown* colleague. (Dunaway, it should also be noted, was and remains a fine actress and a model of endurance in an industry that tends to jettison its leading ladies in early middle age.) There was reportedly an incident early in the production of *Chinatown* in which Nicholson, in a characteristic prank, saw fit to relieve himself in a paper cup. Exasperated by some professional misunderstanding between them, Dunaway allegedly threw the contents into Polanski's face. 'You cunt, that's piss!' he observed. 'Yes, you little putz,' Dunaway replied.

Generally speaking, Dunaway seems to have been irritated as much as anything else by Polanski's reluctance to discuss the 'motivation' of her character with her. Although explicitly clear about the least technical detail, he generally left such questions of interpretation to the individual actor or actress. When Dunaway forcefully repeated the point to him, Polanski is said to have replied, 'Motivation! I'll tell you motivation! All the money you're being paid to do it. That's motivation.'

All this was but a prelude to the scene in which, in a bid to keep the day's production on track, Polanski leant over and extracted a rogue hair from Dunaway's head. In the subsequent eruption, Dunaway referred to her celebrated director as a 'motherfucker' and retreated to her dressing room to summon her agent Freddie Fields. According to a knowledge-able source, the actress' subsequent list of demands was 'long – very long'. It included the specific stipulation that the 'little putz' be replaced on *Chinatown* by a film-maker more congenial to herself. Polanski, for his part, readily admitted to Fields that 'I was wrong to do it', but then rather spoilt the apology by adding that his client was 'nuts'. At that, Dunaway delivered another expletive-laden monologue, including some medical advice to Polanski that 'Doc' Erickson characterises as 'not very practical'. Although filming eventually resumed, Erickson recalls that 'for a while, Roman directed Faye by turning to Freddie Fields and saying, "Tell Miss Dunaway to do this . . ." and Faye in turn would say to Fields, "Ask Mr Polanski what my character does now."' In a notice-ably bitter review of her experience on *Chinatown*, Dunaway would say that 'What [Polanski] did to me throughout the film bordered on sexual harassment.' She also made note of the director's tendency to dally socially with young, compliant 'chicks'. For some years afterwards, Polanski referred to Dunaway as '*meshuga*', the Yiddish for 'crazy, foolish or clinically insane'.

NEARLY A YEAR AFTER HE FIRST READ ROBERT TOWNE'S SCRIPT, Polanski was still rewriting the final scene of *Chinatown* the night before he shot it. Sensing the 'necessary tragedy' of the Dunaway character's death, he insisted that this was one film 'where the good guys *can't* triumph in the last reel'. Towne, who graciously conceded the point, later referred to Polanski's unique vision of the ending as 'the tunnel at the end of the light'. The writer adds that, at the time, he assumed that 'for Roman, that was life – beautiful blondes always die in LA. Sharon had, just years earlier.' It's arguable that the 'catharsis' of the Manson murders was to be found here rather than in *Macbeth*. As the villainous Cross walks off into the night, the detective, and by extension the audience, are left as helpless bystanders. In a crisp five-word summation of the injustice of it all, a colleague leads Gittes away with the attempted consolation, 'Forget it, Jake. It's Chinatown.'

Thanks to both hard work and the good fortune of having the head of the studio as a producer, Polanski was able to bring in *Chinatown* six days ahead of schedule and only a 'few thousand dollars' over budget. For the most part, post-production proved equally smooth. Polanski and Sam O'Steen, the editor who deftly cut *Rosemary's Baby* to half its original length, managed a similar feat on *Chinatown*, which they condensed into 130 minutes. In its final version, the film would be perfectly pitched between intricate and coherent. It's also superbly economic; there are no long expositions, and the backstory is given away by minute degrees. There is not a superfluous frame.

On a whim, Polanski then commissioned some 'all-American' music from 38-year-old Phillip Lambro, an army veteran turned composer known for his rousing, percussion-driven marches. Lambro's soundtrack for *Chinatown* proved a disappointment. Although Polanski was prepared to honour the commission, Bob Evans stepped in to replace Lambro with Jerry Goldsmith, whose doleful, jazzy score proved the perfect accompaniment. Some weeks later, Evans gave an interview in which he claimed that Polanski had hired 'a rinkydink friend' to write the music and that he, Evans, had been forced to intervene. The director was 'brilliant if channelled properly', he added. Just as it had on *Macbeth*, Polanski's friendship with his producer was strained to the breaking point. In the thirty-three years since *Chinatown*'s release, he and Evans have yet to work together again.

According to Evans' subsequent memoir, everyone apparently thought that after the out-of-town previews of *Chinatown* they had an expensive flop on their hands. Polanski himself modestly considered the film 'not bad', if still a 'bit long . . . It seems never-ending'. Speaking to *Première* magazine in April 1995, the director gave a colourful account of *Chinatown*'s first screening for Charles Bluhdorn, the head of Gulf+Western, at which Evans had turned up the air-conditioning in his private cinema in a failed effort to keep Bluhdorn awake. (According to another Paramount executive present, it was a 'strangely depressing' experience. For once, there had been no buffet or bar; instead, Bluhdorn occupied 'a sort of raised throne' in the rear, while the other guests seated themselves in the front two or three rows, where they reclined 'almost horizontally' for a view of the screen, their backs, awkwardly, to the most powerful man in the room.) This may be another pardonable lapse of Polanski's memory. Eleven years before his *Première* interview, he had told the same story about Bluhdorn and the air-conditioning, only this time the screening had been of *Rosemary's Baby*.

Chinatown opened in North America on 24 June 1974, and became one of the summer's commercial hits alongside the likes of *Papillon*, *Blazing Saddles* and the first in the *Death Wish* franchise. A few reviewers got crabby, making it a point to knock the film by denouncing Polanski's own role in it as an 'unsavoury thug' who 'lowered the tone' of this 'hideous experiment in self-direction'. Paying customers, meanwhile, lined up around the block to witness the result. The film was to be equally popular, if critically disdained in Western Europe and elsewhere. In time there were particularly harsh words spoken about *Chinatown* behind the Iron Curtain, where it was released as йхрюияйхи йьюпрюк some three years later. The Paramount clippings file contains an amazingly acid criticism from one of the Polish newspapers, every sentence of which indicates that the reviewer was a fellow Lodz graduate driven almost to madness by envy of Polanski's wealth and success.

Like *Rosemary's Baby* before it, *Chinatown* would also come to be recognised as part of the revolution in film-making that took place in the late Sixties and Seventies, when a few visionary directors managed to break free of their audiences' long-held expectations about what a movie should feel like, and specifically that it deliver the requisite happy ending. That *Chinatown* managed to be forward-looking while simultaneously evoking an era more than thirty years in the past only adds to Polanski's achievement. The traditional cinematic structure, the old tricks and conventions that even a Welles had employed, was being undermined by a small number of restless, television-savvy figures tunnelling along their own separate routes from several different directions. Their work was continuing and the repercussions from it were beginning to be felt, with once 'alternative' themes becoming mainstream. (Even five years earlier, it would have been hard to imagine a conglomerate like Gulf+Western underwriting a project whose plot twist concerned the incestuous relationship between a father and his daughter.) Arguably the two titles to have done more than any others to advance the process were 1967's *Bonnie and Clyde* and 1969's *Easy Rider*. In a chronological, logical progression, each film contributed a star, Dunaway and Nicholson respectively, to *Chinatown*.

ONE OF THE REASONS POLANSKI'S DARK VISION worked so well in *Chinatown* was that it touched on a world that had gone wrong. In Britain that winter millions sat, belted and shivering in unheated offices and factories, waiting out a miners' strike and the tripling of oil prices. The United States had been brought to a virtual civil war by Watergate and the ignominious departure of White House aides accused of perjury, deception and fraud, culminating in the president's own resignation just six weeks after the film's release. It's admittedly unlikely that many Americans consciously decided to drive out to their local mall to watch the film because of its supposed allegorical insights into the culture. But it would be fair to say that Polanski's themes struck a nerve. According to the critic John Parker, *Chinatown* 'presented a metaphorical view of a [country] where nothing was ever what it seemed', and thus captured its times 'just as *Blow-Up* had done in another way in its sardonic view of Swinging London'.

Chinatown was nominated for eleven Academy Awards at the ceremony held on 8 April 1975, and failed to win ten of them. Polanski lost in the category of Best Director to Francis Ford Coppola for his *Godfather* sequel. Nicholson and Dunaway were beaten by, of all people, Art Carney and Ellen Burstyn respectively. *Chinatown*'s sole success of the evening was Robert Towne for his screenplay. It is arguable that Polanski might have shared the award. Leaving the Los Angeles Music Center, Towne found himself in a car with Jack Nicholson, Bob Evans and Anjelica Huston, and had to 'practically hide his Oscar under the limo seat', the actor recalls. Polanski himself was apparently skiing in Gstaad, and so sent regrets. He also failed to attend Faye Dunaway's celebrity-studded wedding to the rock singer Peter Wolf, always presuming that he was invited. The director did, however, bank not only his *Chinatown* fee, reportedly $300,000, but, for the first time ever, the all-important profit percentage points, earning himself a tidy annuity for life.

AT LEAST ONE CURRENT MAGAZINE PROFILE has praised Polanski for his 'uniformly excellent taste in films', with their 'instantly recognisable throughline [in] terms of themes, obsessions and characters'. In the Sixties and Seventies, however, his career rarely made the mistake of consistency. As recently as 1995, the director told *Positif*, 'I always immediately react against the work I've just done.' Over a six-year period that had also seen the Manson murders, Polanski's CV had included a memorably deranged Dracula spoof, a satanic-cult blockbuster, a faithful adaptation of Shakespeare, an ill-advised excursion in soft porn and the definitive Thirties thriller. In the same vein, he followed

Chinatown not by another Hollywood spectacular but by directing Alban Berg's opera *Lulu* at an arts festival held on the cobbled streets of Spoleto, outside Rome. Berg's piece had caused a sensation on its pre-war debut, where the performance was interrupted by a rioting public seemingly inflamed by the composer's anti-fascist sentiments. Polanski's adaptation failed to stir comparable emotions, although there was what he calls a 'typically Italian pandemonium' about the preparations. On the day before the premiere it was apparently found that all the scenery was still in Milan, and the stage resembled a building site. That was at least one account; but the accounts are as various and confused as the muddles they claim to describe, and the only certainty is that Polanski earned a standing ovation, followed by numerous offers to direct operas around the world.

ONE MORNING EARLY IN 1975, William Hobbs, the fight director on *Macbeth*, was asked to call in for a drink at West Eaton Place Mews. An 'excited' Polanski wanted to discuss a 'rollicking adventure-comedy' that he and Gérard Brach had been writing in the villa on the via Appia Antica. Self-explanatorily, it was called *Pirates*. Jack Nicholson was to be the lead, and Polanski himself would play a character named 'The Frog'. Hobbs listened to an outline of the plot and then asked how many fights there were in it. 'It's one long fight,' said Polanski, with a chuckle.

Unfortunately, the same could have been said of the film's business negotiations. Andy Braunsberg and Jean-Pierre Rassam, *Pirates'* original producers, both fell prey to drug use and a corresponding tendency to procrastinate on the project. Shortly after *Chinatown*'s release, the 32-year-old mogul Barry Diller had taken over Robert Evans' job at Paramount, with a brief to increase revenues by a minimum of fifty per cent over three years. Diller reportedly liked the script of *Pirates* but blanched at the estimated $14 million budget. Eventually, Polanski put together a deal with United Artists, though here, too, there were to be issues. The studio wanted the director, who had already bought a sixty-foot barge and several smaller craft in order to simulate the pirates' manoeuvres in Los Angeles harbour, to personally put up a 'completion guarantee' to insure them against any cost overruns. Moreover, they had no intention of letting Polanski act in his own movie. According to the studio memo, he was to assemble instead a 'hugely talented cast of recognised stars'. Polanski was thus forced to make enquiries of Dustin Hoffman, who turned him down, not 'car[ing] to play second banana' to Jack Nicholson. Meanwhile, Nicholson himself, who had recently enjoyed another skiing holiday with Polanski in Gstaad, was steadily raising his fee from $750,000 to $1 million and upwards to appear in *Pirates*. Not long after receiving the actor's final demand of $1.5 million (and $50,000 a day in overtime) Polanskiput the whole project on hold, where it remained for the next ten years.

ALTHOUGH SEVERAL STUDIOS had been clamouring for another commercially attractive 'packaging' like *Chinatown*, they cooled appreciably once Nicholson was out of the picture. After two Oscar nominations, a Golden Globe and at least six festival awards, Polanski, as he remarked to a sympathetic John Huston, was 'still knock[ing] at Mr Goldwyn's door'. The Hollywood consensus was that, while talented, he needed 'handling' – as Robert Evans had said of his experience on *Chinatown*, 'It takes guts to be a producer, and eventually Roman realised I was right all along.'

Mirroring his career frustrations, Polanski appears to have also been reassessing his life in Rome, where he had now been based for three years. The voluntary exile had begun happily enough, as a welcome antidote to his ordeal in post-Manson Hollywood. The via Appia Antica house that Polanski shared with Gérard Brach, Andy Braunsberg, the Caliban Films crew and a domestic staff of six was one of the most luxurious in Rome. Complete with its own vineyard and swimming pool, the estate was set in a walled, nine-acre park that struck one visitor as 'like a model village'. A charming, old-world sleepiness hung over its winding lanes and tree-lined driveways, unpaved and posted with a 5 kph speed limit. The whole place struck the visitor as 'unnaturally quiet' by day, although Polanski maintained his hectic nightlife. In his early forties, he still appeared singularly fit and boyishly energetic. A woman now called Valli Pfohl briefly knew Polanski in Rome, where she remembers him as a fixture both on the floor of the Il Matriciano club and at the local cinema a door or two away. 'He actually adored watching films,' Pfohl says, not universally the case with directors. At the end of one 'exemplary' evening on the town together, she teasingly asked Polanski whether he always tried to get a date to go to bed with him.

'I used to,' he said. 'I don't anymore.'

There was a moment's pause as a 'thin smile' played on his lips.

'To be quite honest, sometimes I do.'

For all its charms, however, Polanski was apparently growing weary of life in Rome by the middle of 1975. For one thing, Andy Braunsberg had acquired an 'attractive but unstable' American girlfriend who moved in with him on the via Appia Antica. The couples' increasingly violent rows, perhaps exacerbated on Braunsberg's side by drug use, would frequently rattle the villa roof. Although Polanski himself was largely abstemious, pot, LSD and on occasion heroin circulated freely among his immediate circle. Meanwhile, liberated by the 'communal vibe', Caliban's once superbly formal chauffeur, Armand, had discarded his suit and cap in favour of jeans and a tie-dyed T-shirt. In short order he was calling his employer 'Roman' and 'swagger[ing] around Rome and London', telling people that he was a producer. Armand's fall from grace was complete when he first seriously damaged Caliban's Rolls and then somehow misplaced their other car, a Ferrari.

A more general threat to Polanski's welfare was to be posed by the Red Brigades, the militant leftist group founded by students at the University of Trento whose operations soon expanded into Rome. The Brigades' manifesto in March 1975 claimed that their goal was 'a concentrated strike against the heart of the state, because the state is an independent collection of multinational corporations.' Later that year, the Rome Brigade issued its supplemental 'guide to the working class', a six-point document paving the way to the 'Marxist-Leninist ideal' that specifically included the kidnapping and torture of 'prominent foreign capitalists', among whom, presumably, were the residents of Lady Warwick's sumptuous hilltop villa. Having already had bitter personal experience of Manson's programme of 'urban guerilla warfare' Polanski was understandably wary of its latest mutation. His fears were well grounded; the Red Brigades are said to have ultimately committed some 14,000 acts of violence, most notoriously the murder of the former Italian prime minister Aldo Moro. Not long after two members of the Rome judiciary were shot dead in a restaurant around the corner from the via Appia Antica, Polanski left the city and took the lease on an apartment on the avenue Montaigne in Paris.

On 2 October 1975, Polanski placed a phone call to Barry Diller, the chairman and chief executive officer of Paramount. In another tribute to his formidable powers of persuasion, he hung up twenty minutes later with a mutual commitment for him to direct the film version of Roland Topor's novel *Le locataire chimérique* (retitled *The Tenant*), which the studio happened to own, and which Diller reportedly budgeted at a modest $2.2 million. Punishingly faithful to the source material, Polanski's and

Brach's screenplay was a return to the contemporary horror of *Repulsion* and *Rosemary's Baby*, with which *The Tenant* forms a loose trilogy.

Trelkovski, a Polish émigré to Paris, rents a rundown apartment, whose previous tenant, Simone, has attempted suicide by throwing herself out of the window. We are party to no more information than that, but Polanski, within the first few moments of the picture, signals to his audience that this is to be another case of identity breakdown, the camera catching a face that turns from Simone's into his own peering out from behind the curtains. In time, Trelkovski, too, descends into a Kafkaesque world where nothing is quite what it seems. In the course of the film, he has several bizarre interviews with his landlord, obsesses over some mysterious Egyptian hieroglyphics in the lavatory, extracts a tooth from the wall and, dressed in drag, sits by his bedroom window outside which a ball bounces up and down, gradually coming to resemble his own head. (As a Paramount memo notes of *The Tenant*, 'it's not Walt Disney'.) When, like his predecessor, Trelkovski prepares to leap to his death, the building's other occupants stand at their windows, which have become theatre boxes, and applaud.

In an inspired piece of casting, Polanski himself played the unhappy tenant. Although Trelkovski's behaviour was 'self-destructive', the director noted, there was 'plenty there', and several levels of disaffection, he could relate to. 'In Paris,' Polanski told the New York *Daily News*, 'one is always reminded of being a foreigner. If you park your car wrong, it is not the fact that it's on the sidewalk that matters, but the fact that you speak with an accent.' As someone who saw himself as a permanent alien, there was little in his portrayal of Trelkovski that required the Method approach. Polanski was not only currently living in Paris, but had inhabited just such a grungy, one-room walk-up when he had first come to the city in the early Sixties. 'I know that atmosphere of the [French] apartment building,' he noted, 'with the twin menaces of the concierge on the ground floor and the landlord upstairs.'

A co-star in the film is the tenement itself – notionally located at 19 rue de Calais in the Pigalle district but actually built, at a cost of half a million dollars, on the stage at Épinay studios. In order to make the facade look twice as big, Polanski had his crew lay a vast mirror flat on the ground outside the front door. Conversely, the director of *Knife in the Water* knew just how important physical confinement can be. Trelkovski could never have held our attention had he lived in a house. His crackup is that of someone whose nights are spent cooped up in a small flat, with neighbours, landlords, muffled voices behind closed doors, and garbage in the stairwell. Put him in a 'contemporary American home', as Paramount had suggested, and it would have been just another sitcom.

The female lead in *The Tenant* was 21-year-old Isabelle Adjani, who had won rave reviews in Truffaut's *The Story of Adele H.* With Diller's help, Polanski was able to recruit the veteran American character actors Melvyn Douglas, Jo Van Fleet and Shelley Winters, the last of whom played the concierge. Winters arrived in Paris looking 'pig fat', she cheerfully allowed. Polanski reportedly told her that there was no problem, since he saw her character as 'not innately attractive'. Winters saw the humour in the remark and later referred to 'my all-time god, Roman', high praise from an actress who had worked with the likes of Howard Hawks and Stanley Kubrick. In February 1978, at a time when many of those performers who normally flock to a cause were suddenly remembering pressing appointments elsewhere, Winters would continue to loyally call Polanski her 'hero'.

The Tenant was shot, edited and released at wild speed by today's standards: Polanski signed his contract in late October 1975 and the film was premiered at Cannes on 26 May 1976, just seven months later. Unfortunately, the same undue haste applies to Trelkovski's mental collapse, which takes place in an abrupt gear change midway through the picture. There would be none of the suggestive characterisation of, say, Martin Scorsese's *Taxi Driver*, another film to debut at the same festival.

Although his pacing is off, Polanski does successfully capture the tone and assorted petty indignities of Parisian apartment life, and *The Tenant* contains some of his most arresting images: the hospital scene, for instance, where Trelkovski meets the grotesquely injured Nicole, bandaged almost to the point of mummification, a look that may have been drawn from his memory of visiting Krzysztof Komeda on his deathbed. ('He had tubes up his nose and down his throat. His head was shrouded. His eyes were open but unseeing.') Trelkovski himself while in drag looks disturbingly like David Bowie in his *Space Oddity* phase. There are many other vivid set pieces in *The Tenant*, which generally confirms that claustrophobia is to Polanski as the frontier is to John Ford. The screenplay is not only literate, but with an absence of cliché unusual in suspense films, and with some good satirical jokes. Hitchcock had brought a roughly similar style to 1954's *Rear Window,* another psychological thriller set in an apartment building which approaches the most hideous subject in the most deceptively matter-of-fact way.

The Tenant was nominated for the Palme d'Or at Cannes, although Polanski remembers his experience there unhappily. After the events of 1969 he had ceased virtually all contact with the press, or at least that part of it he described as 'the sewer'. Although he made an exception for *Macbeth*, he no longer liked to do promotion, rarely stopped to chat or sign autographs and found the festival atmosphere as a whole oppressive. One writer who did briefly meet Polanski in 1976 says that 'It really was like pulling teeth. At that stage, I still didn't know what Roman thought of me ['a fink ratbag', he discovered later], but it was pretty clear that he would rather have been elsewhere. He hate[s] people like us.' Reciprocally, *The Tenant* was widely reported as a failure – one of those 'honourable' failures, however, that rather endear a director to his critics, at least some of whom acknowledged that it had had the thankless job of following *Chinatown*. Several reviews helpfully pointed out that the film might have solved the problem of making the mysterious – almost preposterous – Trelkovski convincing by letting his insanity emerge gradually over the course of the two hours. Instead, the *Today* correspondent wrote, 'it's all weird and intense and a bit spooky. But, unlike *Repulsion*, it's also completely unbelievable.' *The Tenant* was released in the summer of 1976 and did only modest business. For its North American premiere the Paramount PR department came up with a memorable tagline, if one that was to prove mildly unfortunate a few months later. It ran, 'No one does it to you like Roman Polanski.'

SEVEN YEARS EARLIER, after being detained at the airport and effectively deported from Italy, Polanski had impetuously decided to apply for British citizenship. He subsequently changed his mind and decided to become a Frenchman. Although he appears to have then forgotten about the whole thing and continued to travel the world on his new Polish 'consular' passport, his return to Paris in 1975 finally settled the issue. Polanski's naturalisation papers were issued the following August, in the week of his forty-third birthday. 'I was born French,' he noted factually. Yet no matter how hard he tried, even the self-made cosmopolitan couldn't undo what twenty-six years' residence had done for him. 'I'll always be Polish,' he confirmed a year or two later, 'although I try and distance myself from what's happening there.'

There was a 'squat, female' concierge at the avenue Montaigne, too, but in all other respects Polanski's new home, part of a modern, seven-storey block just off the Champs-Élysées, was a marked improvement on

Trelkovski's. As well as hosting his normal quota of overnight guests, the director was subsequently invited to be a judge of that year's locally staged Miss Universe pageant. At least one critic would later note that this was perhaps ill-advised. Polanski may have also seen something of Mia Farrow, who had continued to be a loyal friend since *Rosemary's Baby*.

Early in October 1976, Polanski flew to Munich to direct the Bavarian State Opera's production of *Rigoletto*. The commission was all the more striking since he had never seen the piece performed, a 'state of innocence' he considered vital to the success of the enterprise. On his first night off from rehearsals, he went out on a double date with a German arts critic and two young women. After the familiar round of dining and dancing, the four found themselves in Polanski's luxurious hotel suite, part of his package deal with the opera's organisers. The director took one girl to bed and the arts critic took the other. Some time later, Polanski walked out into the sitting room to find that the critic had gone home, leaving his date, who had introduced herself only as 'Nasty', sprawled in an armchair. Doing the gallant thing, he invited Nasty to join his girlfriend and him in bed, which she did. Her real name, Polanski learnt, was Nastassia Kinski. An aspiring actress, she shared a birthday with Sharon Tate, to whom she bore a passing resemblance. Kinski was, however, only 15.

AFTER HIS SUCCESS WITH *RIGOLETTO*, Polanski decided to spend Christmas with his father and stepmother in Krakow, his first time on Polish soil in nearly fifteen years. Fog forced his plane to divert to Prague, where he rented a car and drove east through the same border crossing by which he had left in 1962. It was a generally happy reunion. After a sentimental visit to Wysoka, where he had sheltered from the Nazis thirty-three years earlier, Polanski collected his friend Renek Nowak and spent several hours walking around Krakow's market square. Over the next few days, he circulated through his home town and seemed delighted, unlike his recent practice, to pose for pictures and sign his name on scraps of paper. When he saw someone he recognised, his face, in one newspaper account, would 'flash up'. Polanski would stride over, ungainly in his haste, and blurt out a name. 'Our Tad,' he'd say. 'How goes it?' He'd put his arm around Tad's shoulder. 'How *are* you?' Polanski's charm offensive both revived old contacts and made new ones. Even at potentially awkward moments, as when one elderly man asked him solemnly, 'What have you been up to then, lad?', he kept his good humour.

After leaving Krakow, Polanski spoke to an audience of between four and five hundred at the Warsaw film club. Here the atmosphere seems to have been noticeably cooler. Polanski began the proceedings by announcing that, instead of making a speech, he would answer the audience's questions, which he was confident would be 'very personal' and 'very mean'. Sure enough, several eager young men leapt up one after another to enquire why Polanski had 'gone west' and 'sold out'. 'Well, I can see how worldly *you* are,' he snapped back at one of them. 'And I was prepared to take you for a bunch of provincials.'

Just before leaving for Paris, Polanski gave an interview to Janusz Glowacki for the prestigious weekly magazine *Kultura*. The director began by complaining about his grilling at the hands of certain 'surly' audience members at the film club. Glowacki listened politely, and then asked a red-faced Polanski his first question. 'Why did you leave Poland?'

'Why did Erich Von Stroheim leave Germany?' Polanski said. 'Why did Hitchcock leave England? If you were a director you'd like to work in Hollywood, too. Now go ahead and ask me if I'm still Polish. You people keep asking me this question. You want Polish artists to make it in the world, but when they do, you accuse them of treason.'

Tactfully changing the subject, Glowacki asked the director whether he considered himself successful.

'I never made a film which fully satisfied me,' Polanski said.

'Why?'

'If I knew, I'd make it.'

'Do you think you'll find out making *Pirates*?'

Polanski reddened again. 'You treat commercial films as treason,' he said, 'but millions of people want to see them.'

'But what do *you* want?'

'I want people to go to the movies. I am the man of the spectacle. I'm playing.'

Rue Saint-Hubert, Paris. Number 5, Polanski's first home, is part of the 1930s apartment block on the left.

Krakow's Wawel Castle, the historic centre of the town and headquarters of the occupying German high staff 1940–44. Bula Polanski worked here as a cleaning woman shortly before being deported to Auschwitz.

A group of refugees, seen wearing arm-bands which identify them as Jewish, flee Krakow by horse-drawn cart in the last days before the imposition of the ghetto, March 1941.

A young Polanski. 'Charismatic, trim, boyish, [with] a vaguely feral air ... A brilliant monologuist and never a martyr to false modesty'.

The cover of *Time* magazine of 20 September 1963, showing a still from *Knife in the Water*. Although Polanski affected not to care, it was the ultimate media accolade for the young director.

Polanski dancing with the actress Françoise Dorléac at a Paris nightclub in early 1964. The relationship would rarely be as warm once they came to film *Cul-de-Sac* the following year.

Polanski's London home at 95 West Eaton Place Mews. The quintessential sixties bachelor pad was furnished with a coffee table consisting of a nude female mannequin on all fours supporting a sheet of glass. On the mantelpiece were two busts, one of Napoleon, the other of Polanski himself.

Polanski's wedding
to Sharon Tate on
20 January 1968 was
the event of Swinging
London, although the
various receptions
that followed reminded
one guest of nothing so
much as 'the cattle-call
for some transvestite
Broadway revue'.

The newlyweds at the 1968 Cannes film festival. The occasion ended in some disarray when several jurors and guests organised a boycott in solidarity with the rioting students in Paris. Polanski was to remark of his fellow directors Jean-Luc Godard and François Truffaut, 'they are like little kids playing at being revolutionaries. I've passed through this stage. I was raised in a country where these things happened seriously.'

A heavily pregnant Sharon Tate shortly before her death.

Charles Manson, whose campaign of urban guerrilla terror, or 'helter skelter', was supposed to have started a race war – leaving himself as the world's sole authority.

Shaven-haired Manson 'family' members sit outside the courthouse and speak with reporters during his trial for murder.

Eight days after the Manson atrocities, Polanski visited the murder scene and allowed himself to be photographed sitting on the front porch, immediately in front of the white door still daubed with the word 'PIG' in his wife's blood.

Polanski and *Playboy* publisher Hugh Hefner announce their production of *Macbeth* in the summer of 1970. Hefner was eventually called on to advance a further $500,000 to keep the troubled film afloat.

Shooting some 'castle footage' for *Macbeth* on location in Northumbria.

Princess Anne attended the film's British premiere, reportedly because of 'all the riding sequences' involved. 'I hated them,' Polanski told her in the receiving line. 'I'll never make another film with horses in it.'

In an iconic scene from *Chinatown*, Polanski slits open Jack Nicholson's nose. According to the actor Roy Jenson, seen on the right, 'Roman did it explicitly because of Sharon Tate . . . He wouldn't let any other actor handle a knife if he could help it.'

Polanski outside the Santa Monica courtroom, just after having been sentenced to 90 days' 'evaluation' in a California jail.

Superior Court Judge Laurence J. Rittenband, 71, the enigmatic figure who presided over the Polanski case. The judge was not pleased when his prisoner – then already in London, en route to Paris – failed to appear for his final sentencing.

43 Avenue Montaigne, just off the Champs-Élysées, where Polanski fled in February 1978. It remains his home thirty years later.

CHAMBERS OF
The Superior Court
1725 MAIN STREET
SANTA MONICA, CALIFORNIA 9040:
LAURENCE J. RITTENBAND, JUDGE

February 1, 1978

MEMORANDUM

TO: Mr. Roger Gunson
         Deputy District Attorney

FROM: Judge Laurence J. Rittenband

SUBJECT: Roman Polanski case

Please instruct the District Attorney's investigator to make an effort to try to locate the whereabouts of Polanski and report to me the details of what was done to locate him.

                              L.J.R.

LJR:ah
cc: file

With Nastassia Kinski at the
Cannes festival, promoting *Tess*.
The subsequent press conference
consisted of reporters bawling
questions at Polanski about his
being an 'escaped convict' among
his other 'legal problems.' 'I have
no problems,' he assured them.

Polanski played a very plausible
Mozart in both Polish and French
productions of Peter Shaffer's play
Amadeus. He had less success with
the film rights.

Pirates. Although Polanski (stage centre here, acting out a scene for the cast) 'gave my blood' for the film, it sank without trace at the box office. The real star of the show was the larger than life-size galleon the *Neptune*.

Emmanuelle Seigner, who co-starred in 1988's *Frantic* despite relatively modest prior experience. 'Jean-Luc Godard told me I could make it big in pornography', the actress later recalled. 'He reckoned I had a great ass.'

By then married to Polanski, Seigner in a scene with Peter Coyote in *Bitter Moon*.

Although Polanski (here on location with Johnny Depp and the city mayor) had big hopes for *The North Gate*, the film was plagued with a variety of production problems. It ended in a lawsuit.

Polanski, watched by Adrien Brody, lays a wreath at the Warsaw Ghetto Memorial during production of *The Pianist*.

On location of *The Pianist*. As usual, the director was also frequently his own props man, and personally 'did the blood' for the most graphic scenes.

Just short of his seventieth birthday, Polanski became the oldest person ever to win the best-director Oscar. Prudently declining to return for the ceremony, he later accepted the award from Harrison Ford at the American Film Festival in Deauville.

Ever the visual perfectionist, adjusting his wife's dress on the red carpet in Venice.

Polanski, still in the saddle in his mid-seventies. As he has said, 'I am the man of the spectacle. I'm playing.'

CHAPTER 7
THE TRIAL

Back in Paris, Polanski was ready to cash in on his fame. The 'new Hollywood' had become a mecca for gritty, character-driven dramas whose 'superbly hirsute' directors, as Orson Welles called them, could command million-dollar salaries. All around him, Polanski saw Scorsese, Coppola, Friedkin and De Palma in some cases 'literally nam[ing] their own price'. Why not him? After his latest 'worthy flop', as he sardonically called *The Tenant*, Polanski acquired a new, powerhouse Los Angeles agent, 40-year-old Sue Mengers, and signed a contract with Columbia to adapt and direct Lawrence Sanders' cop thriller *The First Deadly Sin*. Polanski's combined fee was to be $625,000, and in all probability he would have earned it. The film's star was Frank Sinatra, who was making a comeback after the ill-fated production of *The Detective* in 1968. His leading lady was Faye Dunaway.

As a sideline, Polanski had also accepted a commission to guest-edit the Christmas 1976 issue of *Vogue*'s French edition. Its central pictorial was of Nastassia Kinski, who, presumably in homage to the becalmed *Pirates*, was seen on a beach in the Seychelles being borne away by a swarthy buccaneer, among other vaguely nautical set-ups. To complete the assignment, a photographer named Harry Benson took a picture of Polanski buried up to his neck in sand with the waves breaking over his head – a popular form of eighteenth-century capital punishment, and one the director ruefully compared to his real-life ordeal over the next fifteen months.

In the end, *Vogue* decided not to use Benson's photograph. However, Polanski's alluring shots of Kinski, with whom he had begun a brief but intense affair – sometimes giving what a guest calls 'children's parties' for her, at which he gamely (and, it should be stressed, innocently) tried to mix with her friends, some of whom were as young as Kinski – were a stunning success. His guest-editorship of *Vogue* led to a meeting with Gerald Azaria, the editor of the magazine's brother publication *Vogue Homme*. While eminently respectable, this particular title was pitched less at the fashion conscious per se and more at an audience of men between the ages of 21 and 45 primarily interested in photographs of scantily clad women in exotic locations, and subjects such as sports, films, television, cars, crime and alcohol. Anyone familiar with today's *Maxim* or *FHM* magazines, with a more 'arty' veneer, can readily picture the format. Polanski told Azaria that he would accept a commission to photograph 'several adolescent girls' around the world in order to 'show them as they really are', which he defined as 'sexy, pert and thoroughly human'. By 'adolescent' the director meant 13 or 14 years old. Azaria reportedly jumped at the idea. The promise of 'Illustrations by Roman Polanski' was one guaranteed to instantly attract both readers and advertisers to his production. Nor was this merely one of those cases, not uncommon in the arts, of the talented man who longs to be acclaimed for something else. Polanski's interest in still photography went back at least as far as 1955, when, as part of his first year's course at Lodz, he had accumulated a highly regarded portfolio of 'eighty or ninety' stylised black-and-white pictures. Most were of street scenes, the elderly or nude girls.

Before flying to Los Angeles to begin work on *The First Deadly Sin*, Polanski had dinner with Henri Sera, the would-be singer who had briefly installed himself first at the Santa Monica house and then Cielo Drive in 1968–9. Sera had the 'perfect candidate' in mind for Polanski's photographic spread of pubescent girls. A year earlier, the two men had been in a Sunset Strip club called On the Rocks, where they met a pleasant-looking woman in her mid-thirties who told them that she wanted to be an actress. One subsequent, though unproven version was that the woman, named Susan, had come on to Polanski, complimenting him on his after-shave and generally signalling how positively she would react to any romantic overtures he might choose to make. The director later informed a state-appointed investigator that she had been 'trying to get an agent'. At some stage in the proceedings, Sera had learnt that the woman also had two daughters. He was currently dating one of them, and suggested her younger sister for Polanski's magazine layout. Her name was Samantha Jane Gailey. She was 13 years old.

Polanski and his supporters would seek to put his subsequent action in its 'broader context', to quote Shelley Winters, if not excuse it altogether. At what was called the 'sociological' level, the director's conduct was to be seen as a gesture of revolt against the stifling conventions and paralysing inhibitions of the American bourgeoisie, and a blow for swingers everywhere. Such things were 'routinely accepted' in Europe, they argued, and, besides, switched-on young women like Gailey were frequently known to be sexually active by their early teens. There was some merit to this twin defence. Just weeks earlier, Nastassia Kinski had happily introduced Polanski to her mother, who appears to have been in no doubt about the nature of her daughter's relationship with the man twenty-eight years her senior, in order for the three of them to discuss the young actress' career prospects. This was the 'mature, Continental' approach later applauded by the *New York Times*. Gailey herself, furthermore, wasn't quite the naif sometimes portrayed. In her Grand Jury testimony, she noted that she had had sex twice in the year before she met Polanski, that she had been drunk, and that 'yeah, once I was under the influence of Quaaludes when I was real little'. However precocious, Gailey, it should also be noted, was a seventh-grade schoolgirl who 'had a Spider Man poster on the wall and kept pet rats', she recalled in a magazine interview. Born on 31 March 1963, she was fully four years under the age of consent then required by the state of California. Polanski was later asked by the district attorney how old he had believed Gailey to be when he met her. 'She was 13,' he said.

In trying to assess the overall reporting of what followed, we have to acknowledge that, in the case of Roman Polanski and the media, both parties had 'form'. That the director enjoyed the company of young girls was no newsflash. Since Tate's death eight years earlier he had consciously shied away from women of marriageable age and instead concentrated on 'chicks' – 'for fear of betraying Sharon's memory', he told a reporter. For its part, the press had a history of gleefully pouncing on Polanski's 'gladiatorial' love life, which they couched in headlines like the *Globe*'s 'MAGNETIC POLE' or 'the babe and the beast'. Particularly in the mid-Seventies, certain tabloid correspondents, then going through one of their cyclical fits of patriotism, seemed to actively enjoy the opportunity to denounce a foreign-born director or actor in their midst. If, like Polanski, he appeared to be singularly unapologetic for his crimes, the stage was set for high drama.

The widely disseminated story of Polanski's behaviour in February and March 1977 has it that he not only accepted a dubious assignment to take salacious photographs of underage kids, but that to do so was unprecedented in the annals of modern civilisation. This account requires correction. Appearing just two years after Jodie Foster's Oscar-nominated performance as a pre-teen hooker in *Taxi Driver*, Paramount was busy touting its 'searingly graphic' period drama *Pretty Baby*, celebrating the relationship between a 12-year-old girl and a middle-aged photographer who insinuates himself into her home, which happens to be a brothel. In broadly similar vein, the 11-year-old actress Eva Ionesco, whom Polanski cast in *The Tenant*, had just controversially graced the pages of the Italian edition of *Playboy*. The pictures in question were taken by the child's mother. Meanwhile, another glossy Condé Nast publication named *Vogue Beauté* had gone on sale in late 1976 with the 14-year-old Doushka Petit splashed inside in a series of erotic poses, and had quickly become the most successful issue in the magazine's history. In the UK, there was a perennial vogue, at its peak in the Seventies, among magazines as diverse as *Tatler* and *Penthouse* for models in their mid-teens shown in a variety of unorthodox schoolgirl uniforms. Even the august editors at *Life* had seen fit to commission a lavishly illustrated article enquiring into the current popularity of 'the nymphet'. Questionable as some or all of these projects were, they lend weight to Polanski's claim that the strictly artistic part of his assignment from Azaria was 'nothing new'.

AT AROUND 2 P.M. ON 'BLOODY SUNDAY' FOR POLANSKI, 13 February 1977, the director left the Beverly Wilshire Hotel, where he occupied a penthouse suite across from both Steve McQueen and Warren Beatty, and drove down Highway 101 to his appointment at the Gailey family's small, nondescript house in the western Los Angeles suburb of Woodland Hills. It was an unlikely setting for an internationally acclaimed Hollywood film-maker in which to find himself. Although Woodland Hills has subsequently enjoyed something of a renaissance, for much of the Seventies it was a shabby, predominantly Hispanic-American neighbourhood whose civic highlight was a 'Dynamite Chile Cook-off' contest each September, and whose one surviving cinema was currently showing the late Bruce Lee's *Enter the Dragon* for the third straight year. To add to the incongruity, Polanski, who was driving a silver Mercedes, had recently received the first six-figure instalment of his fee from Columbia for *The First Deadly Sin*. As well as having a major film in development, he was busy on a number of related fronts. Over the previous week, Polanski had had no fewer than eight sessions with his new agent, had met individually with his accountant, lawyer and real-estate broker, and was actively negotiating with the immigration and naturalisation authorities to obtain a coveted 'green card', which would have allowed him to continue to live and work in the US while retaining his dual Franco-Polish citizenship. There were some grounds for optimism that his application would be granted. Just as in mid-1969, immediately before the Manson horror, Polanski had ample cause to be cheerful as he set out that Sunday afternoon.

Once inside the Gaileys' home, Polanski was introduced to 13-year-old Samantha, with whom he was mildly disappointed. She was 'a good-looking girl, but nothing sensational', of about his own height and with an unexpectedly husky voice. Photographs of Gailey at the time show a slim, sandy-haired child with a passing resemblance to an extremely young Diane Keaton. Though her gruff tone and generally unresponsive manner didn't bode well, Polanski walked back outside to his car and returned with a copy of the Christmas issue of *Vogue*. The Gaileys duly admired his glossy photographs of Nastassia Kinski. The district attorney would later imply that this had been a ruse by Polanski, designed to persuade the family that Samantha could expect similarly glamorous results. 'We have this man,' the court was told, 'coming in, showing an elaborate, slick paper magazine – Paris *Vogue* – with beautiful photographs of beautiful girls and scenery and background. Photographs with beautiful settings and backgrounds, almost like a movie setting . . . Mr Polanski shows these articles and this issue of *Vogue* to the family and asks if their daughter, who he has been told is 13 years old, would like to be photographed for a future article in that same magazine. [She] agrees, and Mr Polanski comes back at a later time, and there is a photo session at that time. And, looking at the photographs, they are not near to the type or quality that was shown to the family originally.'

The following Sunday, 20 February, Polanski returned to Woodland Hills, armed with cameras and film. Thirty years later, there are still differing versions of what precisely happened next. Polanski's own some-time claim to have been the victim of an elaborate mother-daughter 'sting' can, perhaps, be dismissed as another piece of self-fabulism. Making what-ever allowance possible, a 43-year-old man who opts to have sex with a 13-year-old girl is, at the very least, complicit in his own downfall. At the same time, there are so many discrepancies, distortions and outright falsehoods in the various accounts of the case that the whole thing has come to resemble one of those morally ambiguous tales like *Rashomon*, only with a modern twist – *The Accused*, perhaps. The version that follows is taken from the mutually accepted facts, as well as Samantha Gailey's grand-jury testimony of 24 March 1977, the unsealed transcripts of

Polanski's subsequent court hearings and the district attorney's report to the trial judge of 5 August 1977, with corroborating evidence from the US Department of Justice, all published here for the first time.

When Polanski returned to the Gaileys' home, he found Samantha waiting for him at the door, wearing a pair of jeans and a patchwork blouse. The girl's mother and elder sister had helpfully laid out a variety of other clothes for her to change into during the photographic session, which he assured them would be 'fun', and last 'at most an hour'. Polanski chose three or four items from the pile, then he and Samantha got in the Mercedes and drove a half mile or so into the hills immediately behind the house. Parking the car, they made their way up a narrow dirt pathway to an isolated spot from which they could look down over the rooftops to the Pacific Ocean. Polanski took some test pictures and, in a bid to relax his subject, started asking her about her home life. Gailey told him that she had a boyfriend with a black belt in karate. Unfazed by this news, Polanski asked her to remove her blouse and change into a shirt that he had chosen for her at the house. After a few further shots, he asked her to remove the shirt. The published photos, he assured her, would be tastefully cropped; there would be no 'boobies', as he called them.

Roger Gunson, the deputy district attorney, later pressed Gailey on this particular turn of events.

Q At any time did you pose without a top?
A Yes.
Q At that time were you wearing a bra?
A No.
Q So you were bare from the waist up?
A Yes.
Q Was that at his request or did you volunteer to do that?
A That was at his request.
Q What did Mr Polanski say with respect to posing without anything on your top?
A He said, 'Here, take off your top now.'*

---

* Polanski writes that, at this stage, Gailey was 'entirely at ease' and 'posed with professional aplomb ... She had nice breasts.' Shortly afterwards, Gailey herself was asked in court why she had failed to mention the topless photos to her mother. 'I wasn't sure if I was going to tell her or not,' she said. 'I was just going to say I didn't want to get any more pictures taken [by Polanski] again.'

Although Gailey fails to mention it, Polanski apparently expressed concern that the light was fading, and that in order to do a 'really professional job' for *Vogue Homme* he would have to schedule at least one more session with her. Around six that evening, he drove his young model back down the hill and delivered her safely to her mother. In their hour together, Polanski had taken two rolls of film, or seventy-two shots, of Gailey. These were later described in court as 'rather below' the technical quality a magazine like *Vogue Homme* would have expected. As the pair were approaching the front door of the house, in a scene oddly redolent of one of Polanski's own films, they passed a 'toothless' man and a woman, 'both apparently in their late seventies or eighties', walking a poodle. Gailey leaned over to Polanski so that the elderly couple couldn't hear her. 'That's our dog,' she said. A moment later she said, 'No, it isn't.' Polanski remarked that it was either her dog or it wasn't. 'It, like, hangs around here,' she told him.

Polanski was invited into Samantha's home, where he sat down in the small front room between Mrs Gailey, who was divorced from both the girl's natural and adoptive fathers, and her live-in boyfriend. The latter revealed that he was on the editorial board of a periodical called *Marijuana Monthly*. Would Polanski help him to arrange an interview with Jack Nicholson, or for that matter take out a subscription to the magazine? Apparently as an inducement, the boyfriend then produced several issues of *Hustler*, which he passed to Polanski for his professional assessment of the 'great photographs of male and female genitalia'. The director expressed non-committal interest in both publications. Samantha herself then reappeared, having changed back into her original jeans and blouse, flourishing a copy of *Playboy* with this 'cool picture' of a girl in a wetsuit on the cover. Again Polanski dutifully admired the layout and then left the house, promising to return for a follow-up session when time allowed. If there were any reservations about their meeting again, they seem to have been more on his part than the Gaileys'.

The next morning, Polanski flew to New York in order to observe the police department at work as part of his research for *The First Deadly Sin*. He stayed in a top-floor suite at the Plaza Hotel, paid for by Columbia. According to the memo, the studio had asked that their director 'be person-ally acquainted with arrests, booking procedure [and] interrogation', since much of the film's action would take place in a Manhattan precinct house. A retired officer named Sol Rizzo was one of those delegated to chap-erone Polanski, and once escorted him to watch an autopsy at the city morgue, where, much to the professionals' admiration, 'Roman stood casually munching an apple'.

Polanski notes that he returned to Los Angeles on 26 February 'after an interval of ten days', although it was more likely to have been the 3rd or 4th of March. In any event, he soon called the Gaileys and arranged for another session with Samantha. Polanski arrived two hours late on the date in question, Thursday 10 March, after spending the afternoon in more 'dreary' interviews with his lawyer and others, discussing his various immigration issues. As a consequence, he was again concerned about the light. According to Gailey, 'He was in a rush. He went, "Let's go. All the light is going to go down. Hurry up. Get your clothes."' In their haste, there was little or no chance to consult with the girl's mother or her partner, the latter of whom was apparently 'sprawled out' in front of the television, still surrounded by various copies of his chosen reading material.

Once on their way, Polanski insists that he told Gailey they were 'go[ing] to Jackie Bisset's place on Mulholland Drive, [which] would make an ideal setting for our pictures.' Gailey denies ever knowing their destination – only that there were 'three guys and two girls' at the house and that she spent an hour there posing for Polanski by the swimming pool while Bisset's friends watched them through a French window. Samantha notes that though she'd omitted to wear a bra for the occasion, the fifty or so photos taken at the actress' residence were all 'straight' – nothing topless – and that she alternated between wearing her best white blouse and a rugby shirt. Polanski then made a phone call to his friend Jack Nicholson, whose home was only a five-minute drive away, to ask if they could continue the shoot there. Nicholson himself happened to be at his ski lodge in Aspen, enjoying an early spring break with Polanski's old flame Jill St John, but his neighbour Helena Kallianiotes, who was house-sitting for him, told Polanski to 'come right over'.

At that the photographer and his young model got back in the Mercedes and drove further up Mulholland to Nicholson's remote hilltop estate. The court was later told that Mrs Gailey had asked to 'accompany the party [on 10 March], and it was Mr Polanski who suggested and who indicated that the mother should not go, because it might inhibit the girl in the photo session.' As noted, he had also extracted his subject from her home with pronounced speed, after expressing concern about the light. There is some further evidence that the conversation took a distinct, and critical turn while the couple were in the car on their way up the canyon road. Polanski is reported to have asked Gailey whether she was 'still a virgin and [if she] knew anything about masturbation'. The idea, according to the district attorney, was that the subsequent act was 'almost planned', a 'sexual atmosphere' having been established some time in advance of the criminal offence. This partly contradicts Polanski's own version of events, in which Samantha herself had volunteered some information about her love life, and he, merely to keep his end up, as it were, had asked her when she first started having sex. 'When I was 8,' she replied.

Once inside Nicholson's mansion, Polanski exchanged shop talk with Kallianiotes, a strikingly attractive, dusky former professional belly dancer and sometime actress who was currently writing a screenplay. Samantha wandered around the property and reappeared to announce that she was thirsty. Opening the refrigerator, which was 'full of juice and wine and soda and all this stuff', Polanski removed a bottle of Cristal champagne and poured a glass for each of the three of them. This was the exact moment when his assignation with Gailey crossed the line from the merely incautious to the potentially criminal, California law making it a specific offence to 'have and accomplish an act of sexual intercourse with a minor, she being rendered temporarily incapable of giving legal consent to the commission of said act by the administration to her [of] intoxicating liquor.' After Kallianiotes excused herself, Polanski began photographing Gailey against the bay window in the living room, with the lights of West Hollywood steadily coming on in the valley below them. Whatever else one makes of the whole affair, it's easy to believe that someone could have chosen that particular spot in which to take pictures. After another sip or two of Cristal, Polanski once again asked his subject to pose topless for him, which she did, playfully holding her champagne glass beside her breasts and generally 'behav[ing] with complete aplomb'.

At Polanski's request, Gailey then changed into a formal blue dress belonging to her sister and walked out on to the patio where there was a pool and jacuzzi. Despite his habitual lack of introspection, the director may have noted the fact that his old house on Cielo Drive, though no longer illuminated by Christmas lights, was only a mile or so away, and still dimly visible, immediately across the canyon. On her way out of the kitchen door, Gailey paused for four or five photos, among them a vivid pose in which she was seen licking an ice cube. Polanski then asked the girl to get into the jacuzzi for him, and at this point she decided to phone her mother. According to Gailey's testimony, 'She went, "Are you all right?", and I said, "Uh-huh." She said, "Do you want me to come pick you up?" and I went, "No."' Polanski then took the receiver and solicitously told Mrs Gailey that Samantha might be late home for dinner. After he hung up, the director went into the bathroom and produced 'this little yellow thing – some kind of container – in [which] he had a pill broken into three bits.' Polanski gulped down one of the pieces, and the girl did the same. The combination of the champagne and the pill, a Quaalude, disorientated her. 'I can barely remember anything,' Gailey told the grand jury two weeks later. 'I was kind of dizzy, you know, like things were kind of blurry . . . I was having trouble with my co-ordination, like walking and stuff.'

Gailey nonetheless undressed and got into the jacuzzi, while Polanski stood on the patio above her snapping more photographs. Again there's some discrepancy between his account, in which Samantha 'continued to move around, spontaneously adopting various poses' and hers, in which the combined effect of the hot water, the tranquilliser and the alcohol had all but stupefied her. According to the grand-jury testimony, Gailey had removed the blue dress but retained a pair of panties when she stepped out of the kitchen door to the pool area. 'I was ready to get in and [Polanski] said, "Take off your underwear." So I did,' she recalled. The prosecutor then asked her about the precise order of the events that followed.

Q At some time did Polanski stop taking photographs of you in the jacuzzi?
A Yes.
Q What did he do after that?
A He said that he was going to get in.
Q What did you see him do?
A He went in the bathroom and he came out and got in.
Q When he came out was he wearing anything?
A No.

At this stage, Gailey appears to have rapidly reconsidered her position. When Polanski 'sat down at the deepest part' of the spacious jacuzzi, the girl 'scoot[ed] up to the other end of it' and ignored his requests to join him. She then feigned an asthma attack convincing enough to have fooled the director, who tenderly put his arm around the girl's waist and helped her out of the water before suggesting that she join him for a dip in the adjacent pool. After swimming a lap, Gailey got out and went to the nearby bathroom to dry off. A moment later Polanski joined her there, asking if she were all right. According to her testimony, Samantha 'told him that I wanted to go home because I needed to take my medicine'. Polanski replied, 'Yeah, I'll take you home soon.' She repeated the request. At that, Polanski 'told me to go in the other room' – a guest cabana, furnished by a sofa and a bed – 'and lie down'.

Gailey was asked what she had done next.

'I was going, "No, I think I better go home," because I was afraid. So I just went and I sat down on the couch.'

'What were you afraid of?'

'Him.'

POLANSKI TELLS US THAT GAILEY then assured him she was feeling better, after which 'very gently, I began to kiss and caress her'. The child's contemporaneous account is significantly different. When Polanski asked her if she felt all right, she replied, 'No'. Asked what happened then, Gailey recalls, 'He reached over and he kissed me. And I was telling him "No," you know. "Keep away."' The next few questions and answers between Gailey and the prosecutor reportedly made at least one of the grand jurors wince. 'It was the moment you realised,' the man was to say years later (thus speaking as a private citizen), 'that she was just, you know, a kid ... Everyone looked at each other, I remember, and I think the general feeling was "That could be my daughter".'

Q After Polanski kissed you did he say anything?

A No.

Q Did you say anything?

A No, besides I was just going, 'No. Come on, let's go home.'

Q What was said after you indicated that you wanted to go home when you were sitting on the couch?

A He said, 'I'll take you home soon.'

Q Then what happened?

A And then he went down and he started performing cuddliness.

Q What does that mean?

A It means he went down on me or he placed his mouth on my vagina.

Polanski omits this episode from his narrative, but notes that Gailey then 'spread herself and I entered her. She wasn't unresponsive.' Gailey again has a different recollection, insisting that 'I was saying, "No, stop,"' and that Polanski had merely enquired whether she was on the pill. On being told she wasn't, he first asked Gailey when she had last had her period and then volunteered 'to go in through the back', an offer she declined. Polanski refers to their having been 'making love'. Gailey's testimony seems to suggest a notably less consensual process, in which Polanski did, in short order, 'put his thing in my butt'.

Gailey was asked whether either party had said anything at that point. 'No.'

'Did you resist?'

'A little bit, but not really because ...'

'Because what?'

'Because I was afraid of him.'

Both sides agree that someone had then knocked on the door and a woman's voice called, 'Roman, are you in there?' At that, the girl had 'frozen', perhaps unavoidably, as she remained pinned face down on the sofa. Polanski went to the door, opened it a crack and muttered a few words. The caller was Anjelica Huston, with whom Jack Nicholson had been conducting an on-off affair. Huston, who had never taken to Polanski, asked him what he was doing there. 'I'm doing a picture session for *Vogue*,' he replied.

Polanski then closed the door, walked back to the couch and continued to sodomise Gailey. After climaxing, he let her up to go into the bathroom, reportedly advising her to 'Clean yourself good.' 'I put on my dress,' Gailey recalls, 'combed my hair and I walked ... I sort of was walking out and he said, "Now, wait for me," but I didn't. I went out. I got my clothes and there was – that woman was sitting there on the phone. And I said hello to her and I just went out and got in the car.'

Gailey sat and cried for the next five minutes, at which point Polanski reappeared and drove her home. He says that they talked about movies on the half-hour journey to Woodland Hills, and that he offered to take Gailey and her family to see *Rocky* the following week. 'My motives weren't particularly altruistic,' he notes. 'It was one way to be sure I'd see her again.'

Polanski accompanied Samantha inside, where he showed the family some of the photographs from their previous session and convivially passed around a joint, before continuing on his way as though nothing out of the ordinary had happened. (Although the director notes that the Gaileys had 'seemed to like' the pictures he showed them, Samantha would later recall that 'jaws had dropped' when her mother and sister first saw the topless shots, and that in the domestic furore that followed the family's dog had 'peed on the floor'.) A member of the district attorney's office would later tell reporters, speaking off the record, that it had been a 'merely routine day for Mr Polanski' thus far: some lawyers' meetings, one or two phone calls and visits to friends, followed by sex with a young girl and, finally, a quiet dinner at his hotel. 'By his standards, that qualified as normal,' the prosecutor remarked. The only hint of impending trouble came later that night when Henri Sera rang to say that Mrs Gailey thought the photographs Polanski had taken of her daughter were 'horrible'. This contradicted the director's own impression. Brushing aside the mother's apparent change of heart, Polanski kept a late-night appointment with Robert De Niro, who was keen for them to work together, and spent most of the next day in meetings on *The First Deadly Sin*. Photography was due to begin in early May, with a final release date in November. Late in the afternoon a friend dropped by with a gift of some Quaaludes for Polanski, who was using them to unwind after his habitual twelve- or fourteen-hour workdays. He had a date that night with his fellow director Frank Simon and some young women, including his current girlfriend, 19-year-old Lisa Rome, with whom he was excitedly planning to see a play and then visit this 'fantastic club' on Sunset Strip where they could enjoy a floor-show and drink complimentary champagne served to them in a VIP box. 'It's like being royalty,' he chuckled.

This was Polanski's mood when, at seven o'clock that Friday evening, he rode down in the lift to meet his friends in the hotel lobby, the very room through which Julia Roberts later sashayed in *Pretty Woman*. Everyone was in high spirits. As the party was proceeding through the exquisitely furnished hallway to the front door, a middle-aged man, rather incongruously dressed in jeans and a bowling shirt, strode up to them and flashed a badge. After apologising to Polanski for the intrusion, he added, 'I have a warrant for your arrest.'

In the lull that followed, the policeman formally introduced himself as Detective Phillip Vannatter. He was a ten-year veteran of the force, whom a former colleague describes as 'the perfect square-jawed cop from Central Casting', and who went on to be the lead investigator in the

O.J. Simpson murder case seventeen years later. Vannatter and three plain-clothes deputies briskly ushered Polanski back into the lift and up to his suite. Three other officers and two representatives of the district attorney's office, bringing the total number of arresting officials to nine, remained behind in the lobby. On their way up, Polanski enquired calmly, 'Is this going to take long?' Vannatter replied that they had a warrant to search his room, and a 'complaint of rape' to investigate. Even that seemed not to shake Polanski's composure, although he did slip a Quaalude out of his pocket and try to discreetly drop it on the floor. One of the officers spotted what he was doing, grabbed Polanski's wrist and relieved him of the pill, which he then put in his own pocket.

Once in the suite, the police took possession of several rolls of undeveloped film, some cameras and a full vial of Quaaludes. Polanski still remained calm, inviting his guests to sit down and politely asking Vannatter, 'What's this all about?' A moment later, one of the officers turned up a sheaf of 'twenty or thirty' photographs lying on top of the sitting-room desk, all of them studies of young girls apparently destined for the pages of *Vogue Homme*. 'That's what we're here for,' he remarked. According to the report, Vannatter then asked 'the suspect', by now rapidly crossing and uncrossing his legs, if he had 'the slightest idea' why he was being arrested.

Polanski's chief emotion was perplexity. 'I honestly don't know,' he said.

One of the officers read Polanski his rights, a procedure he was familiar with from his research for *The First Deadly Sin*, and asked if he would accompany them back to Jack Nicholson's house. They also had a search warrant for the 'crime scene', Vannatter added. Polanski agreed to do so, but asked if it was necessary for all four officers to escort him back down in the lift and through the lobby, since 'everyone will be watching'. They agreed to be discreet. Vannatter, who had been peripherally involved in the Manson case seven years earlier, found himself momentarily sympathetic to Polanski. By now, in an eerily familiar reaction, the director had begun pacing around the floor, muttering rapidly. 'The guy was genuinely astonished,' Vannatter recalls. 'He started talking a blue streak. I tried to shut him up. I told him that anything he said I might have to testify to, if there was a hearing or trial. But he wouldn't listen. He had no idea of what being arrested in America meant.'

Taking two cars, all ten men returned to Mulholland Drive, where Polanski startled his escort by promptly jumping over a wall and opening the gate to Nicholson's house from the inside. After some delay, Anjelica

Huston appeared and agreed to be searched. The police relieved her of a small quantity of cocaine and a bag of marijuana which they found in a chest of drawers in her bedroom. Two officers then sat down to interview Huston in the kitchen, where she reportedly told them that Polanski was 'a freak'. Recalling the events of the previous day, Huston added that she had gone around the house calling 'Roman, Roman!' until she heard noises from the poolside bedroom. Opening the door, she had seen the two of them 'going at it'. Polanski had gotten up and walked over to her, naked from the waist down. 'We'll be a few minutes,' he said.

After an hour's questioning, Polanski and Huston were taken separately to the West Los Angeles station house. Ten years later, the actress recalled, 'I was victimised in the situation. And so was Roman. It was absolutely absurd that I should have been arrested. I still try to figure where the justification for any of it came in.' Polanski told Huston that he felt 'awful' about her getting involved.* Considering the gravity of the charges, and that this was a major metropolitan police station on a Friday night, the atmosphere remained surprisingly congenial. The authorities never handcuffed Polanski, and one of the DAs who accompanied him downtown remarked that he had seen *Knife in the Water* twice; he was a 'great artist'. Someone else asked for his autograph. Perhaps in consequence, the director himself remained singularly composed. In the admiring phrase of a retired law enforcement official present that night, 'he never lost his lunch'. The only note of censure came when, around one o'clock on Saturday morning, Polanski was formally photographed and booked. Staring down at him from his lectern 'like a Victorian judge', the desk sergeant asked, 'What in hell do you think you're doing, going around raping kids?'

Polanski was released on $2,500 bail, and his lawyer, a Wally Wolf, arrived to drive him back to the Beverly Wilshire. By the time they were halfway up Santa Monica Boulevard, every radio station they tried was carrying a newsflash about the arrest. After a hurried conference, the lawyer turned the car around and headed for the home of a hairdresser friend named Maurice Azoulay, who lived in a remote part of Coldwater Canyon. They could lay low there from the press, Wolf said. Listening to the radio reports linking his client to a 'child rape', the lawyer had

* Huston would later agree to testify against Polanski in return for being granted immunity on all charges of drug possession, a decision he concedes left him feeling 'slightly bitter'.

apparently done his best to reassure him, wondering if it would even go to a trial. As they arrived at their destination, Polanski spoke up: 'I'm finished.'

Early the next morning, Polanski hired a highly regarded criminal attorney named Douglas Dalton. Reflecting the unusual nature of the case, their first meeting took place on a Sunday morning and lasted until well past nightfall. Dalton was able to supply some of the particulars of the twenty-four hours that had followed Polanski's departure from the Gaileys' home late on the previous Thursday evening. Samantha, it appeared, had gone upstairs to her bedroom and phoned her 17-year-old boyfriend to tell him that she had been at Jack Nicholson's house, where Roman Polanski had sex with her. It was an implausible story, and the boyfriend seems not to have quite known what to make of it. Later that evening, Samantha repeated her version of events to her elder sister. The sister informed their mother. Mrs Gailey in turn rang the police, to tell them that her 13-year-old daughter had been raped.

After taking a statement, the authorities escorted Samantha downtown to Parkland Hospital. At about the same time that Polanski had been sitting down to talk to Robert De Niro, his victim was submitting to a particularly intimate physical examination. This reportedly revealed minor bruising to the girl's anus, with no sign of vaginal rape. There was, however, 'seminal residue' found in Samantha's underwear. This was enough to bring two representatives of the district attorney's office to the hospital, where they met with the police, Mrs Gailey, her boyfriend and the family's hastily summoned lawyer. While this sombre parade debated how to proceed, Samantha herself walked across the road for a late-night snack at McDonald's.

Polanski would spend the next fortnight holed up at Azoulay's and other friends' houses, much as he had done immediately after Sharon Tate's death. Following his brief, formal arraignment in a downtown courtroom, he had wandered off, apparently in a state of shock, and was found some hours later sitting by himself in a dark corner of the Hamburger Hamlet restaurant on Hollywood Boulevard. Samantha Gailey's grand-jury hearing took place in a closed session of the Superior Court on Thursday 24 March. That same afternoon, the state indicted Polanski on six counts: furnishing a controlled substance to a minor; unlawful sexual intercourse; raping a child whom he had previously intoxicated; committing a 'lewd and lascivious act upon and with the body and certain parts and members thereof [of] a 13-year-old girl';

perversion, by 'copulating his mouth with the sexual organ of the girl'; and an 'infamous crime against nature upon the person of a human being', as the state called sodomy. The offences carried a potential sentence of fifty years.

The news that Roman Polanski had been arrested and charged on a morals rap sent the press into another feeding frenzy. Over the next few days and weeks the prevailing tone of the coverage would rival anything seen in August 1969, with the critical distinction that the media was no longer under any obligation to even pretend to be sympathetic to the director. The more or less factual reporting of the case, with its litany of sexual dramas, was one thing; but the accompanying commentary, editorials, analysis, opinion and hearsay soon turned the story into one of those self-sustaining tabloid serials that appear on the front pages every morning and on the television news every evening. 'POLANSKI THE PREDATOR' and 'NAMES DIRECTOR OVER SEX ROMP' ran two representative headlines in the *Enquirer*. It was perhaps fortunate that these were the days before the internet. Polanski, of course, had also connived in his own image (that of an 'evil, profligate dwarf', as he put it), whatever one makes of the vilification that ensued. Leaving aside his personal appetites, he seems to have had a distinct professional, or aesthetic perspective on the subject. Speaking to *Cahiers du Cinéma* in 1979, Polanski would name three of his 'all-time favourite' films in descending order as being 1947's *Devil in the Flesh*, 1946's *Beauty and the Beast* and 1951's *Forbidden Games*. The first concerns the illicit wartime affair between a married woman and an underage high-school student; the second, at least in its original version, is the arresting tale of a teenage girl who, in order to save her father, sacrifices herself to an ogre; and in the third, a young Parisian waif is taken in by a peasant family, whose son introduces her to a fantasy world. All three films are exquisitely made, and can be innocently enjoyed on any number of levels. If one were to summarise their common theme, it would be the corruption of innocence, and, more specifically, of barely pubescent children.

WITHIN TWENTY-FOUR HOURS OF POLANSKI'S ARREST, the stand-up comedians were competing to crack jokes about him. No one who had access to a television, radio or paper could possibly avoid them. 'Heard the title of the Pole's new film?' Johnny Carson would ask of his *Tonight Show* audience. '*Close Encounters with the Third Grade*.' Reporting on the criminal indictment, the possible sentence and the distinct likelihood of a separate civil suit against him by the Gaileys, *Life* used the cover line 'Polanski in Peril!' Inside, an anonymous friend was quoted saying: 'Roman is afraid this is the end of the line . . . After all he has been through, it seems ironic that he could go to jail for the rest of his life for making love to a girl.'

Smaller things were not going all that well either. Since Polanski could no longer go for his daily run without attracting a crowd of bystanders, he took to exercising alone in a Polish friend's ballet school after the young dancers had gone home for the day. Leaving the premises after one late-night session, Polanski walked out on to Melrose Avenue while still dressed in a black leotard, over which he had thrown a thick-collared sheepskin coat, with a baseball hat pulled far down over his forehead. It must have seemed like an effective disguise. A middle-aged couple reportedly chose that moment to leave a nearby restaurant and walk to their car. As they passed Polanski, the man turned to his wife and remarked matter-of-factly, 'There goes the Hollywood rapist.'

POLANSKI'S CELERITOUS FALL FROM PUBLIC GRACE was fully matched by the reaction from within the industry. Hollywood as a whole had rarely been as united against one of its own since 1921, when, during a wild drinking party at a San Francisco hotel, a starlet named Virginia Rappe was seized by violent convulsions and later died, allegedly after having been sexually assaulted by the 320-pound 'Fatty' Arbuckle. Although acquitted of manslaughter, Arbuckle, a national pariah, was forced to adopt a pseudonym and continue his career in Europe. He died, disillusioned and bankrupt, aged 46.

In a broadly similar backlash, Columbia now informed Polanski that a decision had been made 'not to proceed' with him as director of *The First Deadly Sin*. His own agent Sue Mengers was quoted saying, 'We can't have a rapist in our midst.' As part of their standard contract, every major studio required that their employees 'conduct [themselves] with due regard to public convention and protocol, and not do or commit any act or thing that will degrade or subject [them] to public hatred, contempt, scorn, ridicule or disrepute, or shock or offend the community, or violate public ethics or decency, or prejudice their standing in the community'; the so-called 'morals clause', which had been introduced as a direct result of the Arbuckle scandal. As Polanski himself is said to have ruefully noted, he failed to meet 'almost all' the admittedly 'antiquated' criteria.

Early in April, Polanski moved into a suite at the Château Marmont, the hotel which had been his home in happier circumstances with Tate ten years earlier. One caller found him alone in his room at eleven o'clock at night, 'listen[ing] to some doleful jazz' on the stereo. Seated in a 'huge leather armchair' which seemed to 'swallow him up', Polanski launched into a disjointed monologue which lasted nearly two hours. Three or four other visitors, apparently including Lisa Rome, appeared at regular intervals. Gathered in a semicircle around him, Polanski's guests exchanged troubled glances as he darted from subject to subject, sometimes lucid and logical, at other times veering into seemingly wild conjectures and bursts of anger at 'the people who won't rest until they get me'.

On 15 April, Polanski appeared for a preliminary hearing at the Superior Court in Santa Monica. This was his first encounter with the judge in charge of the case, Laurence J. Rittenband, who was to prove a major presence in his life over the next ten months. A party of teenage schoolgirls happened to be visiting the courthouse that morning and provided a shrill, and somehow fitting chorus, giggling and jeering as Polanski was led in. Theirs were to be by no means the only raised voices heard in and around the drab municipal building that Friday. Extra police had been drafted in to control the surrounding melee of fans, reporters, TV crews and what were described mysteriously as 'dark-suited observers from the Polish government'. Two news helicopters circling overhead contributed to the atmosphere of Colosseum-type frenzy. Amidst the commotion, one enterprising young man stationed himself at the front door, selling T-shirts inscribed with the slogans 'FREE POLANSKI' and 'JAIL POLANSKI'.

Judge Rittenband, having gavelled his court to order, immediately made it clear that the hearing was 'a formality', designed merely to 'read the defendant the bill of indictment'. The proceedings, even so, allowed a brief but vivid precis of the prosecution case, including some of the more graphic details of the alleged rape. At this the court was plunged into spellbound silence, broken only by the noise of a man, denied access to the public gallery, but fully audible from his position in the corridor outside, who shouted 'Bastard!' before being evicted from the premises. The judge himself took a seemingly benign view of Polanski at this stage, renewing his $2,500 bail and even allowing him to travel outside the country 'should he so wish'.

He did. Twenty-four hours later, Polanski quietly left his hotel and flew to London. Even here, however, there were unwelcome reminders of the stigma attached to being the notorious 'Hollywood rapist'. Among the letters awaiting him at West Eaton Place Mews was one from his insurance company, brusquely cancelling their policy on the house. When Polanski subsequently tried to phone the offices of *Vogue Homme* in Paris, nobody there was available to take his call. After several days' delay, he was finally able to arrange a meeting with the man who had commissioned him to guest-edit *Vogue*'s Christmas 1976 issue, Robert Caillé. Caillé told Polanski, 'We've already been questioned by a man from Interpol. He came to ask about your assignment. We said we knew nothing about it.'

It is not impossible to feel sympathy for Polanski as he returned to Los Angeles later that spring, where a small but vocal mob awaited him at the airport. The news coverage if anything now deteriorated, with pages of 'analysis' in broadsheets and tabloids alike, accompanied by endless gossip and reconstructions of the crime as well as the inevitable recyclings of the Manson murders. The fatuous, sententious tone infested all the major reports of the case. Certainly no one appears to have been overly concerned with the concept of presumption of innocence. Polanski and his accuser did not have sex or make love – instead, he 'demanded' sex; she 'gave him' sex or allowed him to 'perform a sex act' on her. Every word written was designed to imply that the unnamed victim was a total innocent in the affair, helplessly yielding up her body to the ferret-faced Pole. Although subsequent events would bear out most of Gailey's testimony, much of what was written at the time struck even Judge Rittenband as inept. 'It was prurience,' he allegedly noted, 'masquerading as journalism.'

Many of the American papers, in fact, seemed to be gripped by an advanced form of schizophrenia when it came to reporting the Polanski case. On the one hand, there were constant editorials rightly deploring that a 13-year-old girl had been violated, in a 'grotesque breach', to quote the *Globe*, of her 'rights and privacy'. On the other hand, these same guardians of Samantha Gailey's dignity felt able to engage in an almost psychotic discussion of the most clinical details of the case, including, but not limited to, the exact state of the child's panties. Detective Vannatter's grand-jury testimony, as leaked to the media, had reportedly shown that Samantha 'was not wearing the garment at the time the [police] officers arrived' on the night of 10 March. She had 'gone to another part of the house, got the garment, and gave it to the officers'. Could the panties (variously described as 'pink', 'rust', or 'copper-coloured', and either 'French-cut' or 'loose-fitting') have belonged to someone else, for instance her sister? Might the 'seminal residue' thus be that of the sister's boyfriend? Although the undergarments themselves remained under seal, at least one popular tabloid saw fit to display a photograph of 'panties identical to those worn by the Polanski victim', with arrows helpfully locating the 'Semen traces' and 'Crotch'. As the media commentator Marshall McLuhan later observed, this was 'voyeurism dressed up as a public service'.

Polanski took much of the coverage of the case as a personal affront, noting that 'they had been after' him ever since he had had 'the bad taste to have a wife who was murdered'. In that context, it's interesting to compare his experience at the hands of the press in the spring of 1977 with that of his friend Keith Richards. The Rolling Stones guitarist had been arrested in Canada on 27 February, just twelve days before Polanski, and was currently facing charges of 'possession of heroin for the purpose of trafficking', an offence which carried a potential life sentence. Yet, with one or two notable exceptions, 'Keef' was treated with a deference conspicuously lacking in Polanski's case. Travelling around with a 'shedload of smack' was fine, even rather endearing, as that was the sort of thing a proper rock star would do. Besides, as the *Globe* insisted, Richards' was a 'victimless crime' that 'heightened kids' awareness' of hard drugs. The paper seems not to have grasped the inherent contradiction: what 'kids' perhaps more obviously need when it comes to heroin is lowered awareness.

At the same time, it would be fair to say that Polanski never exactly courted popularity in the media. Some of his behaviour in the weeks immediately following his arrest appeared not so much perverse as wilfully self-destructive. He is reported, for instance, to have driven back to the Gaileys' house three days after his indictment in order to 'confront the mother of the 13-year-old'. Finding no one at home, Polanski allegedly then sat outside in his Mercedes until a concerned neighbour phoned the police. When the officers arrived, the director was ordered out of the car, searched and subsequently advised of the relevant statute relating to witness intimidation. According to one published version of events, the interview had concluded with one of the officers squeezing Polanski's crotch 'to see what all the excitement is about', before advising him to return to the car and 'get your ass outta here pronto'.

Although Polanski eventually acknowledged, in his 1984 memoirs, that 'I caused [Gailey] considerable pain', he made little or no visible show of contrition at the time. One credible source quotes Douglas Dalton as warning his client to limit his number of public appearances in the company of 'nubile young actresses', and Polanski replying, 'I am not guilty, so why should I act guilty?' Damien Thomas, the co-star of *Pirates*, recalls 'Roman said something very much along those lines' about the case when they worked together eight years later. It is harder to establish whether, as one biographer claims, the director cracked jokes about his crime and once lewdly referred to his victim's pubic hair. Polanski did, however, remain supremely confident of his acquittal should the matter ultimately come to trial. 'I wouldn't [flee the country]' he assured the *Los Angeles Herald-Examiner*, when asked about his travel plans. 'First of all, I have faith in the judicial system. I know I am innocent and I am not going to shy from it.' Speaking to a second reporter, he added that he was a 'hard-working professional', who was obliged to 'deal with these distractions'.

This observation, which he repeated in several interviews, was how Polanski most wanted to see himself. It was also a key to the negative press coverage. Let others wallow in the squalid details of what had been, at worst, a technical lapse on his part. To Polanski, the whole, drawn-out prosecution of the case was 'risibly self-indulgent' and a 'waste of time' (although he may have felt an artistic interest in some of the more Kafkaesque judicial proceedings). At the very height of his powers, he was 'never, for a single day' free of 'abuse' and 'victimisation' in the matter, which seems to have struck him as yet another of the cruel blows in an already blighted life.

When Columbia fired Polanski as the director of *The First Deadly Sin*, his generous expense account went with it. As a result, he was scraping by on residuals from *Chinatown* and his few investments, at a time when he was maintaining homes in London and Paris, in addition to his suite at the Château Marmont. Douglas Dalton, meanwhile, was reportedly charging him $110 an hour, with an ultimate legal bill estimated at $150,000 – equivalent to the director's entire fee from *Rosemary's Baby*.

Polanski thus accepted with alacrity when, in a notable show of loyalty, the producer Dino De Laurentiis asked him to remake John Ford's classic 1937 drama *The Hurricane*. Following the failure of his 'Dinocittà' studio complex in Rome, the 57-year-old Italian mogul had moved his operations to Hollywood, where he had recently been responsible for a successful, if critically derided remake of *King Kong*. He was said by one magazine to be 'richer than King Farouk' as a result. Apparently overcoming her earlier misgivings, Sue Mengers was able to win her client a $960,000 contract, the fee to be paid in a typically complex series of eight pre- and post-production instalments. Polanski spent some of his first cheque footing the bill for Nastassia Kinski and her family to fly to California, where 'Nasty' would learn English. After that he enrolled her in acting classes at the Lee Strasberg Institute. Polanski was apparently resolved to launch his 'dear friend' (though no longer his lover) with a starring role in *The Hurricane*. She was to be given the 'full studio treatment', he insisted, and to enjoy equal billing to the seasoned professionals on the film like Jason Robards and Trevor Howard. Douglas Dalton reportedly congratulated Polanski on his commission, but advised him not to talk too much about his latest protégée. Kinski, though talented and undeniably lovely, was still only 16 years old.

POLANSKI WAS BACK IN COURT ON 20 MAY, sitting with a deadpan expression while Dalton debated procedural matters with the deputy district attorney, Roger Gunson. The exchange was said to have become 'heated'. Judge Rittenband then denied the defence's petition for a dismissal, and appeared to take a dim view of their motion asking that they be allowed to introduce 'known facts' regarding Gailey's previous sexual history. 'It is clearly contrary to law,' said Rittenband, 'and I therefore have no authority to grant your request. And even if I did, I would not, Mr Dalton. It is not my function to serve as your pathfinder.' Following the hearing, Dalton drove Polanski back to his office on the thirty-third floor of a downtown skyscraper. Whilst there, he evidently first raised the subject of a plea bargain. It was a not unfamiliar defence tactic in sexual misconduct cases, and had certain obvious attractions. Polanski might, for instance, admit to a single count of sodomy, an offence that, while ripe with comic potential for the talk-show hosts, most Californian courts punished by only a nominal one- to three-month sentence followed by probation. (In January 1952, the 17-year-old Charles Manson, then in a young offenders' centre, had taken a razor blade and held it against another inmate's throat while he sodomised him, an offence for which he lost ninety days' 'privileges'.) Providing the prosecution co-operated, everyone could thus be spared a costly and embarrassing trial. In the best case scenario, Polanski might avoid jail altogether and perhaps just be given community service and a fine – although, as Dalton was at pains to point out, 'ultimately [it] would all depend on the bench'.

The bench, Laurence Rittenband, was an enigmatic figure whose drab, accountant-like appearance concealed a lively private life. Aged 71, and a confirmed bachelor, he was a popular member at the Hillcrest Country

Club in Beverly Hills, where he liked nothing more than to give and attend fancy-dress balls. A fellow member recalls that Rittenband asked him and three or four other male members to 'drive out one Halloween to a house in Brentwood. He had garment [bags] with him, and, before we went in, we had to take off our own costumes and change into drag', a disguise the judge himself was more than capable of carrying off. Whatever the implications of this particular proclivity – quite possibly no more than a visual style appreciation – the judge was something of a closet swinger, who is reliably said to have conducted an 'intense relationship' with a 20-year-old woman while he himself was in his mid-fifties, and who still enjoyed the company of several, more mature female companions at the time he encountered Polanski.

Rittenband, it should also be noted, had by then had a long and distinguished legal career spanning nearly fifty years. Of a modest background in Brooklyn, New York, he's agreed to have been knowledgeable and personally unassuming – in one account, 'not one of those judges who always thinks he's in the movies' (although by the same token, also not above keeping his own press cuttings file). In his memoirs, Polanski implies that Rittenband was star-struck by the proceedings, and, after initially exercising due judicial restraint, was 'clearly enjoying his first excursion into the limelight'. This was not quite fair. By the time he met Polanski, Rittenband had already presided over a host of high-profile Hollywood cases, including Elvis Presley's divorce, Marlon Brando's child-custody battle and a paternity suit against Cary Grant. Nor could it be concluded from these proceedings that the judge was in any way prejudiced against his celebrity defendants. In the case of Grant, for instance, Rittenband had made the eminently sensible suggestion that both the actor and the alleged mother of his child submit to a blood test, 'after which we will determine what to do'. When the woman in question had failed to appear for her scheduled test, and for two subsequent appointments, Rittenband curtly dismissed her suit. As well as being a stickler both for the letter and the spirit of the law, regularly advising plaintiffs and defendants alike of the need to be 'decorous' and punctual in his court, the judge was vastly well read in a variety of fields, which enabled him to make pertinent and original connections in his rulings. Regarding Elvis, for example, he quoted Jonathan Swift, observing to the bemused singer that 'Censure is the tax a man pays to the public for being eminent.' Looking back on the Polanski case years later, Rittenband puckishly told the press, 'It reminds me of a line from Gilbert and Sullivan: "I've got him on my list."'

While the judge and lawyers discussed the terms, if any, on which Polanski might be allowed to enter a plea, a no less heated debate continued to rage between the director's apologists and others, like the Los Angeles *Facts*, calling for him to be 'chemically castrated'. (Even this was mild compared to some of the subsequent internet opinion.) On Douglas Dalton's advice, Polanski himself had little to say on the matter, which is perhaps why so few people got a sense of any real regret on his part. In one report, 'the Pole's shrugging, on-with-the-show' reaction to the charges 'prove[s] that he just doesn't get it . . . He's accused of drugging and raping a 13-year-old child, and he's out parading around with his friends.'

Speaking to Franz-Olivier Giesbert of *Le Nouvel Observateur* in April 1984, shortly before a civil-suit settlement permanently muzzled him on the subject, Polanski seemed to confirm some of his critics' misgivings.

'Do you regret having made love to this young girl?' Giesbert asked.

'I regret everything I had to go through afterwards,' Polanski replied.

'She was 13 years old.'

'She was about to turn 14. Three weeks later to be exact.'

'That's no excuse.'

'If you had seen her, you would have thought she was at least 18,' said Polanski, omitting to mention that, by his own sworn testimony, he had known exactly how old Gailey was on the first day he met her.

One intriguing possible explanation for Polanski's unapologetic stance is that he genuinely felt himself to be a victim of the piece. It was he, not the other party, who had been led on. According to his friend Mike Fenton, the casting director on *Chinatown*, 'I know from my personal experience that [Gailey's] mother was ambitious for the girl, and was only too happy for her to meet someone like Polanski. That's not to say that Roman behaved like a knight on a white charger, and clearly the whole thing went too far. But it's absurd to say that he was a predator who single-handedly forced himself on the family. In my opinion, more than one person was guilty of poor judgement.'

The press hostility seemed unjustified to Polanski, and it's said 'completely perplexed' him. He had basically done nothing that 'countless men' had not done before him. 'When Mr Smith or Mr Brown sleeps with 14-year-old adolescents who look 18, it doesn't interest anyone,' he told *Le Nouvel Observateur*. 'But when a famous film director does, the law and the media sound the alarm.' The animus hurt not least because the judge and potential jurors in the case were being exposed to a barrage of headlines like 'REPULSION' and 'POLE, ON PERV CHARGE,

FACES 50 YEARS'. From 11 March 1977, it became an axiom among the media to be either pro- or, more often, anti-Polanski. Only the filmgoing public, it seemed, could hold in its head concurrently the ideas that a morally equivocal situation, however regrettable, had existed; that Polanski had taken full advantage of it; and that he remained a director of genius. While Judge Rittenband reviewed proceedings in Los Angeles, one enterprising film club 3,000 miles away in Princeton, New Jersey, organised a weekend festival in a disused Catholic church which promised 'screenings of *Rosemary's Baby*, *Macbeth* and *Chinatown*, along [with] panel discussions and seminars on the work'. On the night of Saturday 9 April, some 2,700 fans queued up for admission; well subscribed, for a room seating 300.

While Polanski himself maintained a discreet silence, a number of surrogates were busy jousting on his behalf. To some of these, the prosecution of the case appeared to be nothing less than the result of a vast right wing, and by extension puritanical conspiracy. Everyone was in on it: the Vatican, the Mafia, the FBI, the KGB, Opus Dei and P2. One particularly well known British film critic categorically assured me that 'the Republican administration in Washington fitted Roman up because, like John Lennon, they wanted to deport him', a thesis which overlooks one inconvenient fact: the US president at the time was Jimmy Carter, a liberal Democrat. It's a tribute to the loyalty Polanski engenders among his colleagues that he was able to call on the support of a number of actresses who, under normal circumstances, might be expected to rally to the feminist cause. To Mia Farrow, it seemed that 'maybe Roman's judgement was off on this occasion', but that he was 'hounded' as a result. Shelley Winters similarly felt that there was a 'witch-hunt involved . . . Roman was persecuted because, being foreign, talented and opinionated, he was an easy mark.' For her part, Catherine Deneuve believes that 'a very young girl can look much older than she is, and that was the case here'. Jacqueline Bisset, who had actually briefly seen Polanski and his victim on the afternoon of 10 March, notes that 'a lot of these kids are really hip – they know exactly what they're doing', apparently echoing the key defence position that Gailey had been 'precocious' when it came to sex and drugs.

Curiously enough, while most of the women in Polanski's life remained broadly sympathetic to his plight, not all the men were as tolerant. To at least one of them, speaking, perhaps wisely, on condition of anonymity, he was an 'evil tosser' whose fate, however tragic, deserved little pity.

Richard Sylbert, a long-time friend who had worked on *Rosemary's Baby* and *Chinatown*, was more openly critical, describing Polanski's original photographic commission as being 'more vague than *Vogue*' and characterising the director as a 'Svengali figure' for whom sex was about 'power and control ... Roman is uncomfortable with women over 30,' Sylbert concluded. One or two others in Polanski's immediate circle were similarly unimpressed. Their numbers grew once a German magazine's photographs of Gailey – showing a skinny child who looked, if anything, younger than 13 – began to appear in a few domestic outlets, a factor that did not help the defence.

Douglas Dalton was, nonetheless, ultimately successful in his efforts to negotiate a plea bargain for his client. The Gaileys' family lawyer, Lawrence Silver, had already noted that a public trial would provide 'a circus', with Samantha herself being cross-examined 'in clinical detail' about her sexual and pharmacological history. 'My primary concern,' Silver added, 'is the present and future well-being of the girl', who had since made clear her 'extreme reluctance' to testify. As seasoned prosecutors, both the district attorney, John Van de Kamp, and his deputy, Roger Gunson, would have recognised the classic pattern to California child sexual-abuse cases, in which, at the time, some eighty per cent of the young plaintiffs ultimately declined to appear in open court. Polanski himself remained stubbornly opposed to 'admit[ting] I am a rapist', but gradually came to see the merits of what he reportedly called a 'creative deal' – at one stage he formally proposed that he should fund an arts school for teenage children by way of restitution – with the proviso that he avoid any 'significant' jail time. As a subplot to the discussions, Douglas Dalton was apparently briefed to protect his client's already delicate immigration status as best he could. Polanski currently enjoyed a multiple-entry visa to the US, and had been negotiating for a green card up to and including the very day he had taken Gailey into Jack Nicholson's jacuzzi. As part of any 'fix', he reportedly insisted, he should be allowed to continue to 'live and work wherever [I] choose'.

With so many traps along the route to a viable compromise, and the media, meanwhile, clamouring for 'justice', the parties had to proceed gingerly. After several weeks, in which Roger Gunson, a clean-cut young Mormon, not only worked twelve-hour days but then 'sat and scrutinised the defendant's films' by night, an arrangement was reached that was minimally acceptable to all sides. Polanski would plead to a single count of unlawful intercourse, or statutory rape, a crime which could be punished by anything from probation to the full fifty-year sentence.* The remaining five charges would be dropped. In his classified report on the case, Gunson noted that 'though this office considers the major underlying offence to involve the rape of a minor by use of alcohol and drugs', there appeared to be 'unusual and extraordinary circumstances that require acceptance of the single-felony plea'.

Among the salient factors were: '1) *Family concern*: From the time the case was reported, the family of the victim has requested that our office seek to the extent possible to protect the victim from publicity and maintain her privacy. 2) *Victim's reluctance*: The 13-year-old victim in this case was the object of a most traumatic crime. Her extreme reluctance to testify and her fear of further trauma in and out of the courtroom has been communicated to us by her attorney. 3) *Office experience*: Our office is aware of and most concerned with the extreme stress experienced by all rape victims. The news coverage as a result of Mr Polanski's role in this case, the age of the girl, and the entire aura of another "Hollywood Babylon" trial can only serve to intensify such trauma. 4) *Fair resolution and public protection*: The fact that the family believes that Roman Raymond Polanski's admission of guilt is a satisfactory solution and [other] points indicate that the offered plea constitutes a fair resolution of the case of *The People* v. *Polanski* and gives appropriate public protection.'

As part of the deal, Polanski agreed to be 'examined by court-appointed psychiatrists to determine if he is a mentally disordered sex offender. If such a finding is made, he may be committed to a state hospital for treatment and required to register following his release.' Critically, too, the formal recommendation subsequently presented to the court on 6 August did 'not in any way involve a sentence commitment'. Judge Rittenband had it at his sole discretion to send Polanski to jail or not, as he saw fit.

LATE ON THE AFTERNOON OF 7 AUGUST (not, as he wrote, the 8th), Polanski went to Holy Cross cemetery to put flowers on Sharon Tate's grave. The

---

* As the law stood in 1977, the California Community Release Board provided a penalty ranging from sixteen months to three years for the crime of unlawful intercourse. However, it also carried a term of zero to fifty years under the Attorney General's current legal interpretation. A sentence of anything over a year in state, as opposed to county, prison would have automatically been referred to the immigration and naturalisation service, with the distinct possibility of immediate deportation on release.

following day was the eighth anniversary of her death. While he was kneeling there he caught sight of a paparazzo snapping pictures of him from behind a hedge. Polanski confronted the man, who appeared to be a German, and remarked with some justification that this was an 'intolerable intrusion' on his privacy. The photographer replied that he was merely 'following orders'.

By now completely incensed, Polanski seized on the phrase.

'Fucking Nazi!' he yelled. 'FUCKING NAZIS! FUCK OFF! ALL OF YOU!' At that an undignified struggle had taken place at the gravesite. After some mutual pushing and shoving, Polanski eventually wrenched the camera from the photographer's neck and removed the film. A complaint promptly lodged with the district attorney, accusing the director of theft and assault, came to nothing, as did a petition by several newspapers that they be allowed to witness his next day's hearing. 'We have to protect everyone's rights,' said Judge Rittenband, who had made the ruling himself.

At 9.25 the following morning, Monday 8 August, Polanski appeared in Santa Monica to enter his plea of guilty to the sole count of unlawful intercourse. The judge appeared in a benevolent mood. 'Why don't you get a chair for Mr Polanski and let him sit next to you?' he enquired of Douglas Dalton, favouring the defence team with a 'broad smile'. A moment later, Polanski was seated at the front and centre of the court, a 'tiny, dark-suited figure' in one account, 'swinging his legs like an antsy child at the dinner table'.

After some brief preliminaries, the Gaileys' lawyer Lawrence Silver spelt out, in detail, the suffering endured by the family to date. 'I am mindful that they, and more particularly she, have been harmed by the unlawful acts committed by the defendant. My view, based upon advice from experts, and the view of the girl's parents, is that a trial may cause further serious woe to her. Long before I had met any other attorney in this case, my clients informed me that their goal in pressing the charges did not include seeking the incarceration of the defendant, but rather the admission by him of wrongdoing.

'Whatever trauma has come to the victim would be exacerbated in the extreme if this case went to trial. The reliving of the sorry events, with their delicate content, through the vehicle of direct and cross-examination in this courtroom laden with strangers, would be a challenge to the emotional well-being of any person. The potential for harm is even greater with one of tender years.'

Silver concluded, 'The public disclosure of identity in such a charged atmosphere can only harm – and seriously harm – the child. Relationships with friends, and indeed her family, would never be the same. A stigma would attach to her for a lifetime. Justice is not made of such stuff.'

In the matter-of-fact back and forth that followed between Silver and the judge, it seemed that Rittenband, too, sought 'not specifically incarceration [but] a clear statement' by the defendant. Polanski then left his seat and made his way, apparently with reluctance, to the stand. He would enter his plea, under oath, in a series of terse exchanges with Roger Gunson. As the proceedings continued, 'the defendant spoke in a voice so low' that the court reporter, Roger Williams, 'strained to hear it from four feet away'. Polanski was now formally admitting to a criminal act.

Q Are you in fact guilty of this charge?
A Yes.
Q What did you do in this case?
A I had sexual intercourse with a female person not my wife, under the age of 18.
Q And was this female person the complaining witness in this case?
A She was the complaining witness.
Q And did this occur on 10 March 1977?
A That's correct.

Gunson concluded with a series of pro forma questions, each of which a now 'barely audible' Polanski was required to answer. The exchange took some twenty minutes, involving sixty-two procedural points in all. Reading only a few of these would seem to refute the later claim that Polanski was 'misled' into believing that his plea bargain precluded the threat of his serving jail time.

Q Mr Polanski, who do you believe will decide what your sentence will be in this matter?
A The judge.
Q Who do you think will decide whether or not you will get probation?
A The judge.
Q Who do you think will determine whether the sentence will be a felony or a misdemeanour?
A The judge.

Q Do you understand that at this time, the court has not made any
   decision as to what sentence you will receive?
A [No response]
Q Mr Polanski, do you understand that the judge has not made any
   decision?
A Yes.

POLANSKI REMAINED AT LIBERTY, based in his suite at the Château Marmont,
pending the sentencing hearing scheduled for 19 September. He spent
part of his time casting *The Hurricane*, a film he later described as 'never
a particularly worthwhile project', and part of it meeting with his two
court-appointed psychiatrists, Doctors Markham and Davis, to determine
whether he was a mentally disordered sex offender. (They eventually
concluded he wasn't.) As part of the process, the director was able to
supply glowing testimonial letters written by friends such as Dino De
Laurentiis and Mia Farrow. Polanski also submitted to 'seven or eight'
hour-long interviews with his probation officer, Irwin Gold. Their early-
afternoon sessions generally took place in a small consulting room in City
Hall, but sometimes moved to a luxuriously furnished office supplied by
De Laurentiis in his studio complex on Canon Drive, in Beverly Hills. At
their first meeting, Gold reportedly told Polanski that he meant to take
him, step by step, over his entire life, 'particularly the war tragedy', and
eventually provided a highly sympathetic report. Some time later, Judge
Rittenband would allegedly come across an elderly female secretary, who
was Jewish, at the courthouse, in tears as a result of typing the relevant
passages 'concern[ing] the defendant's experience in the Holocaust'.
   Polanski, Gold concluded, 'expressed great remorse regarding any
possible effect the present offence might have had upon the victim. He
expressed great pity and compassion for her, stating that he knew the legal
proceedings had been extremely difficult for her. He stated that because of
the many tragedies that he, himself, has known in his own life he feels
great empathy for a youth in distress.' The director's specific account of
the events of 10 March included the observations that the girl had 'talked
about sex', 'was not inexperienced' and that they had only gone to the
poolside bedroom because he thought he had heard a car coming; there
were 'some maniacs who used to come to the compound', he noted, a tacit
allusion to the Manson murders. After providing a moving precis both of
his wartime ordeal and the events of August 1969, Polanski, it was said,
had remarked how often he had been 'kicked' in life. 'Haven't *you* kicked

anyone, Roman?' Gold asked, whereupon Polanski allegedly 'looked down and wept'. According to a knowledgeable source, Gold subsequently described this as a 'genuinely sad' and 'poignant' moment, and one which perhaps tinged his final report. Certainly it took a commendably bold, progressive view of the offender in a child-sex case. Some cynics later wondered whether the mild-mannered Gold might possibly have been outwitted by the former professional actor, whose fellow-feeling for a 'youth in distress' – the implication being that he, too, was damaged in adolescence – was open to doubt on several levels. When talking to the press, Polanski himself invariably went out of his way to mock the whole idea that he had somehow been scarred by his experiences as a young man. 'I wasn't particularly unhappy,' he had assured Dick Cavett, referring to his wartime exile. Speaking to a second enquiring television interviewer, Charlie Rose, he added that 'Kids accept life as it is . . . The hardships I went through seemed quite normal to me.' Rose had then proceeded to ask his guest whether he ever thought about 'the connection between losing [his] mother, experiencing that sense of fear' and its effect on his later life.

'Never,' said Polanski.

'Never?'

'Absolutely never. I'm not even interested in it.'

On Friday 16 September, Judge Rittenband called a meeting of the prosecution and defence teams in his chambers. Laid out on the desk in front of him were three identical manila folders. The first, from Dr Davis, reportedly summarised Polanski's crime as 'an isolated instance of transient poor judgement and loss of normal inhibition in circumstances of intimacy and collaboration in creative work'. (This was later satirically abridged as '"The girl was asking for it" defence'.) The second, from Dr Markham, broadly agreed that 'the present offence was neither a forceful nor aggressive sexual act'. After reviewing the psychiatric opinion, Rittenband turned to the probation report, whose conclusion he read aloud:

> It is believed that incalculable emotional damage could result from incarcerating the defendant, whose very existence has been a seemingly unending series of punishments.

Leaning back in his red leather armchair and putting his feet up among the folders, Rittenband told the two sets of lawyers exactly what he thought of the professional recommendations. The 'head-doctors' might well know their business, he conceded, but the probation report was a 'whitewash'.

The judge then announced that he intended to send Polanski to the California Institute for Men at Chino for a ninety-day 'diagnostic study'. Even Roger Gunson, the prosecutor, appears to have questioned whether such a 'supplemental exam' was strictly necessary, given that two mental-health professionals had already reported to the court. Rittenband repeated his decision. Polanski, who wasn't present, writes that the judge then 'implied he would sentence me to probation' on release from Chino, although there is no record to prove it.

At the formal hearing on 19 September Douglas Dalton argued eloquently for his client's release, despite knowing it to be a lost cause. Polanski may have had a 'lapse of judgement', but 'shouldn't be treated any more harshly than any other defendant who stands before the court with a conviction of unlawful intercourse . . . This particular offence doesn't have the connotation of rape. It's not even an offence, a criminal offence, in about thirteen of our states and in many places of the world . . . The defendant has no other criminal record. He is not a sexual deviate. He is not a man of criminal bent . . . I feel he is a criminal only by accident,' Dalton concluded, 'and that there are many complex social and psychological factors that were involved in this situational event which otherwise was a complete departure from his normal mode of conduct.'

The judge disagreed. Although, it was true, 'the prosecutrix in the case [was] a well developed young girl, regrettably not unschooled in sexual matters', this was 'not a licence to the defendant, a man of the world, in his forties, to engage in an act of unlawful intercourse with her'. Polanski would be taken away for 'evaluation', the better to enable the court to 'reach a fair and just decision as to the sentence to be finally imposed'.

In a notable volte-face, there was something of a media backlash against the judge, whose 'protracted' and 'increasingly surreal' handling of the case achieved the seemingly impossible feat of making Polanski into a more sympathetic figure. The *Hollywood Reporter* conjectured that Rittenband was 'soft in the head', and the *Star* declared him a 'rambling and vindictive old man who [was] clearly out to get Polanski'. If so, he appears to have been curiously indulgent of a whole series of unusual defence motions. Rittenband had allowed Polanski to travel freely on nominal bail following both his April and August hearings, for example, and no effort was ever made to deprive the director of his two passports. Rather than 'see [him] led away', Dalton now asked for a three-month stay in order for Polanski to complete pre-production work on 'a film budgeted for many millions of dollars' (*The Hurricane*), which required him to 'conduct business in [Bora-Bora and other] locations in the South Seas'. Once again, Rittenband cheerfully agreed to the defence's request.

On his way to Polynesia, Polanski (travelling the long way around) enjoyed a layover in Munich, where he was photographed seated at a café table, smoking contentedly, in the company of several lovely women. The picture went out over the wire services, and eventually found its way into the *Santa Monica Evening Outlook*, which happened to be Judge Rittenband's home paper. The accompanying caption read: 'Movie director Roman Polanski puffs a cigar as he enjoys the companionship of young ladies during a visit to the Munich Oktoberfest, the world's largest beer festival. Sources say Polanski came to Bavaria's capital as a tourist and just wants to relax. A Santa Monica court ordered Polanski to undergo a ninety-day diagnostic study at a state prison but permitted him to finish a film first.'

Polanski later complained that the offending picture had been taken without his permission, and, more to the point, cropped in such a way 'that only girls were visible around me'. The occasion had been a perfectly decorous night out with a number of friends from the West German film industry. Although it might have looked differently to a casual observer, 'it was a scene of pure innocence'. None of which greatly impressed Judge Rittenband, who swiftly summoned half a dozen journalists to his chambers, where he brought them to order by loudly banging his hand down on the top of his desk. As one of those in attendance wrote, the ensuing press briefing 'went ahead in a strained atmosphere'. According to the judge, he had agreed to the three-month stay of the defendant's sentence only because of the 'serious consequences to others, [the] many innocent people who would face economic hardship' in the event *The Hurricane* was cancelled. However the photograph in question had been edited, there was no way in which it could be 'construed as show[ing] Mr Polanski hard at work directing a film'.

Rittenband had first seen the critical issue of the *Evening Outlook* while being chauffeured to the annual Columbus Day costume ball at the Hillcrest Club. He himself was magnificently attired as a fifteenth-century seaman for the occasion. So incensed was the judge by what he read that he slipped into the club through the basement entrance from the parking garage, to avoid the party, and immediately went upstairs to the library to draft a formal letter to Douglas Dalton. Polanski was to report back to the court for a further hearing on 21 October. What was more,

Rittenband, so he later complained, had apparently been under the impression that the 'defendant would [use] the three-month stay to execute his project', rather than merely to scout locations and complete the pre-production process. The judge was not pleased to learn that Polanski was currently scheduled to shoot *The Hurricane* in March 1978, the implication being that he would either be released after his time at Chino or, at worst, be given another stay. This now struck Rittenband as a 'miscalculated assumption'. Early in the morning of Monday 17 October, the judge summoned yet another reporter from the *Los Angeles Herald-Examiner* to announce that 'Roman Polanski could be on his way to prison this weekend'. He added, 'I didn't know [last month] that the movie would be impossible to finish in ninety days. I do feel that I have very possibly been imposed upon.'

Dalton phoned the news to Polanski in London, where the director was enjoying a working holiday with Nastassia Kinski. His lawyer told him to fly back immediately. Unfortunately, there happened to be a British air traffic controllers' strike that week, and Polanski was able to report to Santa Monica only on 24 October. The subsequent hearing was held in camera, but by all accounts there were three distinct phases to it. Firstly, Polanski himself assured the judge that his visit to Munich had been 'strictly business', a version of events Dino De Laurentiis corroborated. There had been 'no abuse whatsoever' of the court's goodwill. Douglas Dalton and Roger Gunson had then further debated whether Polanski's enjoying a night out at the Oktoberfest was sufficient representation of his role as a 'hard-working director' on whom 'hundreds depended for their livelihoods'. Finally, Rittenband had allowed the ninety-day stay to run, but warned that there would be no further postponements. Polanski was to report to Chino on 19 December, and to remain incarcerated there 'for ninety days or until the completion of a diagnostic study, whichever is the sooner'.

Polanski spent the next six weeks in Bora-Bora. While his small accompanying crew stayed at the local Club Méditerranée, the director preferred a more secluded resort on the extreme northern tip of the island. The compound contained a number of guest houses, small, mushroom-like structures set apart from each other with views of the sea, and elegantly furnished, according to one visitor, 'with Gauguin prints, wicker chairs and a white fan turning slowly in the ceiling'. Towards the end of his stay, Polanski met a 'stunningly beautiful' 18-year-old Tahitian girl named Aloma, who lived with him for several days. On 5 December, the

Associated Press moved a story claiming that the district attorney's office were 'concerned' that the 'guilty party in a rape case' remained at liberty outside of US jurisdiction. The government of French Polynesia had seen no call for an extradition treaty relating to the crime of unlawful sexual intercourse. Polanski, however, voluntarily left his tropical haven on 14 December on the direct flight from Papeete to Los Angeles, arriving around 9.30 the following morning. Despite everything being booked at the last possible minute, he had fretted about the publicity the 'jail thing' could bring, and quickly realised how much he'd underestimated it when two camera trucks rolled up to meet him on the runway before his jet had even come to a stop.

Polanski spent the night of 16 December at the director Tony Richardson's house, where there was a small party in his honour. Jack Nicholson, generously overlooking the personal fallout from the events of 10 March – which had included his satisfying the police that he knew nothing about any drugs found at his home – was among the guests. The evening might conceivably have reminded Nicholson of the plot of *The Last Detail*, in which his character 'Bad Ass' Baddusky had given a young offender a royal send-off on his way to the brig. Indeed, there was something 'jaunty', it's said, in the friends' parting in the early hours, the salutation of two men who had gone through some tough times together but were coming out of it now. 'It's never dull, is it?' Nicholson asked. 'Never,' said Polanski.

Douglas Dalton had negotiated for his client to begin his sentence two days early, on the morning of 17 December, meaning that Polanski, with only a quick stop for breakfast, went directly from the party to jail. The thinking seems to have been to get the ordeal over as quickly as possible, as well as to avoid the crowd of reporters expected at the prison on the 19th. Dalton himself drove Polanski to the facility, located some thirty miles east of Los Angeles in the foothills of the Santa Ana mountains. Built in 1941, it was a sprawling, 2,500-acre complex which housed up to 6,000 short- to medium-term inmates in the central cell blocks, which were surrounded by a series of outlying wooden barracks and smaller chalets, earning it the nickname of the 'Chino Country Club'. To others, the more obvious comparison was to the layout of a Second World War German prison camp. Either way, it must have seemed less than welcoming to Polanski, as he was led through the narrow front gate, which a guard then banged shut behind him, while an enterprising television news crew filmed his arrival from atop a hydraulically operated crane which, judging from its logo, they had bought or leased from Paramount studios.

After being intimately searched and fitted with regulation blue overalls, Polanski was formally processed into Chino. Much of the admissions drill was conducted not by guards but by 'trustys', the slightly more benign modern equivalent of the wartime kapo. One of them hung a card around the new arrival's neck identifying him as CALIF PRISONER B88742Z and took his mugshot, a grim portrait looking as if it belonged on an old 'Wanted' poster and hardly boding well for the comic film Polanski had perhaps facetiously said he would make of his stay. His living quarters were revealed as a private, six-by-ten-foot cell, not entirely devoid of comfort: there was a metal bunk, a flush toilet and a washbasin with hot and cold running water under a large vanity mirror, a barred window and even piped music – 'no worse than the average Soviet hotel room' one visitor remarks. Polanski spent most of his first afternoon inside methodically scrubbing every square inch of his new accommodations with toilet paper. After dinner, he repeated the process. Over the next few days he seemed to display an almost fetishistic interest in sanitation and hygiene generally, as a result of which he was issued a mop and broom and assigned to clean the prison day room each morning, when the other residents were exercising. Due to fears that he could be raped or worse, Polanski remained in protective custody throughout his sentence. Although occasionally able to watch television, he was denied access to communal areas like the library and the gym. When he showered, the entire wing was closed off from the general prison population. Christmas dinner that year was a plate of stew and potatoes, with bread and margarine and a carton of milk, which Polanski took with a blunt spoon, in solitary confinement.

For all that, life in Chino settled into a routine that seemed to be more tedious than strictly punitive. Polanski was able to enjoy an unlimited amount of correspondence to and from the outside world, and reportedly took the opportunity to write to a fellow Krakowite named Karol Wojtyla, the future Pope John Paul II, requesting a character reference. Several Hollywood colleagues and friends sent sympathetic 'Thinking of you' cards, although it is thought that there were few producers among their number. Polanski also adds that there was a series of 'heartbreaking' letters from his father. The official prison censor, though fluent in Spanish and to a lesser extent English, simply handed over the family correspondence, written in idiomatic Polish, with a resigned shrug. Among

Polanski's visitors were two psychiatrists and a psychologist to further evaluate his mental health, various clergymen and rabbis and at least one journalist posing as 'Roman's cousin'.

Polanski was later to describe his time in Chino in glowing terms. 'Being in jail was an interesting experience,' he told *Le Nouvel Observateur* in 1984. 'To be honest I found life as a convict fascinating. I got a much stronger understanding of why the people we call re-offenders, once released, look for new ways to get back behind bars. Since then, like those guys, I've found myself missing the time I spent in there.' Writing in his autobiography later that year, Polanski added, 'I was a happy man after a few days in Chino. I was out of the public eye. I felt secure and at peace.'

On a less nostalgic plane, Polanski was later to portray his fellow inmates at Chino as 'the scum of society'. According to his near-neighbour, a 24-year-old parole offender named Terry Lee Koker, 'As time went on Roman got lonelier and lonelier, and more and more depressed. He was told there were guys in the regular cell blocks who were just dying to get him for being a "baby-raper". He was isolated from the real hard-core cons.' Polanski also evidently continued to see himself as a victim of circumstances. The siren that had lured him on to the rocks 'looked at least 18' he assured several of his fellow residents of Z block, the psychiatric observation wing. It had all been a 'bum deal' Polanski further noted, in a perhaps inadvisable turn of phrase. 'Roman was very self-deprecating,' adds an English friend who visited him. 'He was great at teasing and joshing – even inside, we were taking the piss out of each other. He's extremely self-aware, and most people in that situation are, in my experience, high on self-delusion.'

Exactly ten years earlier, the actor Dean Jones had auditioned unsuccessfully for the lead in *Rosemary's Baby*. Jones had since gone on to fame in Disney's *The Love Bug* and its various sequels, while undergoing a well-publicised conversion to Christianity. In late December 1977 he was starring in a film called *Born Again*, some of which was being shot in the town of Chino. After seeing the 'terrible' news footage of Polanski's arrival at the prison, Jones quickly arranged to visit him.

I was escorted in to a typical institutional meeting room, furnished largely with vending machines to dispense these bite-sized bags of candy and potato chips. After a while Polanski strode in, all in blue, as cocky as I've ever seen anyone in my life. His first words to me were, 'Gimme some change.' He then armed himself with half a dozen items from the coin machines, which he sat munching throughout our interview . . . I'll tell you something about Roman: He was the only man I knew who could sit there in prison denim, with arrows on, and completely dominate the room. It wasn't just that I didn't get a word in. Even the guards were hovering back, neatly to attention. They seemed more like waiters.

After completing location work on *Born Again*, Jones went back to the facility for a second and final visit.

Polanski came in, and again talked up a storm about how well he was doing . . . Everything was great. No sweat. Roman sat there, basically doing his Jimmy Cagney impersonation, occasionally throwing in some jail slang for effect. It was all 'deez, demz and doz' and that hard-nosed attitude. After twenty minutes or so of this, I finally leant over the table and said, 'Roman, you've made so many cold films. Without forcing it, do you think you could ever do one that was warm and positive?' Strangely enough, the question seemed to completely stun him. Abandoning his horizontal slouch, Polanski sat straight up in his seat. He was obviously giving it some thought. I don't think either of us spoke for at least a minute. Then Roman looked me in the eye for the first time, as if just now realising why I was there. 'No,' he said quietly. 'I've lived in the dark too long.'

A week later, in mid-January 1978, Polanski was visited by Dino De Laurentiis. Given all the 'flap' and 'uncertainty', the producer was reluctantly removing him from *The Hurricane*, at least on a provisional basis. It was a tragedy. But it was just business. The film, foreshortened to *Hurricane*, and budgeted at $22 million, would eventually be directed by a Swede named Jan Troell. Over the years it went on to grace all the Worst Movies in History lists.

Having once again satisfied the mental-health experts, Polanski was released from Chino on 29 January. Looking thin and haggard, and wearing a thick beard, he paused at the front gate only to confirm that he was 'ecstatic'. He had served forty-three days out of a possible ninety-day sentence. Under the provisions of article 1203.03 of the California penal code, Judge Rittenband was now at liberty to discharge Polanski unconditionally; to place him on probation; or, the least likely alternative, to commit him to the sexual-offenders unit of a state prison. The judge had publicly announced that he would determine the matter at a meeting in his chambers scheduled for the morning of 30 January.

The hearing went particularly poorly from Polanski's point of view. Judge Rittenband reportedly asked both sets of lawyers to again argue their cases, after which he advised them that he would call a session on 1 February in order to return 'the inmate' to Chino for the outstanding forty-seven days of his term there, followed by an 'indeterminate' jail sentence. This, the judge noted, could be cut short at any time should Polanski agree to voluntary and permanent deportation. The Gaileys' attorney Lawrence Silver, who was present in the room, recalls that both sets of opposing counsel and he himself had been 'stunned' by this development. Roger Gunson, the prosecutor, was sufficiently taken aback by the latest judicial twist to reportedly argue against 'any further incarceration' over and above the original ninety days. Polanski later told the interviewer Charlie Rose, 'I did my time in prison. That was supposed to be it . . . The judge then reneged on the bargain-plea that was accepted by all sides and wanted me to go back.' In fact, Rittenband, as the transcripts prove, had never agreed in open court that the diagnostic study would necessarily serve as the full sentence. The only possible occasion on which he could have given that impression was at his off-the-record conference of 16 September, at which Polanski believes that the judge had 'implied' he was inclined towards probation. There is no minute to that effect. For all that, an 'indeterminate' spell in jail was a peculiarly cruel blow: in the worst case scenario, Polanski could have spent longer behind bars than the Manson women, some of whom were already eligible for parole and, unlike him, enjoyed widespread support in the media.

By all accounts, the judge's disposition towards 'the inmate' had, during the course of the previous month, undergone a distinct change for the worse. Rittenband is said to have remarked to the writer and producer Howard Koch, while in the men's room of the Hillcrest Club, 'I'll send him away forever. I can't imagine anything more terrible, more disgusting, having sex with a 13-year-old girl. I'll see that the man never gets out of jail.'* Whatever the truth of this particular exchange, the judge made a number of no less inflammatory remarks, in both public and private,

---

* Howard Koch, who died in 1995, was a highly regarded figure in Hollywood, with a string of screenwriting credits that included *Sergeant York* and *Casablanca*. The story of his encounter with Judge Rittenband appears to have been circulated by his son, Howard Koch Jr. The younger Mr Koch, it's only fair to say, declined to specifically confirm the incident (or, indeed, anything else about Polanski) when I contacted him in 2006.

which in time led Douglas Dalton to file a 'statement of disqualification' against him, citing 'partiality, prejudice and [other] violations of the California judicial code'. 'I'm getting too much criticism,' Rittenband had said at the 30 January hearing, an apparent reference to the numerous editorials and commentaries calling for Polanski to be locked up without further ado. In subsequently denying any impropriety, the judge only succeeded in reinforcing the impression of bias. 'I wanted that man – the prisoner – out of the country' he announced at a press conference held in his chambers the following month. If so, Rittenband was to achieve his ambition through an unorthodox route. Polanski himself clearly felt that his case was less to do with the dispensation of justice and more to do with appeasing a press which had 'loathed' him since 1969. (One veteran Hollywood correspondent, who professes 'great respect for Roman's films', remembers catching his first glimpse of him after Sharon Tate's murder – 'that hunched figure trying to skulk off down the back ways of the Paramount lot . . . We just didn't like him. The feeling was mutual and [we] could sense it.') 'Don't you realise that the media took over the judicial system in your country?' Polanski later asked Charlie Rose. 'In [my] case it was all because of the press. The judge himself said at one point, "They will have what they want."' When Rose had enquired what, exactly, they had wanted, Polanski replied, 'My head.'

The day after Rittenband's in-camera hearing with the lawyers, 31 January, Los Angeles was in the grip of the worst thunderstorm in recent memory. The traffic along Flower Street, and downtown generally, proceeded at a crawl. News vendors had laid plastic sheets over their supplies of that day's *Herald-Examiner*, whose inside headline promised 'DIRECTOR TO BE GIVEN "MORE TIME IN JAIL"'. Shortly after ten that morning, a half-hour later than scheduled, Polanski arrived for a briefing with Douglas Dalton and his civil lawyer, Wally Wolf. After listening to a precis of the previous day's session, he wandered over to the plate glass window, thirty-three floors up, and stood staring out into a storm 'altogether more impressive' than that subsequently seen in *Hurricane*. By his account, Polanski had then asked his criminal attorney words closely to the effect of, 'Why should I go back to jail until I have to beg to be deported? Why not just leave?' Dalton had reportedly looked down at the papers on his desk and begun to make a dignified speech about the necessity to remain calm, and that, in time, he would seek to have the judge removed from the case. He might as well have been reciting the legal small print in a mortgage advertisement. When, after several moments, he glanced up,

Dalton found that he was addressing only his fellow attorney. Polanski was already on his way back to the Château Marmont.

After packing his bag at the hotel, Polanski got in his Mercedes and continued down Sunset Boulevard to Dino De Laurentiis' office in Beverly Hills. According to a secretary's diary entry, he arrived there at 1.06 p.m. Polanski told the producer, with whom he had evidently remained friendly, that he had decided to leave the country. Other than a tentative enquiry from a 'picture house in France', he now had 'no professional or personal life' and thus 'nothing to stay for'. De Laurentiis hugged his guest, and agreed that it was the best solution. The judge, before whom he had appeared himself, was a *cazzo*, or prick. An assistant was summoned to collect all the cash on the premises, approximately $1,000, which was thrust into Polanski's pocket. The staff had then assembled in an informal receiving line to shake his hand and applaud him. Polanski left the building at 2.25 p.m. and continued to drive westward toward Santa Monica, home not only to Rittenband's courthouse but a small airport, where pale sunshine was now breaking through over the ocean. Hurriedly revising his plan to charter a plane and pilot it across the border to Mexico, he made a U-turn, headed south on the San Diego freeway and arrived at the departures terminal of LA International sometime between 3.30 and 4 p.m. Polanski left his Mercedes in the short-term parking lot and went inside to the British Airways reservations desk, where, after standing 'interminably' in line, he used a credit card to buy the last remaining first-class seat on Flight 508 non-stop to London, departing at 5.57 p.m. The ticket agent accepted his French passport as valid for travel, having no reason to do otherwise, and advised him to go directly to the gate. Polanski barely had time to phone his secretary to tell her about the car, and then Dalton, to let him know that he wouldn't be in court the following morning.

Polanski had first landed in Los Angeles on 13 April 1964, and been met by a black stretch limousine bearing a Polish flag, before being feted at that night's Oscars ceremony. He arrived a local hero and departed fourteen years later a fugitive from justice. Polanski had 'always seen everything in front of him and nothing behind, his eyes firmly fixed on a future he always seemed to be hurtling toward – and for him that was California', his friend and fellow director Andrzej Wajda recalled. And now the whole experience had come full circle. Quite apart from his legal woes, there was the fact that Polanski had come, in an almost affectionate way, to utterly and completely loathe what he called the

Hollywood 'factory' – or at least its corporate stupidity, its inverted pyramid of talentless middle managers and ever-expanding legion of 'flaccid lawyers and accountants' whose job, apparently, was to wilfully stifle creative souls like himself. So there were few regrets about his hasty departure. Polanski admits only to being 'exhilarated, almost manic' as he watched the lights of the city vanish below him. If in fleeing America he had hoped not only to make a new artistic start but also to leave behind that press creation, the 'evil dwarf', he was mistaken, however. He was chained to it.

Polanski arrived at Heathrow shortly before noon on 1 February. At 2 p.m. local time, 6 a.m. in Los Angeles, he rang Douglas Dalton to confirm that 'Rittenband has seen the last of me'. Three hours later, Dalton stood up in court and announced, 'Your Honour, I received news from Mr Polanski advising me he would not be with us this morning.'

'Where is he?' the judge asked.

'I do not believe he is in the United States,' Dalton replied.

At that point, Rittenband issued a bench warrant for Polanski's arrest and sent the district attorney a memo formally requesting that his investigator look into the matter. Later that morning, a Stephen Trott of the DA's office reportedly assured the press, 'We've got the dogs out, the hounds are on his trail . . . We will extradite Polanski from anywhere, as long as there's a treaty.'

Precisely what happened in London that long Wednesday has always been difficult to establish. Polanski himself writes only that, after sitting alone in his damp and unheated house for several hours, 'I felt I wasn't safe even now.' Other accounts insist that he made a hurried appointment with a lawyer, who advised him that a British court, as opposed to its French counterpart, could 'send [him] back to America in chains' within as little as a month. In fact, the relevant treaty as it stood in 1978 was open to interpretation, guaranteeing merely the 'provisional detention' of a properly identified suspect such as Polanski, who would enjoy the 'full and unrestricted right of appeal' against any subsequent ruling. It would be another twenty-five years before, prompted by the 9/11 atrocities, the UK government introduced proposals specifically intended to 'facilitate the swift removal of terrorist suspects and [other] criminals, including those considered fugitives from law, from these shores to the United States, and vice versa,' to quote David Blunkett. Even so, Polanski can hardly have relished the prospect of spending the next several months or years fighting probable extradition proceedings. At six that same evening, without having unpacked, he took a cab back to Heathrow, where he again presented his credit card and passport to an obliging British Airways ticket agent. The Los Angeles district attorney's dragnet had evidently not yet extended to the world's busiest airport, because Polanski was able to board a scheduled flight to Paris, where he arrived shortly after 10 p.m. local time.

Some weeks later, an incident took place at the Fulham home of Polanski's friend and producer Timothy Burrill which seemed to confirm the wisdom of his onward flight. As Burrill recalls, 'One afternoon a car skidded to a halt outside, parking on the double-yellow line. Two plain-clothes gentlemen got out, rang the doorbell and enquired if Roman was with me.' On being told that he wasn't, the officers had made it 'very clear' that Polanski would be arrested should he ever again set foot in the United Kingdom.

The 'picture house' mentioned to Dino De Laurentiis turned out to be Renn Productions, which, along with Burrill's own company, was amenable to financing a new adaptation of Thomas Hardy's *Tess of the d'Urbervilles*, a project Sharon Tate had also urged on her husband. From his sanctuary on the avenue Montaigne, Polanski threw himself into the 'welcome relief' of pre-production meetings, while issuing a series of defiant statements to the media. 'I've been tortured by this thing for a year, and that's enough,' he told the BBC by phone. The director spoke to at least one friend 'in all seriousness' about his holding a full-scale press conference to 'give [his] side of the story'. The friend in question 'affectionately told Roman he was nuts, which I rather gather was the consensus elsewhere'. There never was a press conference, but Polanski's generally unapologetic comments, his caustic humour and his increasingly tart remarks about 'Tinseltown' made him more than ever Hollywood's ogre – that necessary figure – whose 'snub nose', to quote *Time*, was 'being gleefully thumbed at America'. Not that, even now, he was entirely free of the threat of retribution. On 2 February, a spokesman for the ministry of justice in Paris confirmed that, as a French citizen, 'Polanski may not be extradited under any circumstances.' However, the spokesman added, 'the judicial authorities may decide to try this case in France'.

On the morning of 4 February, Douglas Dalton and his colleague Wally Wolf appeared at avenue Montaigne and attempted, for the next several hours, to persuade their client to return with them. Polanski listened politely, then told them that they had wasted their time. Before they departed, he treated them to dinner and a nightclub.

Two days later, back in Santa Monica, the parties reassembled in front of Judge Rittenband, who was told that 'Mr Polanski feels there is a degree of animus operating toward him' and, as a result, would 'not be available' for sentencing. Rittenband spoke to reporters later that afternoon, allowing that Polanski was 'guilty of moral turpitude' and thus (surely a non sequitur) had 'no place here in the United States'. Dalton then moved that Rittenband be disqualified from the case, citing 'bias and prejudice'. The judge vehemently denied any such thing, but agreed to stand aside 'for the sake of expediency'. The case of The People v. Polanski was removed from the court calendar, though, as the district attorney noted, 'the process will resume promptly when and if the defendant returns to our jurisdiction'.*

In the end, the French authorities declined to prosecute Polanski, who at last began to enjoy some notably more positive press coverage. The Paris daily Le Matin referred to America's 'excessively prudish petite bourgeoisie' in its account of the case, while other reports compared the director's ordeal to that endured by Nelson Mandela or the 'great Soviet dissidents'. Polanski was still compelled, nonetheless, to answer the eventual 1988 civil suit in which Samantha Gailey, identified only as 'Jane Doe', sought damages for 'physical and emotional distress'. Even this strictly private hearing brought several days' worth of headlines. In a precedent-setting ruling which anticipated the High Court's contentious decision seventeen years later allowing Polanski to give evidence by videolink, and thus avail himself of British justice without the risk of arrest, California's Second District Court of Appeal announced that he did not forfeit the right to contest Gailey's claims through his attorney because of his 'reprehensible, irresponsible and unlawful absence'. The terms of the subsequent judgement were sealed, but are said to have involved Polanski paying his victim a six-figure sum, as well as agreeing not to discuss the case in public.

If so, the reported confidentiality clause appears not to have been mutually binding. Some years later, Polanski's accuser, now named Samantha Geimer, threw herself headlong into a series of press interviews. The director 'took advantage of me' she confirmed to the Los Angeles Times in 2003, before repeating the widely held theory that 'a plea bargain was agreed to by his lawyer, my lawyer and the district attorney, and approved

---

* 'It remains an outstanding matter between Mr Polanski and the court,' the district attorney's office added to me in 2007. There's 'no question' of an amnesty.

by the court. But to our amazement, at the last minute the judge went back on his word and refused to honour the deal.' (Twenty-six years after she launched her complaint, Ms Geimer would appear to be labouring under the twin misapprehensions that the penalty in cases like hers is set purely to suit the victim, and, indeed, that there was ever any such 'deal' to be dishonoured in the first place.) Both then and in subsequent articles, Geimer seemed to become an unlikely champion of the man she once alleged had 'raped and perverted' her. 'I have to imagine,' she said, 'Mr Polanski would rather not be a fugitive and be able to travel freely. Personally, I would like to see that happen. He never should have been put in the position that led him to flee. He should have received a sentence of time served, just as we all agreed . . . Who wouldn't think about running when facing a fifty-year sentence from a judge who was clearly more interested in his own reputation than a fair judgement? If Roman Polanski could resolve his issues, I'd be glad.'

Those issues notwithstanding, Polanski appeared to be a relatively happy man during the early days of his chosen exile. When he strolled outside on the Champs-Élysées, a large crowd invariably gathered around him to applaud. The men signified their approval by clapping and the women by jostling among themselves to touch the hem of his coat, and frequently much more. Once or twice, when particularly moved by the occasion, Polanski would lunge eagerly at his audience, flinging his arms high above his head, his fingers extended in a Churchillian V-sign, his familiar impish face split wide in what no one could doubt was a victory smile. Noting the incongruity of the scene, it struck the visiting ABC News correspondent as 'oddly like Nixon's perky departure from the White House', another occasion when 'a man some saw as the villain apparently saw himself as the hero'.

For all that, it would continue to irk Polanski to be denied entry to America and other countries because of 'one old man's intransigence'. Thanks exclusively, as he saw it, to Judge Rittenband, he could no longer work in 'the world's film capital' (whatever else he thought of Hollywood), or stroll down the King's Road in London or even visit his wife's grave. 'Here in France, people like me more than America,' Polanski quite factually told the New York Times in 1987, before adding that his legal situation was being 'actively examined' by lawyers on both sides of the Atlantic. 'I want to do something about it, yes, [for] my peace of mind,' he said. These negotiations reportedly foundered as a result of Polanski's insistence that he not serve any further time in Chino or an even worse facility. As the district attorney had long since noted, 'no one would [make] such a guarantee'. For his part, Judge Rittenband, having once vowed to remain on the bench until Polanski returned for sentencing, finally retired in June 1989, aged 83. 'I can't wait that long,' he told reporters at a packed press conference. The judge then held forth on a variety of his celebrity acquaintances, admitting that, while Elvis was 'a nice man', his memory of Polanski was 'less fond'. Rittenband died at the home of a female companion in Los Angeles in December 1993.

The folk memory of this self-admittedly 'outspoken' jurist is of an eccentric and increasingly vindictive fogey who, in reneging on the terms of a mutually binding agreement, drove an internationally revered artist into exile. It's a caricature, if one that has a grain of truth. Rittenband may well have led the lawyers to believe at their meeting of 16 September that Polanski would ultimately seem to be well qualified as a candidate for probation. It's further possible that he may have been influenced by some of the simulated moral outrage in the media, and among his own friends, at the time he originally sent the director to Chino. Nor had the picture taken at the Munich Oktoberfest improved his overall disposition. Several of the judge's public comments on the case were at best tactless and at worst brazenly injudicious. As noted, he may conceivably have given counsel to tacitly understand that Polanski would avoid jail, although Rittenband reportedly later insisted that these 'well-compensated mouthpieces' simply hadn't listened to him with sufficient care. 'I celebrate myself and sing myself/And what I assume you shall assume,' he remarked, citing Walt Whitman. For all that, however, Rittenband never 'went back on his word', to quote Samantha Geimer, and 'refused to honour the deal approved by the court'. There never was any such deal. Even had he seemed to offer some encouragement to the non-custodial line of argument, Rittenband neither proposed nor accepted it as a contractual commitment. At the hearing of 8 August 1977, at which Polanski pleaded guilty on the basis of a supposed prior 'understanding' with the judge, the prosecutor, Roger Gunson, had put a series of questions both to the defendant and his attorney.

Among them was this exchange:

MR GUNSON: Mr Polanski, has anyone threatened you or threatened anyone near and dear to you, in order to get you to plead guilty?

THE DEFENDANT: No.

MR GUNSON:	The district attorney will make a motion to dismiss the remaining pending charges after sentencing. Other than that promise, has anyone made any promises whatsoever to you, such as a lesser sentence or probation, or any reward? Immunity? A court recommendation to the immigration and naturalisation service, or anything else, in order to get you to plead guilty?
THE DEFENDANT:	No.
MR GUNSON:	Counsel, have you fully discussed with Mr Polanski his rights, his defences, and the possible consequences to him of his plea of guilty?
MR DALTON:	Yes.
MR GUNSON:	Are you aware of any promises whatsoever that have been made to your client, that have not been stated on the record and in open court today?
MR DALTON:	No.

THROUGHOUT THE SPRING OF 1978, the French media became increasingly more fulsome toward the distinguished refugee in their midst. As Judge Rittenband himself noted a shade tartly, 'Solzhenitsyn in Siberia didn't derive more moral credit than Polanski did for living in Paris.' Over the years, the director had had something of an ambivalent relationship, even so, with his adopted home. When he had first lived there in 1960 he was a struggling film-maker who could, and did, walk about without being recognised, and who was still treated by the world in general as an ordinary human being rather than as a *monstre sacré*. Polanski appears not to have relished the experience. Recalling an incident when his wife had been robbed on the Métro, he writes in his autobiography, 'My rage transferred itself from the thief to the French in general – to the snooty coiffeur who wouldn't set Barbara's hair unless she let him cut it as well; to the supercilious neighbourhood grocer who sneered because we always bought the cheapest brands; to every callous, arrogant, sarcastic, cocksure Parisian I'd ever met.'

Eighteen years later Polanski's opinion had evolved significantly, although some of his earlier qualms remained. When a journalist asked him what he most liked about Paris, he replied, 'Everything, apart from the behaviour of Parisians, the arrogance of the newspaper vendors, and the rude toilet attendants.' In answer to another reporter's question,

Polanski denied missing anything about America in general and Hollywood in particular. 'I'm basically European, and everything I love is here in Paris,' he said. 'I don't know of any other city of the world where you can see so much.' There was the added advantage, he later told Charlie Rose, that 'I don't want to be all over the tabloids [and] here in France we have wonderful[ly] strict laws regarding privacy.' 'Paris vibrates,' Polanski summarised it to *Le Nouvel Observateur*. 'You need five lives to keep up with what's going on. For anyone interested in culture or who works in show business, it's heaven on earth.'

Polanski certainly found the life on avenue Montaigne more congenial than his probable next residence had he remained in America, a cell in the sexual-offenders wing of a prison like Folsom or San Quentin. His fourth floor apartment above an Iranian bank building is described by visitors as simply furnished and impeccably modern – 'all glass and spotlights'. Polanski could if he so chose look out from his balcony, over a long row of horse chestnut trees, on to some of the world's most fashionable retailers. Christian Dior, Bulgari and Chanel were among his immediate neighbours. For a month or so in early 1978 the high-rise directly opposite played host to a 'seedy' collection of photographers and reporters, some of whom would periodically stride up to the glass front door of Number 43 and tell the concierge they were 'friends of M. Polanski', but eventually even the most tenacious paparazzi, perhaps deterred by those 'wonderfully strict' privacy laws, abandoned their perch.

After Polanski's arrest, later compounded by his flight, most media opinion of him had, he rightly noted, 'soured appreciably', for the good reason that a whole catalogue of alleged sexual crimes and misdemeanours had necessarily been exposed – as much by events as by any diligence on the reporters' part. Primarily for that reason, there was a 'morbid' press interest in the subject of Polanski's next film. If *Macbeth* had seemed to some to peculiarly echo the Manson murders, then *Tess* would strike at least one critic, Pauline Kael, as a 'wilfully macabre' partial retelling of recent real-life events, with its 'self-pitying' leading man and 'defiled heroine'. 'You'd have thought Roman Polanski would have had the decency to do a war film or something,' the *Hollywood Reporter* remarked.

Polanski spent several days that spring photographing Nastassia Kinski in a series of romantic poses designed to promote both her and their new film together. The tastefully staged and soft-focus results, reminiscent to one arts correspondent of the 'erotic daydreams of David Hamilton' (with the critical distinction that the young model remained fully clothed) and suggesting to another a sort of 'Victorian Pirelli calendar', appeared in a double-page spread in *Variety* to coincide with the Cannes festival. The caption read simply, 'Tess, by Roman Polanski.' The layout brought the attention not only of would-be investors but of a large number of critics around the world. Back in Santa Monica, Judge Rittenband is said to have remarked to a reporter from a weekly newspaper that it was perhaps just as well Polanski had decided to relocate to Europe. Publishing photographs of a teenaged girl, however chaste, 'wasn't exactly an exercise in contrition' after what had happened a year earlier. 'Someone like that,' the judge sadly concluded, 'forfeits his right to live in America.'

CHAPTER 8
FRANTIC

Thomas Hardy's *Tess of the d'Urbervilles: A Pure Woman Faithfully Presented* had caused 'a furore', Polanski told one of the cast of his film, because the author had 'challenged the moral code' of the 1890s. The actor in question adds that he drew his own conclusions as to 'why Roman might have been drawn to that particular text'. As well as the violent seduction, or rape of the heroine, there was the 'masterly evocation [of a] simpler, peasant life' that put the director 'fondly in mind', he noted, of the Polish countryside. Polanski would also have recognised the book's central conflict between good and evil, as personified by Tess' two suitors, the alternately caddish and weak-willed Alec and the kindly but overweeningly self-righteous Angel. Perhaps it would be fairer to say that each of the men is a composite of attractive and repulsive qualities; each is at odds with himself as much as he is with his rival. There is a concomitant degree of satire in Hardy's book about the only limited opportunities for social mobility in late Victorian England. Over recent years, a good deal of earnest academic effort has also gone into portraying the character of Tess as something of an earth mother. She begins the story by participating in a festival for Ceres, the goddess of the harvest, and ends it lying down, as though engaging in a pagan fertility ritual, on a slab at Stonehenge. This, too, may have resonated with Polanski, who at this stage still tended to see women as 'gorgeous' and 'fecund' creatures rather than as dogged careerists like himself.*

The actor-cum-producer Claude Berri had first met Polanski in Paris in 1960, had expressed interest in *Pirates* fifteen years later and 'now more than ever wanted to back Roman'. Like Timothy Burrill, Berri received a number of official or quasi-official warnings about his collaborating with 'somebody on the FBI's fugitive list'. To be a friend of Polanski in the late Seventies was to be a candidate for this sort of treatment, which both men loyally ignored. The 43-year-old Berri had had mixed professional fortunes over the years, although his early comedy *Le Poulet* had won an Oscar for Best Short. His most recent project was a mildly scabrous film called *One Wild Moment* (remade with Michael Caine as *Blame it on Rio*) in which a middle-aged man has sex with his best friend's teenage daughter. Berri had formally committed to *Tess* after Polanski arrived at his house in Paris one evening accompanied by Nastassia Kinski. By all accounts, the young actress had cut a striking figure. 'Seeing her in her skirt and little blouse,' Berri told *L'Express*, 'I understood immediately that I was going to accept.' The next morning, the producer opened negotiations to buy the film rights to *Tess of the d'Urbervilles*, which were held by the estate of David Selznick of *Gone With the Wind* fame. Although the book would again be in the public domain in December 1978, just seven months away, Berri paid $50,000 in order to secure the property immediately. It would be by no means the greatest of his extravagances over the next year. Polanski and Gérard Brach then locked themselves up on the avenue Montaigne and began work on a screenplay. Bowing to the challenges of 'a Pole and a Frenchman adapt[ing] a novel set in Victorian Wessex', they eventually hired an English writer named John Brownjohn who, by a happy coincidence, actually lived in Marnhull, the 'Marlott' of Hardy's novel. On the front of the finished typescript, Polanski added the dedication, 'To Sharon'.

---

* The author, for all that, disowned some of the more fanciful symbolism attributed to his book. Replying to a reader in December 1909, Hardy noted that '*Tess of the d'Urbervilles* was not written to "prove anything" about Heaven or Earth ... To be sure, Tess is called on the title page "A Pure Woman", but that statement was in no way meant as a challenge (though it was taken as such in some quarters). It was added in at the last moment after reading the proofs as a mere description, unlikely to be disputed, as one might say "an accomplished lady" or "a man of wealth".'

Nastassia Kinski, for her part, was entrusted to a dialogue coach in London in an effort to master a Dorset accent, a stiff task by most people's standards let alone those of a 17-year-old German actress whose English had been charitably described, just a year earlier, as 'limited'. Critics were in two minds about the final results. Although 'Kinski's vocal experiment [was] a disaster', the *New York Post* found her 'a good-looker, with a touch of Ingrid Bergman'. She seemed 'somewhat hesitant in her manner', perhaps understandably so under the circumstances, and was still 'far from being in the great man's league'. The 'great man' was Klaus Kinski, Nastassia's father, who had left the family when she was just 8 years old. By her own admission, 'Nasty' had subsequently grown up 'too fast', embarking on relationships with older men because, as she once concluded, she was 'always a child longing for that authority figure'.

While Claude Berri applied himself to the twin challenges of securing his financial backing and lining up a galaxy of talent in the hectic period following his pre-announcement of *Tess*, Polanski ensured that parts were found in the film for the likes of 60-year-old Richard Pearson, the doctor in *Macbeth*, and other comparatively unsung British television performers to whom he became an unlikely patron. John Collin of *All Creatures Great and Small* was signed to play Tess' father John Durbeyfield, Rosemary Martin of *The Sweeney* played his wife and Peter Firth (*Equus*) was Angel Clare. The role of Alec, Tess' seducer, went to a young stage actor named Leigh Lawson, who, before committing to the part, asked his agent, 'Where's the script?' 'Read the book,' she advised him. In the event, Polanski would still be 'frantically revising' the text each night in his hotel room, then bringing the pages to the set a few hours later to be filmed.

By early summer, the producers had scoured Normandy and the surrounding areas of northern France in order to find a look as close as possible to the English countryside, eventually involving some seventy locations in all. Berri's estimated budget rose from $6 million to $8 million. As on *Macbeth*, production assistants were dispatched to remove 'TV ariels [and] any other twentieth century obtrusions', as one of the film's publicists recalled. 'On that spend, nothing was too much trouble. Highways were made straight for Roman [and] rivers were forded lest he get his feet wet.' A superlative technical crew had been engaged, among them Geoffrey Unsworth, the Oscar-winning cinematographer whose numerous credits included *A Night to Remember*, *2001* and *Cabaret*, and the venerable costume designer Anthony Powell. Everyone assembled 'in high spirits' says Leigh Lawson, fully convinced, after a week's intensive rehearsal, that 'we were in the hands of a master craftsman' for whom 'no detail was too small ... Roman quite rightly insisted, for example, that I spend my every waking hour when not actually in front of the camera walking around in jodhpurs, smoking a cigar, because that was what Alec would do.' Other cast members were similarly 'living their way into their characters', and following the eve-of-production dinner Polanski climbed up on a stage to happily announce that they were 'fantastic ... the best prepared team' of his experience, before throwing several bunches of red roses down to the crowd.

Now all that remained was the shoot, which did not go well.

Aside from the familiar hazards of making a period film even in rural surroundings – next to the quaint labourers' cottages would be a village shop lit with a neon sign – *Tess* presented a whole series of its own perverse, if not fully unique challenges. The first day of filming, 7 August, involved a particularly elaborate set-up in which Alec was to feed Tess a strawberry while lying together in a field on what the script describes as 'a perfect summer's day'. Polanski awoke to find it pouring with rain. Despite advance requests, no 'full-scale repairs' had been made to a large greenhouse essential to the scene – nor repairs of any description. Once the union labourers supplied by the state-owned film agency had departed for the day, promptly at 3 p.m., the director and a volunteer crew of actors, technicians, costume designers, stuntmen and others picked up the discarded paintbrushes and finished the job themselves. In the weeks ahead, an assortment of other natural or man-made obstacles brought about repeated and costly stoppages, and frequent shifts of location. Just as had been the case on *Macbeth*, the weather was atrocious nearly throughout, and all too many mornings began with the props boys shinning up trees to erect a waterproof canopy over the actors' heads, while Polanski fumed at the resulting delay. The production was interrupted more than once by the noise of French air force jets and other traffic screaming out over the Channel. Nastassia Kinski repeated one short speech twenty-seven times before the sound crew deemed it technically passable. Leigh Lawson remembers doing a particular exterior shot 'thirty or thirty-five times, grow[ing] increasingly pissed off until I heard Roman's voice booming out over the loudhailer, "Don't worry, Leigh! It's fantastic! Keep doing what you're doing. We're just trying to get the birds to behave."'

As Richard Pearson says, 'Much of *Tess* was a nightmare, and would be a prime candidate for one of those behind-the-scenes documentaries.

Having said that, I never had any problems with Polanski himself. His only real direction to me was to underact. He never wanted you to turn to the camera and declaim. It was always less, less, less. And to achieve that Roman would literally film you all day.'

Leigh Lawson also refers to *Tess*, for all its problems, as 'one of those golden memories an actor has . . . Polanski was *very* clear about what he wanted, and prepared to be quite ruthless in order to get it. People's feelings weren't spared. If something was wrong, he told you so. At the same time, you always had the feeling that, as a professional, you were going to be well looked after by Roman. You knew that all the hassle and repetition was in the interests of making a great film. "Tired but happy" would be a fair description of my emotions most evenings. I distinctly remember driving back to the hotel with Roman and three or four others, singing "We are the Champions" at the top of our lungs.'

When it came time for Lawson, as Alec, to ravish Tess, 'Polanski didn't offer any particular direction or insight, although it's conceivable it may have struck him as uncomfortably near the bone. Roman certainly didn't refer to his own predicament with the girl in California. I just remember him calling for take after take of that particular scene in order to "get the balance right", although that was his standard practice.' Thanks to the timely intervention of some artificially created fog, it would be left for the audience to decide whether Tess was in fact raped or merely 'taken', as the script rather ambiguously put it.

Although Polanski declined to impose his recent personal experience on the scene, he was 'uniquely hands-on', adds Leigh Lawson, 'when it came to most of the film's set pieces. Being an actor himself, he wasn't shy about "doing" your part for you in rehearsal. But it went further than that: in one shot, I had to gallop downhill on a trap, a heart-thumping experience for me because of the obvious risk on these occasions that the cart will crash into the horse. People have been killed doing it. Anyway, I survived the scene, and, a few minutes later, passed by Polanski on my way in to lunch. "Good fun," I said. "You know, Roman, the general wisdom is that you should never race a horse and cart downhill like that." I meant it more or less humorously, but perhaps the gauntlet was down. In any case, when I looked up again, there, on top of the hill, was Polanski, cigar in mouth, sitting in the very trap I'd just driven. As the entire cast and crew watched, he careened down at roughly twice my own speed, drew to a halt, dismounted and calmly walked in to eat. He never said a word.'

Lawson further notes that Polanski 'though always competitive' was 'a very different personality off set, where I found him to be a fantastic host. Everyone would be entertained royally with the best food and drink. Nothing was too much trouble. Roman actually *liked* actors, which is by no means universally true of directors.' Towards the end of filming *Tess*, Polanski was 'ecstatic' at an apparent visit by Peter Sellers, with whom he did an impromptu waltz in front of the cast. Alas, his partner turned out to be Sellers' latest stunt double, a Birmingham-based salesman and occasional performer named John Taylor. When he discovered his error, Polanski, to his credit, 'laughed as loudly as anyone'.

On 28 October, eleven weeks into production, the cameraman Geoffrey Unsworth suddenly fell ill in his Brittany hotel room. Polanski and others tried to revive him by snapping ammonia poppers under his nose until the emergency services arrived. The full gravity of the situation was brought home when, after rapidly assessing the patient, an ambulance man promptly began to pound Unsworth's chest with all his might in an effort to restart his heart. 'It was a bizarre atmosphere,' one crew member recalls. 'Two or three women were running up and down the stairs in hysterics, which the hotel manageress seemed to think was in some way part of the film, while Roman himself briskly exchanged views with the medical personnel, concerned, apparently, that they might break one of Geoffrey's ribs.' Despite their best efforts, Unsworth was pronounced dead later that night. He was 63. Though understandably shaken, Polanski elected to carry on filming as scheduled the next morning, with Ghislain Cloquet, a colleague of Claude Berri, ultimately replacing Unsworth. (In a macabre coincidence, which one or two Polanski watchers have fancifully attributed to a 'curse', Cloquet himself died shortly thereafter, aged 57.) Richard Pearson believes that 'Roman and Geoffrey Unsworth in fact didn't always see eye to eye on *Tess*, but losing someone like that, so unexpectedly, was obviously tragic for all concerned. I don't think the production was ever quite the same again.'

Polanski continued to painstakingly choreograph the film for another five months, sometimes reshooting a scene sentence by sentence or even on occasion phrase by phrase. There was also a 'lot of hanging around' says Leigh Lawson, 'waiting for the light to behave, at which point Roman would assemble everyone in a blur of activity.' After the ensuing shot, the cast and crew would wait expectantly. 'Fantastic!' Polanski routinely enthused, followed by the inevitable, 'We go again.' Having gone through an entire summer and autumn, the production then ran into the worst winter in northern France of the last sixty years. As a result, Polanski was able to show with 'total verisimilitude' the marked change of season integral to the plot of *Tess*. After enduring a freak early November snowstorm in Boulogne, the entire company moved back to the studio in Paris. Claude Berri's projected $8 million budget was consequently revised to $10 million.

Before *Tess* was finally wrapped, Polanski would, among other flourishes, order the construction of a plywood replica of an entire Dorset village, a complex of farm buildings, thatched cottages, spired churches, greenhouses and shops, all surrounded by immaculately trimmed hedges and innumerable stone walls, and criss-crossed by at least a dozen roads. As on *The Tenant*, he sometimes cleverly distorted his set with a large mirror, although many of the nineteenth-century dwellings seen in the film were built to scale. Perhaps not surprisingly, Leigh Lawson sensed a 'certain occasional tension between Roman and his financiers', with 'faintly sinister men in black overcoats, whom I took to be the producer's envoys, hovering around the place, making for an uncomfortable atmosphere.' Polanski's final supposed extravagance was his lavish recreation of Stonehenge in a field some forty miles north of Paris. The director later told Max Tessier of *Ecran* that he had been forced to take this step primarily because the actual site 'is a tourist attraction that's gradually wearing away; it's surrounded by barbed wire and there's even a caretaker's house sitting there', although this was to tactfully overlook the fact that Polanski himself would have been arrested had he travelled to the United Kingdom. When all the figures were added up, *Tess* would cost its producers $12.2 million, making it the most expensive film ever shot in France.

With that much money at stake, Polanski made himself available for a number of interviews, ostensibly to promote *Tess* but actually to rehash his recent 'unpleasantness' in Los Angeles. It has to be said that, by and large, he failed to cut an immediately sympathetic figure. Fortunately, in order for his films to succeed, it had never been necessary for his audiences to love Polanski personally. And now they didn't. He assured the highly rated American news show *60 Minutes*, for instance, 'The girl [Samantha Gailey] is not a child. She is a young woman. She's had, and she testified to it, previous sexual experience. She wasn't unschooled in sexual matters. She was consenting and willing. Whatever I did wrong, I think I paid for it. I went through a year of incredible hardship, and I think I paid for it.' It was perhaps unfortunate that a second interview appeared in the pages of the men's magazine *Club*, where Polanski's views on his ordeal, and the nuances of sexual etiquette, were juxtaposed with images of glossy young women fondling their breasts. Although the facts of his case could be made to fit almost any agenda, the general perception of him, at least in North America, remained what a fellow distinguished director summarises as a 'talented shit'. It was later reported that Polanski's name was one of those considered for an eleventh-hour pardon by Jimmy Carter on his last day in office in January 1981, but, if so, the departing president evidently thought better of it.

Polanski's performance at the 1979 Cannes festival – where Claude Berri had insisted that he and Kinski put in an appearance – did not find him at his best. It was, as he later confided, a 'fucking mess'. Shortly after their arrival, the pair were spirited into a small reception room in the Carlton Hotel, where a mob of eighty reporters and cameramen was waiting for them. Standing beneath a large poster showing Kinski posing in a white bonnet and the word 'Tess' incorporating a livid red heart dripping blood, Polanski, wearing a black silk shirt open to his midriff, began to expound on the 'moral paradox' and other aspects of his latest project, while periodically interrupting himself to appeal for 'calm' before again resuming his seminar on the as yet unfinished film. It wouldn't have mattered had he in fact been reciting the Polish national anthem, because nobody could hear him. After several angry chops of his hand, the director finally abandoned his prepared remarks and instead started a Q&A session, which essentially consisted of reporters bawling at him about his being an 'escaped convict', facing the 'threat of jail' and 'other problems'. 'I have no problems,' Polanski assured them. 'I want to talk about my film.'

Tactlessly asked to comment, moments later, on whether he would consider 'doing the honourable thing' by returning to America, Polanski repeated that 'I'm here to talk about my picture. Ask me about my work.' The same British reporter squeezed forward a few feet, then put his follow-up question: 'Tell us why you made *Tess*. It's the story of a very young girl who is sexually violated by an older man. Did you make it because of the parallels in your own life? The girl in your film kills the man who raped her. That is justice, is it not? You approve of that—'

'Wait!' Polanski snapped, rising to his feet. 'That's a stupid question! You're not asking a question, you're making a speech. Can't anyone ask an intelligent—'

'It's a question.'

'No—'

'My question is: you approve of Tess killing her seducer. So how can you complain all the time to the press that you got a raw deal in the United States? Isn't a couple of months in prison a lot better than getting killed?'

Without formally replying, Polanski suddenly dropped into a simian crouch, screwed up his face and emitted a long, high-pitched noise like that of a monkey, evidently to mock the reporter, if not the absurdity of the whole occasion. There was considerable laughter. From out of the din an elderly male French journalist asked Polanski, 'How do you feel now about young girls?' Putting his arm around Kinski's waist, the director replied affably, '*Je ne me suis jamais caché d'aimer les jeunes filles. Simplement, maintenant, je disai encore que j'aime les très jeunes filles.*' ('I've never hidden the fact that I like young girls. I will say again, once and for all, I like very young girls.') At that, Polanski turned to Kinski and planted a kiss on either her cheek or the corner of her mouth, depending on reports. There was again widespread laughter, although now mingled with a few jeers and catcalls. After giving it several seconds, Polanski then rolled his eyes in apparent rapture, and placed his hand over his crotch, as if masking an erection. That concluded the press conference.

THE EDITING OF *TESS* IF ANYTHING ECLIPSED THE ORDEAL OF ITS FILMING, involving the cutting of three separate versions, in English, German and French, which were elaborately mixed in quadrophonic sound. The whole process took so long that at one stage Polanski left the film in the hands of Sam O'Steen, the editor of *Rosemary's Baby* and *Chinatown*, and flew off on an extended walking tour of the Himalayas. When he returned to Paris, he found O'Steen lying exhausted on a cot in the studio, with Claude Berri loudly protesting that a running time of 172 minutes spelled commercial death for the film and bankruptcy for him personally.

On purely artistic grounds, it's arguable that *Tess* would have been better without both the formal, static shots of its heroine that reminded one critic of 'stills of the sort Polanski took of Sharon Tate for *Playboy*', and some of the other mundane day-to-day details draped over the film like a vast, obscuring dust sheet. There appears to have been a heated creative debate on the subject, with Berri at one point repeating his key assertion to Polanski across the floor of a crowded restaurant, 'It's *too long!* Nobody is going to buy it!' As the post-production problems mounted, so inevitably did the producers' investment. The various challenges of bringing *Tess* to the screen were so widely reported that, to one observer, a traditional review of the film when eventually released 'seem[ed] unnecessary ... all that was really needed was to publish the accounts'.

Tess was premiered in West Germany on 25 October 1979, to widespread derision. The film's reception in France six days later was marginally better, though the subsequent box office was disappointing. There were still no distribution arrangements in place for most other countries, including the United States and United Kingdom. At one stage Francis Ford Coppola expressed interest in marketing the film through his Zoetrope studios, although his eventual offer came with a number of conditions. Not the least of these was that *Tess'* opening credits should show the pages of Hardy's book being turned by hand, a device popular in screen adaptations of literary classics in the Hollywood of the Forties, after which a voice, 'something like Orson Welles'', would narrate the story. That terminated discussions between Polanski and Coppola. *Tess* was ultimately released by Columbia (the studio that had ejected Polanski from *The First Deadly Sin*) in both North America and Britain after Charles Champlin of the *Los Angeles Times* wrote a leading article describing it as 'the best film of the year', which had been 'scandalously ignored' as a result of apparent prejudice against the director.

At nearly three hours, *Tess* resembles nothing so much as a long series of colour-supplement photographs, gorgeous in themselves, but necessarily slow-burning when seen alongside the likes of *Stir Crazy*, *Airplane!* and the latest *Star Wars* saga, its primary contemporaneous competition in American cinemas. Its understated eloquence has worn well over the years. With one or two notable exceptions, the prevalent critical view in 1980 was that Polanski's 'film morality tale', to quote *Variety*, was 'pretentious and slow'. The consensus today is that *Tess* is one of those sumptuous period pieces whose deliberate pace is part of its charm, and a major achievement by a director who, whatever one makes of the rights or wrongs of the case, had effectively been on the run at the time he made the film, and under acute pressure of another sort right up to and beyond its initial release.

Tess won three Oscars at the 1981 Academy Awards, though Polanski lost as Best Director to Robert Redford for *Ordinary People*. There were also a host of Golden Globes, Baftas, Césars and other glittering prizes over the next two years. Thanks to the awards and word-of-mouth recommendation, it became a belated commerical success, recouping Claude Berri's investment and enabling the cast to travel on various promotional junkets. On one such tour of Latin America, Nastassia Kinski excited some interest by her habit of sunbathing in the nude, while Polanski himself cut a swathe through the nightclubs of Rio. *Tess* did exceptional business in Brazil, where much of the adult population had followed the Gailey affair as avidly as they did *Dallas*. On another night in Amsterdam, Leigh Lawson picked up the phone in his hotel room 'and, much to my surprise, heard Polanski's voice. Assuming the answer would be somewhere in France or Poland, I asked him where he was. "Down the hall," he said. He'd somehow slipped into Holland, where there was a treaty with the US, and, I gathered, actually sat in the back row at the premiere completely unrecognised. Roman assured me that he would be out of the country again before there was any "legal nonsense". In the meantime, he intended to take everyone out on the town to celebrate. Even in those circumstances, he wanted to party. It was a great night.'

THE LEGAL, TECHNICAL AND FINANCIAL CHALLENGES of making *Tess* took their toll on Polanski. For the first time in twenty years, he neither had a new film project on the horizon, nor was he looking for one. In interviews, he began referring to himself as a 'former' director. The loss of momentum in his career around the turn of the Eighties, together with the continuing fallout from the rape case, combined to create an especially vulnerable state of affairs in which he alternated between bouts of 'megalomanical self-confidence' and the conviction that his best days were behind him, with only 'repetition and self-parody' ahead. In the event, Polanski had two offers of work in the early weeks of 1980: another satanic-worship film, to be produced by a mortuary- and parking lot-based conglomerate underwritten by junk bonds, and scheduled to be shot in Albania, and a cameo role in Steven Spielberg's *Raiders of the Lost Ark*. He declined both invitations.

One frequent visitor to avenue Montaigne describes the Polanski of the early Eighties as a 'mildly eccentric' character who spent much of his time obsessively making notes about his life for a proposed autobiography, in order to 'counter all the lies written about him'. By all accounts, it was a particularly intense research process. 'Roman [was] a master at blocking the world out, ignoring everything except what he considered a priority. Although he's normally the most efficient man, that wasn't necessarily the case when he was on a mission. Phones rang and messages weren't returned. Faxes never received replies. He'd eventually get around to dealing with what he felt was most important in the pile, he'd always make good on a promise, but the rest of it could wait forever.' Polanski continued, even so, to enjoy an active social life; indeed, merely to leave the apartment was an adventure, according to a friend and future collaborator named Jeff Gross, as 'women would approach him every few yards as he walked down the street, expressing their love of his work, or other endearments'. When Polanski stepped out of a taxi or alighted from a train, reporters crowded round him, and there were impromptu press conferences at curbside and station – 'this was a man', the *Herald Tribune* wrote, 'more famous, [and] a more guaranteed source of good copy, than any film star'.

Polanski remained a notably popular figure in his local haunts, where, Jeff Gross adds, his party pieces included 'telling an endless stream of stories and blue jokes, and a pet trick where he would tip a glass of wine off the edge of the table and then catch it before it hit the floor – impressive, if a little lacking in *gravitas* for a 50-year-old man.' Another acquaintance similarly recalls the 'public Polanski' as exuding 'millions of volts of synthetic charm', and 'always ensuring he was the centre of attention, whether by telling the most outrageous stories or ostentatiously leaving the biggest tips'. One American magazine columnist went to lunch with the 'notorious masher' fully determined to 'loathe him on sight [but] began to weaken from the moment we sat down, the signal for Roman to call for champagne while leaning forward to relate an uproariously obscene story about the late John Wayne and two nuns'. When the party eventually broke up around 4 p.m., 'the waiters lined up and applauded, unabashedly paying their respects to a great man in a way you somehow couldn't imagine them doing in the States'.

On average two or three nights a week, Polanski took a taxi down the rue de Rivoli to an ultra-hip, split-level basement club called Les Bains-Douches, where one English admirer remembers him 'chugging out on to the dance floor, wearing a hat, dark shirt and shades, looking a bit like a Hofmeister bear without the fur'. The same neon-lit cellar also provided the director with a controlled environment for his still-frequent dealings with the 'non-sewer' end of the media. Throughout the Eighties, Polanski typically used the club as a venue in which to meet both would-be producers and, more often, reporters. It was an inspired choice on his part, as even the most cynical interviewer tended to warm appreciably to his subject when plied with the finest food and wine. A distinguished British film critic went over to Paris in 1981 for 'a serious Q&A session with Roman, and instead found myself lapping up bowls of caviar and other goodies at his booth'. Around two the next afternoon, the journalist woke up with what he calls an 'ideological hangover', having been 'completely seduced by the man's extraordinary personal charm'.

A roughly similar combination of charisma and good humour did wonders for Polanski's love life, which showed no signs of decline in middle age. One afternoon while visiting Paris in the winter of 1981, Jack Nicholson happened to meet the model Tara Shannon and a friend named Lisa Rutledge leaving the George V Hotel. After exchanging pleasantries, the actor invited them to join him at 'a little party around the corner', by which he meant Polanski's apartment. Finding the place to be already 'full of 14-year-old blondes', the two women soon made their excuses and left. One self-described 'Polanski groupie' who later spent a night with him at avenue Montaigne recalls that 'girls like me were told they were the love of his life, before being ditched with the same self-loathing as an empty tub of Haagen-Dazs'.

One popular theory of post-*Tess* Polanski was that he had joined the long line of artists embittered by unsatisfactory fame, and become, to quote *Today*, 'more sparingly available', if not reclusive, as a result. Instead of making movies, he was 'mooch[ing] around Paris, working on his tan, playing chess and bedding an unfeasible number of young women'. It's true that a certain degree of professional disillusion had set in, as the mainstream film industry now went through another of its cyclical crises. 'When I started out twenty years ago,' Polanski told *Le Matin de Paris*, 'the job of the director involved about thirty per cent of dreary but unavoidable discussions with producers ignorant of artistic demands. Today the figure is ninety per cent and these never-ending conversations have become so demoralising that I just can't stand them. The film business has fallen into the hands of profiteers who are only interested in prestige, honour, and, to put it crudely, cheap sex.' It's also true that Polanski was constrained by the American justice system from working in Hollywood even had he wanted to. Shortly before the 1981 Academy Awards ceremony, the Los Angeles district attorney informed the press that 'should Mr Polanski choose to attend, he will be arrested [and] brought before a judge for sentencing'. But the legend that the director had, to again quote *Today*, 'thrown it all away, sabotaging his career for a life of guilt-ridden exile' involving 'solitary evenings in front of the TV' was something of an overstatement. Polanski was probably enjoying himself more than at any time since the late Sixties. Not coincidentally, he was also steadily going broke, forcing him not only to sell his London house but to cast around for such work as he could get.

In the five years since *Rigoletto*, Polanski had fielded a number of offers to direct operas in Italy, Germany and Spain (none of which countries presented any legal obstacles), as well as the chance to do 'straight' theatre on the Paris stage. What was more, he told the enquiring parties that he would also star in the eventual production, an artistic revenge, perhaps, for his rejection thirty years earlier by the Krakow drama school. 'We do not have many parts which call for people of your build,' Polanski had been told. There was also talk of his accepting further commissions as a 'glamour' photographer, the occasion for a long, anonymous syndicated newspaper profile calling him 'immensely talented, a man of charismatic quality, in some ways genuinely an idealist, [but] suffering from a megalomaniac rejection of anything he sees as hostile criticism . . . He apparently still doesn't understand why anyone would reasonably take exception to his posing half-dressed teenaged girls.'

Polanski also set to work on his memoirs. This monumental task, accomplished with the help of a *Newsweek* stringer named Ed Behr, was sold to the American publisher William Morrow for a reported $500,000, with half as much again offered for the foreign rights. This was serious money for a celebrity autobiography in the early Eighties, particularly since Polanski had made only a relatively modest $300,000 for his two years' hard labour on *Tess*. There had been some fears that the US authorities would attempt to attach the publisher's advance, under the laws prohibiting a felon from profiting 'whether directly or indirectly [from] the monetary exploitation of his crime', but these proved groundless. Polanski and his amanuensis wrote a book that was by turns exhilarating and, on the occasions when moral indignation set in, faintly dull.

In the meantime, Polanski suffered through a few desultory meetings with visiting Hollywood executives, who brought him proposals that could have been done 'by a couple of drunks during five minutes of a night in the bar and sketched out on the back of a beer mat'. In fact, most of the ideas were hardly complex enough to require even that, dealing as they did exclusively with 'UFOs [and] lesbian vampires'. When resting between films in the past, Polanski had cheerfully quoted the Polish proverb, 'I hear the bells ringing, but I don't know from which church they're coming', meaning that something, somewhere would turn up. From around 1980 to 1984, the bells were silent. The pity was that so much of his time was taken up not with working but in futile negotiations that somehow never translated 'property' into 'product'.

One or two of Polanski's professional suitors, it has to be said, flew home from their discussions apparently unimpressed by the man, whom a particularly well known studio chief depicts as 'humourless'. (This was tame compared to the visiting press agent, apparently dispatched to assess Polanski's suitability for a project that would have invited an unusual degree of media interest, who reportedly found his host 'the most snooty, cocksure, anal person. He made me ill.') Perhaps it would be fairer to say that Polanski did not project the kind of locker-room joviality that, among American men, often passes for wit. He was well informed and a prolific monologuist on everything from world politics to the correct protocol for eating a kiwi fruit. Nor was Polanski ever a martyr to self-modesty. He was, however, extraordinarily generous and loyal to a wide range of people, even those with whom there may have been a temporary cool-ness over the years. In April 1981, Hugh Hefner abruptly fired Victor Lownes as part of a wholesale 'restructuring' of the Playboy empire, a prelude to Hefner's closure of the landmark London club. Lownes had fallen out with Polanski ten years earlier, when the director had given an unhelpful interview at the time of *Macbeth*'s release. There had subse-quently been a sulphurous exchange of letters and a mutual return of gifts, among them that 22-carat gold appendage. So Lownes was unprepared when the phone rang one evening shortly after his dismissal and a voice announced, 'I have Roman Polanski on the line. Will you take the call?'

According to Lownes, Polanski was 'extremely gracious' in his remarks. 'I'm in Paris and I've been hearing about what happened at Playboy,' he said. 'I want to tell you that I'm very sorry to hear what they've done to you.' It was a central fact of Polanski's life that even some of his most ardent supporters, as well as those on the other side of the fence, so often saw him as a performer, a man not only trying to make an impression, but calculating to a fine degree exactly what impression he wanted to make – including, on occasion, that of a big-hearted friend. Lownes, an extremely astute judge of character, thought Polanski's call 'completely sincere', without side, and would remain 'deeply moved' by the gesture.

IN THE SPRING OF 1981, Polanski flew home for the Warsaw premiere of *Tess*. This, more than his 'private' visit in late 1976, was the triumphant return he had promised to Josip Sats and his fellow border guards when he had left Poland nineteen years earlier. Following the screening there was a glittering vodka reception attended by a number of cabinet ministers and other high-ranking government officials. One Western journalist recalls having approached Polanski and offered to fetch him a drink, 'only to hear Roman's superb reply, "No, thanks, the minister of culture's getting me one."'

As an aspiring young student, Polanski had hero-worshipped the actor Tadeusz Lomnicki, whose performance as Puck in *A Midsummer Night's Dream* had been the talk of Polish national theatre in 1949. Now 56, Lomnicki was both a member of the central committee of the Communist Party and rector of the state drama school in Warsaw. In 1976, he had been able to open his own, artistically 'liberated' playhouse, the Teatr na Woli, to some an encouraging sign that Poland itself might be emerging from thirty years of Soviet bullying and cultural repression. After watching *Tess*, Lomnicki 'literally ran across the room [to] ask Roman, whom I considered to be our greatest national artist, to return to Warsaw and direct a play'. Although the fee was 'negligible', Polanski immediately accepted the invitation.

For his first home stage appearance in thirty-one years, Polanski chose Peter Shaffer's *Amadeus*, a tale of a hedonistic young boor who happens to be a musical genius. For once it seemed that the critics might be right when they made the inevitable connection between the director's life and his work. 'Like Mozart,' Polanski noted, 'I was deformed by childhood success. I was forced to succeed early, to become an adult before my age and so everybody thinks you are unbearably arrogant.' To underline the point, Polanski himself played the title role, making up in a powdered wig and capering around the stage to give a very passable imitation of the man he described as 'a person [who] could make sublime art and still use swear words and baby talk, still be childish and sometimes gross'. *Amadeus* was an unqualified commercial and critical success with sold-out houses for six weeks, after which Polanski handed over to an understudy.

Unfortunately, the much heralded wider 'normalisation' of Polish life proved illusory. On a winter Sunday night just four months after Polanski's final performance in *Amadeus*, the army and the secret police rounded up some 20,000 Solidarity trade union activists or other so-called 'gendarmes, spies [and] counter-revolutionaries' and herded them into internment camps. The military regime effectively invaded its own country, stationing tanks at every city street corner, reimposing strict press controls and ensuring that organisations like the Teatr na Woli conform to the stated goal of 'national salvation'. Tadeusz Lomnicki promptly resigned his Party membership and was replaced at the state drama school by a hard-line bureaucrat whom the soon-to-be-expelled AP correspondent sardonically described as 'a chip off the old Bloc'. Lomnicki went into retirement and died in 1992. Following his success in *Amadeus*, Polanski had admitted that he still 'occasionally dream[t] of returning home to live', if only during the summer months. That dream ended with the shocking reports of 14 December 1981, which he saw as the 'latest episode in our national tragedy'.

Although chided by some in the media for his 'garbled command of French' and 'mongerel accent', Polanski brought *Amadeus* to Paris, where it enjoyed a highly satisfactory run of 246 performances at the cabaret-style Théâtre Marigny, playing to a total of 172,000 customers. The film critic Iain Johnstone, on assignment for the American programme *Entertainment Tonight*, was one of those to be given an interview. 'I found Roman utterly charming and a very smooth performer indeed, right up until the moment I asked him about his legal problems.' At that, Johnstone recalls, Polanski had become 'a bit ratty' and suggested that they change the subject. This 'marked huffiness' was one of the qualities that many journalists or other outsiders tended to note in the director. In fact, Polanski was a man closed to critics but, generally speaking, open to criticism – as long as it was private, and strictly related to his work. Most days while making a film, dozens of pages of technical advice, analysis, professional grievances, warnings and frequently bitter memos from the producer came his way. Polanski ignored or brushed aside much of them, but responded enthusiastically to what he called 'constructive' complaints. Sven Nykvist, the award-winning cinematographer on *The Tenant*, for example, had had occasion during filming to dash off a note protesting that 'I am not sure whether we are making a comedy or a horror story'.

Polanski's scribbled response was reportedly, 'I know. Good, good. Too many mood swings?'

'We seem to be falling between two stools,' Nykvist continued. 'T[relkovski]'s . . . insanity appears to drop on him from the sky.'

'Yes! Yes!' Polanski wrote.

'Roman was very approachable [and] open to criticism, provided it was in the right context,' Nykvist noted.

After the final performance of *Amadeus*, Polanski enquired whether the screen rights to Shaffer's play might be available. He learnt that he had been beaten to them by a matter of days by the producer Saul Zaentz, who in turn had signed a contract with Milos Forman, the Czech-born director of *One Flew Over the Cuckoo's Nest*. *Amadeus* was released to great popular and critical acclaim in September 1984. It won eight Oscars, including those for Best Picture and Best Director. Polanski subsequently described his reaction to Laurent Vachaud of the magazine *Positif*. 'I think I would have made a better film,' he said.

Instead, Polanski accepted a number of lesser jobs, including a role in Arielle Dombasle's comedy feature *Chassé-croisé*. He continued to lead the social life of a man half his age, as illustrated by a new top-of-the-range Mercedes coupe and a young English model named Sabina. Polanski and his partner spent some of the summer of 1982 at a rented villa in Ramantuelle, an almost excessively quaint fishing village perched on a rock overlooking the Bay of Pampelonne near Saint-Tropez. When the Rolling Stones performed in Nice on 20 July, Mick Jagger and some young fans reportedly came to the house for a late dinner. Polanski's neighbours' view of the fleet of limousines and motorcycle outriders seemingly necessary for this engagement was the village's major talking point, though the sight, early the next morning, of Jagger casually strolling into the local tobacconist's clad in American football tights and a pink jacket made a strong bid for runner-up.

When Polanski got back to Paris, Robert De Niro was there with another script that he reportedly wanted them to develop together. Just as in March 1977, on the night Samantha Gailey and her family had been giving their statements to the police, the two men's discussions, though 'very warm', ended without a tangible result. Six thousand miles away in Los Angeles, the Gaileys and their lawyer Lawrence Silver were beginning the process of suing Polanski for damages. One morning, the concierge at avenue Montaigne phoned upstairs to warn the director that half a dozen 'reptiles' were outside waiting for him, wanting to discuss the latest rumours that, as part of any civil settlement, he would return to face the American court system. Polanski came down, listened to the reporters' speculations, and rebutted them one by one. That done, he said quite coldly: 'This has been a great pleasure for me, but now I am going to breakfast.' Adjourning across the road for a cognac, the ABC News correspondent was left to remark ruefully to a colleague that Polanski had 'run rings' around them.

When contacted by BBC Radio's *The World This Weekend*, Polanski remained unapologetic. It was 'total nonsense', he said, that he had brought any of his troubles on himself. Noting, rather, that he had had a 'raw deal' over the years, he added, 'I don't think I would exaggerate if I said I was one – or maybe the person – who has suffered more abuse from the press than anybody else. If I showed you the trunks full of clippings which I keep down in my cellar you would be truly surprised. And it continues – there seems no end to it. I wrote my autobiography to tell it as it really was from as far back as I remember. But even this seems to be a vain effort.'

The book, even so, brought some consolation, going on to become an international bestseller. Before moving on it's worth mentioning this project once more, if only because of its obvious importance to Polanski, who invested three years' work in it, effectively the equivalent of two full-scale films. If not quite the 'whole shocking truth' as promised by the publisher's advertisements, it was unusually frank for a living celebrity's account of his life. The index offered a representative flavour. Under 'Polanski, Roman', the reader would find references to 'Sexual initiation', 'First sexual experience', 'Sexual involvement with a minor', 'Rape charge', and so on. For the most part, the director's memoir was 'well written, uninhibited and crisply phrased', to again quote the advertising, with 'sudden, disquieting jolts of insight' and 'candid stories'. Anecdote was a place where Polanski felt very much at home. It was praised by the *Washington Post* in its Christmas round-up as the most 'conspicuously alive thing' among the annual pile of 'vacuous tripe' emanating from 'so-called famous authors'.*

Between the time Polanski finished the book and its publication, he invited his father and stepmother, whom the Polish military authorities had prevented from attending the French opening of *Amadeus*, to visit him in Paris. Now past 80, Ryszard had become a gaunt, hollow-eyed old gentleman who bore a passing resemblance to Nastassia's father Klaus Kinski. Those who saw him in and around avenue Montaigne agree in

---

* There is a small mystery about one copy of the book. Shortly after its publication, Polanski had given a specially boxed first edition to his close friend and fellow director Jerzy Skolimowski, his co-writer on *Knife in the Water*. A full-page inscription in the author's bold hand read, in translation, 'So, you see what transpires. I am signing my biography for you. And it is in English. You could not have forseen this during those hot evenings on Narutowicra Street when we were served fruit juices by Kuba. Love, Romek.' On the surface, it would seem to have made the perfect gift. But twenty years later, a Los Angeles book dealer would offer this same copy for sale, priced at $8,000. At the time, Skolimowski was still active as a director and performer.

their description of him as an infirm, somewhat stooped figure, with a hoarse voice, ashen complexion, shuffling gait and trembling hands. Mentally, however, he was still recognisably the same Ryszard, gently ticking off his son for extravagances such as his electric curtain-openers and not hesitating to question his choice of friends. One visitor to the apartment would vividly recall how movingly Polanski had 'nursed' his father, how, without being asked, he lent a hand when Ryszard needed to stand up, how gently he sat him down again and, in general, exuded a 'quiet affection' for the older man.

Towards the end of his second week in Paris, Ryszard was reportedly prevailed upon to visit a doctor, who referred him to a specialist. Advanced cancer was diagnosed. Ryszard declined to be admitted to hospital, and stayed on in the apartment with his son through his final days. His death is said to have been peaceful. Roman accompanied his father's coffin back to Krakow, where it was placed in the modest tomb Ryszard had built for himself.

'For me, the death of my father was very terrible,' Polanski told Lawrence Weschler of the *New Yorker* ten years later. 'It was, in a way, my last connection with Poland, with that which makes you feel still young. I always had this feeling of still somehow being juvenile until my father died. Afterward, that was somehow no longer the case.'

By all accounts, Ryszard's death was only one of the blows that contributed to a 'knockout midlife crisis' for Polanski, who had turned 50 on 18 August 1983. At about the same time, he had finally divested himself of his remaining American and British assets, among them his London mews house, and would use at least some of the proceeds to eventually settle with Samantha Gailey, as well as both taking the lease on a second apartment at avenue Montaigne and buying a winter home on Ibiza. Polanski's autobiography could also be read as a sort of summation of what he now referred to as his 'old self'. His relationship with Sabina, his English girlfriend, had apparently cooled, leaving what one observer described as 'a rather forlorn middle-aged man who was frequently charming to passing acquaintances and, to be frank, a pain in the arse if, having got to know him, you inadvertently set him off on a rant on one of his pet subjects – the US justice system being an obvious example. It was like standing in a wind tunnel of abuse. Another bad sign was that he began to refer to himself, at various times, as "Polanski". Something would be a "bad rip-off of a Polanski film" or, more charitably, it "showed the Polanski touch".'

It was into this already somewhat charged atmosphere that Emmanuelle Seigner strode. According to the early press handout, she was a 'stunning figure, [with] very delicate features, very fine blonde hair and very green eyes' whose wardrobe at that time seemed to consist entirely of black and red leather miniskirts. Even in a city renowned for its glamorous women, Seigner, it was said, could 'literally stop traffic' merely by walking up the Champs-Élysées. What was more, she was the granddaughter of a distinguished classical actor, Louis Seigner, and had some film experience of her own, including a bit part in the forgettable *L'Année des Méduses*, shot almost exclusively on a topless beach, and a slightly more exalted role in Jean-Luc Godard's crime drama *Détective*. Godard was apparently quite taken by the young actress. 'He told me I could make it big in pornography,' Seigner later recalled. 'He reckoned I had a great ass.'

Born on 22 June 1966, at about the time Polanski had been dating Sharon Tate, Seigner had had a traditional Convent education before, in something of an abrupt switch, she became a part-time model at age 14. It's possible that she was encouraged in her ambitions by her father, a professional photographer, if not her mother, an interior designer and occasional journalist. The family, completed by a younger sister, enjoyed a 'normal, Bohemian' existence and mingled comfortably within a circle largely composed of writers, artists and musicians. In the autumn of 1984, while looking around for further acting work, Emmanuelle had met a casting agent who arranged for her to audition privately for Polanski at avenue Montaigne. Remarkably, she had never even heard of the director's name until then. At the time Seigner went up to Polanski's home to read, she had just turned 18 years old. *Rocky* was a 'classic film' to her, and she 'wasn't the slightest bit interested' in discussing art theory or 'pretentious junk'.

It appears that she did her homework, even so, because on entering Polanski's apartment she declined to drink the champagne or eat the cake he offered her 'in case he had put drugs in it'. Despite these inhibitions, Seigner apparently impressed her host as not only physically striking and technically accomplished but, for all that, refreshingly innocent. Speaking of her performance three years later in *Frantic*, Polanski described his latest discovery as 'so French – cool, tough and graceful', before adding, 'Of course, she is nothing like that in life. She's sweet.'

It is a tribute to both parties' discretion that Polanski and Seigner went out on several dates before the paparazzi even noticed them. That the relationship remained private was no accident. When the couple went to dinner, a Mercedes with blacked-out windows first deposited Seigner at the restaurant. The car then snaked around the block and returned to discharge Polanski. Often this strategy was not necessary, as they reportedly spent most of their evenings alone at avenue Montaigne, where Seigner was able to enjoy private screenings of films like *Repulsion* and *Cul-de-Sac*. Family, colleagues and neighbours were all sworn to secrecy, well aware that any breach of the *omerta* would be the end of their friendship.

Seigner herself had seemingly been in two minds when Polanski initially invited her out. 'Originally, I didn't want to go,' she revealed, 'because I knew he just wanted to fuck me.' However, she had been won over by his 'respectful nature and honesty'. Although Polanski was older than her own father, the 'age thing' was not a problem. 'Anyway, it's not about that,' Seigner noted. 'It's about soul, and Roman's is beautiful.'

Friends smiled that Polanski's 'special ladies' had become, like Russian dolls, diminishing or at least younger versions of the same basic type. Seigner, as some cynics noted, seemed to particularly resemble a latter-day Sharon Tate, a 'ravishing beauty' and 'modestly gifted actress' who was apparently putty in Polanski's hands. One American acquaintance who visited the couple at avenue Montaigne recalls that 'Roman clearly adored her, and played a sort of "Uncle Romek" role. He would tell her to dress up warmly, and then to hang up her coat in the proper place when they came back inside.' A second visitor from the West Coast broadly agrees that the couple were 'kind of cute' together. It would prove to be one of Polanski's major relationships.

There was encouraging professional news, too, when Claude Berri, who had finally recouped his personal $6 million-plus investment in *Tess*, introduced Polanski to a Paris-based financier named Tarak Ben Ammar. Within a few days, the long-moribund script of *Pirates* was back in circulation. Thom Mount, formerly the so-called 'baby mogul' president of Universal Pictures at the age of 26, and the Tunisian-born Ben Ammar, a then 35-year-old oil baron and business partner of the former lounge singer and future Italian prime minister Silvio Berlusconi, acted as co-producers, with Polanski's friend Dino De Laurentiis modestly describing himself as having later 'chip[ped] in' some $15 million to a budget that eventually topped $40 million. Polanski himself was to be paid a fee of up to $1 million, provided he delivered on schedule. 'Rather typically for a big movie,' says William Hobbs, to whom the plot of *Pirates* had been explained ten years earlier as 'one big fight', 'when things finally happened, they happened quickly.' As the figures duly rose, with over $8 million earmarked for the construction of a larger than life-size Spanish galleon, Polanski was heard to remark that he devoutly hoped that the making of *Pirates* 'wouldn't be as bad as *Tess'*. His producers assured him that there would be no comparison between the two films. They were quite right. *Pirates* was much worse.

In November 1984, Polanski, Gérard Brach and John Brownjohn, the creative team on *Tess*, met in Paris to convert a screenplay that had long been in 'turnaround' in Hollywood – where, one executive notes, the director's 'lifestyle choices' had effectively killed it – into a brisk, ninety-eight-page shooting script. What emerged was, on paper, a rollicking good tale with a full set of piratical accessories: Jolly Rogers, cutlasses, lashings, plunder, peg legs, grog, scurvy and a generous minimum 'Arrr' quota. The specifics of the story hardly mattered, but concerned a Captain Red and his loyal assistant The Frog who are shipwrecked and taken aboard a passing galleon, the *Neptune*. After discovering that the *Neptune* is also carrying a solid gold Aztec throne, the captain raises the crew to mutiny and commandeers the ship himself, only to lose it again after hosting an intemperate all-night party. A subsequent attempt to retrieve the booty fails disastrously, and the captain and his lieutenant end the proceedings as they began, adrift on a raft, Polanski being a great believer in the 'rondo narrative form . . . It invites you to reflect, at the end, on your starting point.' For the record, the intended tone of *Pirates* was jocular, and its three authors, perhaps ominously, are said to have 'laughed themselves silly' when writing their script.

Jack Nicholson, Polanski's original choice to play Captain Red, was committed to making *Prizzi's Honor* for another *Chinatown* alumnus, John Huston, and so declined the offer. Both Michael Caine and Sean Penn were similarly unavailable. Polanski finally settled on the 64-year-old Walter Matthau, whom he viewed as an 'acceptable compromise' to play a swash-buckling action hero, despite Matthau having undergone triple-bypass heart surgery eight years earlier. A young English character actor named Damien Thomas was cast to play the captain's chief adversary, the *Neptune*'s first lieutenant Don Alfonso de la Torré. The clean-cut Thomas was initially told that Polanski was looking for 'grotesques' to inhabit his film, but overcame this obstacle to win a small non-speaking part. 'Some time later I had a call saying that Polanski didn't get on with Timothy Dalton, who was originally due to play Don Alfonso. Needless to say, I was overjoyed.'

Polanski once again enlisted a group of actors who had acquitted themselves with credit on British television without ever quite having threatened an international breakthrough. There were parts for Jack MacGowran's friend David Kelly (the feckless Irish builder in *Fawlty Towers*) and Richard Pearson, setting a record by appearing in his third Polanski film following *Macbeth* and *Tess*. Pearson remembers 'Roman being very much at the helm of a movie, like himself, bubbling over with energy, wit and mischief, and frequently giving a broadly comic interpretation of the action for you before each day's shooting.'* Polanski had had himself firmly in mind to play the captain's young sidekick when *Pirates* was first optioned by United Artists in 1975. Nine years later, now aged 51, the director was forced to concede that he was too old, and instead gave the part to a teenaged French pop-singing hearthrob, Cris Campion, appearing in his first film.

While a crew of 600 shipwrights, carpenters and assorted technicians laboured over the construction of the 14,000-ton *Neptune* in a dry dock in Tunis, the cast were flown first-class to Rome for their costume fittings with the designer Anthony Powell. David Kelly, more used to playing 'some rough and ready Irish navvy type', remembers the novel experience of putting on a £25,000 gold-trimmed period frock coat, a fitted silk shirt and handmade satin shoes, all of which typified the painstaking detail, and soaring expense, of a Roman Polanski film. While the principal characters took an intensive course on pirate etiquette, including instruction in both proper table manners and the all-important rolling gait, a second unit was preparing elaborate sets in a variety of locations in Tunisia, Malta and the Seychelles. Meanwhile, William Hobbs was hard at work in a sports centre in central Warsaw, where he was training dozens of young Polish stuntmen how to wield a cutlass while shinning up and down a rope, thus to simulate battle conditions on the *Neptune*. When the cast and crew finally came together on the eve of filming, Polanski assembled everyone over dinner and told them, 'Until now, pirate movies have just been cowboy films set on water. This one will be different.'

'Technically, it was difficult,' Polanski was later forced to concede of *Pirates*. 'The group wasn't very cohesive – no more in nationality than in mentality. We were limited financially and hardly spoilt by the weather.

---

* Expounding on his vision for the film, Polanski later told Damien Thomas that *Pirates* was intended to be family entertainment. 'There'll be a rape scene,' he noted. 'But it will be rape for children.'

You know that the bigger a budget is, the more problems there are.' Despite all the preliminary team-building, it seemed that not all the crew were of one mind even before the first day's shooting. When the core, sixty-three-strong company landed at Zarzis airport on their way to the primary location in Tunisia, they were asked by immigration officials to fill in a card stating their personal details and the nature of their visit. Sixty-one of the party said 'Filming' or 'Acting', Walter Matthau put 'Paid Vacation', and Polanski tersely wrote 'Work'.

The crew hotel was majestic, with sweeping views of Djerba harbour and the Mediterranean, but with few pretensions to modernity. 'The lavatories were like something out of Hieronymus Bosch,' one actor remembers. As usual on location, Polanski was in early to work the following morning. 'Evidently regarding himself like God on the first day, Roman was a blur of activity,' the same colleague recalls. 'He shouted and applauded, sent round enthusiastically obscene notes – "FUCKING FANTASTIC!" if specially pleased – and wasn't above shinning up masts, wielding a sword and personally demonstrating the most dangerous stunts.' What Polanski chiefly did, however, at least in the initial stages of *Pirates*, was to wait.

Working outdoors in the Tunisian rainy season proved equally vexing to anything Polanski had encountered on *Tess*, and Damien Thomas recalls 'endless standing around, waiting for the right conditions, after which the Polish technical crew would elaborately light the scene while Roman paced up and down muttering, "Will somebody tell me when I can start the fucking cameras going?"' As a result there were frequently 'only minutes' left before dusk fell and everyone got into the buses to return to the hotel. A near-disaster befell the *Neptune*, which was all but lost in a tropical storm just hours after being launched, and consequently had to turn around and put in for extensive repairs before even reaching the location. 'Not a good start,' Thomas notes. Between the rain and the clouds and the man-made delays, Polanski counted himself fortunate to get through one or, at most, two set-ups a day, the average quota for a smooth-running film being six or seven. Problems of a 'quite bewildering' variety seemed to pursue the production. An entire night-time sequence later shot in the Seychelles had to be abandoned when it was discovered in the cutting room that a swarm of fireflies had flown into shot and ruined the effect. Walter Matthau, too, though still a formidable actor, had clearly reached that golden stage towards the tail end of a distinguished career when he could dictate terms without fear of contradiction. 'Walter,' says Damien Thomas, 'was very genial company and I liked him a lot. He also had one of those airtight contracts the rest of us can only dream of. My memory is that he left the set *exactly* at clocking-off time every evening.'

By contrast, Polanski put in his usual long hours on location, and in addition to turning the 'fucking cameras' found time to discuss his or her role with very nearly every member of the full 200-strong crew. (The one exception to this rule was the senior cast. True to form, Polanski expected his 'well paid' actors to essentially 'get on with it', as Damien Thomas recalls. 'At the beginning of the shoot I asked Roman how he saw my character and what his motivation might be and it was as if I'd asked him to explain the cricket LBW law. He just shrugged.') That Polanski, under the most trying conditions, should have gone on worrying and obsessing over the smallest technical detail left a particular impression on the English actor Michael Elphick (later television's *Boon*), who had a small role in *Pirates*. 'Roman was a little bugger,' Elphick recalled, not without affection. 'He must have known halfway through that the film wasn't going to be the blockbuster that everyone had hoped, but he still flogged both us and himself into the ground. Basically it was a case of, if a thing isn't worth doing, it's worth doing well.'

Polanski took particular pains in staging a hand-to-hand combat scene involving Matthau and various adversaries, a two-minute sequence which apparently drove William Hobbs nearly to despair, and took the best part of a week to film. After each take, there would be a spirited cry of 'Fandastic! Fandastic!' from behind the camera, followed by the now familiar sequel, 'We go again.' After the twelfth consecutive take, Matthau unbuckled his sword and asked, still in his cockney accent, 'Can we do something else?'

'One more time,' said Polanski.

After seven or eight further takes, with Matthau making increasingly voluble reference to his heart-bypass surgery, the cinematographer Witold Sobocinski announced that the light had gone. As the cast packed up for the day Polanski and Sobocinski began to debate the matter in animated Polish and were apparently still going at it two hours later over dinner in the marina restaurant. Midway through the meal, a young waiter then dropped a heavy serving bowl full of meat and gravy on Polanski's lap; after the fuss had died down, Michael Elphick had the feeling that both parties were 'mutually unimpressed' by the encounter. The hard-won fight sequence was later cut almost in its entirety from the finished film.

One of the most impressive speeches in *Pirates* was delivered by Matthau on set a day or two later and it, too, was not in the final cut. 'Fuck! Fuck! Fuck! I may never get out of this fucking desert,' he remarked after yet another 'pissy' retake of an exterior scene. Turning to David Kelly and two or three other cast members, Matthau then enquired, with perfect timing, 'Do you find the camels are starting to look good to you?' 'Everyone duly fell about,' Kelly recalls, 'but I sensed resentment because Roman's painstaking style clearly wasn't to his liking.' Matthau himself later confirmed this impression. 'I'll just say Polanski wasn't my kind of director,' he recalled. 'There were all kinds of mishaps and problems that weren't his fault, but frankly he did fart around a lot.'

Matthau was at least being well compensated for his troubles, earning some $4 million, with generous expenses, for his six months' work on *Pirates*. Damien Thomas, who cheerfully allows to having made 'about £70,000' over the same period, recalls that 'the actors' pay got so behind that our agents were urging us to take some action in the early weeks of shooting'. Collective loyalty to Polanski averted a real-life mutiny, although Thomas reports that there was a certain amount of understandable 'muttering' as filming dragged on through the spring and summer of 1985 with no real improvement in conditions. As a relief from the mounting pressure of completing *Pirates* within budget, Polanski treated himself and a small group of mainly Polish cronies to weekend breaks in Ibiza. Of this inner circle, Damien Thomas particularly remembers Arnold, 'the one-legged Paralympics high-jump champion' who doubled for Walter Matthau, and a 'Cape Verde professional soccer player with a recently broken neck'. Polanski also occasionally liked to disappear to the hotel bar with the Warsaw-based stuntmen, most of whom enjoyed a vodka.

On the occasions when the company as a whole met socially, Polanski again proved to be both a strikingly generous and thoughtful host. As David Kelly recalls, 'Roman gave an apparently fabulous party which, for some reason, Richard Pearson and I missed. Two nights later, he repeated the whole exercise for our benefit. We were in a room somewhere in rural Tunisia eating caviar and drinking champagne that Romek had had flown in from Paris.' Damien Thomas remembers an exuberant moment on location when Polanski enlivened proceedings by pulling down the shorts of a notably well endowed male member of the company, and 'invited me to take a look'. On another off-duty occasion, says Thomas, 'Roman playfully shouted across the table, "Hey, Damien, why don't you screw Charlotte [Lewis, the love interest in *Pirates*]?",' thus giving voice to

Polanski's theory that a 'fucked woman is a happy woman'. (In the event, neither party took up the suggestion, which nonetheless got a 'big laugh'.) Although his language and humour could be as coarse in private conversation as they were, in general, correct on set, Polanski was 'basically very sweet', Thomas insists. 'Emmanuelle flew in on occasion to join him, and Roman was extremely tender to her. You somehow expected him to be a satyr, and he wasn't.'

As a result both of the enforced delays and Polanski's meticulous style, *Pirates* inevitably went over budget. The first obvious sign of trouble came with the arrival on location of Dino De Laurentiis' representative, a 'cheerful and smiling' Italian who shook the director's hand before announcing that his employer 'had some suggestions'. These were words Polanski would hear often over the next twenty-four hours. De Laurentiis evidently remained unsatisfied, because some days later David Kelly looked up from where he was working on the *Neptune* and saw 'two large men in dark suits and sunglasses standing on the beach, each with a briefcase at his feet, staring out at us. Talk about a spectre at the feast.' After calling for a break and conferring with his visitors, 'Roman walked away and got in his car. At that Walter Matthau yelled out, "Where are you going? You're not leaving me out here in the fucking desert." Polanski assured him that yes, he was. And he did. Everyone assumed that Roman would be back in an hour or two, but later that night we heard he had flown to Paris.'

After 'vigorous' and 'prolonged' discussions between Polanski, his agent and the film's backers, the production resumed fifteen days later. The total cost of the shutdown, whoever bore ultimate responsibility for it, was reported to have been $700,000. After filming concluded in the Seychelles, Polanski shot a few final scenes in the studio in Paris, where he again lavishly entertained members of the cast, both at avenue Montaigne and in sundry nightclubs. Even then, Damien Thomas reports, 'Roman was enthusiastic about the project, and distinctly mentioned the prospect of a sequel.'

Whether because, as some said, Polanski's reflexes had gone, or for other human or technical reasons, *Pirates* was catastrophically badly edited; *Tess*, though nearly an hour longer, seems dissolutely fast by comparison. As just one example of the film's *longueurs*, there is a scene in which Captain Red confers with his friend Dutch, played by Roy Kinnear, while the latter reclines in his bathtub. Nothing particularly happens. It takes up six minutes of screen time, and, as Damien Thomas says 'seems to last forever, to the point where you almost assume someone had made an error.' At the other extreme, a much needed action sequence in which Thomas was involved 'was cut in its entirety by the distributor in order, I was told, to shorten the film so as to allow time for "concessions". A pirate movie without action . . . but let's sell some ice cream.' One well known British arts reviewer wrote that *Pirates* was a 'symphony with several mini crescendos but no climax. Immediately on the regulation two hours, it doesn't end. It stops.'

Pirates was given a limited release in February 1986, and officially premiered at Cannes three months later. It was a critical disaster, roundly panned by highbrow (*The Times*), middlebrow (the *Express*) and lowbrow (the *Sun*) alike. The *Today* correspondent made reference to its 'DVT-inducing length.' In America, it enjoyed some of the most vitriolic reviews of even Polanski's career, with comments such as 'One of the most unintentionally hilarious movie[s] of all time', 'So bad it's actually enjoyable' and 'A bomb . . . uniquely appalling'. After some initial morbid curiosity, audiences were thin, not to say gaunt. Damien Thomas went to the British first night and 'sat in a silent and very sparsely populated cinema in Chelsea, before leaving deeply depressed.' *Pirates* lost some $35 million for its producers. Alexander Walker, the London *Evening Standard* critic, considered it to be a 'nautical "epic" that sank with all hands', while *Time* wondered whether Polanski's career could even be salvaged from the wreckage.

But was the film such a wreck? For all its inept editing, *Pirates* still delivered on sheer spectacle, and the sight of the full-sailed *Neptune* (today a popular museum, berthed in Genoa) heaving majestically into view was impressive enough to be the finale of a less ambitious film. Polanski also proved to be seventeen years ahead of his time in reviving the whole pirate genre, and more specifically in his depiction of the lead character, as ably interpreted by Walter Matthau; the actor's estate should send Johnny Depp a bill. As in *Tess*, there are some sumptuous colour-supplement-like shots, and, as Damien Thomas admiringly says, 'In some ways, it's a marvel to behold. There are no digital tricks; everything you see on screen happened in front of the camera.' Several of Polanski's fellow directors, including Stanley Kubrick, would pay tribute to the film's technical ingenuity and visual flair. (Kubrick is reported to have both compared *Pirates* to a 'Turner seascape' and called it 'a balls-out masterpiece'.) Finally, and critically, it's a story, however outlandish, you can believe in. Thanks in roughly equal parts to the script, the direction and the pathological attention to detail, it all 'rings well', as Walter Matthau later reflected. 'It may not be realistic, but it feels real and it feels right . . . If it isn't what pirates are like, it's what audiences like to *think* they're like.' The movie did, in later years, enjoy something of a cult and even collected three Césars and an Oscar nomination, among other awards. 'My job,' Polanski once remarked, 'is to make you forget you are sitting in a cinema.' At its best, *Pirates* comes tantalisingly close to achieving the ideal.

Perhaps what was missing in the reviews, many of which read like full-scale obituaries, was a sense of perspective. When Barry Norman sat down to interview Polanski at Cannes, 'I certainly didn't get the impression of a man who had just had a $40 million disaster. After all Roman had been through, he was just happy to be alive and working.'

POLANSKI HAD ENOUGH SELF-AWARENESS TO KNOW that he could come across as a 'bit brash' – something he attributed to 'a question of my personality . . . and fate', that he lacked a certain quality of feeling, and that, thanks to 'extracurricular events' many if not most critics were 'actually review[ing] me and not my films'. He seems to have been commendably thick-skinned about it and, as Barry Norman suggests, refused to see *Pirates* as anything more than the latest commercial setback in a career that had already included such box-office flops as *Macbeth*, *What?* and *The Tenant*. Once having extracted his still 'very acceptable' fee from Dino De Laurentiis, Polanski was again able to enjoy life in Paris with Emmanuelle Seigner. He was clearly proud to be seen with a 20-year-old woman who was physically stunning, well dressed and appeared to worship every word that dropped from his lips. The affair escalated when Polanski decreed that his new protégée would take a starring role in his next film. Like Nastassia Kinski before her, Seigner was duly enrolled in a language school in London. Polanski used some of his ensuing spare time to direct a revival of Peter Shaffer's 1964 play *The Royal Hunt of the Sun*, a lively enough tale of Spanish explorers in the Incan empire, freighted with a rather heavy-going subplot about the death of God. Such themes aside, there was no denying the production's artistry. For one scene, Polanski lit up the set with what appeared to be a highly polished wall of glass dizzily winking back the blizzard of gold coins strewn over the stage – an Eisensteinian visual collision.

In the summer of 1987, the *New York Times*, a loyal friend to Polanski in his continuing struggle against the American justice system, sent its star reporter Joan Dupont to interview him at avenue Montaigne. She appears to have been suitably impressed by her subject, whom she described for her readers as seeming 'incredibly fit. He is all lean meat, with features carved to the bone. Fast on his feet, dressed boyishly in jeans and a sweater, a polka-dot kerchief sticking out of a pocket, Mr Polanski looks like a streetwise Peter Pan, with his open, impudent face and not one gray hair.' Later in the grilling, Ms Dupont would report that Polanski 'leads a high-power, hectic life; he drives a Mercedes, goes to a gym, and dances at Les Bains-Douches.' It was true that he had 'broken some taboos' (as she called the child-sex laws) in 1977, but was now ready to settle down and 'can see himself [becoming] a father'. Perhaps reflecting this new-found gravity, Polanski told friends that he was more concerned about the Cold War, and specifically the role played in it by the Soviet Union, than when he had formerly lived behind the Iron Curtain. 'God knows where this will end,' he said to the writer Jeff Gross, reflecting on the latest Soviet adventures in Latvia and elsewhere. Even while sitting under the mirrorball at Les Bains-Douches, Polanski was frequently heard to discourse gloomily on the general state of the world – 'We'll blow it up eventually.'

Six months earlier, the French newspaper *Libération* had published a bulky special feature in which 700 directors around the world answered the question 'Why do you make films?' Many of the respondents had taken the opportunity to send in impassioned essays on the subject that in one case ran to 12,000 words. Polanski's succinct reply was, 'I wonder.' Notwithstanding those doubts, he and Gérard Brach were soon to approach Thom Mount, the co-producer of *Pirates*, with their latest venture, an efficient Hitchcock-style thriller they called *Frantic*. Mount loyally rejected the widespread criticism that Polanski was a spent force. 'When I watched him on the set of *Pirates*,' he recalls, 'I saw an extraordinary performance by a director. He acted, helped stuntmen, worked on lights and was even his own script girl when he had to be. He knew as much about the craft of film-making as anyone I'd historically worked with,' a backlist that included the likes of Steven Spielberg, Oliver Stone and Brian De Palma. Mount's effusive patronage was enough to attract Warner Brothers, who happened to be awash with money from the *Lethal Weapon* and *Police Academy* series, among other recent triumphs. The studio generously agreed to invest $20 million in the project, on condition that there would be none of the foreign buccaneering associated with *Pirates*, a proviso Polanski was happy to accept. 'From the start the idea was to make a film in the city where I live,' he told *Le Nouvel Observateur*. 'I wanted to stay at home after being away for two years in Tunisia.'

Polanski's script took as its starting point a 1985 news report about the theft from a San Francisco-area electronics company of a krytpon high-speed pulse generator that in theory could be used to trigger a nuclear weapon. The fictional story would follow a middle-aged American heart surgeon whose wife vanishes while the couple is visiting Paris. Encountering only Gallic shrugs from the hotel employees and local police, he reluctantly enlists the help of a disco-bopping young woman who appears to know more about the affair than she lets on. The doctor's mood is unimproved by the realisation that the girl is involved with a mysterious cell of Russo-Arab terrorists smuggling parts for a bomb. This leads to kidnapping and murder, and eventually to a chase of sorts, with some scenic high jinks on various Paris rooftops. In a somewhat histrionic ending, which Polanski himself later criticised, the doctor and his wife are reunited, the rather underwritten villains flee and the girl is shot dead in the melee.

A normal life turned upside down is the familiar but still compelling hook of Hitchcock yarns like *The Man Who Knew Too Much* and *North by Northwest*, in which, like *Frantic*, a quiet American is caught up in a world of international intrigue and violence. This being Polanski, and it being the Eighties, there was also a generous amount of postmodern, ironic comment involved, not least in showing the mundane details of contemporary ordeals such as checking into a Parisian hotel. The director would only half-facetiously insist that *Frantic* was 'a film about jet lag', thus anticipating the critically highly regarded *Lost in Translation* by fifteen years. Among several deft characterisations, Polanski was able to convincingly portray the essential hostility or, at best, indifference of the average French security professional, having, he said, 'met several of these people' over the years. There was particular sport, too, at the expense of the at once feckless and exquisitely condescending dolts at the US embassy, where the doctor initially goes for help in finding his wife. One could fairly readily believe that Polanski might have taken a mischievous pleasure in drawing on some of his own experiences at the hands of American officialdom.

The first-draft screenplay of *Frantic* reportedly shocked the Warner Brothers quality control department, who found it potentially interesting but full of 'troubling' and 'crass' illogicalities. Over the next three months the studio sent Polanski a succession of fetching young female aides, none of whom proved a sufficiently astute script doctor. Finally the director turned to a 29-year-old American expatriate author and former semi-professional soccer player named Jeff Gross. Gross went up to avenue Montaigne and 'listened to Roman outline the story of *Frantic*, after which he asked me what I thought. "It's full of holes," I told him. "Good," Polanski said. "The more sceptical you are, the better. You're hired."'

The next fifty-six days were an 'ecstatic experience' for Gross, who typically went up to Polanski's apartment 'around eleven in the morning. We'd sit opposite each other working for a couple of hours, break for lunch, and then I'd keep going until late at night. Roman himself would leave around 6 p.m. and I'd stay there with the script. The idea was to tune up the dialogue, and, more specifically, to insert the right American idiom and that sort of French fuck-you attitude I knew only too well. Polanski hadn't been in the States in ten years, and Gérard Brach was a recluse who was on his way to becoming a full-bore agoraphobic; he rarely if ever left his flat. The guy was an expert on the Paris of 1969, not of 1987. Brach would send us pages which I was meant to translate. Most of his ideas were useless, and I told Polanski so. Eventually there were two full-scale synopses of *Frantic*, one for us and one for Warner Brothers. Roman knew exactly what it took to get around a Hollywood studio. He was brilliant; I mean, great to work with, not least for his sense of humour. Polanski always had a fund of jokes at his disposal, which he would try out on a small audience. If he got a specially big hand, he'd turn to me and say, "*That's* one for the film." Although I didn't get credited for *Frantic*, I never complain about it. When I met Roman I was living in a tiny room, completely broke. Suddenly I was being taken out to lunch on the Champs-Élysées *and* getting paid for two months.'

After Gross departed, Polanski flew in his friend Robert Towne, at Warner Brothers' expense, for some three weeks' work on a final shooting script. Having just issued an excitable press release predicting that *Frantic* would be the 'most dazzling of all Freudian thrillers' not excepting Hitchcock's *Spellbound*, the studio was apparently delighted to finance this reunion of the creative team behind *Chinatown*. In 1973, Polanski had been an unforgiving editor of Towne's 'intricate and almost incomprehensible' original screenplay, leading to some occasionally harsh words between the two men. Towne is reported to have said he would never work with 'the Pole' again. Fourteen years later, there was a marked shift, if not a complete role reversal, in the professional relationship. 'Bob cut out quite a lot on *Frantic* because he could see things with a fresh eye,' Polanski said. 'He noticed a lot of things that didn't seem obvious to us because I knew the story so well and couldn't look at it objectively.' With the final script approved, Polanski calmly informed Warner Brothers that he wanted to build a full-scale replica of Les Bains-Douches on the sound-stage at Studios de Boulogne, as the real one was 'a problem' for him. Again the home office sympatheti-cally agreed to the request. One of Warners' senior executives sent down a fulsome accompanying memo that deplored the standards of an industry that 'penny-pinches its great geniuses', and said of Polanski, 'the most brilliant director we have, we own.'

With that sort of unstinting corporate support, the casting process proved refreshingly straightforward. For his lead, Polanski considered what he called various 'all-American boys' including Kevin Costner and Jeff Bridges, before settling on Harrison Ford, whose last film, *The Mosquito Coast*, had been greeted with critical restraint. Ford went up to avenue Montaigne and listened to a synopsis of *Frantic*, after which he said, 'Thank God I don't have to read any more scripts.' The 40-year-old singer-actress Betty Buckley (of *Carrie*) was signed to play the doctor's wife, necessarily absent for much of the action. Jacques Ciron, the hotel proprietor in *The Unbearable Lightness of Being*, returned to play the same role here. The key part of Michelle, the miniskirted waif, went to Emmanuelle Seigner.

Storytellers have the right to pick and choose as they please, but it seemed curious to some that Polanski would revert to a Cold War melo-drama, however topical compared to the likes of *Tess* and *Pirates*, in the very year in which the conflict was drawing to a close. Although *Frantic* already seemed faintly dated on its release in 1988, and the film only sporadically lived up to the promise of its title, it was still a competent thriller, tough and intense, and on occasion even exciting. It also proved to be one of the smoother shoots of Polanski's career. Early in the process the director decided that the lobby of the Grand Hotel, where they were filming interiors, was painted an altogether too cheerful shade of beige to suit the noirish story. Polanski made arrangements with the hotel management to redecorate their premises with all-grey furniture and carpets (the production notes call for the 'battleship look'), although Thom Mount subsequently vetoed this move as 'gratuitously depressing' to the audience. It appears to have been the one creative dispute between Polanski and his producer in the course of their year-long collaboration on *Frantic*. The cast and crew, many of the latter veterans of *Pirates*, knew what was expected of them and performed accordingly. Polanski complained to Mount about one French actor cast in a minor part, who he said had 'ruined' a scene, and added facetiously that the actor should either be killed, maimed or thrown in the Seine, although ultimately he settled on simply reassigning the man.

The film's deceptively cheap and grainy look suited its tone, and Polanski clearly delighted in showing the murky corners of Paris rather than the gilded city of a Gene Kelly or Audrey Hepburn. The Eiffel Tower appears only fleetingly, although there are some apparently satirical references to the Statue of Liberty, a pocket-sized version of which serves as a hiding place for the terrorists' gizmo, a plot device the film shares with 1951's *The Lavender Hill Mob*. 'I wanted to get rid of everything that was too obviously quaintly Parisian and tried to show the town of today,' Polanski would recall. 'It was the way I see it and not as Americans might imagine it to be.'

In a private conversation before the first day's shooting, Polanski confessed to his returning cinematographer, Witold Sobocinski, 'The screenplay is your bible. I already know exactly where I want the camera to be for every shot.' It was the same sort of rigid blocking of, again, a classic Hitchcock film, a connection Polanski further confirmed by choosing to play a Hitchcock-like cameo as a taxi driver who passes a vital clue to the doctor. (It's perhaps no accident that *Frantic*'s main action begins in the shower.) The one significant departure from the plan was the film's climax, which, not coincidentally, was something of a mess. As on *Chinatown*, there was a heated debate about which of the various characters should die, right up to the moment one rainy Friday afternoon when Polanski, crouching behind the camera, simultaneously fired a flare gun in the air and called 'Action!' The original screenplay called for the doctor and his wife to escape, only for him to find the nuclear trigger in his pocket and the Arabs still in hot pursuit. Warner Brothers reportedly wanted a more 'positive' conclusion, in which the krypton is tossed into the Seine and the Emmanuelle Seigner character rather flamboyantly dies on the riverbank. Polanski pulled off one *coup de théâtre* by ensuring that Seigner's wound look sufficiently gory, with the 'guts actually pour[ing] out on to her dress'. When Betty Buckley, playing the doctor's wife, unsuspectingly knelt over the dying girl, she 'nearly vomited' at the sight, an effect vividly captured in the film.

Polanski spent December 1987 editing *Frantic* down to the regulation two hours and, as usual, supervising the film's every technical detail.

A member of the production crew admiringly recalls that 'Roman would be in the cutting room jabbering away to his Polish friends. In mid-sentence he'd pause, glance at the monitor and issue a stream of highly complex instructions in rapid French before again breaking off to field a phone call from the studio head in Hollywood. One day Ennio [Morricone] came in to score the music, and Polanski outlined the story of *Frantic* to him in fluent Italian. You want to know how much of a Renaissance man he was? I remember him dancing around to the music while someone from a gallery came in with these oil paintings for him to inspect, I presumed for [avenue Montaigne]. There was Roman bopping up and down, and meanwhile still carefully appraising the paintings. "Yes, that one . . ."' While Polanski edited *Frantic* by day, at night he adopted a fetal crouch to play Gregor Samsa in Steven Berkoff's acclaimed stage produc-tion of Kafka's *Metamorphosis*. After the curtain fell, the 54-year-old dynamo would then typically take in a club or late-night restaurant with his young girlfriend. It was a full workload, even by Polanski's standards. 'The Kafka makes me irritable,' he admitted to a reporter. 'I find myself doing bug motions constantly.'

With one or two notable exceptions the critics were kind to *Frantic*, which opened on 26 February 1988. Harrison Ford brought more than a dash of Indiana Jones to the proceedings by apparently doing his own acrobatic stuntwork in the action set-pieces and frowning photogenically through most of the lesser sequences. He also glowered, scowled, fretted and pouted, and there were long stretches in many scenes when he did little else. It was a bravura performance, in which, as the critic Janet Maslin said, 'Ford conveys great determination, as well as a restraint that barely masks the character's mounting rage. He makes a compelling if rather uncomplicated hero.'

It wasn't that *Frantic* was a bad film, as even its detractors allowed, merely that it was faintly derivative and predictable. To one of the *Los Angeles Times'* many correspondents, 'The villains could not have been any more obvious had they each been wearing a black cape and carrying a bomb . . . I frequently had the eerie sensation that I had seen the whole movie before.' (Seeming to confirm Polanski's poor impression of it, the same paper had recently carried a series of outraged readers' letters reacting to the rumour that he was negotiating a return to the US.) To concentrate merely on the plot was, however, to overlook *Frantic*'s many atmospheric charms. The opening sequence establishes the note of quiet foreboding that lasts virtually to the final frame; the doctor and his wife are in a taxi travelling into Paris, a superficially banal passage that would have been sleep-inducing in the hands of a lesser director but one that exudes menace here, not least because of the Arab radio music droning into the cab. Similarly, Polanski invests the otherwise mundane early scenes in the Grand Hotel – in which he directed the actors to 'do nothing' – with a sense of impending danger, the beige decor notwithstanding.* Despite the bland surroundings, the hotel is clearly established as hostile territory for a mildly gormless, sleep-deprived American tourist.

Frantic would earn some $17 million at the US box office, and as much again around the world. It did particularly well on its mid-August release in West Germany, where *Der Spiegel* called the movie a work of genius. Polanski, the magazine concluded, was 'a great artist' whose film could be compared to a Mozart symphony 'with its small and suspenseful touches as important [as] the main work'. The review was a nice birthday present for Polanski, who, after several years of silence broken only by commercial disaster, seemed to have achieved the hardest trick in show business: the comeback.

---

* As the filming of this sequence had worn on, involving some forty-five takes, many of the extras playing desk clerks and hall porters had had no problem feigning boredom. As one of them recalls, 'If I look glassy-eyed, it may be because they had to wake me up for the shot.' One of Polanski's 'many backstage tricks' on *Frantic* was to immerse his cast, as far as humanly possible, into their fictional characters' lives.

CHAPTER 9

ROMAN HOLIDAY

O N 30 AUGUST 1989, Polanski married Emmanuelle Seigner. He was 56, and had been a widower for just over twenty years. His 'third and last' wife, as he sometimes affectionately called her, had recently turned 23. The news, when it was eventually released, was greeted by much the same press reaction as that summer's wedding of Bill Wyman and Mandy Smith (thirty-four years his junior) in England and inspired some waggish cartoons, including one showing a beaming Polanski holding an infant with a face like Seigner's and saying, 'Nurse, she's just said "Daddy."' Unsurprisingly, the couple's friends saw their prospects quite differently, although opinion seems to have been divided on Seigner. One recent acquaintance of Polanski insists that he was 'hardly aware' of her existence at avenue Montaigne, although he could apparently hear her scurrying into hiding when he called, or catch a glimpse of her hands nimbly passing a drink through the serving hatch. To a rather closer friend, 'Emmanuelle [was] a wonderful woman, and quite clearly the love of Roman's life since Sharon Tate. She teased him a lot, which I think he adored. Physically, too, she wasn't just gorgeous, but with a touch of Slavic class about her. A certain refinement and delicacy of manner occasionally suggested a miniskirted Polish princess.'

Shortly after his wedding to Seigner, Polanski appeared as Lucky in a film adaptation of Samuel Beckett's *Waiting for Godot*. Beckett himself supervised the piece, his last public act before his death four months later. Polanski had owed the playwright a professional debt that went back to *Two Men and a Wardrobe*, and few of his major films were free of at least one character, scene or individual speech that could have graced the pages of *Godot* or *Endgame*. One critic had even found a variant of the 'Beckettian master-slave theme' in the knockabout relationship between Captain Red and his sidekick The Frog in *Pirates*.

One hot Saturday afternoon that September, a family doctor named Alain Haultcoeur was having his hair cut at a salon not far from avenue Montaigne. At some stage he looked up, noticed something familiar about the man in the next chair, and said to the reflection in the mirror, 'Are you Monsieur Polanski?' The two customers struck up a conversation, and Haultcoeur remarked that he had greatly admired Harrison Ford's performance as a surgeon in *Frantic*. This was well received. 'Polanski was charm itself, and favoured me with a number of stories and facial impersonations. We continued to address one another in the mirror. It went on for some time. I was happy to be the audience. One felt almost that one had been part of a private stage performance.'

Meanwhile, Polanski entered one of his cyclical troughs of professional frustration and mutual disgust with Hollywood, notwithstanding the modest profit shown by *Frantic*. Between the summer of 1989 and the spring of 1990 he was said to have been under consideration to direct screen adaptations of the bestselling books *Perfume* and *Mary Reilly*, as well as *Les Misérables*, and was in 'advanced talks' on three untitled projects variously starring Jack Nicholson, Robert De Niro and Mickey Rourke. In the end all six properties were either dropped or assigned to another director. To at least one well informed studio chief, part of Polanski's latest alienation could, in his opinion, be 'directly linked to his megalomania', often a source of strength on the set but just as likely to be counterproductive in negotiations. The executive remarks that '"Thou shall have no other gods but me" has always been the first and most important of Roman's commandments. Taken alongside his legal problems, it cost him a lot of work for which he was otherwise eminently qualified.'*

In early November 1989, Warner Brothers approached Polanski to adapt and direct Mikhail Bulgakov's Thirties novel *The Master and Margarita*. As well as being mordantly funny in its own right, it was the definitive satire of the old-style Soviet system, with Stalin's regime juxtaposed to that of Pontius Pilate. (Following its 'limited' publication, the book would be

---

* Twenty years earlier, at the time of *Rosemary's Baby*, Robert Evans had remarked of Polanski, 'There were two points of view – his and his' and 'he had quite an ego'; high praise from one famously robust in that area himself.

unavailable in Eastern Europe for the next forty years.) Polanski reportedly called this 'the one I was born to direct' and put in long hours writing the script. With some understatement, he pronounced himself 'displeased' when Warners then abruptly dropped the project, apparently believing it was no longer relevant following the fall of the Berlin Wall. For a man who had already suffered a series of well-publicised reverses, it was the final insult. Polanski was 'bouncing off the walls' according to a close friend and colleague who visited him in Ibiza. 'It was all "How could they be so fucking dumb?" and other generally unappreciative remarks about cancelling his movie. To Roman, it was further proof that Hollywood was in the hands of morons who knew as much about the Soviet empire as they did about the dark side of the moon.' Three years later, the young Russian director Yuri Kara filmed a $15 million version of *The Master and Margarita*, which recouped its costs within the first week of release.

'What people forget,' Kenneth Tynan had remarked of his collaborator on *Macbeth*, 'is that Roman is a writer, and therefore prey to the usual writerly neuroses.' Even when astonishingly successful and critically acclaimed, Polanski had fretted constantly about work and often wondered what he was doing making films anyway, as his reply to the *Libération* questionnaire had made clear. Yet it would be wrong to imagine that he was one of those peculiarly sensitive artists too finely wired for the rough and tumble of modern movie-making. Polanski had a clear and unshake-able belief in his place at the top of the directors' league table, a boast that by and large proved more justifiable as time went on. One had only to compare *Chinatown* with its eventual sequel *The Two Jakes*, again starring Jack Nicholson and which Paramount released, reportedly after years of internecine struggle, in August 1990. Nicholson himself directed. The *Washington Post* spoke for many when it described the latter film, a commercial flop, as a 'scrambled mess, which only makes us long for the original, [for] Faye Dunaway and John Huston, for the old style, and most of all for Roman Polanski'. A projected third instalment of the *Chinatown* story, to be called *Cloverleaf*, subsequently went into turnaround.

The following May, Polanski's friend and sometime critic Jerzy Kosinski took a fatal dose of barbiturates with his usual rum and Coke, taped a plastic bag over his head and then stepped into a warm bath. Kosinski's last note read, 'I am going to put myself to sleep now for a bit longer than usual. Call the time eternity.' He was 57. Many of Kosinski's friends believe that he had never recovered from sensational allegations published in 1982 accusing him of plagiarism and intellectual dishonesty, specifically of having embroidered his experiences as a boy in wartime Poland, although there were other contributory pressures on him at the end. Polanski had nothing public to say on the subject, but a mutual associate describes it as 'the ultimate love-hate relationship' of both men's lives. They had known each other for some thirty-five years. In the early Seventies, Polanski had introduced Kosinski to Peter Sellers, who had promptly embarked on a relentless and ultimately successful campaign to bring Kosinski's novella *Being There* to the screen. Perhaps less agreeable was the fallout from Polanski's later appearance on *60 Minutes*, in which he had portrayed Samantha Gailey as a 'consenting and willing' partner in their lovemaking.

Kosinski, who had also been interviewed on the programme, reportedly took the trouble to phone Polanski on location in France to inform him that he had missed 'the issue' and, what was more, was 'an idiot'. From this point on, the conversation appears to have deteriorated rapidly. As Kosinski recalled, 'Roman [had] said on camera that the girl wasn't a child. She had the mind and the body of a young adult. I correct[ed] Polanski. The girl's appearance, I told him, wasn't the point. The point was that she was 13. When you yourself were 13, I said, in spite of your experiences, you were a child.' According to Kosinski, Polanski had merely replied, 'Well, I had to talk about *something*,' before abruptly ringing off.

Later that year, Jeff Gross was invited to stay with Polanski and Seigner on Ibiza, where they lived in a 'gorgeous split-level house with a pool and all the trimmings'. Despite this idyllic winter retreat, 'Roman seemed increasingly frazzled. He was having trouble finding work, and meanwhile Emmanuelle was complaining of being bored. She didn't want him to go off on location for six months and leave her.' Polanski, it's agreed, had been attentive and generous to his young bride, and she, in her turn, was coquettish and lively – an energetic 25-year-old who, in one assessment, 'wasn't the kind of girl who liked to be tucked up early with a good book'. Although Seigner didn't actively encourage it, Polanski continued to look for a suitable new film project for them both. After rejecting several live-action equivalents, he apparently considered directing a full-length animated feature based on a series of erotic cartoons, remembered as having chiefly involved soft-core lesbianism and other variants, executed by a well known Italian artist, though ultimately the idea foundered.

Perhaps the strangest proposal to come Polanski's way was a screenplay called *Morgane*, on which both he and Jeff Gross put in several weeks' work. The tale was set in the Eighties and was about a working-class teenager from the American Midwest who goes to Paris. There, he somehow finds himself house-sitting a luxurious modern flat which bears a passing resemblance to avenue Montaigne. One evening the boy settles down to watch television and is gratified when a beautiful and scantily clad young woman appears on screen; this is what he came to France to see. In the first sign that something unusual was happening, the girl then stretches out a hand and pulls the boy into the television set to join her. Jeff Gross remembers Polanski being 'enthralled' by this fable, which the two of them eventually developed into a treatment which they delivered to the producer Alain Sarde.

In the autumn of 1991, Polanski was at last able to fulfil some of the hopes dashed by Warners' cancellation of *The Master and Margarita* by starring in a so-called 'satirical thriller' entitled *Back in the USSR*. Alas, the author of this undistinguished spy yarn was no Bulgakov. Released in February 1992, *Back in the USSR* was severely panned by the few critics who noticed it, and accumulated just $400,000 at the American box office over the next fifteen years.

At about the same time, Polanski is alleged to have illicitly returned to the US for several days, where he supposedly directed the likes of Nicole Kidman, Anjelica Huston and Warren Beatty in a fresh adaptation of Daphne du Maurier's *Rebecca*, with rather more emphasis laid on the story's S&M potential than was the case in the classic 1940 film starring Laurence Olivier and Joan Fontaine. Polanski's version, which, if it exists, remains unreleased, is said to have been shot at the Beverly Hills home of the investor and philanthropist Max Pavelsky. While there is absolutely no hard evidence, as opposed to widespread rumour, that the project ever took place, it's not inconceivable that a determined individual could find his way around the notoriously officious and inept US immigration authorities, particularly in those lax pre-9/11 days. The case of the Buenos Aires National Wildlife Refuge, located on the border of south-central Arizona and Mexico, is a representative example. As well as harbouring several rare plant types and exotic animals, the refuge is also used by up to 3,000 so-called *alambristas*, or wire-hoppers, nightly, an estimated 1,200 of whom are able to make their way around the few watchtowers and walk unimpeded into America. That isn't by any means to suggest that Polanski would ever avail himself of this particular option, which conjures up an admittedly unlikely mental image of the 58-year-old film-maker skulking around under cover of dark through the Arizona desert. There are several other such opportunities for the undocumented migrant, some of which would involve nothing more arduous than driving down one of the many invitingly open roads from Canada. Of course, it may all be one of those unsubstantiated rumours that tend to gather around Polanski, and two of the people closest to him in the early Nineties, when interviewed for this book, declined to be named or even quoted on the subject.

When Polanski delivered his script of *Morgane* to Alain Sarde, he happened to notice a paperback novel, with a picture of a voluptuous, bare-backed young woman on the cover, lying on the producer's desk. Entitled *Lunes de fiel*, it had been published in 1981 by Pascal Bruckner, a prolific author, essayist and political thinker who later became a rare French literary champion of George W. Bush and Donald Rumsfeld. Sarde remarked that he had recently bought the rights to the property, but had no specific plans for it. Polanski took the book home, read it overnight and the next morning phoned Sarde to tell him that he wanted to film it immediately. Inside a week, with Timothy Burrill's participation in London, the parties had agreed on a modest $5 million budget for what was now called *Bitter Moon*, and sets were being built at Paris Studios Cinéma in Boulogne-Billancourt. As Jeff Gross says, 'Roman was given to sudden enthusiasms. He was never really one for a ten-year plan.'

The script that emerged, largely faithful to the novel, revolves around an embittered and literally paralytic drunk, Oscar, an American, who button-holes an Englishman named Nigel on a Mediterranean cruise ship and tells him the story of his life. From that faintly unpromising start, the film would unspool in a series of long flashbacks set in Paris. Many of these touch on Oscar's once vibrant sex life with his young wife-to-be Mimi, who enjoys a touch of sadomasochism when the occasion calls, and which tend to the clinical. 'Steady on, old chap,' the Englishman remonstrates at one point, as Oscar favours him with a prolonged rhapsody on his partner's clitoris. There are a number of passing references to the couple's age difference; in the early scenes Mimi walks around in a schoolgirl's ra-ra skirt, plays hopscotch and drinks only water and milk, of which more later. Eventually we learn how Oscar ended up in his wheelchair. The Englishman (Hugh Grant, in his last pre-bouffant role) is 'strangely interested', he confesses, and on ground well beyond that when he subsequently meets the vora-cious Mimi. Apparently enjoying the prospect of some voyeurism, Oscar blithely invites his new friend to help himself. In another mildly over-wrought climax, Nigel's tweedy wife Fiona then seduces Mimi before he can, at which point Nigel remonstrates with Oscar, who produces a pistol, shoots his wife, and turns the gun on himself. Nigel and Fiona are left to console one another on the boat deck while the bodies are carried off and the credits roll. A tentative conclusion would be that Polanski, by now happily married himself, was actually making a moral point about the futility and general self-destructiveness of loveless sex, although most critics were more struck by the preceding lesbian romp.

Jeff Gross was again engaged on the screenplay, putting in thirty-six days in a noticeably more strained working environment than had been the case on *Frantic*. 'Essentially,' he says, 'I'd go to avenue Montaigne in the morning and spend an hour or an hour and a half poring through the novel scene by scene with Polanski. We'd agree on what we needed for that day's bit. Then I'd go home, write it, and fax the pages back to Roman. Meanwhile, in another part of Paris, Gérard Brach was simultaneously writing his own unique version of the screenplay. It took him another two months to deliver it. To compound the problem, John Brownjohn was then brought in as the "British idiom expert". That made for a three-way creative battle, and the eventual shooting script was liberally marked with blue ink. At that stage Alain Sarde grabbed me and said, "As you can see, there's virtually nothing left of you. If you insist on an on-screen credit, I'll make it so small that no one will even see it." Roman had said that he would negotiate for me, and he did. The billing at the end of the film says, "Script collaboration: Jeff Gross". I settled for that. A full screenplay credit would have made me a few more thousand, but I was naive. When everything was fixed, Roman gave me the famous line, "Maybe we can work together on the next one."'

Bitter Moon proved a godsend to Polanski's critics, who accused him of having made a grotesque porn film, with an impossibly tasteless plot line about a young woman, really no more than a girl, involved with a louche expatriate old enough to be her father. It seemed to be the most brazen example yet of the director's alleged tendency to adapt personal events for his films. Polanski himself, however, was having none of it. Speaking as recently as 2001, he would assure the journalist Octavi Marti, 'I don't want to analyse anything, including myself', having already consistently denied that there were any autobiographical references to be found in any of his work over the previous forty years. Sharp-eyed critics, even so, didn't miss the striking similarity between a key scene in *Bitter Moon* and a passage from Polanski's memoirs in which he gives a rather full account of making love to his first wife. In the film, Oscar, a failed writer, watches Mimi slip from their bed and stand at the window, naked, while a voiceover intones, in the protagonist's over-the-top prose style, 'Nothing ever surpassed the rapture of that first awakening. I might have been Adam with the taste of apple fresh in my mouth. I was looking at all the beauty in the world perfected in a single female form.'

Recalling his first night with Barbara Kwiatkowska in 1958, Polanski had written, 'I still remember . . . when she slipped out of bed that dawn and stood looking down into the street, naked. I'd never seen such utter perfection before.'

The lead in *Bitter Moon* was offered to James Woods (*Salvador*), who expressed initial interest but was reportedly 'horrified' when he came to read the script. The names of Jack Nicholson and Michael Douglas were both subsequently mentioned, and one can only regret that Jeremy Irons, who was born for the role, was either overlooked or unavailable. In the end Polanski gave the part to Peter Coyote, a 49-year-old jobbing actor with the right hint of moral ambiguity, if not out-and-out sleaze about him. As one critic wrote of his character, Oscar, he was 'someone you would want to touch only while wearing a pair of latex gloves', even though he 'somehow elicited our pity' by the end of the film. After Coyote had read the script, Polanski sent him a fax asking, 'Do you know the difference between eroticism and pornography? In the first you just use the feather. In the second you use the whole chicken.' Coyote immediately faxed back to enquire, 'What do you call it when you use the entire ostrich?'

Alongside Hugh Grant, establishing his persona as the definitive upper class English twit but with an added sexual veneer undreamed of by Bertie Wooster, Polanski cast Kristin Scott Thomas (*A Handful of Dust*), Victor Banerjee (*Foreign Body*) and the child actor Sophie Patel. The part of Mimi, the schoolgirl-turned-femme-fatale, went to Emmanuelle Seigner.

Although Polanski was able to engage his usual top-flight production crew, the process took significantly longer than on *Frantic*. The original screenplay of *Bitter Moon* proved too strong even by the standards of some of the hardened French technicians. As Polanski recalled, 'The so-called golden shower talk [in which Oscar had eulogised about Mimi's urinating on him] was originally a scene, as it is in the book; but I realised that leaving it in caused controversy. An editor whom I wanted to hire said that he would absolutely not work on a film like that, and a director of photography just dropped out.'

It is a curious fact that despite the recent reassessment of the Roberto Rossellini-Ingrid Bergman working relationship, the tastemakers of *Cahiers du Cinéma* listing their *Journey to Italy* (1954) as one of the top ten films of all time, even the greatest directors have struggled when it comes to collaborating with their wives. Polanski's experience on *Bitter Moon* was no exception. His home life in 1991 and early 1992 was 'difficult', he admitted to the journalist Stephen O'Shea. 'When you direct and you live with someone who worries about the work, you have to be reassuring. But sometimes you have a tendency to say, "So, please, now stop it. Let's live for a while."' The end result was a perfectly competent performance by Seigner, who did what she was supposed to do, which was to look ravishing, even if there was noticeably less in the way of emotion, animation or expressive speech.

On top of the challenge of combining his professional and domestic lives, Polanski also faced the added complication of directing Seigner in some singularly potent love scenes. One senior British member of the crew still admiringly recalls the 'cool and phlegmatic' way in which 'Roman cast his wife and soon-to-be mother of his kids in a role that called for the morals of a bisexual alley cat.' In one strikingly unorthodox breakfast ritual, for example, Seigner's character drools a mouthful of milk on to her bare breasts for Peter Coyote's benefit, the prelude to some energetic fellatio. In a subsequent scene the young actress would appear clad in a black plastic mac, which she doffs to reveal the classic ensemble of high-heeled shoes, stockings and a suspender belt. It being a Polanski film, she was also carrying a razor. One morning, Jack Nicholson visited the set of *Bitter Moon* and was rewarded by the sight of Coyote writhing around on the floor wearing only a pig mask, while Seigner, *sans* panties, flogged him with a bullwhip.*

As usual, Polanski laboured over the ending of his film, which bears little relation to the final pages of Bruckner's novel. Instead of the book's more nuanced climax, we're treated to a New Year's Eve ball which, much like 1957's *Breaking Up the Party*, ends in a drunken riot – closely followed by the emotional pile-up of a gay tryst that in turn gives way to a murder-suicide and the necessarily sombre fade, in which the English couple cling to one another in an apparent triumph of traditional marital values over those epitomised by the deceased swingers. To further emphasise the point, Polanski would have a sweet young girl appear on deck to wish

---

* Although many journalists and other guardians of public morality later expressed horror that Seigner, to cap her already 'shameless' performance, had apparently also been pregnant at the time of *Bitter Moon*, simple arithmetic would seem to refute this theory. The Polanskis' first child was born on 20 January 1993. Nine months earlier, in April 1992, the couple had already finished work on what they called their 'other production'.

the adults the season's compliments, a scene one critic interprets as an 'angelic messenger [proclaiming] a more life-giving course'.

Bitter Moon was released on 12 July 1992. It would do some $2 million worth of business at the US box office, and eventually turned a small profit for its producers. As a soft-porn melodrama it works well enough, and it has the added distinction of being a one-stop anthology of classic Polanskian themes: in just over two hours we get moral corruption, violence, voyeurism, black comedy, escalating claustrophobia and, as in *Frantic*, some enjoyable cultural satire involving an American abroad. The descent into sexual infatuation followed by full-blown madness seems convincingly done; as Jeff Gross remarks, 'Just prior to writing the script I'd had a rather torrid affair with a German woman which more or less followed the pattern of *Bitter Moon* ... Although hopefully I'm not as morose, cowardly or sadistic as Oscar in the movie, many of the fictional details came straight out of my situation at the time.' For a film that supposedly plumbed new depths of tastelessness, *Bitter Moon* is both deliberately paced and in many ways reassuringly old-fashioned, with a number of obvious references to Polanski's past work. The flashback formula was one he had used thirty-three years earlier in *When Angels Fall*, while the basic theme of sexual intrigue on a boat recalled *Knife in the Water*, if on a slightly higher budget. There was also some familiar-looking but beautifully shot tourist footage of Paris of the type Polanski had denied himself on *Frantic*. As in all 'arty' erotica, the film's principals went about their business with a kind of sophisticated ennui, and even while naked on all fours Peter Coyote seemed to break new ground in glassy-eyed torpor. Despite or because of the bad reviews, *Bitter Moon* went on to become something of a late night cult classic. It remains Polanski's most notorious public act.

'If you have a great passion it seems that the logical thing is to see the fruit of it. And the fruit are children,' Polanski announced in 1993. As a younger man, this same consuming passion had existed solely in terms of film-making, and even now he liked to file away lines or other ideas suggested by his scripts to be carefully polished for future use in interviews or elsewhere. The Polanskis' daughter, born that January, was named Morgane, the title of the abandoned screenplay about a young woman who comes alive inside a television set. It proved to be the first in a year of several significant milestones. Sharon Tate, had she lived, would have turned 50 that same month, and her son would have been 23. It was exactly forty years since Polanski had first appeared on screen as an actor, in *Three Stories*, thirty years since *Time* had given him his major break in

America, and twenty since he shot *Chinatown*. The director celebrated his own sixtieth birthday later that summer, an occasion he marked with a party for himself, Emmanuelle and some 200 of their closest friends.

IN A REMOTE, RUN-DOWN POLICE STATION, a jaded, self-loathing inspector confronts the amnesiac, has-been author who is brought in one stormy night charged with murder. The latest Roman Polanski film? Despite the resemblance, it was actually a low budget and critically ignored Italian drama called *A Pure Formality*, directed by Giuseppe Tornatore, the auteur of the Oscar-winning *Cinema Paradiso*. In an imaginative bit of casting, Polanski played the inspector, his first ever appearance as an authority figure. Gérard Depardieu was the washed-up writer. Although he gave a superbly taut performance, Polanski 'loathed' the tedium and discomfort of working on location for six weeks, which reminded him yet again of what he most disliked about the business of film-making. 'Don't forget that for a director, a movie represents a whole year of his life, sometimes more,' he told the magazine *Positif*. 'I remember it was pretty horrible on [Tornatore's] set. The place was cold and dank, and there were candles and water strewn all over the floor. It was a very depressing scene.' Even so, the Kafkaesque atmosphere and palpable tension of *A Pure Formality* were to prove the ideal warm-up for Polanski's own next feature. Nor could any project he graced ever be entirely free of light relief. A French journalist who visited him on location in Abruzzo recalls that 'Although Roman was dying to get back to Paris, he was still his usual irrepressible self. For some reason, a group of nuns had been invited on to the set to watch him in the film's final scene with Depardieu. When it was all over, Roman walked over and greeted the Mother Superior with a warm embrace on both cheeks. I don't suppose she had been kissed for fifty years.'

There was renewed speculation in the winter of 1993–4 that Polanski would somehow negotiate an amnesty with the American authorities. His well-connected agent Jeff Berg, the chairman of ICM, and a local lawyer are said to have approached the newly elected Los Angeles district attorney to determine if there might be grounds for a review of their client's case. Evidently the DA was still reluctant to offer the sort of guarantee that Polanski had in mind. To Robert Evans, who had reportedly lobbied on the director's behalf, both at the time of *The Two Jakes* and subsequently, 'It was too intense . . . It became not just a justice factor, but a media one. It doesn't take much to imagine the outcry that would be drummed up against him. The pressure would be too great. Roman wouldn't last five days in jail, and no one's going to give him an airtight agreement that he wouldn't have to do time.' Polanski himself later seemed to harden against the idea of a return, remarking that he had his family to think of and couldn't possibly risk depriving Morgane of her father.

THE YEAR 1991 HAD MARKED A NADIR IN POLANSKI'S CAREER. It was a high, however, for the Argentinian-born author Ariel Dorfman, who enjoyed a transatlantic *succès d'estime* with his morality play *Death and the Maiden*. Dorfman, born in 1942, had briefly served in the administration of the Chilean president Salvador Allende before going into long-term exile following the bloody military coup of 1973 that brought General Augusto Pinochet to power. *Death and the Maiden*, written shortly after Pinochet's ill-tempered departure from the scene in March 1990, deals with the encounter in an anonymous Latin American country between a former political prisoner named Paulina Escobar and the man she believes tortured her. After a brief but critically acclaimed run at the Royal Court Theatre in London and subsequently in the West End, the play transferred to Broadway in 1992, with Glenn Close (just before her triumphant turn as Norma Desmond in Andrew Lloyd Webber's revival of *Sunset Boulevard*) in the lead. The opening night house in New York was so involved with the story that several female members of the audience applauded when the heroine exacted her partial revenge by first bashing her alleged tormentor senseless and then tying him to a chair.

As Ariel Dorfman recalls, 'At about the time we opened on Broadway, I was getting all sorts of movie offers from prestigious directors. Then Thom Mount appeared and told me that he had someone "particularly apt" in mind, and that that someone was Roman Polanski. The logic was that Roman's personal history fitted the piece. He was an exile. He knew something about oppression, both under the Nazis and the state of California. And artistically, his stocks-in-trade were claustrophobia, enigma and terror. What's more, his heroines had almost always been "tortured". The more I thought about it, the more I liked the idea, especially once Warners got behind it. Anyway, I was invited to Paris for a meeting. Although I'd heard stories about Polanski, I also knew that he was a great artist. I didn't need a writ.'

Shortly after his arrival at avenue Montaigne, Dorfman concluded that he and Polanski were 'unlikely' to be friends. 'I don't like hurting people, whereas Roman . . . let's say, had a cruel streak in him.' Like many guests before him, Dorfman was also shown the director's 'charming, effusive' side, and recalls a particularly lavish meal in a Paris restaurant 'with Roman doling out the caviar, delighted to be making the production company pay for it all'.

Polanski also impressed Dorfman with his intuitive grasp of the play, which, reversing the formula of *Bitter Moon*, he insisted should be shot entirely without flashbacks. Instead of 'opening up' the film with a series of graphic torture scenes or other exposition, 'Roman was content to rely on the work's inherent tension. He had an amazing insight into the process of turning this dark, claustrophobic chamber piece into a big-budget movie, not to mention a strong affinity with both the torturer and his victim. There were elements of each of them in his personality. From early on, it was pretty obvious that he was the man for the job. Polanski obviously felt the same way, because Thom Mount reported back that Roman was desperate to do it.'

The original plan was for Polanski to first direct *Death and the Maiden* on the Paris stage, thus adding to an already impressive number of such productions. By 1993 there had been some thirty Paulinas in stock companies around the world, and it became a part that every actress wanted to play. Polanski seems to have changed his mind about this 'reconnaissance job', as he called it, although three months later he invited Dorfman back to avenue Montaigne for a script conference. This went well, by all accounts, the two men working side by side over the course of several days and occasionally playing Schubert's *Death and the Maiden* quartet on the stereo for additional inspiration. Dorfman then flew back to his home in America and finished the script, which Polanski rejected. As far as could be ascertained, 'Roman seemed to feel that we'd strayed too far away from the original play. We could fix it, he said, but it would take at least a couple of months of solid work. I couldn't make that commitment, so Rafael Yglesias [the author of Peter Weir's film *Fearless*] came in as a co-scenarist. I like the job he and Roman did on *Death and the Maiden*.'

With typical attention to detail, Polanski phoned Dorfman 'continually' over the next several weeks, bombarding him with 'incredibly precise' questions about, for instance, the exact decor of Paulina's house, right down to the brand of her cutlery. The playwright also sent in 'about forty pages of notes cover[ing] the fine points'. In late October 1993, Dorfman once again flew to Paris, where he persuaded Polanski to change the ending of his screenplay. 'I thought it essential that Paulina, her husband and her torturer, having gone through this whole ordeal, then meet up in the audience at the same concert hall, listening to Schubert's quartet.

You had to show some of the love between the three characters, I told Roman – who would always push up the tragedy – or at least how they coexist. That's the real world. Polanski listened to my pitch, walked over to the stereo and again put on *Death and the Maiden* at peak volume, before sinking into an armchair with his eyes closed. Presumably he was conjuring up the scene. When the music ended, no one spoke for a moment. Then Roman looked at me and said simply, "OK, we'll do it." That one decision added $400,000 to the budget, and it was worth it.'

With the material agreed, Polanski cast Sigourney Weaver, who worked for a third of her normal fee, as Paulina and the English-born Stuart Wilson (of *The Jewel in the Crown*) as her lawyer husband. The quality of the villains had been something of a disappointment in both *Pirates* and *Frantic*, in which the hero had only occasionally seemed to have a worthy adversary, let alone to be in any danger. There were no such problems in *Death and the Maiden*, where Polanski signed Ben Kingsley to play the torturer.

Even without the fluorescently bright credits, it would have been fairly easy to guess the name of the film's director from its first scenes. The action opens in a remote beach house on a cliff where, in classic gothic-horror tradition, a violent rainstorm makes the lights flicker and the phone work erratically. Gerardo, the husband, appears out of the storm with the kindly Dr Miranda, the Ben Kingsley character, who has given him a lift home after his car broke down. Paulina hears the doctor's voice from the next room and instantly recognises it as that of the man who, fifteen years earlier, having been sent to examine her while in custody, had instead applied electrodes to her body and repeatedly raped her while Schubert's music played in the background. Or so she thinks. Although the New York audiences had cheered the heroine on from the start, it's an important part of the plot that she might be mistaken about the stranger's identity. Kingsley denies everything, including the suggestion, offered by his hostess as an impromptu plea bargain, that he had been merely a passive, just-follow-orders man, a Latin version of a Nazi functionary. Having first slipped outside to push the doctor's car over the cliff, Paulina returns to knock him unconscious, drag him across the room and tie him up. In a scene missing from Dorfman's play, she then removes her panties and gags him with them, before straddling his lap in order to tape his mouth shut, leaning straight into his face to tear the tape with her teeth. The effect is unsettling, sexual and distinctly Polanskian. Paulina then puts the doctor on trial, with herself as judge and executioner, while her husband, the lawyer, initially protests at the breach of hospitality before gradually coming to believe and help her.

Actors seem to love this sort of edgy, confrontational drama, very much the stuff of workshop classes, and Polanski would report that all three cast members had been 'a joy' to direct. The ten-week shoot again took place at Paris Studios Cinéma in Boulogne-Billancourt, with the clifftop exteriors added on location in north-west Spain. In a break from normal practice, Polanski shot the film entirely in chronological order, and at reckless speed by his own standards. By all accounts there were few resulting technical or continuity problems, although the shape of Ben Kingsley's moustache varies appreciably from one scene to another.

The veteran cinematographer Tonino Delli Colli, the cameraman on Sergio Leone's *The Good, the Bad and the Ugly* and other spaghetti westerns, had worked under Polanski on *Bitter Moon* and been invited back by him to film *Death and the Maiden*. 'I immediately agreed, with reservations,' he recalls, joking that 'I was probably also attractive to Roman because I was so short.' On the positive side, 'Polanski was absolutely the best *technical* director I'd known in fifty years in the job, including those old masters Malle and Fellini. They were good, but Roman was better. [Polanski] knew as much about cameras and lenses, which he could identify at a glance, as I did, and I frequently had the impression that he could have easily made the film with just himself, the three actors and maybe a wardrobe assistant.' Delli Colli's only doubts were that, at 72 'I couldn't keep up . . . You know Roman's schedule: ten rehearsals and twenty takes, sometimes many more, and one went straight from the set to the latest nightclub. Even there, you'd find yourself discussing the movie with him. Unlike many great visionaries, he loved the bits and pieces of film-making.'

Polanski, in short, threw himself into the production. Few jobs were too menial for him, and he's remembered as much for his obsessive craftsmanship as for his aesthetic vision. When it came to the scene where Paulina knocks the doctor out cold, Polanski, perhaps drawing on his experience at the hands of the murderous Janusz Dziuba, was happy to show exactly how the victim should fall, first by discussing the matter and then by rolling around on the dirty floor, moaning pitifully. As seen on *Macbeth* he had a particular passion for fake blood, and brushed aside his make-up artist to personally apply the wicked-looking gash to Ben Kingsley's forehead. When Kingsley was subsequently about to be bound and gagged, Polanski snatched the packing tape out of Sigourney Weaver's hands and wound it tightly around his own face to demonstrate the proper technique.

Ariel Dorfman was on hand in the studio throughout the shoot, 'mainly doing rewrites for Sigourney', and was suitably impressed that the director was 'frequently also his own stuntman'. Dorfman's only reservation was the more artistic one that 'I continually suggested to Roman that there be more sense of the connection, or even love, between the three characters. He told me that he'd fix this, but he didn't . . . It all went back to the early meetings we'd had in Paris, when Roman had expressed surprise that I was so "sunny", in stark contrast to himself . . . That was really the first hint of how he might see *Death and the Maiden* . . . When the producers came to look at a rough cut of the film, they duly thought it "too cold" an ending, with the characters wandering off in a daze, and nothing apparently resolved, before meeting again in the concert hall. There was some talk of flying the cast back to Spain just to shoot an extra thirty seconds of footage. But Roman wouldn't have it. To his credit, he didn't give a damn about the critics or the box office. Literally couldn't care less. Everything had to be true to his vision of the work. You could disagree with him, but you couldn't fault his integrity.' As Polanski himself had noted, when promoting *Rosemary's Baby* twenty-five years earlier, 'If you show your hero triumphant, the audience leaves satisfied. And there's nothing more sterile than the state of satisfaction.'

For all the various creative differences, *Death and the Maiden* comes neatly full circle to the final concert scene, which Polanski filmed in a balletic sweep of the camera from over the heads of the musicians, on to Paulina and her husband seated in the stalls, then floating upwards to Dr Miranda, enjoying the performance in a box with his wife and two young children. The feeling of weightlessness matched the celebrated opening long shot of Andrzej Wajda's *A Generation*, or of Polanski's *The Tenant*. In all three cases, there were no breaks or cuts of any kind. *Death and the Maiden* may have ended on the note of moral ambiguity that was anathema to the average studio, but it did so with immense visual style.

Released in December 1994, *Death and the Maiden*, like *Bitter Moon* before it, took some $2 million at the American box office. The reviews were mixed. A general criticism was that the film was punishingly faithful to the play and, if anything, even more tightly coiled. Sigourney Weaver did Paulina proud, delivering a full-out caricature of a female avenger just this side of her role in the *Alien* saga, but neither of the men, despite Kingsley's character again proving the adage about the banality of evil (and being a voluble witness in his own defence, when not muzzled by the gag), ever really emerged from her shadow. To the *Washington Post*, *Death and the Maiden* was a 'wrestling match interrupted periodically by moral debate. Polanski stages some lovely moments [but] he also undercuts the high-minded ideals of Dorfman's play by exposing its radical chic pretensions.' The *New York Times* agreed the material was 'well meaning [if] pretentious', but felt Polanski 'treads lightly on the clumsier lines, and sustains tension by creating an elegant, unobtrusive dance with the camera . . . It all suggests the discipline of *Frantic* rather than the go-for-broke excess of *Bitter Moon*.'

According to one plausible but unverifiable story, a then senior manager at one of the film's distributors sat alongside Polanski and several of the cast and crew at *Death and the Maiden*'s French premiere in March 1995. It was apparently the first time the executive had seen the final cut, and at the subsequent party he was tight-lipped and censorious. Among other things, he disapproved of the 'grey' feeling to the film, thought that Ben Kingsley had been wasted by spending 'too much time trussed up like a turkey', and made ironic comments about Sigourney Weaver's under-wear. The crew were amused after the man departed to hear Polanski say of him: 'He's so wonderfully encouraging, isn't he? That's just the sort of support that makes it all worthwhile.'

It would be wrong to suggest, though, that the corporate reaction to *Death and the Maiden* was totally negative. There was a professional pride in being associated with Polanski, whose name, according to the produc-tion company's year-end report on the film, 'ensured certain worldwide attention [and] a certain quality of product' beyond that of a lesser figure. Polanski was quite sincere when he said that he never knowingly turned out a film that he wasn't proud to see his name stamped on, even if 'one or two individual scenes or whole sequences' had inevitably fallen flat, and notwithstanding the wholesale 'butchery' once inflicted by Marty Ransohoff. Fine Line Features and their co-distributors went on to under-write a series of promotional junkets involving the cast and crew that lasted through the summer of 1995. Ariel Dorfman recalls some 'enjoyably lavish' tours of the south of France, New York and California, the last two necessarily without the film's director. There was also to have been a weekend trip to Iceland, where Polanski had enjoyed major cult status ever since *The Fearless Vampire Killers*, known locally as *Vampyrintappajat – anteeksi, hampaanne ovat niskassani*, had caused a sensation at the 1968 Reykjavik Film Festival. At the last minute, however, as Dorfman recalls, 'the lawyers advised Roman not to get on the plane'. For all its deep-seated admiration of Polanski, Iceland was one of the dozen or so countries where he risked being arrested on arrival.

By 1995, Polanski had gone fifteen years since his last solid commercial success with *Tess*, and even that had been a pyrrhic victory. He was still obsessively creative, writing or adapting a screenplay every few months, but producers no longer beat a path to his door. During a break from filming *Death and the Maiden*, he took a cameo role as himself in Michel Blanc's comedy thriller *Dead Tired*. They were to prove to be his last two screen credits for five years. 'I'm in that strange time in between films,' Polanski remarked in mid-1995. Although he would insist that he had 'several projects simmering', including fresh discussions about *The Master and Margarita*, none of them came to the boil. With no other firm offers, at some stage in 1996 Polanski again apparently considered shooting a full-length animated film based on a series of erotic lithographs. Paul Mayersberg, the writer-director of *Captive*, a 1986 'sex thriller' starring Oliver Reed, reportedly produced a screenplay, of which one industry figure who read it chiefly remembers a scene 'involving a young maiden and a bull'. In the end, even the more independent-minded studios rejected the idea, and, other than staging a brief run of Terrence McNally's play *Master Class*, Polanski was out of circulation, professionally speaking, until co-producing a small Italian war comedy called *Castelnuovo* in early 1999.

Well before then, although still an artistic force in world cinema, if for no other reason than that he was more famous than the stars who appeared in his movies, Polanski had slipped into another of those creative funks in which he liked to refer to himself as an 'ex-film-maker'. He was in his mid-sixties now, an age at which a director grows tired of being jerked around by some Hollywood accountant posing as a producer. As Peter Coyote of *Bitter Moon* says, 'This is a guy who knows every aspect of film-making. Can you imagine Roman taking script notes from a 28-year-old MBA? He would commit homicide.' Polanski's legendary self-confidence was apparently unimpaired by prolonged bouts of unemployment. 'I can only say that whatever my life and work have been, I'm not envious of anyone, and this is my biggest satisfaction,' he noted. Elsewhere he was to reflect that his versatility was 'much like that of Picasso', and to compare his artistic struggles to those of Michelangelo.

Clearly, a happy marriage and a family, a recurring theme in all Polanski's interviews, had had their effect. Shortly after starring in the 1997 sci-fi film *Nirvana*, about a video-game character who comes to life, Emmanuelle Seigner gave birth to a son. Perhaps reflecting his father's love of American pop culture, if not of its justice system, he was named Elvis. When talking to journalists, Polanski proudly referred to his two children as 'my best productions'. A well known British actor and occasional house guest at avenue Montaigne remembers waking up at the flat early one morning in the spring of 1998. 'Roman first became visible to me,' he says, 'in an unfastened silk bathrobe over a hairy chest; he wore a cherubic grin and carried a small baby in his arm.' To another visitor, Polanski seemed 'more like the proprietor of a boutique hotel for kids [than] a traditional Victorian authority figure. He struck me as immensely patient and courteous.' When his daughter Morgane was old enough to enquire about Santa Claus, Polanski paid her the compliment of being 'totally honest' and disabusing her on the subject.

According to an interview he gave *Die Woche* in late 1998, Polanski took 'much, much more pleasure now in film-making than I ever have', presumably because it was no longer his sole preoccupation. But pleasure had been in short supply just eighteen months earlier, when the director had announced plans to shoot an extravagantly budgeted drama written by Gérard Brach and himself called *The Double*, starring John Travolta. Travolta was to be paid $17 million. Sparks flew immediately on the star's arrival in Paris, at the controls of his own Boeing 707. Still attired in his personally designed pilot's uniform, Travolta complained in the course of a heated production meeting that his part had been 'totally rewritten' (*'fucking totally'*, in some accounts) without his consent. A witness to the scene remembers 'John hav[ing] sat there and gone very slowly and methodically through every one of the lines with his name next to it like a tortoise chewing an unpleasantly tough bit of cabbage,' before having 'erupted.' Polanski countered that he was completely within his rights, indeed under an obligation, to change the script as he saw fit. At that stage, Travolta left the set and flew himself and his family back to Los Angeles on his 210-seat but, it is believed, substantially modified jet. This abrupt 'withdrawal of labour', to use the term in the subsequent lawsuit, brought about a hurried call to Steve Martin, who reportedly agreed to step in as a replacement. Before he could do so, *The Double*'s female lead, Isabelle Adjani, also apparently had cold feet and left the film. The project was then scrapped. Back in Hollywood, Travolta's publicist initially announced that his client's departure was solely to do with his 4-year-old son Jett undergoing unspecified surgery. Speaking to the press a week later, Travolta stuck by the surgery but admitted that he had had 'creative differences' with Polanski. Two years on, the director 'still [hadn't] forgiven that man . . . So many people had put so much effort into the project when all of a sudden everything fell apart. Pierre Guffroy, my long-time designer, cried when we tore down the set.' In May 2001, Travolta and two production companies reached an out-of-court settlement of their mutual lawsuits arising from *The Double*. He declined to say anything at all about Polanski or their brief association when contacted for this book.

More unwanted headlines followed in the wake of the Travolta debacle when several US news organisations reported that Polanski had agreed to surrender to authorities in Los Angeles. Under a deal supposedly brokered 'in secret meetings between the judge and the admitted sex abuser's lawyers', the court would impose only probation, accompanied by a heavy fine, instead of jail time. The ensuing coverage rekindled a lively debate about the rights and wrongs of the case, with the suggested remedies running the gamut from a full executive pardon for Polanski through to his surgical mutilation. Samantha Geimer, now a 34-year-old mother of three living in Hawaii, went public to say that she had 'forgiven' the director. 'I want him to be able to come back and just let it all be finished,' she added. 'I want it to be over.' A number of leading industry figures similarly went on record to call for 'closure' in the affair. One anonymous star explained to *Vanity Fair* magazine that his support for Polanski had 'something to do with forgiving talent their excesses . . . I'd feel different if either the girl or the girl's family felt strongly about putting him in jail.' The interviewer had asked the man how he would feel if Polanski had sodomised his own 13-year-old after giving her champagne and pills. 'I'd pull out a gun and blow his fucking head off,' he said.

Ultimately the amnesty talks broke down, if they had ever begun in the first place. According to court session minutes, a Judge Larry Fidler and the original prosecution and defence attorneys had met in a closed-door hearing on 31 January 1997, coincidentally the nineteenth anniversary of Polanski's flight to London. But this was just as likely to have been a purely procedural affair to renew the outstanding bench warrant as it was any material review of the case. When contacted in 2007, the Los Angeles district attorney's office denied that there had been any change to Judge Rittenband's long-standing order for Polanski's arrest, and nor was one anticipated. 'It remains a matter between the defendant and the court.'

By the spring of 1998, Polanski later admitted, 'I needed work. I had to do something. It was too long a time since my last film, and a lot of projects were cancelled.' After reading Arturo Pérez-Reverte's bestselling novel *El club Dumas*, relating the fortunes of a professional 'book detective' on the trail of two rare, satanic texts, and of a secret society obsessed with Alexandre Dumas – with an overall flavour broadly similar to *The Da Vinci*

Code – Polanski was able to package a deal for the property, which he renamed *The Ninth Gate*. His principal backers were Artisan Entertainment, the distributors of the *Rambo* and *Terminator* series, who led a Byzantine consortium of Franco-American financiers which eventually put up $38 million, bringing it close to the astronomic budget of *Pirates*.

While at the Cannes festival in May 1997, Polanski had met Johnny Depp, the seemingly ageless but in reality 33-year-old *Edward Scissorhands* star who was there plugging his acclaimed Mob drama *Donnie Brasco*. Two years earlier, *Variety* had announced this film as a so-called 'come-back tool' for John Travolta, who lost the role as a direct result of his defection from *The Double*; the same Mandalay Entertainment was the producer in both cases. In May 1998, Polanski signed Depp to appear in *The Ninth Gate*. The director then flew to Ibiza with John Brownjohn, the co-scenarist of *Bitter Moon*, for what was called a 'typically intense' bout with the script. What emerged was the tale of Dean Corso, the Depp character, who travels from New York to Europe in pursuit of his prize while in turn being tailed by the recently widowed Liana (Lena Olin) and another interested party, an unkempt but apparently angelic blonde played by Emmanuelle Seigner, whom at one point we, but not he, see fly. Along the way Corso also encounters a wheelchair-bound baroness, a pair of comic-opera identical twins (played, in a neat digital trick, by the same man) and a climactic black mass that crosses the finale of *Rosemary's Baby* with that of its immediate predecessor, *The Fearless Vampire Killers*. The whole thing ends in a blaze, not necessarily of glory, when Corso's client, the amoral Boris Balkan, accidentally cremates himself after rashly pouring a can of petrol over his head while attempting to invoke the devil. After energetically making love to the blonde with the inferno still raging around them, Corso sloughs off to discover the truth both about the books and possibly evil itself. As played by Depp he's a peculiarly grungy, slouching sort of bibliophile, who smokes non-stop, carries priceless editions around in his tatty shoulder bag, and not infrequently looks as if he's been airlifted in from another movie. In the original novel, Corso had been a middle-aged businessman in a bespoke suit. Polanski also dispensed in its entirety with the Dumas club, a major subplot of the book.

The Ninth Gate led to inevitable comparisons with *Rosemary's Baby*, as well as to the charge that Polanski truly was 'obsessed' with the satanic. Nothing could be further from the truth, he assured reporters. 'I don't have a relationship to evil,' Polanski told the magazine *Der Tagesspiegel*.

'I've never believed in occultism or the devil. I'm not at all religious. I'd rather read science books than something like that.'

The interviewer had then asked Polanski how he explained the current popularity of 'demonic themes' in the cinema.

'It sells,' he said.*

When visiting the Warsaw film club in December 1976, Polanski had expounded his artistic theory in three simple sentences. 'I want people to go to the movies,' he said. 'I am the man of the spectacle. I'm playing.' He was true to his word in *The Ninth Gate*, where there could be little more arresting sight than that of the extreme close-up of Polanski's bulging-eyed wife in flagrante on the diabolist's funeral pyre. Her character's dialogue by that stage consists predominantly of feral yelps, which would be accompanied in the final cut by a thunderous symphonic crescendo. Although the couple's children were frequent visitors to the set, and 5-year-old Morgane took an uncredited cameo in the film, it's not known if they were present for that particular shot.

One Las Vegas-based reviewer wrote in December 1999 that this scene was 'unbelievably cheap and gaudy', while several others expressed more technical reservations about Seigner's acting. Many felt that, once again, the beginning of Polanski's film was better than its ending. The same had been true of his last three outings, and arguably ever since *Chinatown*, enjoyable as they all still were. As even Polanski's critics allowed, his work, however flawed, was fully informed with the tradition that preceded it, and his mastery of his medium was unsurpassed by any other living director. *The Ninth Gate* opens with a spectacularly fluid title sequence involving a suicide by hanging, a pitch-perfect Hitchcockian note not quite sustained by the lurid climax.

After negotiating the budget for *The Ninth Gate*, Polanski had divided his time between Ibiza, adapting the 'difficult' source novel, scouting locations in Spain and Portugal, and finally Paris, where he devoted most of his working hours to selecting his cast.

Johnny Depp aside, Polanski's actors were once again extremely able performers who weren't currently household names. Barbara Jefford, the 68-year-old veteran of *Lust for a Vampire* and other Hammer-horror fare, signed to play the baroness, and Frank Langella, himself a former Dracula, was Balkan. The undeniably attractive if glassy Emmanuelle Seigner as

* While not conventionally religious, Polanski is said to have not been above one or two minor superstitions, including, allegedly, the use of a 'lucky coin'.

noted gave her usual turn as the girl. A 45-year-old character actor named James Russo took the key part of Bernie, a book-dealing friend of Corso who ends up murdered and hung upside down in a macabre parody of a figure in one of the satanic texts. Polanski didn't know the man, but he was aware of Russo's work from *Donnie Brasco*, and Depp pushed him strongly as the consummate 'non-actor' who would make something of a reality of Polanski's need for 'total plausibility' in *The Ninth Gate*.

Polanski's first question about Russo was characteristic. 'But can we count on him to be loyal?' the director wanted to know. 'I don't mean a yes-man. I mean – you know – one of us.' Reassured that he was a team player, Polanski phoned Russo in Los Angeles. The two men hit it off. Russo, like most actors, was drawn by Polanski's gift of the gab, by his sharp wit, by his obvious enthusiasm, by his pixie qualities and, above all, by his 'utter originality' of style. 'I would have done the film for nothing,' he says.

Polanski's attention to detail struck Russo even more than the technical mastery which 'was pretty well understood, given Roman's reputation'. Early on in the proceedings, the cast and crew waited patiently while their director spent the best part of an hour preparing a particular scene by fussily rearranging the books on a shelf, as one actor recalls, 'pulling one out, putting another in its place – sometimes seemingly satisfied, but then drawn back to it, totally lost in the job.' Eventually, one of the cast had the temerity to ask, 'Roman, is this shot about the people or about the props?' Without stopping what he was doing, Polanski snapped back over his shoulder, 'It's about both.' In the same vein, James Russo remembers examining 'several dozen pairs of expensive glasses, laid out on a table, one of which I was going to wear in the film. There was Armani, Porsche, Prada, Gucci – you name it. It literally looked like an optician's store. Various technical people came by and expressed their preferences. Finally Polanski himself appeared, glanced at the selection and said, "No. None of them are right for the character." Instead I was to wear this shitty, five-dollar pair from the local drugstore, and, of course, they were perfect for the part. All the designers and prop guys were wrong, and Roman was right.'

Polanski's artistic template for *The Ninth Gate* was *A Touch of Evil*, Orson Welles' 1958 cinema noir classic set on the Mexican-American border. Throughout all the revisions and refinements to the script, and consequent production delays, 'Roman was adamant about getting his vision of the film up on the screen,' says James Russo. 'I mean, *whatever* it took. Thirty or thirty-five stabs at a scene weren't unusual. We took all day to do one set-up where the camera was looking over my shoulder . . . The film was very much done on Roman's time, and anything or anyone who interfered could go screw themselves.' As a result there were to be persistent difficulties with the front office at Artisan Entertainment, representatives of which took to regularly phoning the set from Hollywood, complaining bitterly about the overages. 'By the second week in, they'd already read Polanski the Riot Act,' an actor recalls. The director's unhurried technique appears to have eventually tried the patience even of Johnny Depp – a model professional, it should be stressed – who later noted of the experience that 'Roman is pretty set in his ways'. It wasn't all gloom for the actor, however. According to reports, the female lead of *The Ninth Gate* was originally to have been Vanessa Paradis, the 25-year-old actress-singer and former 'teenage vamp' responsible for 'Joe Le Taxi', an almost guiltily enjoyable Top Ten hit in 1988. Although not ultimately required in the film, Paradis found herself sitting in the lobby of the Hôtel Costes in Paris one evening just as Polanski and the cast came in the door. She and Depp had struck up a friendship; within a few weeks, Paradis was pregnant with their daughter, Lily-Rose, and soon thereafter the couple were ensconced in a $2 million villa in Saint-Tropez.

Three weeks into the production, Polanski apparently got into an unseemly dispute with one of the Artisan representatives who was visiting the set. The executive had reportedly studied the production log, which is thought to have shown something less than the Stakhanovite quota of six completed scenes a day that the company had requested. According to one source, the visitor had 'banged down' the log before turning to the director and remarking, 'You're already a week behind.' Polanski had begun to explain the various reasons for the delay, at which point the man, it's said on good authority, 'went fucking berserk. He told Roman that he didn't give a shit about any arty excuses, and Roman in turn went ballistic. There was a hell of a scene. The set was cleared.' The details of what followed are unclear, but it seems fairly certain that the executive remonstrated with Polanski, and that the two fell into a noisy quarrel. At one point there was the sound of a chair hitting a wall. A witness to the fracas insists that the company man ultimately 'aimed a wild punch at Roman, missed and fell into a bowl of dip on the buffet'. Shortly after that, the executive took his leave of the set.

A few moments later, a 'huffing and puffing' Polanski appeared in Johnny Depp's trailer, where Depp had been waiting out the storm with James Russo. The two actors looked at their 'obviously rattled' director and asked him what had happened. 'I got into a fight,' Polanski said simply.

According to James Russo, a 'dark cloud' had perhaps inevitably hung over the remainder of the shoot. 'Artisan brought in a new line producer to watchdog the production, which wasn't a happy experience,' he notes. Despite or because of the heightened scrutiny, Polanski completed *The Ninth Gate* on schedule. As with *Pirates*, the real problem seems to have begun in the editing room, with the final cut enjoying a whole raft of post-production tricks but suffering from a series of continuity glitches and other errors that would never have been allowed in, say, *Chinatown*. The finished $38 million film is framed by two such blunders: when Corso meets Boris Balkan for the first time, we see a crouching crew member, possibly Polanski, reflected in a window; when the same two characters finally part, on Balkan's self-immolation, the light turns from dusk to bright sunshine in the space of a few fictional minutes. And as a real bibliophile remarks, 'I gave up counting the howlers in the ways these alleged professionals treat their books', the 'constant dropping of fag ash on to the volumes' being only the most egregious lapse. There also appears to have been a breakdown, at several key points in the film, in the all-important synching of the sound effects to the accompanying action.

The Ninth Gate was premiered in August 1999, and went on general release the following Christmas. Polanski's contribution to *fin de siècle* dissolution was judged only a modest success by the critics. *Today* thought it the 'flawed work' of a 'still talented' director. The *New York Times* agreed about the flaws but questioned the talent, calling the movie 'about as scary as a sock-puppet re-enactment of *The Blair Witch Project*, and not nearly as funny'. One little commented-on possibility is that *The Ninth Gate* was spoiled by its own lavish budget. Compared to *Rosemary's Baby* (shot for $2.3 million, or roughly $12 million in 1999 prices), it all seems strangely artificial. New York looks like a film set (which it was – the Manhattan scenes were shot in Paris), the weather always gives the impression that it was added in digitally, and Seigner's flying stunt is a sham. 'I don't know if it's senility,' Polanski had remarked to *Cahiers du Cinéma*, 'but I do observe a phenomenon in older film-makers that's quite irritating, almost obscene. It happens to certain artists who realise that everything going on around them is changing and moving further away from what they're doing . . . So they end up performing somersaults which, for them, is quite undignified. Something odd always happens to older artists . . . [It's] really annoying.' Although Polanski had said this in 1968, it would be as insightful and relevant thirty years later as it was at the time.

On the other hand, Polanski's control of his material, as opposed to his special effects, remained peerless. His use of pause and nuance injected a much-needed tension into several scenes, and belied the theory that, at 65, he'd somehow lost his grip. With rare exceptions, Polanski had always been more successful when simply directing an actor or two on a bare stage than when straining to choreograph a cast of dozens and their support group, including, in this case, a seventy-six-strong visual effects department and no fewer than 155 accredited 'Miscellaneous Crew and Stuntmen'. *The Ninth Gate* cuts back and forth between these two stylistic extremes, never quite deciding if it's Harold Pinter or Busby Berkeley, but in the end confirming Polanski's reputation for elegant horror.

Polanski won a European Film Award for *The Ninth Gate*, among several lesser prizes. He later referred to his fifteenth feature as 'fun' and 'nice', but agreed that 'it doesn't make any important statement'. In July 2000, Artisan Entertainment sued Polanski in Los Angeles District Court, alleging that he and his production company had pocketed some $700,000 in refunds of France's value-added tax instead of turning them over to International Film Guarantors, Artisan's completion bond company. Rather than place the funds in one of the third party's bank accounts, the complaint noted, Polanski had 'brazenly deposited the money in his private account' and had 'refused all requests to return it'.

Whatever the rights and wrongs of this case, whose outcome, if any, would remain sealed, and which elicited no further public comment, Polanski perhaps had the last word in the matter. *The Ninth Gate* eventually went on to gross $57 million worldwide, making it one of the most profitable films of his career. He had rubbed his lucky coin, gambled on the devil and won.

CHAPTER 10
OSCAR

THE NEW MILLENNIUM BROUGHT A FAMILIAR-SOUNDING flurry of rumours that Polanski would return to take his chances in the United States. It had been twenty-three years since what the *New York Times* called the 'unpleasantness' of Judge Rittenband's hearings, and as the paper noted in the midst of a generally glowing profile, the director 'want[ed] nothing more than to make important films', an opportunity apparently denied him by America's stuffily puritanical views on child sex. (It was perhaps possible, even so, to misjudge the scope of Hollywood's reported 'mass corporate boycott' of Polanski, which since 1978 had driven him into the arms of such fringe organisations as Columbia and Warner Brothers.) 'On the whole,' the monthly *Republic* concluded magisterially in its year-end review of 1999, 'the balance of Americans are probably of the opinion that some way should be found [to] allow Roman Polanski to work here.'

Not for the first time, the rumours of a negotiated deal were 'pure baloney', as Polanski observed. 'Every now and again [the press] propose the notion that I am doing something about it. Then there is a new round of articles about my coming return. There's nothing!' One possible reason for the 'loopy' speculation was that Polanski himself, despite this denial, had sometimes seemed to encourage it. 'I don't know if [I'll return],' he told the interviewer Charlie Rose in March 2000. 'I didn't say I'm not going to do it . . . The most important aspect for me would be to get it over with. It's rather for my peace of mind than any other reason.' But there remained 'unfortunate obstacles'. Judge Rittenband having died, Polanski saw a new barrier to his ever getting a fair deal at the hands of the US court system. 'A lot has changed, but the main thing is that the media has taken over American justice ... The outcome depends entirely on what they say and show about you on television ... I think it would be hell, if not from the system itself then from the media. I don't want people hanging outside my door and antenna dishes in front of my window.'

Though Polanski had never been particularly good at keeping secrets about his private life, he tried hard now. Reasonably enough, he specifically didn't want 'some goon point[ing] cameras at my kids', and liked the fact that, in France, 'even the paparazzi show some taste' – one of several advantages of life in his adopted home. Polanski cheerfully corrected an interviewer who remarked that he led a 'rather comfortable existence' by telling him, 'Not "rather"; a *very* comfortable existence.' There was also the gratifying professional respect of what Polanski called his 'Paris community', notwithstanding some negative local reviews of *The Ninth Gate*, including one in *Libération* calling the film 'painful to watch'. On 15 December 1999, France's illustrious Academie des Beaux Arts had inducted the director as an 'eminently distinguished' life member. The master of ceremonies, Peter Ustinov, told the star-studded audience gathered for the occasion that Polanski was a 'great genius' whose films had earned him the 'well-deserved immortality' of a place 'among the gods'. As one reporter remarked, it would have taken 'almost suicidal skills' to have willingly sacrificed such personal and professional kudos for the 'cold confines of a California jail cell'.

Nor were there exactly compelling artistic reasons for Polanski to return. In forty years, he had only ever made two films on American soil, and bitterly summarised his dwindling prospects there as being 'remakes of the same story – *The Son of Rosemary's Baby*', or something equally dire. Polanski's ambitious plan to film *The Master and Margarita* was reportedly again rejected in 2000, prompting another colourful rebuke of the 'cretins' running the typical Hollywood studio. An acquaintance and occasional collaborator in Paris says that from time to time, 'Roman would simply announce that he had quit.' At 66, 'he'd lost the drive essential to success, was bored by the in-fighting and, ultimately, didn't give a damn.' Few of the people who knew Polanski best would have agreed with any of this, and at least one of them insists that the exact opposite was true. 'But for Roman, this sort of thing was a necessary part of gearing up for a major film. Every decision had to be a crisis, every decision had to be a part of a larger drama. If you look at his very best work, it's all tended to come out of a sense of rejection, which is where he's at his happiest.'

It's worth dwelling on the state of Polanski's career in early 2000 if only to show that, having long been the epitome of a director who was more critically feted than commercially successful, the very opposite applied in the wake of *The Ninth Gate*. Not that he suddenly found himself being pursued by the major studios as a result. Thanks either to his proverbial reputation for being 'difficult', or to the negative publicity from his feud with Artisan, Polanski again seemed to be entering one of his cyclical periods of underemployment, if not professional ostracism. At the same time, he would never be completely without what he called a *divertissement* or two on the side. In the early weeks of the new century he appeared in an award-winning short called *Hommage à Alfred Lepetit*, briefly directed an Italian stage version of *Amadeus* and even managed to adapt *The Fearless Vampire Killers* as a Viennese musical. For Polanski, however, none of these projects could take the place of a full-length film, if only because they lacked a sufficient audience. Recycling his 1967 Dracula spoof was unlikely to win him new fans in any appreciable numbers, or to excite the big men of Hollywood. As the producer-director Stanley Kramer put it later that year, 'Had you sat a hundred industry chiefs in a room and asked them if Roman was still a significant player, at least eighty of them would have said no.'

So one can see how much in the balance Polanski found himself walking the streets of Krakow on a 'profoundly nostalgic' family visit that Easter. Although he'd been back before, this was his first time there as a father, perhaps lending a sharper perspective on what his own parents had suffered sixty years earlier. 'I went to the area where the ghetto was,' Polanski recalled. 'It's the place that suddenly makes it all live again in my memory ... Those places are sacred for me. What one can still remember is important.' The visit appears to have served as what he called a 'freeing exercise'. Shortly after returning to Paris, Polanski read the recently reissued Polish edition of Wladyslaw Szpilman's book *The Pianist*, originally published in 1946 under the title *Death of a City*. It was the powerfully dispassionate, autobiographical account of a Jew who survived the Nazi occupation of Warsaw by going into hiding while his family members were successively murdered. In September 1939, Szpilman, then a 27-year-old pianist and composer, had been playing the last live music heard on free Polish radio, Chopin's *Nocturne in C sharp minor*, before German bombs destroyed the transmitter. Six years later he returned to the studio, finished the piece, and shortly thereafter wrote his memoirs. 'It's the story I've been looking for for years,' Polanski said later that spring, announcing that it would be his next film.

There was a certain amount of industry surprise at the news, which one trade paper characterised as an 'act of artistic despair'. The cynical view was that Polanski had called the Nazis to the rescue of a career that had seemed to be quietly drawing to a close. Now, suddenly, he was back with a $35 million production, largely underwritten by France's Canal Plus cable television channel, and co-financed by his old Cadre Films partner Gene Gutowski. Why, after so long, this obviously evocative subject? Just eight years earlier, Steven Spielberg had offered Polanski the opportunity to direct *Schindler's List*. According to Gene Gutowski, 'Roman turned it down because he felt that filming in the remains of the Krakow ghetto would be too painful.' A key advantage of *The Pianist*, other than its Warsaw location, was the book's deceptively simple style and underlying moral ambiguity, familiar hallmarks of Polanski's own best work. The warring parties are treated with an honesty and an emotional maturity which are a rebuke to their partisans. Szpilman describes not only the horrors inflicted by the Nazis, but also by the indigenous Polish population on the Jewish minority, and indeed among the Jews them-selves. In a final paradox, it's a German officer who ultimately saves Szpilman's life by offering him food and shelter. (In the original version of the film, made shortly after the war, Soviet censors had deleted this last scene and substituted a shot of Warsaw residents deliriously welcoming the Red Army.) Polanski, who had briefly met the author thirty years earlier in Los Angeles, thought the book 'stylistically, not that well written', but was impressed by its sense of detachment. 'It breaks lots of stereotypes and is told without the desire for revenge,' he said at a news conference. 'Though the subject matter is bleak, it's treated objec-tively, which is what I like . . . It's also a very positive story in the way that the person telling it is himself a survivor. Szpilman's book makes a very strong impression through the details. It has that peculiar brand of precision and distance that the survivor often carries with him.'

As his scenarist Polanski chose Ronald Harwood, the 66-year-old, South African-born author of *Taking Sides*, another morally complex war story with a musical protagonist. Based on the life of Wilhelm Furtwängler, Hitler's favourite conductor, Harwood's original play had examined the notion of the 'good Nazi' who does what he can for the Jews in his orchestra. *Taking Sides* was subsequently adapted into a film starring

Harvey Keitel. Striking the right note of artistic detachment, Harwood would recall that while 'some people said I was hard on Furtwängler, his widow was very nice about it . . . She saw the play in German-language productions around Europe. Afterwards she would often hold the hand of the man who played her husband, particularly if he looked like him. It was quite touching.'

Polanski and Harwood spent six weeks in the summer of 2000 at a rented house outside Paris, adapting Szpilman's book, allegedly with some faxed input from Gérard Brach. It was a surprisingly congenial experience given the source material. 'The children played in the garden, we had a fabulous cook, and my wife came home every night from the theatre where she was performing,' Polanski said. They had gotten through the process by 'work[ing] with a positive attitude, laughing a lot, making bad jokes . . . talk[ing] about the hundreds of Jews we had to kill in the next scene.'

After studying dozens of audition tapes, Polanski cast 27-year-old Adrien Brody (*The Thin Red Line*) in the lead. It was an inspired choice given the demands of the role, for which the actor would shed thirty pounds from an already thin frame. Brody's process might best be described as Method, and broadly in the school of a young Al Pacino. Thomas Kretschmann, the East German star of *U-571*, signed to play Hosenfeld, the *Wehrmacht* officer who saves Szpilman's life, and Maureen Lipman, somehow forever Beattie from the British Telecom advertisements, was the pianist's mother. Polanski had a long tradition of taking competent but occasionally obscure British television actors and giving them major roles in his films. The part of Szpilman's friend Yehuda went to 45-year-old Paul Bradley, who had been Nigel Bates in *EastEnders* before going on to tackle Chen in *Red Dwarf*.

As Bradley says, 'In this business there are two kinds of director: the ones who do their homework and the ones who don't. Polanski wasn't just in the former category. He defined it. Before even setting foot on location, each of us got an hour-long "enunciation tape" compiled by the man himself. The idea was to ensure that everyone pronounced certain key words – "Nazi" being an obvious example – the right way.'

Polanski was also 'supremely positive' about the tone of his film, which, if not exactly sympathetic to the Germans, set things in a broader context. A number of critics of American foreign policy would later come to see it as a prescient study of how good intentions can be perverted when patriotic expedience rules the day. More specifically, Polanski wanted nothing 'sentimental and gimmicky', either from his cast or from his cameraman. The director's wholesale ban on 'showing off' reportedly extended to refusing repeated requests from various of his backers that he include explanatory on-screen notes about the progress of the war, to be intercut with graphic archival footage of German concentration camps. One or two of the frustrated moneymen subsequently gave him the at least half-admiring nickname of 'God'. 'As Roman made very clear, *The Pianist* was to be a "neutral" film, one that didn't hit you over the head with its morality,' says Paul Bradley. 'At several points in the story the actors would have to walk past small kids pretending to be corpses lying in the street. Polanski's direction was always to just pass by, without looking down at them or showing any emotion at all. That sort of desensitisation comes across far more powerfully than a big theatrical reaction.'

Polanski had told the production crew that, logically enough, *The Pianist* would be shot entirely on location in Poland, making it his first feature there since *Knife in the Water*. It was then discovered that there were only three buildings remaining of the original Warsaw ghetto, so the exteriors were filmed in the city's outlying Praga district, and the interiors of Szpilman in hiding on a sound-stage in Berlin. Several of the most harrowing sequences were thus shot in the former Reich capital, with other ghetto scenes added at an abandoned air force base in Jüterbog, East Germany, once the centre of operations for the Luftwaffe's attacks on Poland. Polanski may have particularly relished having the facility dynamited to create sufficient rubble.

Although 'God's' voice was quieter now, less that of an angry demagogue than of a wearied artist, no one ever doubted who was in charge on the set of *The Pianist*. As a cast member says, 'When Polanski snapped "Action" he clearly meant it as an order ... You'd look up and he'd always be in the same spot, crouched over the camera, as opposed to over by the video monitor, which is fifty feet away from the actors. Roman wanted everyone there to know who was directing.' Another long-time colleague adds that 'I knew Polanski was serious about the movie when he arrived on the first morning with his glasses on. In ten years I'd only ever seen him wear them once before, and that was to read a wine list.' As the story progressed, and the Brady character degenerated from a cocky young man into a human scarecrow, Polanski was seen to break away on occasion and stand off in a corner by himself in between takes. Some scenes in the filming, like that of the train being loaded for the death camp, were so potent that 'there were times when Roman was visibly upset', Gene Gutowski says.

The average film crew being heavily unionised and Polanski making as he did demands on everyone's time and patience, one or two of his sets over the years had come close to defining the term 'hostile working environment'. Anyone not meeting his exacting professional standards could expect a lecture, if not an abrupt dismissal, and offenders were rarely invited back to the next project. In the Sixties and Seventies, Polanski had had a disdain for 'incompetents' and 'ass-draggers' that had excited even Charles Bluhdorn's admiration. 'Roman is good at drowning the kittens,' the famously hard-bitten mogul had once said.

The Pianist engendered a very different atmosphere. Polanski later told *Premiere* of the 'casual [workers] who came at four in the morning, and stayed in the sun all day . . . [There] was never a word of complaint, never any bad humour or temper. 1,400 people were around me, each one of them playing a role. It was phenomenal.' Along with the extras, several hundred elderly residents of Warsaw came to watch parts of the production, and many applauded, often in tears, at the conclusion of a scene. In another break from recent tradition, Polanski was rarely if ever forced to squabble about money with his backers. 'I wish every film I've made could have been done in such a way,' he said.

For their part, the cast were fanatically loyal: when he was given the part of Szpilman, Adrien Brody moved out of his apartment, sold his car and as he says, 'lived the role' for the next year. As well as learning to play Chopin, he dropped from eleven stone to less than nine stone under Polanski's dietary supervision. 'Roman wanted that,' Brody notes. 'He knew being truly hungry would change me psychologically and emotionally as well as physically, and he was right.' The actor's immersion into the role also included his drinking fetid water out of a fly-covered barrel and other privations that eventually reduced him to a near-animal state. Paul Bradley remembers that 'at one point Adrien's mum visited the set and was quite distressed about his condition. He was pretty near the edge. When he finally had a square meal again, he threw up.'

Polanski was able to command his actors' uncomplaining respect if for no other reason than that he worked himself equally hard. He swept on to the set before seven each morning, checked the day's call-sheets and for the next two hours installed himself in his trailer where he would brief individual actors about what was required of them. After nine or ten hours' filming, he met with his production crew and worked on the next day's storyboards before retiring to the projection suite until past midnight. One of the cast remembers that 'Roman was also constantly rewriting the script, and my impression was that he added a lot of scenes from sense memory', or personal experience. The Polish militiaman who had once allowed Roman and a young friend out of the ghetto and then hissed at them 'Don't run' has his counterpart in the film, as does the old woman he had seen shot dead by a German officer in the street. As usual, Polanski was also frequently his own props man, and personally applied his patented stage blood to Paul Bradley and other characters. (As Bradley says, 'It did strike me at the time that Roman was "going through" something with the blood. What other major director would do that?') As if not hands-on enough, Polanski would dub his voice for that of a Jew waiting to cross the street who complains about Gentiles living nearby; his daughter Morgane again had a cameo role.

True to his word, Polanski avoided anything 'sentimental and gimmicky' both in the six months of principal photography and the six months of post-production and editing. 'Cinema is often very pretentious ... [Directors] cut the film up, they shake the camera about and they manipulate sound. But for what purpose? Everyone knows things like this are possible. But being simple – now there's a real talent.' Polanski had said this of *Rosemary's Baby*, but it applied equally well to *The Pianist*. The film was affecting, sometimes overwhelmingly so, but never pandered. No soaring choirs marked reunions, no *Jaws*-like thudding signalled the perils. The climactic confrontation, when the Nazi officer asks Szpilman to prove he can play the piano, the stark implication being that he'll be shot if he can't, is exquisitely underplayed. Where another director would have given us close-ups of squinting eyes and sweaty palms, Polanski lets the scene unfold quietly, with just the right note of tension and relief. Instead of the panoramic sweep of a *Schindler's List*, *The Pianist* concerns itself exclusively with a more modest and specific set of events. In scaling down the action to a single, not always heroic figure, it invites the audience members to put themselves in Szpilman's shoes and so achieves an impact that Spielberg's worthy but heavy-going epic had somehow lacked. It remains Polanski's masterpiece, one that surprises through its understated and irresistible power to move.

After wrapping *The Pianist* in September 2001, Polanski flew to Tel Aviv, where he was able to find the original concentration-camp file on his father housed in the Archive of Contemporary Jewish Documentation. 'I went down there,' he told the writer and fellow Holocaust survivor

Jorge Semprun. 'Everything was organised by nationality, and as I walked around these boxes full of papers it was as though I were walking through the opening scenes of *Citizen Kane*.' Wladyslaw Szpilman had died in July 2000, aged 88, but Polanski arranged to host both a number of Szpilman's contemporaries and Hosenfeld's five elderly children for a private screening of *The Pianist* in Berlin. The director was struck by the dramatic possibilities of his guests drinking champagne together and then sitting down in the dark on either side of himself, the Polish ghetto survivor. All parties had been 'very taken by the film,' he said.

The Pianist was premiered on 24 May 2002 at the Cannes Film Festival, where it was given an eight-minute standing ovation. The festival committee awarded Polanski their Palme d'Or, the first of numerous honours from around the world. Ronald Harwood would remember that the producer Harvey Weinstein of Miramax had watched the film 'for three or four minutes and [then] got up very ostentatiously and walked out'.

Harwood was asked if, as a Jew, Weinstein had found the story too upsetting. 'No,' he said. 'He didn't think it would make any money. He was saying, "I am the great Harvey and you guys know nothing."' The art-house division of Universal, Focus Features, eventually bought the American rights to *The Pianist*, which they released only in January 2003. Harvey Weinstein came to the New York opening and introduced himself to the film's principals, telling them that he loved their work. 'He'd forgotten all about [Cannes] by then, of course,' says Harwood.

The American reviews were somewhat slow to come, and when they did a number of Polanski's old foes got tetchy at his foreign success. Quite by chance, *The Pianist*'s New York release coincided with yet another burst of speculation about the director's possible return to the United States. As at least one critic noted, perhaps hyperbolically, leaks and denials of the latest apparent negotiations 'notched up millions in free PR', while stories about 'little Roman' filled more column inches than the Iraq war. There were also one or two more measured criticisms, mainly to do with the 'limiting' device of Polanski's doggedly following the Brody character rather than the 'more inclusive' and 'historical' Spielberg approach to the Shoah. *Today* was able to list half a dozen minor anachronisms in *The Pianist*, for example the scene of the Szpilman family supposedly listening to the broadcast of a speech by Josef Goebbels that he actually gave some four years later. But most notices were all that Polanski and his producers could have hoped for. The *New York Times* was particularly taken by the film's 'bleak, acid humor' and saw Szpilman, as played by Brody, coming to 'resemble one of Samuel Beckett's gaunt existential clowns, shambling through a barren, bombed-out landscape clutching a jar of pickles. He is like the walking punchline to a cosmic jest of unfathomable cruelty.'

Perhaps more to the point, *The Pianist* proved to be a solid box-office success. Despite a mildly disappointing opening weekend in which it took $111,261 (compared to the $6.85 million of *Schindler's List*) in American cinemas, it went on to gross $32.5 million in the US and roughly as much again in the rest of the world, with first-month figures of $1,757,000 in Germany, where it was shown as part of the history curriculum at all state secondary schools. These were figures of which even Harvey Weinstein would have approved. Polanski had not only fully repaid his backers but had embarked on a Late Period. Just short of his seventieth birthday, he was as much or more in demand than at any time since his early forties, during that brief lull between his directing *Chinatown* and meeting Samantha Gailey. The Paris premiere of *The Pianist* in September 2002 must have struck Polanski as particularly satisfying, not only for the standing ovation but for the obvious pride taken by the local organisers in honouring one of their own. Some 300 guests were present for the gala screening and the lavish first-night party. A buffet was laid out, toasts given, promotional gifts exchanged. Fireworks experts were reportedly brought in from Monaco. Everyone's hotel rooms were filled with white roses. 'What's Roman going to do for an encore?' a visiting American critic asked. 'Versailles?'

Polanski was back at the Cannes festival in 2003, this time to enjoy his triumph as the star of Andrzej Wajda's film *Zemsta*. For their first collaboration since 1955's *A Generation*, the grand old men of Polish cinema chose a seventeenth-century farce about two elderly noblemen who inhabit separate wings of a crumbling castle and thrive on making each other miserable. This period version of *The Odd Couple* was distinguished by an unusually subtle lead performance. Of the few American papers to notice the film, the *San Francisco Chronicle*, calling Polanski 'a revelation', remarked that he had 'style and wit . . . he pitches his voice like a nervous, fluttering flute . . . It's his show, clear and simple, [and] a treat to see a new dimension of his talent.'

At about the same time, Emmanuelle Seigner was starring in another erotic thriller, this one called *Body to Body*. She played a retired stripper who has a car accident and emerges from a coma five years later only to find herself in a bad relationship. There appeared to be no such real-life problem, Seigner's marriage having already lasted ten years longer than some cynics had predicted. An admiring witness to the scene recalls that the Polanskis played host one night that spring to Steven Spielberg, his wife and several other guests including Isabelle Adjani at a Paris restaurant. 'At about one in the morning, Roman, waving off all offers to help, paid the bill and blithely announced that we should move on to a nightclub. Spielberg was absolutely knackered by this stage, but Polanski bundled everyone in the car and duly headed for the Bains-Douches. The guy's energy level was off the wall . . . I crawled home at about 3 a.m., leaving Roman still boogieing around the floor with Emmanuelle like John Travolta. Steven appeared comatose.'

In California, meanwhile, several news organisations published a wire report insisting that 'Shamed director Roman Polanski is set to return to stand trial. He will fly home [*sic*] to face charges after striking a deal with state lawmakers to avoid a jail sentence', though negotiations about whether he would face an 'open and possibly televised hearing still continue.' It was hard to say if this was a continuation or a resumption of the rumour that had begun almost immediately on Polanski's flight in 1978, and which reached a crescendo every two or three years. One Los Angeles weekly, and so-called 'bible for Hollywood insiders', enlightened its readers with the information that, failing any such return, 'Polanski's prospects of further work from the major studios look remote'. For a director who had gone freelance, it would be 'a career-limiting move', the paper added.

HENRIK IBSEN'S 1890 PLAY *HEDDA GABLER* proved as polarising of its audiences as Thomas Hardy's *Tess of the d'Urbervilles* did on its appearance just a year later. The character of Hedda, either a proto-typical feminist or a manipulative bitch, according to taste, remains one of the great dramatic roles, graced over the years by the likes of Ingrid Bergman, Isabelle Huppert, Annette Bening, Cate Blanchett, and, in a particularly robust portrayal, Glenda Jackson in the 1975 film *Hedda*. Aside from these glamorous turns, the play has also shown what various directors can do without the box-office allure of celebrity. In 2003 Polanski staged a much admired production starring his wife, at the Théâtre Marigny in Paris, continuing his habit of alternating each film with a less obviously commercial project. After working with a cast of thousands on the streets of Warsaw, the 820-seat venue must have seemed like someone's living room. By then Polanski was again in demand, at least at the major European studios, but he believed that every director needed experience 'working with three or four actors' and not just 'shout[ing] through a megaphone'.

In between his other commitments, Polanski continued to make appearances for *The Pianist*, attending several European screenings whose proceeds went to benefit Holocaust-related charities. By February 2003, the film had accumulated a host of international honours, including the Gold Ribbon from the Italian critics' circle, Césars and Goyas in France and Spain, and the Best Film and Best Director awards at the Baftas in London. After forty years of relative neglect, Polanski was finally recognised in his home country, again winning Supreme Director (*Najlepsza Rezyserla*) and Supreme Film (*Najlepszy Film*) prizes as well as a lifetime achievement Eagle at the 2003 Polish Film Awards.

On 11 February, Polanski received what he called a 'singular compliment': he was tapped by the Academy of Motion Picture Arts and Sciences for the Best Achievement in Directing Oscar. His fellow nominees were Stephen Daldry for *The Hours*, Rob Marshall for *Chicago*, Pedro Almodóvar for *Talk to Her* and Martin Scorsese for *Gangs of New York*. Although not a vintage year, the inclusion of Scorsese's and Marshall's names still made a contest of it, with most of the smart money being on the latter for his $300 million-grossing musical. Scorsese, for his part, was the firm 'sentimental favourite', having failed to win on any of his four previous outings. He also enjoyed a major PR campaign undertaken on his behalf by Miramax. The spoils were worth chasing, if for no other reason than that an Oscar can add $40 million to a film's box-office take.

Polanski's nomination was attended by a fresh barrage of publicity, with opinion sharply divided between those wanting to 'rehabilitate' the director and those wanting to make sure he walked away from the Oscars empty-handed, preferably in chains. (A third group, smaller but quite vociferous, unsuccessfully petitioned a district court to have Polanski's nomination withdrawn, on the alleged grounds that he was a 'convicted felon, child molester and fugitive from justice'.) Several voting members of the Academy received death threats and temporarily left the country or went into hiding; one distinguished former actor, a long-time colleague of Steve McQueen (and thus no stranger to antisocial behaviour) recalls opening his mailbox to find 'an envelope generously full of shit, and the message, "Here's what I think of you and your Polack rapist."' As he adds ruefully, 'I didn't even *vote* for bloody Polanski.'

The more formal objection to the Academy's position, which seemed to some to condone Polanski's crimes, came from columnists like Judith Reisman of WorldNetDaily. 'In 1977, this infamous Hollywood paedophile got caught,' she wrote. 'He was stunned at his arrest, shocked, outraged.

After all he'd done nothing more than drug, rape, sodomise and almost kill a seventh-grade girl he'd tricked into a hot tub . . . In 1948, before Alfred Kinsey strategised with his American Law Institute cohorts to gut our sex-law statutes, half the states in this great nation offered the death penalty for the rape of an adult. By 1977, having been convicted of a ruthless child rape-sodomy-drugged-near-murder, Mr Polanski might have [expected to] spend some ninety-odd days in rehab, then probation.'

Intemperate as this was – the so-called 'Hollywood paedophile', it should be remembered, pleaded guilty to a single count of 'unlawful intercourse', which not even Judge Rittenband had ever construed as a 'ruthless . . . near-murder' – it expressed a view that many people, a significant number of them American journalists, had of Polanski. Particularly in the Deep South, he enjoyed the kind of public opprobrium not seen since the time, thirty-seven years earlier, when John Lennon had remarked that the Beatles were 'more popular than Jesus'. A few rather desultory public burnings took place of books and posters of The Pianist, though these put the perpetrators in the morally equivocal position of vandalising what was in effect a memorial to the Holocaust. The sheriff of one south-eastern Alabama community, apparently also struck by the paradox at the heart of the protest, banned it from his streets.

Polanski himself seemed unconcerned at the debate that raged on about him in Hollywood and elsewhere. He may not even have been aware of it. The director spent most of February skiing in a remote part of the Austrian Alps, returning to Paris only on the 22nd in order to collect his two Césars (among a total of seven for The Pianist), and hear himself described by the presenter Géraldine Pailhas as a 'national hero' and 'a legend . . . film's one acknowledged genius'. Five days later, he enjoyed a closed-circuit conversation with his fellow Oscar-nominated directors – Polanski from Paris, the other four from their Guild office in Los Angeles. The discussion was said to have been 'mutually respectful' and 'warm', with all five men taking it in turns to praise the others' films. Polanski, after another round of American press vitriol, was more rather than less self-assured, announcing modestly that February had been 'a good month for us' and that he wasn't aware of any 'controversy'.

Enlivening the debate in his absence, Samantha Geimer had once again gone public to decry the intrusions on her privacy, and to ask that Polanski's work be judged on merit and not on 'past misdeeds'. In a letter to the Los Angeles Times, she acknowledged 'the unpleasantness' of twenty-six years earlier, noting that 'It was not consensual sex by any means. I said no, repeatedly, but he wouldn't take no for an answer. I was alone and I didn't know what to do. It was scary and, looking back, very creepy.' But Geimer said that she had no hard feelings about the incident, adding that 'Mr Polanski and his film should be honoured according to the quality of the work. What he does for a living and how good he is at it have nothing to do with me or what he did to me.'

Geimer's generosity towards Polanski surprised some observers, not least the director himself, who in a rare reference to the case acknowledged that it was 'very nice of her'. In Hollywood, the Academy, already under fire for one nomination, was also dealing with criticism of the anti-war maverick Michael Moore, up for a Best Documentary Oscar, which in theory – and, as it turned out, in practice – gave him an opportunity to flay President Bush just as the latter sent troops in to Iraq. There were all sorts of guesses as to how the world's so-called 'most prestigious arts body' could have come to simultaneously honour two men like Polanski and Moore. One was that they genuinely admired both *The Pianist* and Moore's film *Bowling for Columbine*. As Samantha Geimer had made clear, it was perfectly possible to separate a film-maker's current professional attainments from other aspects of his life. Another guess, widely circulated, was that the Academy members had wanted to insult the president. Nominating the self-styled 'Bush-baiter' and a fugitive from US justice was a 'defiant open letter' to an 'illegal regime', according to one trade weekly. In yet another version, the Academy had acted as it did precisely because of the anti-Polanski and anti-Moore sentiment seen in much of the mainstream media. Reflecting on this last possibility, the acclaimed director Robert Wise (*West Side Story*) said that, 'However worthy a candidate is, a certain kind of Academy [member] asks himself, "Is this individual truly popular in Kansas?" And if the answer is yes, he votes for someone else.'

It was also rumoured that Polanski was planning to 'jet in' for the occasion, and that, if so, he could expect to be met not by the traditional Academy limousine but by an armed police detail, which would transport him to the nearest jail. 'The warrant against him remains outstanding,' the Los Angeles county sheriff's department confirmed.

However, when the night came, Polanski was not in attendance. Instead he watched the ceremonies on television from a suite at the Plaza Hotel in Paris. Michael Moore won Best Documentary, and duly took the opportunity to share some concerns, soon to be echoed by the likes of Nicole Kidman and Chris Cooper, on the Iraq war. 'I'd like to thank the Academy for this,' Moore said. 'We like non-fiction and we live in fictitious times. We live in the time when we have fictitious election results that elect a fictitious president. We live in a time when we have a man sending us to war for fictitious reasons. Whether it's the fiction [*sic*] of duct tape or the fiction of orange alerts we are against this war, Mr Bush. Shame on you, Mr Bush. Shame on you. Thank you very much.'

Moore's harangue drew mixed cheers and boos, but there was a standing ovation when the presenter, Harrison Ford, then read out Polanski's name as Best Director. Ford himself agreed to 'accept the award on Roman's behalf'. *The Pianist* also won in the categories of Best Screenplay and Best Actor. Adrien Brody loped up to favour Halle Berry with a protracted kiss, before adding his views to a ceremony already awash with the stars' thoughts on war and peace. Although he referred to his 'good buddy' currently serving in Kuwait, and to several other parties, he failed to mention Polanski at any stage of his acceptance speech. One or two critics subsequently wrote that Brody perhaps lacked the 'maturity' befitting an Oscar-winner.

It was 23 March 2003; exactly sixty years earlier, Ryszard Polanski had been led off to the Mauthausen concentration camp, thus exposing his son to the full horrors of the German occupation. On at least one level, the ordeal now finally seemed to have been brought full circle. 'I am deeply moved to be rewarded for *The Pianist*. It relates to the events so close to my own life, the events that led me to comprehend that art can transform pain,' Polanski said in a statement from Paris. At 69 years and 7 months, he became the oldest person ever to win the Best Director Oscar, eclipsing the record previously held by George Cukor (65) for *My Fair Lady*. As one critic observed, 'the *enfant terrible* of film [had] somehow become a senior statesman'. Six months later, Harrison Ford was able to fly to France and present Polanski with his statuette.

IN JULY 2003, at the height of the critical acclaim for *The Pianist*, Polanski announced to friends in Paris that he was once again thinking of retiring. He was too old and too rich to put up with 'the nonsense' that came with working for a major studio, particularly now that they appeared to be run by committees staffed largely by teenaged morons. Reflecting on his forty years of experience in the field, Polanski told *Premiere* of a career spent 'arguing with lawyers, agents, executives, completion guarantors, bank representatives, [getting] midnight phone calls, threats, oh God . . . All things every director knows only too well, and which sap your energy completely.' The only exceptions to this rule had been *Chinatown* and *The Pianist*, for which 'every bit of energy went into their making, and not into fighting'.

The studios, for their part, by and large seem to have resisted the - temptation to belatedly embrace the Oscar-winning director. While eminently respectable, the box-office figures for *The Pianist* had conspicuously failed to excite an auction for Polanski's services. There was also the lingering controversy of his latest award, with headlines such as *Free Republic*'s 'Pervert Recognised' continuing to surface for weeks after the ceremony, unlikely to engender much confidence on the part either of studio chiefs or their shareholders. As one seasoned agent, who prefers anonymity, remarks, 'Never discount the absolute vacancy of the average Hollywood decision-maker. Most of these guys – they're rarely women – are in their mid-twenties to mid-thirties. Their frame of reference begins with *'Crocodile' Dundee* and ends with *Pirates of the Caribbean*. As a group they know more about outer space than they do about a film like *Cul-de-Sac*.'

For all that, Polanski may have had in mind more of a well-deserved sabbatical than full-scale retirement. The same agent says that he knew of 'several proposals from [or] at least involving Roman' that did the rounds in the autumn of 2003. As with any Academy Award-winner, 'you heard his name a lot at meetings. My impression was that he was still very much in the saddle as a working director.' Polanski had known no other life since 1961, for all his occasional forays into the theatre or opera. He later remarked that what he really wanted after *The Pianist* was to make a film that his children could see for a change. 'They come on the set of my movies, they know what I'm doing, they live around all that, but the result of all this work is something so remote from their world they can't identify with it,' Polanski told the *Observer*. 'I wanted something they could, so I started looking for subjects that would be suitable.' Knowing of her husband's affection for David Lean's classic 1948 film version, Emmanuelle Seigner suggested *Oliver Twist*.

It was another striking departure for Polanski, who had once remarked that he liked to 'react against' his most recent film. As even his critics allowed, it would be hard to find a more varied line-up than his 'post-comeback' projects: *Pirates, Frantic, Bitter Moon, Death and the Maiden, The Ninth Gate* and *The Pianist*. Relatively few directors had known so many different ways to make such generally compelling if not unfailingly brilliant movies. To this eclectic body of work was now added Charles

Dickens' 1838 novel, whose plot, perhaps, can be quickly recalled: orphaned by his mother's death in childbirth and his father's conspicuous absence, Oliver is meagrely provided for under the terms of the Poor Law. An interlude in the branch-workhouse ends abruptly when the boy famously asks for a second helping of gruel. After serving an apprenticeship with the local undertaker, Oliver runs away to London, where a struggle for his soul breaks out between the Jewish arch-criminal Fagin on one side and the kindly Mr Brownlow on the other. The latter eventually prevails.

For all its undoubted theatricality, *Oliver Twist* was exactly the sort of period drama where the average studio fears to tread, unless Johnny Depp happened to be playing Fagin and a part could be found somewhere for Julia Roberts. Nor was it, strictly speaking, family entertainment: beatings, shootings, hangings, fornicating couples, whores merry and dejected, chamber pots, vomit, drunkards and pickpockets, quite apart from the implied racism and paedophilia, crowd the pages. But Polanski rose to the challenge. 'From time to time I think about the audience, but I'm not very concerned with it,' he had remarked. 'You can't cater to an imaginary group of people. You have to satisfy your own taste.' Armed with his characteristic self-belief, and with muscular assistance from his agent Jeff Berg, Polanski was able to secure a budget of reportedly $50–55 million, significantly higher than for *The Pianist*, from a consortium of banks, investors and foreign distributors. Sony's TriStar Pictures would release *Oliver Twist* in North America, but had 'virtually no creative input'.

For forty-five years, Polanski had gone out of his way to rubbish the theory that his films in some way reflected his own life. 'I'm not in that business,' he assured *Premiere*. 'I make fiction feature movies. I was never interested in making an autobiographical picture. What would be the point?' Even so, Polanski was again able to call on his sense memory for certain key individual sequences. In his memoirs, he describes having been a 'specialist scavenger' in post-war Krakow. 'I joined a gang of local children who collected and bartered anything,' he writes of an adolescence not that far removed from Oliver's experience as one of Fagin's street urchins. Polanski himself later told journalists that he could 'personally relate' to Dickens' hero. 'You know Oliver's long walk to London? I went through it at exactly the same age that the boy did,' he said, adding that he'd never forgotten his 'blood-soaked' feet, nor the feeling of being hungry, 'eat[ing] boiled flowers, sometimes with a drop of milk' as a

10-year-old war fugitive. (On a pedantic note, Polanski's part rail, part foot journey from Krakow to Wysoka, though undoubtedly arduous and made under the additional burden of the German occupation, was, at twenty-five miles, just over a third of the length of Oliver's march to London.) The director would go on to refer to his 'lifelong' love of nineteenth-century English literature. Like *Tess of the d'Urbervilles*, *Oliver Twist* was 'full of banal events that change [the characters'] destiny', another plot device with personal resonance.

After studying the usual scores of audition tapes, Polanski cast 11-year-old Barney Clark, of television's *The Brief*, in the title role. Jeremy Swift (*Gosford Park*) signed to play Mr Bumble, the part memorably taken by Harry Secombe in the 'freely adapted' 1968 musical *Oliver!*, and Edward Hardwicke, of Granada TV's *Sherlock Holmes*, was Mr Brownlow. Hugh Futcher, who had appeared in *Repulsion*, heard that Polanski was casting and 'wrote to him to ask if I was Dickensian enough to play Fagin'. The job went, instead, to Ben Kingsley. There would be cameos for both Morgane and Elvis Polanski, the latter making his screen debut. Ronald Harwood returned to write the script. 'What Roman told me,' Harwood says, 'was that he wanted to do a film for children – *his* children.'

All this preliminary creative activity took place against a series of board-room meetings in Paris that eventually landed Polanski the biggest budget of his career. Most of the money went not on the cast (Barney Clark received a reported £40,000 for his services) but on recreating Victorian London in modern Prague, selected in part for its 'Dickensian'-looking vistas and in part for its cheap labour. As usual on a Polanski production, there was meticulous attention to detail: the set, which took three months to construct in the spring and summer of 2004, included five full-scale streets complete with period houses, some twenty amply stocked shops and a maze of back-roads and alleys built from authentic 1830's cobblestones, with, looming over it all, St Paul's Cathedral pixilated on the far horizon. 'Take a look at this rot,' Polanski said with unaffected pride, guiding a visitor into the recesses of Fagin's lair. 'You can *smell* the decay.' The film's 200-odd costumes were a virtual parade of the Victorian class system, ranging from Oliver's pitiful rags to the stylish frock coats of his saviour, Mr Brownlow.

On his first morning in Prague, having stopped off to present a festival award to the Italian brothers Andrea and Antonio Frazzi for their film *Certi Bambini*, which delves into the world of child abuse, Polanski assembled his cast and told them, 'This movie isn't *Oliver Twist*. It's *the Oliver*

Twist.' As one of the actors recalls, 'At 71, Roman still had a childlike passion for the work. He was in a class of his own when it came to rallying the troops, and he was also brilliant when he was explaining the story to the Czech extras . . . I watched him in action, and it was a revelation. Polanski would react to the most elementary question as if he was hearing it for the first time. He would ponder a bit, congratulate the questioner on his originality, then give the answer I'd heard him give someone else five minutes earlier, complete with a leer and a funny voice to mimic Fagin, as the extras listened in utter awe. The result was that everyone in that cast and crew, from Kingsley down to the most casual day labourer, was totally under Roman's spell.'

Despite his youthful enthusiasm, Polanski was finally beginning to look older, if still not quite his actual age. He was a little heavier, his face fuller, his hair greyer. On warm days he was to be seen padding about in a pair of baggy shorts, white tube socks and trainers, a combination that one actor thought made him look both 'animated' and a 'bit sad – like your grandad trying to be cool'. As the shoot wore on, Polanski took to buzzing around the set on a motorised scooter, another indelible image that 'somehow reminded you of one of those old boys off to do the shopping at Sainsbury's'. At the same time, he remained a refreshingly actor-friendly director, as Paul Brooke, playing Mr Grimwig, recalls. 'Polanski was very sure of what he wanted and clear about how it might be achieved, which most [actors] prefer to seeing how things fall out. He wasn't at all unapproachable, but he was the boss. Roman was also "aware" of the cast, noticing, for example, when the actors had spent a long period rehearsing and filming in heavy Victorian costume and in bright sunlight, berating assistant[s] who might perhaps have realised this, and produc[ing] something to provide shade. Much appreciated.'

Brooke also notes admiringly that while Polanski's 'reading' of a film remained peerless, his grasp of 'the mechanics' was just as impressive. 'I particularly remember that on the last day [in] Prague, things had gone slowly, and it looked as though we might run out of time. Vibrant and energetic as he was, Roman appeared to go up a notch like a Wimbledon finalist and he powered through the remaining work, ideas sparking off him and with incredible attention to detail. Fairly soon, it was clear that not only would we finish, but we would finish well, with everything in place, nothing skimped.' Michael Heath, playing the undertaker Mr Sowerberry, similarly recalls 'a big set-piece scene with dozens of actors, hundreds of extras and ducks and geese and cats and dogs all being cued in by their respective handlers and up on the hill, surveying all this from a large wooden chair, was Polanski. He looked like Napoleon at Austerlitz.'

'I never have problems with actors, just with stars,' Polanski cheerfully admitted to Heath and one or two others, still, after thirty-one years, occasionally referring to Faye Dunaway by the playfully familiar '*meshuga*'. By common agreement, the only prima donna on the set of *Oliver Twist* was Bullseye the dog, the latest in a series of animals to have tried the director's patience. (As well as 'all those fucking horses' in *Macbeth*, Polanski had had a troubled working relationship with the goat in 1961's *The Fat and the Lean*, which, he wrote, 'though cheap, turned out to have very little camera sense'.) Ben Kingsley believes that 'Roman used his "traumatised soul" to help other people', a particular asset when it came to corralling the film's 200 or so small children. Though reportedly a stickler for 'control, cleanliness, continence and obedience [in] kids', Polanski went to some lengths to relate to his young cast, hosting tea parties, dispensing ice creams and, according to one suitably awed 10-year-old, 'explaining the story by act[ing] out the scenes for you so that you could *see* it and not just read it'. Another young actor remarks that Polanski appeared to 'see through walls'. However well it was disguised, 'he would always know if someone had a problem [and] would say just the right thing'.*

In all, then, a smooth and happy shoot, which concluded on schedule and under budget. The stress on historical accuracy and the overall theme of the story suited Polanski well. His control of his cast and eye for detail were again to the fore, notwithstanding the occasional minor lapse: although the sign 'John Lobb' is prominently displayed in a scene supposedly set in late-1830s London, no one had apparently told Polanski that the well-known cobbler didn't set up shop there until 1850. Michael Heath remembers a more typical shot where, 'after peer[ing] interminably through the camera lens, Roman stood up, then walked to and fro looking at the scenery from every angle, bending down again, squinting, and

---

* Amidst this well-deserved praise, a discordant note is struck by one middle-aged cast member, who, while 'thrilled to have had the professional experience of working with Polanski', nonetheless wondered 'what Roman would have done had some old lag like me invited [his daughter] Morgane, who was 11 but looked 13, out for a drink and a dip in the hot tub.'

slowly shaking his head. "No," Polanski said at length, summoning the carpenters. "The back wall is wrong. It's two inches too low."'

Oliver Twist had its first public screening on 18 August 2005, Polanski's seventy-second birthday, and went on general release that autumn. There were critics who remarked justly on the film's 'fastidious and rather beautiful recreations of Victorian London', and 'respectful treatment of Dickens' combustible black comedy'. Most, however, found the final result faintly anaemic. As Peter Bradshaw wrote in the *Guardian*, it was 'simply a decent, watchable movie, not obviously more powerful or personal than a teatime-telly version'. Despite some bravura touches, 'there's always a nagging disquiet that what Polanski thinks he is giving us is basically a much-loved children's classic . . . His *Oliver Twist* does not flag or lose its way, [but] the book's original power and force have not been rediscovered.' It is a natural human instinct to put a director's films into some sort of order and then offer them to the public as a league table. Many erudite critics have done this with Polanski, some publishing whole books on the subject: in almost every case, *Rosemary's Baby*, *Chinatown* and *The Pianist* take turns at the top of the list and the likes of *What?* and *Pirates* at the bottom, with *Oliver Twist* in between. It remains a worthy addition to the canon.

IN MID-JUNE 2002, just as the French critics were getting behind *The Pianist*, Polanski found himself forced to take action against one of America's oldest and most resourceful publishing companies, Condé Nast, and their flagship magazine *Vanity Fair*. The offending item amounted to a six-sentence anecdote buried within a seventeen-page story on Elaine's, the famed New York restaurant known for its 'literary' clientele, as well as for other celebrities like Mick Jagger and Cher. In a wholly spurious allegation, *Vanity Fair* quoted an Elaine's regular named Lewis Lapham as claiming that Polanski had walked in to the restaurant just after Sharon Tate had been murdered, whereupon he sat down and promptly made a pass at a 'Swedish beauty', sliding his hand up the woman's leg as he began a 'long, honeyed spiel' about making her a star. 'It was an obvious and blatant lie,' Polanski would complain, noting that it was the 'worst thing ever written about me,' all the more so 'because it dishonours my memory of Sharon.'

Polanski chose to sue the magazine for its relatively small-circulation edition published in England, where the libel laws are generally more congenial to the plaintiff. The less squeamish American courts require that an aggrieved public figure prove not only that what the press wrote about him or her was wrong, but that they wrote it with reckless disregard for the truth. This theory – that certain people have chosen to lead highly visible lives and therefore voluntarily sacrifice much of their protection from criticism – comes from the 1964 decision in *New York Times* v. *Sullivan*. Celebrities, the judge in the Sullivan case reasoned, have ample opportunity to rebut any false allegations. It is a different story in the UK, where the law requires that the offending journalist or author prove that what was printed was correct.

Polanski thus lodged his claim with the High Court in London, which was apparently happy for him to give his evidence by video hook-up. This unusual arrangement was made necessary because of the likelihood that he would have been arrested, and subsequently extradited, had he shown up for the trial in person. But after an objection by Condé Nast, the Court of Appeal unanimously ruled that Polanski had to 'physically and materially attend' the proceedings, noting drily that justice was 'just a Eurostar journey away' for him. It appeared to even seasoned show-business reporters, who might have known better, that that concluded the affair. Such observers underestimated Polanski's obstinacy and resilience. In February 2005, the House of Lords, by a majority of three to two, overruled the Court of Appeal, remarking that the plaintiff was 'not a present-day outlaw' and 'not subject to any principle of fugitive disentitlement'. This landmark decision meant that Polanski wasn't bound by what the lower court had called the 'normal processes of the law' and was again free to participate by videolink.

This was particularly high-stakes litigation. If Polanski could exact an apology and substantial damages from Condé Nast, it would prove not only his specific point about the 'horrific saga' of August 1969, but also that he still had a reputation to tarnish. On the other hand, if *Vanity Fair* prevailed he would have achieved nothing except to publicise both the alleged Elaine's incident, and certain other colourful events from his past, to a global audience several times larger than the 70,000 or so British readers of the original story. Rather than face the potential embarrassment and expense of a public trial, both sides appear to have actively considered a behind-the-scenes settlement. In January 2004, *Vanity Fair*'s editor Graydon Carter met Polanski at a dinner party in Paris. 'I talked with him at length about the suit,' Carter says. 'We were still in the process of gathering our information, and I thought there might be a way of resolving it outside of court. There are some cases that are important to fight, but I didn't really think this was one of them. Except for the fact that, once our evidence had been collected, I believed that the gist of our story was true, and I wasn't going to say otherwise.' According to Carter, Condé Nast had been more than fair to Polanski, who had been given a chance to respond before the offending article was printed. The High Court would be told that the relevant section had been 'faxed twice to the plaintiff's agent, after a phone call was made to confirm the number'. (Polanski said he did not receive the piece.) Carter was, however, forced to concede that he and his magazine were mistaken in some of the specifics of the story. The incident could not have happened when Polanski was on his way back to Los Angeles for his wife's funeral, but had occurred 'substantially as written' some two weeks later. The alleged 'Swedish beauty' was actually a Norwegian model named Beatte Telle, whom *Vanity Fair*'s twenty-strong 'research department' had somehow failed to contact before the magazine went to press. Under the circumstances, Condé Nast, while 'not mind[ed] to give Mr Polanski an apology', did agree to publish a letter by him. He declined the offer.

The result was a high-profile trial whose series of precedent-setting decisions made headlines well before the parties assembled in court. Even Polanski might not have been disappointed by some of the moral paradoxes and (another of his favourite plot devices) the mix of nationalities involved. Here was a Franco-Polish citizen suing an American-based magazine in a British courtroom. The director himself hadn't set foot in the UK for twenty-seven years, and would not do so now. The much-debated videolink was criticised by the defence not only on the obvious grounds that it provided a criminal fugitive with a means of defending his good name, but also for the technical reason that it made cross-examination more difficult, and meant that the jury could see Polanski's face only when he was testifying. In Hollywood parlance, there would be no 'reaction shots'. Polanski's legal team had announced themselves 'very satisfied' with the arrangement, noting that it would be widely interpreted as the next step toward the 'virtual trial'. Not surprisingly, *Vanity Fair*'s solicitor, David Hooper, had a very different reaction. It was 'morally outrageous', he said, that evidence should be heard in this way. Hooper was also concerned that foreign litigants would be encouraged to 'forum shop' and bring their own libel actions into English jurisdiction as a result. Sharp-eyed observers didn't miss the point that Polanski appeared to be in the enviable position of being able to 'cherry-pick' those parts of the judicial system that suited him, while ignoring those that didn't.

On 18 July 2005, in the already highly charged atmosphere that followed the London Transport bombings and preceded the shooting of Jean Charles de Menezes by Metropolitan Police officers, the parties in *Polanski* v. *Condé Nast Publications* assembled in room 13 of the Royal Courts of Justice. The jury selection produced what Graydon Carter calls 'one of many disappointments' for the defence. Instead of the American 'interview' process, which can take days or weeks, and is often one of the most hotly contested features of the trial, 'the names of the potential jurors [were] put on pieces of paper, which were then crudely shuffled by the clerk'. Hoping for a female majority, Carter instead got a jury of three women and nine men.

Polanski, or his televised image, made what even his opponents called a 'superb' witness. Neatly dressed in a black suit and tie, he stood for the first hour of his testimony before 'craving the court's permission' to sit down. He denied having attempted to ever seduce a Swedish, Norwegian or any other sort of Scandinavian model, and denounced the story as an 'abominable lie' which showed 'callous indifference' to his wife's murder. 'That's not the way I behave,' Polanski remarked. 'Still I had some honour. Still I have it now.' The whole episode had left him in a 'state of shock', he told jurors.

On the second morning, Mia Farrow appeared in court on Polanski's behalf. The 60-year-old actress testified that she and a 'distraught Roman' had gone to Elaine's two weeks after Tate's death. 'He started telling me about events in California, what he had gone through, and he got very, very upset,' she told the hushed courtroom. 'We had ordered our dinner, but we just left the restaurant. He was that upset, and I, too.' Farrow did concede the possibility that Polanski may have had sexual encounters with other women within a month of his wife's burial. 'I feel there's a big distinction – for men maybe – between relationships and having sex,' she said, adding that any such liaisons 'would in no way detract from his feelings for Sharon'. Tate's younger sister Debra then went into the witness box to confirm that Polanski had been 'an absolute wreck' following his wife's death.

Following Farrow's concession, Condé Nast's barrister Tom Shields was able to demonstrate that Polanski had indeed had numerous incidents of casual or 'therapeutic' sex, sometimes with more than one woman, and that he had 'often' been unfaithful to Tate. These would have been hard facts to refute, since for the most part they appear in the director's own memoirs.

Flourishing a copy of the book from out of a waist-high pile of documents, Shields went on to quote the opening sentence, 'For as far back as I can remember, the line between fantasy and reality has been hopelessly blurred.' Arguing that his memory of 1969 was hazy, the barrister suggested that Polanski had an 'inability to tell the truth when it matters'.

In subsequent testimony, Lewis Lapham, now the editor of *Harper's* magazine, repeated his essential claim that Polanski had sat down at his table at Elaine's one night in August 1969 and begun to talk to 'a fashion model from one of the Nordic countries' in a 'forward' way. 'At one point he had his hand on her leg and said to her, "I can make you the next Sharon Tate,"' Lapham testified. Polanski's QC, John Kelsey-Fry, said that the article implied that, after the death of his wife and unborn child, his client had gone 'on the pull' and exploited her name as a 'tool of seduction'. Tom Shields remarked that it was for the jury to decide what motive Mr Lapham – who was not a Condé Nast employee and came from the US to give evidence on oath – might have had to make up his story.

On the third day, Shields offered the jury a general overview of Polanski, a 'fugitive from morality' who enjoyed 'a well-deserved reputation as a cynical sexual predator', he said. As such, his standing was 'beyond repair' and incapable of being damaged, Shields added. By coincidence, Polanski was represented in court by three women: Mia Farrow, Debra Tate and Emmanuelle Seigner, the last of whom excited some interest by going about the normally staid courtroom braless. In the summing-up on the fourth day, Shields remarked that the key to the libel action was 'Roman's law of morality'. The fact that Polanski had had casual sex within a month of his wife's death revealed a 'certain callous indifference' to her memory. Calling Farrow's recollection of events inconsistent, he suggested that 'if indeed she was at the restaurant, the evening ended early and Mr Polanski must have stayed on'. Shields added that 'An honourable man would come to this court, an honourable man would return to California, an honourable man would not behave the way he behaved – even in the Swinging Sixties.' He urged the jury that, even if Polanski prevailed, he should be given 'a symbolic award', such as 'the price of a cinema ticket or the price of the Eurostar train ticket that could have brought him to you'.

Nonetheless, Polanski was only in court, so far as he was at all, to refute the specific allegation that he had been in Elaine's on his way to his wife's funeral, and that while there he had made a pass at a woman, invoking Tate's name as he did so. He had already established that *Vanity Fair* had gotten the timing of the story wrong, and had since stated on oath that the incident hadn't occurred at all. As even one or two members of the defence team privately conceded, it would be hard to persuade a jury that anyone's memory of what exactly had happened on a given night thirty-six years earlier was entirely reliable. And the opposition can only ever be encouraged by one of the defendants audibly muttering 'Now we're fucked' as Mia Farrow had taken the stand. Furthermore, under English law, the jury had been allowed to hear only the 'formal outline' of the state of California's criminal case against Polanski, and not the salacious details. The UK press were similarly constrained from publishing anything that might have been considered prejudicial to the plaintiff's chances.

On Friday afternoon, 22 July, the jury found for Polanski and recommended he be paid damages of £50,000, a quarter of the maximum the judge had said was appropriate for 'very serious' cases. Condé Nast was further ordered to pay £175,000 costs within fourteen days, and faced an estimated £1 million legal bill. In a statement, Polanski noted that he was 'obviously pleased' with the verdict. 'Three years of my life have been interrupted,' he said. 'Three years within which I have had no choice but to relive the horrible events of August 1969, the murders of my wife, my unborn child and my friends. Many untruths have been published about me, most of which I have ignored, but the allegations printed in *Vanity Fair* could not go unchallenged.' Polanski later told the Associated Press that he had brought the case 'because I don't want this to be part of the material that comes up and is reproduced again each time they write about me'. His 'enormous risk' had been 'totally vindicated'.

The common wisdom, as dispensed by the British press following the verdict, was that Polanski had pursued his case with rare fortitude and skill. The question that remained was how his reputation had been 'materially damaged' in England and Wales, the territories covered by the complaint, when he had set foot in neither country in almost thirty years.

WITH THE PUBLICITY MACHINE FOR *OLIVER TWIST* AT FEVER PITCH, the fact that the headlines were all about Polanski's court case and not the film itself didn't bode well, perhaps, for the box office. The $50 million-plus production took just $68,447 in its opening weekend in North America, part of an eventual US gross of $1,987,000. Effectively, it went straight to Netflix. The figures were better in Europe, where it did the equivalent of $17 million-worth of business in the three months prior to Christmas 2005. 'I said to Roman that we made a cultural miscalculation,' Ronald

Harwood reflected. 'We made a good movie, but we had thought people would still be interested in the nineteenth-century literary tradition. Generations have come up who simply don't read very much.' One or two critics thought that Polanski was possibly a victim of his own success, films like *The Pianist* and even *The Ninth Gate* having led audiences to expect something more from him than a 'teatime-telly' Victorian drama. By April 2006, at least one of the executives at Sony TriStar was ready to discuss his company's investment in *Oliver Twist*. From a 'sordidly commercial' point of view, it was 'a total strikeout', he concedes.

HIS KNOCKOUT LEGAL RESULT, even so, marked a new peak in the Polanski cult: congratulations poured in, and various French newspapers and magazines hailed this 'stunning blow' to the 'brazen' and 'lewd' 'American media barons'. Once victory was his, as a Paris friend recalls, 'Roman changed, even externally. He became more self-assured, more dynamic. His whole manner of speaking altered.' In the right mood, he was a '*very* merry prankster'; when introspection called, '*un homme serieux*'. Speaking of the libel case to the *Observer*, a 'relaxed' Polanski remarked, 'I believe that the way of truth wins. I'm an optimist. I wouldn't be here if I wasn't.' Despite reportedly being 'angry and bitter' over the way the British press covered the case, he now felt 'very well about [the trial], particularly since it was a unanimous verdict. I'm sure the jurors must have felt good, too, when they read an article in the *Mail on Sunday* in which the woman confirmed that it never happened.'

In his eighth decade, Polanski was clearly entering that special place in a director's career characterised by expertly curated retrospectives of his work and the regular acceptance of lifetime-achievement awards. A biographer writing about a well-known figure these days seeks a single event to 'explain' him, but the key in this case would seem to be an inherently fertile, wonderfully childlike imagination tempered by an acquired love of order and the 'clean, professional finish' that often surprised those who knew him only as the disco-loving raver. 'Everyone has their own set of rules,' Polanski once remarked to *Premiere*. 'Some people may not understand why I'm straightening out a tablecloth, or moving a bottle half an inch to the right, not to mention what I want from the actor sitting at the table . . . I never wish I'd been less of a perfectionist, but many times I wish I'd been more of one.' Reflecting on this 'rich mix' of skills, *Time* would nominate 'the man [who] made *Knife in the Water*, *Chinatown* and *The Pianist* [as] our greatest living director', a verdict Polanski himself, it was thought, accepted. The 2003 Oscar had been no more than belated recognition of a career that had arguably peaked thirty years earlier.

According to a well-placed source, Polanski's professional and personal triumphs 'definitely' increased his 'confidence in his own abilities', giving him a 'flushed-with-success syndrome that was quite noticeable in social situations'. All the same, he remained a 'very complex' individual. Jeff Gross, the co-scenarist on *Frantic* and *Bitter Moon*, believes that 'the emotional gates are pretty well shut with Roman. I see him three or four times a year and he's always superficially charming, but it's somehow as though he's "on" the whole time.' (He was an accomplished actor, after all.) A third acquaintance notes that Polanski has 'had an incredible amount of tragedy. As well as the well-known cases, there was a friend in Ibiza who died in a drug-related way, and one or two other private matters. He lost his creative partner, Gérard Brach [to cancer, in September 2006]. After all he's been through, you can hardly blame the man if he's built a wall around himself.' According to this reading, what Polanski was offering the steady succession of writers, actors, musicians, artists and other guests who met him at avenue Montaigne wasn't so much friendship as friendliness.

In 2007, despite yet another flurry of 'American amnesty' stories, Polanski was still living in Paris, a relatively short drive downhill, if distinctly upmarket, from his birthplace. The household was 'dominated' by Morgane, Elvis and their friends, and like a 'more benign version of *Oliver Twist*', one actor from the film recalls. Several other visitors have remarked on Polanski's obvious preoccupation with his two children, and his affinity for children in general. 'The surprising thing which a lot of people wouldn't accept is his quite extraordinary ability to get on with kids,' his long-time producer Timothy Burrill has said. 'Not just his own, though he is a unique father.' Polanski would tell the *Observer* that he had sued *Vanity Fair* in part to spare his family the ordeal of reading the story which would otherwise have 'gone on the record and [been] repeated by people like you'. Elsewhere in the same interview, he revealed that the school run was the 'top moment' of his day. 'It's the best,' Polanski said. 'It's great to see them walking away into this school. It's a moving moment.' Other sources insist that Polanski is 'almost ludicrously mild-mannered', 'nearly teetotal' and even an 'occasional churchgoer'. Lest anyone claim him for the moral majority, though, the *Los Angeles Times* would find 'numerous reminders' of his previous life on a visit to Paris. 'The most prominent visual hallmark of Polanski's office is a huge painting above his desk of an erotically posed nude woman, [while] Ronald Harwood says that Roman's interest in a new project is signalled by whether it gives him "an erection".'

THE LATEST SPECULATION has Governor Arnold Schwarzenegger allegedly preparing to pardon Polanski, primarily in order for him to 'return to work in America', a prospect for which the director himself seems to betray only minimal enthusiasm. 'Today's Hollywood,' he has written, is like 'a spoiled brat that screams for possession of a toy and then tosses it out of the baby buggy.' All too many recent films, he adds, 'are appalling. They are just mindless special effects, sound effects, which rattle your brain, with very little emotion in general.' Asked recently what he missed most about any aspect of life in the United States, he nominated 'a pastrami sandwich at Nate 'n Al's delicatessen'.

A year after releasing *Oliver Twist*, Polanski was back directing John Patrick Shanley's Pulitzer Prize-winning drama *Doubt* on the stage of the Hébertot theatre in Paris. 'What do you do when you're not sure?' a Jesuit priest asks the audience in the opening line of the play, which goes on from there to explore the issues of religious intolerance, paedophilia and racism. It was another critical coup. In December 2006, Polanski returned to Warsaw to be honoured with the Lifetime Achievement prize at the European Film Awards. 'Only good things happen to me in this town,' he remarked, perhaps tactfully choosing to overlook his mauling at the hands of the Warsaw film club exactly thirty years earlier. The professional versatility, or 'career hopscotching', as one critic calls it, was taken to new heights when Polanski appeared in the summer 2007 blockbuster *Rush Hour 3*, playing a post-retirement age Sûreté inspector who teams up with two wisecracking visitors from the Los Angeles police department. According to *Today*, 'this was a brave bit of casting on the part of the producers'. If so, there was something almost heroic in the subsequent announcement that Polanski was to be entrusted with a reported $150 million budget to direct the film of Robert Harris' novel *Pompeii*, due for release in 2008.*

---

* In keeping with his long and frequently troubled history with the film unions, Polanski apparently pulled out of this project after telling *Pompeii*'s backers, Summit International, that his schedule 'would not permit [him] to wait until after industry labour negotiations had been completed' prior to shooting. In early 2008 Polanski turned his attention to Robert Harris' novel *The Ghost*.

★

'YOU SHOULD NEVER UNDERESTIMATE ROMAN,' his fellow Oscar-winner Robert Wise told me. 'He's not only made great pictures, but he never makes the same one twice. Dramas, comedies, sex, the Shakespeare; and who can forget him having a stab at Jack Nicholson? He's done everything except a western. That blend of a slightly kinky imagination and formal, beautifully composed camerawork is beyond seminal.

'Polanski may surprise us yet. A lot of film-makers go to a ripe old age,' added Wise, who died in 2005, aged 91. 'You know, maybe directing keeps you virile.'

FILMOGRAPHY

Roman Polanski's full-length features. The date is for each film's first commercial release in either Britain or North America, whichever was earlier.

1. *Knife in the Water* (1962). Screenplay by RP, Jerzy Skolimowski and Jakub Goldberg. Starring Leon Niemczyk, Jolanta Umecka and Zygmunt Malanowicz. The classic Polanskian brew of claustrophobia, latent menace, voyeurism, class antagonisms and sexual tension, set aboard a small yacht.

2. *Repulsion* (1965). Screenplay by RP, Gérard Brach and David Stone. Starring Catherine Deneuve, John Fraser, Ian Hendry, Yvonne Furneaux and Hugh Futcher. A gripping, if visibly low budget, depiction of a young Belgian woman living in a seedy London mansion block who loses her mind and goes on a homicidal rampage.

3. *Cul-de-Sac* (1966). Screenplay by RP and Gérard Brach. Starring Donald Pleasence, Françoise Dorléac, Lionel Stander, Jack MacGowran and Jacqueline Bisset. Yet more claustrophobia, with added violence, in this sharply observed erotic triangle involving a weak-willed husband, his exotic young wife and a fleeing American gangster thrown together on a remote island.

4. *The Fearless Vampire Killers or Pardon Me, But Your Teeth Are in My Neck* (1967). Screenplay by RP and Gérard Brach. Starring Jack MacGowran, RP, Alfie Bass, Ferdy Mayne and Sharon Tate. While it never quite decides if it's a drama, a satire or a *Carry On* film, offers some winning performances, not least by Polanski himself as a feckless vampire hunter who falls for Sharon Tate.

5. *Rosemary's Baby* (1968). Screenplay by RP, from the novel by Ira Levin. Starring Mia Farrow, John Cassavetes, Ruth Gordon, Sidney Blackmer, Ralph Bellamy and Charles Grodin. Even Polanski thought the story of a fey young woman whose husband, doctor and immediate neighbours are all satanists, and who finds herself impregnated by the devil, a touch implausible; but the direction is crisp, unpretentious and rarely stoops to cliché.

6. *Macbeth* (1971). Screenplay by RP and Kenneth Tynan, from the play by William Shakespeare. Starring Jon Finch, Francesca Annis, Terence Bayler, Martin Shaw, Nicholas Selby, Paul Shelley and Richard Pearson. Most critics saw this violent, well-acted adaptation as a cathartic exercise by Polanski, whose pregnant wife had been murdered some eighteen months earlier; he denies it.

7. *What?* (1972). Screenplay by RP and Gérard Brach. Starring Sydne Rome, Marcello Mastroianni, Hugh Griffith, Romolo Valli and Guido Alberti. Like *Cul-de-Sac*, takes the potentially interesting idea of sending an outsider into a self-contained, perverse world, but loses its way and ends up as a sadly flaccid sex comedy.

8. *Chinatown* (1974). Screenplay by Robert Towne. Starring Jack Nicholson, Faye Dunaway, John Huston, Perry Lopez, John Hillerman, Roy Jenson, Burt Young, Diane Ladd and RP. Hard-boiled but gently paced saga of big-city corruption, peopled by Raymond Chandler-style wiseguys and featuring a memorable cameo by Polanski as a knife-wielding thug.

9. *The Tenant* (1976). Screenplay by RP and Gérard Brach, from the novel by Roland Topor. Starring RP, Isabelle Adjani, Melvyn Douglas, Jo Van Fleet and Shelley Winters. A male version of *Repulsion*, with Polanski himself playing the schizophrenic tenant, set in Paris; literate, with some good satirical jokes, even if the crack-up itself is unconvincing.

10. *Tess* (1979). Screenplay by RP, Gérard Brach and John Brownjohn, from the novel by Thomas Hardy. Starring Nastassia Kinski, Leigh Lawson, Peter Firth, John Collin, Tony Church and Richard Pearson. Visually sumptuous period drama which, like *Macbeth*, invited numerous Freudian, if not overtly auto-biographical interpretations;

Polanski had just fled American justice, having pleaded guilty to a charge of 'unlawful sex' with a 13-year-old girl.

11. *Pirates* (1986). Screenplay by RP, Gérard Brach and John Brownjohn. Starring Walter Matthau, Damien Thomas, Cris Campion, Charlotte Lewis, Richard Pearson, Roy Kinnear and David Kelly. A commercial and critical disaster, which went on to grace some of the 'Worst Films in History' lists; in spite of that, delivers on sheer spectacle and proved to be seventeen years ahead of its time in reviving the whole pirate genre.

12. *Frantic* (1988). Screenplay by RP and Gérard Brach. Starring Harrison Ford, Betty Buckley, Emmanuelle Seigner, Jacques Ciron and John Mahoney. Solid and occasionally exciting Cold War thriller which somehow gives the impression it has all been done before – which it has, in Hitchcock's *The Man Who Knew Too Much* among others.

13. *Bitter Moon* (1992). Screenplay by RP, Gérard Brach and John Brownjohn, with collaboration by Jeff Gross, from the novel by Pascal Bruckner. Starring Hugh Grant, Peter Coyote, Emmanuelle Seigner, Kristin Scott Thomas and Victor Bannerjee. *Knife in the Water* set on a larger boat and a higher budget; wildly funny in parts and notable for some uninhibited sex scenes starring Polanski's wife Emmanuelle Seigner.

14. *Death and the Maiden* (1994). Screenplay by Ariel Dorfman and Rafael Yglesias, from the play by Ariel Dorfman. Starring Ben Kingsley, Sigourney Weaver and Stuart Wilson. Critically acclaimed drama about a torture victim confronting her former captor; never quite shakes free of its theatrical origins – some moments feel undeniably stagey – but a typically efficient performance by Kingsley as the reformed sadist.

15. *The Ninth Gate* (1999). Screenplay by RP, John Brownjohn and Enrique Urbizu, from the novel by Arturo Pérez-Reverte. Starring Johnny Depp, Frank Langella, Lena Olin, James Russo, Barbara Jefford and Emmanuelle Seigner. Polanski's second satanic-worship venture; not as successful as *Rosemary's Baby*, and bedevilled by behind-the-scenes bickering, but with some characteristically deft touches and another robust performance by Ms Seigner.

16. *The Pianist* (2002). Screenplay by Ronald Harwood, from the book by Wladyslaw Szpilman. Starring Adrien Brody, Thomas Kretschmann, Frank Finlay, Maureen Lipman, Ed Stoppard, Paul Bradley and Julia Rayner. Polanski won his first and as yet only Oscar for this affecting Holocaust drama that, as one of the cast says, 'doesn't hit you over the head with its morality', and launched the director on his Late Period.

17. *Oliver Twist* (2005). Screenplay by Ronald Harwood, from the novel by Charles Dickens. Starring Ben Kingsley, Barney Clark, Jeremy Swift, Michael Heath, Edward Hardwicke, Jamie Foreman and Paul Brooke. Distinguished by its meticulous recreation of Victorian London on the streets of Prague, and a possibly over-respectful treatment of the source novel; it's said to have been aimed primarily at Polanski's two young children.

BIBLIOGRAPHY

Bird, Daniel, *Roman Polanski*, London: Pocket Essentials, 2002

Bugliosi, Vincent with Gentry, Curt, *Helter Skelter*, New York: Norton, 1974

Butler, Ivan, *The Cinema of Roman Polanski*, New York: A. S. Barnes & Co., 1970

Cronin, Paul (ed.), *Roman Polanski Interviews*, Mississippi: University Press of Mississippi, 2005

Feeney, F. X. and Duncan, Paul (ed.), *Roman Polanski*, Los Angeles: Taschen, 2006

Kiernan, Thomas, *The Roman Polanski Story*, New York: Grove Press, 1980

Leaming, Barbara, *Polanski: The Film-maker as Voyeur*, New York: Simon and Schuster, 1981

Lownes, Victor, *The Day the Bunny Died*, New Jersey: Lyle Stuart, 1983

Parker, John, *Polanski*, London: Victor Gollancz, 1993

Polanski, Roman, *Roman by Polanski*, New York: William Morrow, 1984

SOURCES AND
CHAPTER NOTES

Author's Note: Endnotes are a necessary evil in a book like this. The following pages show at least the formal interviews, conversations and/or other source material mined in the three years beginning in March 2004. As well as those listed, I also spoke to a number of people who prefer not to be named. Where sources asked for anonymity – often citing a healthy respect for Roman Polanski and his lawyers in the wake of the High Court's July 2005 libel decision in his favour – every effort was made to get them to go on the record. Where this wasn't possible, I've used the words 'a friend' or 'a colleague', etc., as appropriate. Once or twice, I've resorted to the formula of an alias. (The reader should be assured that every fact stated in the book has been sourced, and for obvious reasons corroborated to the very fullest extent possible, before publication.) No acknowledgement thus appears of the help, encouragement and kindness I got from a number of quarters, some of them, as they say, household names.

Chapter 1

Some of the material relating to events in 1962–3 appears in a different form in *Roman by Polanski*. Court transcripts and other material concerning Polanski's legal difficulties in California in 1977–8 were supplied by the Los Angeles district attorney's office. I should also acknowledge the UK Family Records Centre and California Vital Records for archival help. Other sources included Terence Bayler, Judy Flanders, John Fraser, Barry Norman, Josip Sats and Tony Yeo.

A source close to Polanski on the set of *Chinatown* also spoke to me. I made use of previously published articles that appeared in the *Atlanta Constitution*, the *Globe*, the *New York Post*, the *Daily Telegraph*, *Time*, the *Seattle Times* and *Variety*. It's a pleasure, too, to acknowledge Barbara Leaming's *Polanski: The Film-maker as Voyeur*, John Parker's *Polanski* and Thomas Kiernan's *The Roman Polanski Story*; the last, albeit labouring under its author's note of simulated moral outrage, is particularly vivid.

Chapter 2

For events from 1933–46 I'm grateful to two of Roman Polanski's relatives who enlightened me on his family background, and others who spoke to me about his experience in and immediately after the war, notably the late Burton Andrus, the late Alan Bullock, Jozef Ebert, Ernst Jaenecke and Katharina Rae. I made use, too, of the Federal Bundesministerium archive in Berlin – my thanks to Stefan Hansen, and to Fred and Cindy Smith for introducing me to the city – and of R. H. McNeal's *Guide to the Decisions of the CPSU*, which elaborates on both the official and less formal workings of Stalin's government, more specifically of the various Party conferences between 1929–53.

The quotes beginning 'He often hurt my feelings in little ways . . .', 'A great deal of anti-Semitism . . .' and 'unpardonable betrayal . . .' all appear in *Roman by Polanski*. Polanski's remarks beginning 'It was my first contact with the country . . .' and '. . . Hundreds of American planes . . .' are both from *The Dick Cavett Show*, 22 December 1971, © Daphne Productions. The quote beginning 'Romek could never submit to family life . . .' first appeared in the *New Yorker*, 5 December 1994.

Chapter 3

Interviews and/or taped conversations, some conducted at the time of my earlier biographies, took place with the late Alan Bullock, Don Gordon, Norman Jewison, Don Murray, Barry Norman, Harold Pinter, Katharina Rae, Andrei Sbytov, the late Robert Wise, Tony Yeo. Secondary sources included the *Herald Tribune*, the *Daily Telegraph*, the *New York Times*, *Nova*, *The Times*, *Variety*, *Vogue*.

Roman Polanski's quotes beginning 'It was as if an abyss . . .', '. . . in a room with turquoise walls . . .' and '"Well, did that help, you bitch?"' are from *Roman by Polanski*. 'When I woke up . . .' is from *Der Spiegel*,

16 December 1974. His quote beginning 'I met this mad Viennese promoter . . .' is from *Cosmopolitan*, March 1975. His quote beginning 'It was a relaxed and artistic environment . . .' is from *Cahiers du Cinéma*, May 1992. Polanski's quote beginning 'Everything was geared towards . . .' is from *L'avant-scène cinéma*, December 1983. His quote beginning '. . . uses a holiday atmosphere' is from *Les lettres françaises*, 13 January 1966.

Barbara Kwiatkowska's quote beginning 'It was all a question of dominance . . .' appears in John Parker's *Polanski*. The anonymous quote beginning 'I had a feeling . . .' appears in Barbara Leaming's *Polanski: The Film-maker as Voyeur*.

Chapter 4

Polanski's swinging years were recalled by, among others, Charles Champlin, Mike Fargo, Judy Flanders, Jessie Flint, John Fraser, Hugh Futcher, John Gavin, Alan Hazen, Norman Jewison, Dean Jones, David Kelly, the late Michael Klinger, the late Ronald Lacey, Barbara Leigh, the late Donald Pleasence, Robert Relyea, the late Kenneth Tynan, Eli Wallach, Dave Wolfe, Dora Yanni.

For secondary source material I should acknowledge California Vital Records, Companies House, the *Hollywood Reporter*, the *Los Angeles Times*, the *New York Times*, the *Daily Telegraph*, *Vanity Fair* and *Variety*.

Polanski's quotes beginning '. . . short, dumpy, inexpressibly ugly Jewish girl . . .' and '. . . dismayed me by their . . .', his short quotes on the making of *Cul-de-Sac*, and Sharon Tate's quote beginning 'I got one . . .' appear in *Roman by Polanski*. 'In France I wasn't *nouvelle vague* . . .' is from *Cahiers du Cinéma*, May 1992. Polanski's quote beginning 'How can you improve the quality . . .' is from *Cahiers du Cinéma*, December 1979. His quotes beginning 'I'll let her do it next week . . .' and '"Michael, I know she's a nice girl . . ."' are both from Barbara Leaming's *Polanski: The Film-maker as Voyeur*. His quote beginning 'The more fantastic you are . . .' is from *Cahiers du Cinéma*, January 1969. Jacqueline Bisset's quote beginning 'It was a fascinating experience . . .' is from *Hello!*, issue 248, 1993. It is a pleasure to confirm that, despite dancing a protracted preliminary tango with her agent, Ms Bisset and I never spoke. The dialogue between Polanski and Michael Klinger beginning '"Never in all my experience have I been treated like this . . ."' is quoted in Barbara Leaming's biography; Klinger himself substantially confirmed it to me. Victor Lownes' quote beginning 'Telling jokes and watching the reaction . . .' is from his memoir *The Day the Bunny Died*. Robert Evans' 'little Polack', 'This [was] some character . . .' and 'By the end of the first day's shooting . . .' quotes are from the script of the 2002 MCA/Universal Pictures documentary *The Kid Stays in the Picture*. Polanski's quote beginning 'He's no film-maker . . .' is from *Positif*, February 1969. His quote beginning 'I used to give my cast bananas . . .' is from *Penthouse*, August 1974. His quote remarking 'I pep myself up . . .' is from *Polanski par Polanski*, Editions du Chéne, 1986.

Chapter 5

Despite one or two overtures made by well-meaning intermediaries, I did not speak directly to any of the surviving members of Charles Manson's so-called 'Family', although two individuals close to the cult harangued me, at length, off the record. Manson himself declined to answer my letter to him of June 2006. The specific events relating to the murder of Sharon Tate and four others on 8 August 1969, and of Leno and Rosemary LaBianca on 9 August 1969 are based on the grand-jury testimony of Susan Atkins, the statement of Linda Kasabian, and on Charles Watson's book *Will You Die for Me?* A number of short quotes from Manson and his followers that appear in this chapter are from Vincent Bugliosi's and Curt Gentry's book *Helter Skelter*. I'm grateful to Mr Bugliosi, whose tenacious prosecution of the case brought some degree of justice to bear, for taking the time to return my call. Very nearly every British, American and overseas news organisation extensively covered the events on Cielo Drive; I should particularly mention the reports that appeared in *Newsweek*, 18 August 1969 and *Time*, 22 August 1969.

Polanski's quotes beginning 'We were a grotesque sight . . .', '. . . there was a revival . . .', '. . . hugging her tightly . . .', 'Victor banged some chick in his bedroom . . .' and 'His ingrained pessimism . . .' are all from *Roman by Polanski*.

The quotes by Zofia Komeda beginning 'When I arrived . . .' and 'Only then did Romek telephone . . .' appear, in substantially the form given here, in both Barbara Leaming's *Polanski: The Film-maker as Voyeur* and John Parker's *Polanski*. I didn't personally interview Ms Komeda.

The letter from Polanski to the critic Charles Champlin is courtesy of the Margaret Herrick Library of the Academy of Motion Picture Arts and Sciences and quotes, in part, from H. H. Bancroft's *California Inter Pocula* (1888). The quote suggesting that Sharon Tate 'spent an hour in bemoaning

Polanski's absence' is substantially from John Parker's *Polanski*. Another source, reflecting on this, told me that 'Sharon had [had] no illusions' about her husband, but that the couple had nonetheless enjoyed a 'loving arrangement'.

Chapter 6

Polanski's personal and creative highs – and the nadir of *What?* – were crisply brought home by Terence Bayler, Charles Champlin, Paul Darlow, Roger Ebert, 'Doc' Erickson, Mike Fargo, Mike Fenton, John Gavin, the late Hugh Griffith, William Hobbs, the late John Huston, Roy Jenson, Iain Johnstone, Dean Jones, the late Pauline Kael, the late Michael Klinger, Barry Norman, Richard Pearson, Paul Shelley, Damien Thomas, the late Kenneth Tynan, the late Shelley Winters, Eli Wallach, Robert Wise, Burt Young. The screenwriter Robert Towne declined a formal interview, but spoke to me at some length on the phone.

Polanski's quotes beginning 'I made Tynan stretch out . . .' and '. . . grab[bed] a heavy mop', as well as a number of much shorter direct quotes, appear in *Roman by Polanski*.

Martin Shaw's quote beginning 'Making a film wasn't for people . . .' and a small number of quotes attributed to the late Kenneth Tynan, including Tynan's tour de force beginning '"You had garlic for dinner . . ."' are from John Parker, *Polanski*. The quote by the journalist Neil Norman is from the *Independent on Sunday*, 25 September 2005. Victor Lownes' 'hit the roof' quote is from his book *The Day the Bunny Died*.

Chapter 7

The events from January 1977 to the spring of 1978 were vividly recalled by, among others, Mike Fargo, Mike Fenton, Toni Gahl, Jim Geller, Natalie Hawn, Dean Jones and the late Shelley Winters.

The Federal Bureau of Investigation initially turned down my request, made under the Freedom of Information Act, to review at least a portion of their substantial file on Polanski. I appealed the decision. On 4 January 2007, Daniel Metcalfe of the US Department of Justice wrote to tell me that, 'after carefully considering your appeal, and as a result of discussions between FBI personnel and a member of my staff', the Bureau would, after all, make available 'certain records that might be responsive' to my request. I'm extremely grateful to Mr Metcalfe and his staff.

I also made use of court transcripts and other official records kindly provided by Sandi Gibbons of the Los Angeles district attorney's office. As far as I'm aware, this is the first time that these particular papers have appeared in print.

A number of short quotes, shown here for purposes of comparison to the legal transcripts and other court documents, are from *Roman by Polanski*.

Phillip Vannatter's quote beginning 'He started talking a blue streak . . .', the quote stating that 'As time went on, Roman got lonelier and lonelier . . .' and the story relating to Polanski having returned to the Gaileys' home in order to 'confront the mother of the 13-year-old' all appear, in substantially this form, in Thomas Kiernan's *The Roman Polanski Story*.

The partial list of Polanski's favourite films is from an interview conducted by Pascal Bonitzer and Nathalie Heinich that appeared in *Cahiers du Cinéma*, December 1979.

Polanski's quote beginning '. . . the hardships I went through seemed quite normal to me . . .' is from his appearance on *Charlie Rose*, 9 March 2000. His quote beginning 'To be honest I found life . . .' is from *Le Nouvel Observateur*, 13 April 1984. The 'altogether more impressive storm' quote is not by Polanski personally, and in no way reflects on anything other than the excellent 1937 film *The Hurricane*.

Andrzej Wajda's quote to the effect that Polanski had 'always seen everything in front of him . . .' is from the *New Yorker*, 5 December 1994.

The brief remarks attributed to Irwin Gold were repeated to me by a source, who prefers anonymity, then familiar with Mr Gold.

Finally, I should thank both the source at the Los Angeles police department and the party familiar with the late Laurence Rittenband, that self-admittedly 'colourful' but much-maligned jurist. I did not personally interview Samantha Geimer.

Chapter 8

Primary sources included Dale Crowe, the late Michael Elphick, Toni Gahl, Jim Geller, Gene Griffith, Jeff Gross, William Hobbs, Iain Johnstone, David Kelly, Tom Keylock, Leigh Lawson, Barry Norman, Sven Nykvist, Richard Pearson, Damien Thomas.

Polanski's quote beginning 'When I started out . . .' is from *Le Matin de Paris*, 23 September 1982. His quote beginning 'I don't think I would exaggerate . . .' is from *The World This Weekend*, BBC Radio, 22 January 1984. His quote beginning 'Technically, it was difficult . . .' is from *Première*, May 1986. His quote beginning, 'From the start the idea was . . .' is from *Le Nouvel Observateur*, 25 March 1988. There is also a brief quote that appears in the *New Yorker* profile of Polanski, 'Artist in Exile', 5 December 1994.

The brief remarks attributed to Victor Lownes are either from his memoir *The Day the Bunny Died*, or from a source then familiar with the workings of Playboy Productions. I did not personally interview Mr Lownes.

Chapter 9

Help in recalling the era came from Dale Crowe, the late Tonino Delli Colli, Ariel Dorfman, Jeff Gross, Alain Haultcoeur, Jim Hoven, John M. Kelso, Frank Knox, James Russo, the late Kenneth Tynan, Eli Wallach. I should particularly mention the source familiar with Roman Polanski's mid-Nineties life in Paris and a second individual, who also prefers anonymity, who was a regular companion at Les Bains-Douches. Valya Page and Adam Willis Fleming were both invaluable at rue Saint-Hubert. I visited avenue Montaigne.

Polanski's quote beginning 'The so-called golden shower talk . . .' is from an interview with Stephen O'Shea, © Brant Publications 1994. His quote beginning 'If you show your hero triumphant . . .' is from *Positif*, February 1969. His quote beginning 'I don't know if it's senility . . .' is from *Cahiers du Cinéma*, January 1969.

The 'angelic messenger' quote relating to *Bitter Moon* is from F. X. Feeney's *Roman Polanski*, the best by far of a series of such blow-by-blow filmographies. Peter Coyote's 'This is a guy . . .' quote appears in his 2005 interview with Johanna Schneller for *Premiere*.

Chapter 10

Parting comment from Paul Bradley, Paul Brooke, Jeff Gross, Michael Heath, Emily Hunt, the late Stanley Kramer, Barry Norman, Marian Reid, Damien Thomas, the late Robert Wise, Dave Wole. John Pavlik of the Academy of Motion Picture Arts and Sciences also kindly put his organisation's view of Polanski at my disposal. The Academy's statement reads, in full: 'We have nothing to say with regard to Mr Polanski's Oscar win. The membership's vote to award him the statuette is the only relevant statement the Academy could make.' (Asked to comment on his legal status at the Cannes festival in May 2007, the director himself disparaged the 'empty' questioning and left the room.) I'm also grateful to the source, on the whole less well disposed to Polanski, at the Los Angeles sheriff's department.

Polanski's quote beginning 'Though the subject matter is bleak . . .' is from *El Pais Semanal*, 1 December 2001. His quote beginning 'They come on the set of my movies . . .' is from the *Observer*, 2 October 2005.

A number of the quotes attributed to Ronald Harwood appeared in the *Spectator*, 17 June 2006. The *Guardian* review of *Oliver Twist* appeared on 7 October 2005. Graydon Carter's quote recalling that 'I talked with [Polanski] at some length', and other short comments on the libel trial of July 2005, appeared in *Vanity Fair*, under Mr Carter's byline, October 2005. The quote beginning 'The most prominent visual hallmark of Polanski's office . . .' is from the *Los Angeles Times*, 18 September 2005. I also read Neil Norman's article entitled 'Can Polanski escape the shadow of rape?' in the London *Evening Standard*, 23 May 2002, David Rowan's 'Has Polanski wounded Graydon's Vanity?', also in the London *Evening Standard*, 27 July 2005, and Bryan Curtis' 'Where has Polanski been hiding?' in *Slate*, 31 January 2003.

I should acknowledge the help of the staff at both the Public Record Office and the Directors Guild, and that of the source, anonymous but well placed, at the Royal Courts of Justice.

INDEX